Contemporary Water Governance in the Global South

The litany of alarming observations about water use and misuse is now familiar – over a billion people without access to safe drinking water; almost every major river dammed and diverted; increasing conflicts over the delivery of water in urban areas; continuing threats to water quality from agricultural inputs and industrial wastes; and the increasing variability of climate, including threats of severe droughts and flooding across locales and regions. These issues present tremendous challenges for water governance.

This book focuses on three major concepts and approaches that have gained currency in policy and governance circles, both globally and regionally – scarcity and crisis, marketization and privatization, and participation. It provides a historical and contextual overview of each of these ideas as they have emerged in global and regional policy and governance circles and pairs these with in-depth case studies that examine manifestations and contestations of water governance internationally.

Promoting a view of changing water governance that links across these themes and in relation to contemporary realities, the book is invaluable for students, researchers, advocates and policy-makers interested in water governance challenges facing the developing world.

Leila M. Harris is an Assistant Professor in the Institute for Resources, Environment and Sustainability and in the Institute for Gender, Race, Sexuality and Social Justice at the University of British Columbia. She is also Co-Director of the Program on Water Governance (PoWG).

Jacqueline A. Goldin is an Associate Professor at the University of the Western Cape where she leads the Anthropology of Water (AOW) Research Group.

Chris Sneddon is an Associate Professor in the Department of Geography and the Environmental Studies Program at Dartmouth College.

Earthscan Studies in Water Resource Management

Water Management, Food Security and Sustainable Agriculture in Developing Economies
Edited by M. Dinesh Kumar, M. V. K. Sivamohan and Nitin Bassi

Governing International Watercourses
River basin organizations and the sustainable governance of internationally shared rivers and lakes
Susanne Schmeier

Transferable Groundwater Rights
Integrating hydrogeology, law and economics
Andreas N. Charalambous

Contemporary Water Governance in the Global South
Scarcity, marketization and participation
Edited by Leila M. Harris, Jacqueline A. Goldin and Christopher Sneddon

For more information and to view forthcoming titles in this series, please visit the Routledge website: http://www.routledge.com/books/series/ECWRM/

Contemporary Water Governance in the Global South

Scarcity, marketization and participation

**Edited by Leila M. Harris,
Jacqueline A. Goldin
and Christopher Sneddon**

LONDON AND NEW YORK

First published 2013
by Routledge
2 Park Square, Milton Park, Abingdon, Oxon OX14 4RN

Simultaneously published in the USA and Canada
by Routledge
711 Third Avenue, New York, NY 10017

Routledge is an imprint of the Taylor & Francis Group, an informa business

British Library Cataloguing in Publication Data
A catalogue record for this book is available from the British Library

Library of Congress Cataloging-in-Publication Data
Contemporary water governance in the global south : scarcity, marketization
and participation / [edited by] Leila Harris, Jacqueline Goldin and
Christopher Sneddon.
    pages cm. – (Earthscan studies in water resource management)
    Includes bibliographical references and index.
    1. Water-supply – Developing countries – Management 2. Water resources
development – Developing countries. 3. Water rights – Developing
countries. 4. Water security – Developing countries. I. Harris, Leila.
    II. Goldin, Jacqueline. III. Sneddon, Christopher.
    HD1702.C65 2013
    333.91009172′4–dc23   2012048639

ISBN13: 978-0-415-65799-0 (hbk)
ISBN13: 978-0-203-07636-1 (ebk)

Typeset in Times
by HWA Text and Data Management, London

Printed and bound in the United States of America
by Edwards Brothers Malloy

Contents

PART IV
Participation 177

PART V
Conclusion 249

Figures

Tables

Contributors

Samer Alatout is an Associate Professor in the Department of Community and Environmental Sociology, the Nelson Institute for Environmental Studies, and the Graduate Program of Sociology at the University of Wisconsin, Madison. He is also affiliated with the Department of Geography and the Holtz Center for Science and Technology Studies. He has published extensively on water policy and politics in the Middle East, focusing on the relationship between notions of water scarcity/abundance and political identity, state-building and governance. He is conceptually interested in biopolitics, border studies, and the sociology and history of science and technology. At present, Alatout is writing a book manuscript on water politics in historic Palestine.

Lawrence A. Baker is a Research Professor in the Department of Bioproducts and Biosystems Engineering at the University of Minnesota. As an environmental engineer, his research focuses on ecosystem approaches to understanding water and pollution management. He has published more than 100 technical papers and recently edited *The Water Environment of Cities* (2009).

Karen Bakker is a Professor of Geography, Canada Research Chair in Political Ecology and Water Governance, and Director of the Program on Water Governance at the University of British Columbia. Elements of her work focus on water privatization, the human right to water, water security and other dimensions of water governance. In addition, she has a more general interest in political economy, political ecology and environmental politics.

Jessica Barnes is a postdoctoral associate at the Yale School of Forestry and Environmental Studies and the Yale Climate and Energy Institute. Her research focuses on the nexus of water management, agricultural policy and climate change in Egypt and the Middle East. She holds a Ph.D. from Columbia University in Sustainable Development and a Masters in Environmental Management from Yale University. Her first book, *Cultivating the Nile: The Everyday Politics of Water in Egypt*, is forthcoming with Duke University Press and her work has been published in *Geopolitics*, *Social Studies of Science*, and an edited volume on environmental histories of the Middle East.

Annelies Broekman is President of the Catalan Network for a New Water Culture (XNCA) and Coordinator of the Water Unit of Ecologistas en Acción in Barcelona, Spain. She has a Ph.D. in Agricultural Economics from the University of Bologna (Italy) and an M.Sc. in Integrated Water Management at the University of Zaragoza (Spain). Her working experience has focused mainly on following up the European Water Framework Directive (2000/60/CE) implementation processes, active citizen participation, environmental economy related to the water cycle, as well as drought and water scarcity issues. Her current work focuses mostly on facilitating grassroots organizations and capacity-building related to water conflicts in Spain.

Sinan Erensu is a Ph.D. candidate in the Department of Sociology at the University of Minnesota and a graduate student fellow at the Interdisciplinary Center for the Study of Global Change. He holds an M.Phil. degree in Sociology from Cambridge University. His interests lie in the areas of critical development studies, nature–society relations, political ecology with a particular emphasis on emerging landscapes of renewable energy and the water/energy nexus. His regional focus is the Turkish Black Sea coast.

Jacqueline A. Goldin is an Associate Professor at the University of the Western Cape where she leads the Anthropology of Water (AOW) Research Group. The research group focuses on food and water security, and the interface between human and ecosystem well-being, with particular attention to institutions as mediators between society and nature, as well as to the dimensions of gender, trust and relations of power that affect these settings.

Leila M. Harris is an Assistant Professor in the Institute for Resources, Environment and Sustainability and in the Institute for Gender, Race, Sexuality and Social Justice at the University of British Columbia. She is also Co-Director of the Program on Water Governance. Her work focuses on nature–society questions, including inequality and environment and political ecology, particularly through investigation of water politics, access and governance in the global South.

Zeynep Kadirbeyoğlu is an Assistant Professor in the department of Political Science and International Relations at Bogazici University in Istanbul. She holds a degree in Political Science from McGill University, as well as an MA in Economics from Bogazici and an M.Phil. in Social and Political Sciences from the University of Cambridge. Her research interests include transnational networks, democratization, decentralization and citizenship. Her previous work has been published in *New Perspectives on Turkey* and several edited volumes.

O. A. K'Akumu is a senior research fellow and lecturer in the Master of Urban Management Programme, School of the Built Environment, University of Nairobi. His interests are in the area of housing and urban development, including water reforms. He has written extensively on issues related to water governance in Kenya, particularly on debates over privatization.

Ekin Kurtiç is a Ph.D. student in Anthropology and Middle Eastern Studies at Harvard University. Her research interests are in political ecology, environmental anthropology and politics of water. Her work focuses on rural transformations in Turkey by examining the effects of current water and energy policies as they are manifested in hydroelectric power plants.

Basil Mahayni is a Ph.D. candidate in the Department of Geography at the University of Minnesota and a graduate student fellow at the Interdisciplinary Center for the Study of Social Change. His research interests include the dynamics of and relationships between state development policies and state/society relations. His dissertation work focuses primarily on the dynamic interactions between water sector reforms in public institutions, informal water services, and household perspectives of and experiences with water access and governance in Middle Eastern cities.

Cynthia Morinville is a graduate of the Institute for Resources, Environment and Sustainability at the University of British Columbia. Her research interests include questions of access to resources, participation in decision-making and governance processes, as well as their intersection with, and implications for, identity-making and notions of citizenship.

Muchaparara Musemwa is a Senior Lecturer in the Department of History at the University of Witwatersrand, Johannesburg, South Africa. He holds a Ph.D. in History from the University of Minnesota and an MA in History from the University of Cape Town, South Africa. His research and teaching interests lie in environmental, urban and social history of Africa, specifically contestation over resources, and the history and politics of water in colonial and postcolonial Zimbabwe. He has published in journals such as the *Journal of Southern African Studies*, *Environment and History*, and the *Journal of Developing Societies*. He is currently a co-editor of the *South African Historical Journal* and an editorial board member of the *Water History Journal*, the flagship of the International Water History Association (IWHA).

Uygar Özesmi is the Executive Director of Greenpeace Mediterranean, running campaigns against climate change, unsustainable fisheries, pollution and genetically modified organisms in Turkey, Lebanon, Israel, Jordan and Egypt. He holds an M.Sc. in Environmental Science from the Ohio State University and a Ph.D. in Conservation Biology from the University of Minnesota. He is an activist and key figure in contemporary environmental movements in Turkey, having taken a role in founding and developing several important environment- and civil-society-related institutions. Currently he serves on the Board of CIVICUS, the World Alliance for Citizen Participation.

Eric Sheppard is the Humboldt Professor of Geography at UCLA, where he moved after 36 years at the University of Minnesota. Awards include: Distinguished Scholarship Honors, Association of American Geographers; Fellow, Center for Advanced Studies in the Behavioral Sciences; Fesler-Lampert Professor for the Humanities, University of Minnesota. He is author or co-author on a range of books, including *A World of Difference, Scale and Geographic Inquiry, The Capitalist Space Economy*, and *The Wiley-Blackwell Companion to Economic Geography*, as well as over 100 articles in economic geography, urban geography, GIS and society, development and geographic thought.

Christopher Sneddon is an Associate Professor in the Department of Geography and the Environmental Studies Program at Dartmouth College. His research and teaching focus on conflicts over water at multiple spatial scales, with a primary regional focus on the Mekong River basin of South-East Asia.

Shiney Varghese is a Senior Policy Analyst with the Institute for Agriculture and Trade Policy (IATP) where she leads their work on global water governance. Her primary interests have been on the water crisis, its impact on access to water and food security, and possible local solutions that emphasize equity, women's empowerment, environmental justice and sustainability. She co-chaired the UNCSD Fresh Water Caucus – the primary civil society voice on water at the UN Commission on Sustainable Development – for 10 years and continues to intervene in international dialogs on water, food, climate and energy that have implications for local and national water governance. She has previously worked with indigenous groups, civil society organizations and international groups on social and environmental issues in India; she has also been a visiting fellow at the Agrarian Studies Program at Yale University.

Hillary Waters is a graduate student in the Department of Geography at the University of Minnesota. Her research interests include bringing together postcolonial theory, science studies and political ecology to investigate how water is controlled and accessed in urban Africa.

Preface and acknowledgements

Many of the authors for this volume came together at a workshop held by the Interdisciplinary Center for the Study of Global Change (ICGC) at the University of Minnesota in 2010. From that point, we have pursued a number of collaborations that have put us in conversation and contact – sharing ideas and engaging in constructive critique around the common theme of water governance. This book is part of that collaboration. We are grateful to ICGC for creating that space for dialog and engagement (which for many of us, has been ongoing for many years), and for the abiding commitment to sustainability and justice issues in the global South. We are also grateful to the Hampton Fund and the Vice Provost for Research and International Programs at the University of British Columbia for providing needed funds to further the efforts of our network. Of course, we are also grateful to our own institutional homes for also providing the intellectual space to work on these issues. In particular, we gratefully acknowledge the Institute for Water Studies at the University of the Western Cape where J. Goldin directs the Anthropology of Water Research Group and researches issues related to water in rural areas of Southern Africa; the Department of Geography and Environmental Studies Program at Dartmouth College where C. Sneddon is engaged with the study of water conflicts and politics through a political-ecological and historical lens, particularly in the Mekong Basin; and the Institute for Resources, Environment and Sustainability and the Institute for Gender, Race, Sexuality and Social Justice at the University of British Columbia where L. Harris works on issues of water politics, governance, inequality and environment, especially in the Middle East and Africa.

Just as the editors come from distinct backgrounds, the authors for this book also come from different walks of life, and with different disciplinary training, from engineering to anthropology, geography, science studies and history. Despite these diverse engagements, and varied experiences in different regions of the world, we share a common purpose. We share a passion and interest in better understanding key water governance challenges that are increasingly of concern across the global South. Like many other development practitioners from all over the world, we are deeply aware of the dissonance between the global North and the global South when it comes to practices of 'development', the production of knowledge, as well as the knowledge and practice of water governance. However, we are also aware of the danger of holding up analytical models based on simple notions of global/local, good guys/bad guys or Western/non-Western.

By asking all authors to engage with questions of hegemony, as well as linkages across the several organizing themes of the volume, we have necessarily been fairly directive in this project. We are grateful to our authors for tolerating and following through on this, to ensure the promise of the volume as a whole is realized. By doing so, we have endeavored to create a platform for all of the contributing authors to converse with, and critically engage, the framing leitmotivs for the book. Multiple rounds of revisions to ensure this cross-talk have been essential, even if exhausting. In particular, we thank the authors and commentators for their careful consideration and diligent work to consider the range of questions posed, and in so doing to achieve our ambitious goals for the volume. We also are thankful for Routledge/Earthscan for their enthusiasm and support for the book from the beginning, as well as to Lucy Rodina and Cynthia Morinville for editorial assistance. We also are grateful for the reader, understanding that at times it takes considerable effort to read across multidisciplinary and cross-contextual conversations of this type. While every word may not be satisfying, we are confident that the effort of reading across diverse sites, and diverse approaches, will reap dividends.

1 Introduction

Interrogating hegemonic discourses in water governance

Jacqueline A. Goldin, Christopher Sneddon and Leila M. Harris

The litany of alarming observations about water use and misuse is now familiar—over a billion people without access to safe drinking water; almost every major river dammed and diverted; continuing threats to water quality from agricultural inputs and industrial wastes; and the increasing variability of climate, including threats of severe droughts and flooding across locales and regions. These issues present tremendous challenges for water governance. With this volume, our primary goal is to interrogate the prevalent wisdom of the day with respect to water governance by focusing attention on three major concepts and approaches that have gained currency in policy and governance circles, both globally and regionally—scarcity and crisis, marketization and privatization, and participation. We examine these dominant, or hegemonic, concepts to better understand their political, economic and scientific rationale, as well as to open up lines of inquiry with respect to alternative modes of water governance. We are also keenly interested in how these dominant discourses and practices inform one another as well as the contradictions, harmonies and disharmonies among them.

Our three main themes, (1) crisis and scarcity (2) marketization and privatization and (3) participation, are concepts and operational strategies that have become increasingly entrenched into the world of water governance over the past several decades. These concepts are global in their reach whilst having distinctly local impacts. In this volume, we undertake a conceptual analysis, and an analysis grounded in in-depth case studies, to critically examine the uptake, entrenchment and implications of these dominant water governance discourses and practices. Our approach is to raise questions about how decisions over water's management and use – water governance – have increasingly coalesced around this somewhat narrow set of core concepts. Our treatment of these themes is attentive to the complex governance landscape that makes water-related decision-making and 'sustainability' so challenging. This context encompasses scalar mismatches between the sites of water use and decision-making, institutional fragmentation, and varying socio-economic, political or environmental drivers that shape institutions and decision-making structures. The biophysical and socio-political landscape that conditions water realities on the ground is similarly complex. Given these realities, we choose to evaluate these practices not in isolation, but through considering the convergence and disjuncture between them and the ways that they are applied to specific on-the-ground realities in our diverse locales. For instance, government decisions to create water markets or privatize water delivery services are often justified as a response to ideas of crisis or scarcity. Similarly, market approaches are often accelerated by calls for devolution and for more participatory approaches, creating interesting convergences and tensions between theory and practice.

One of our central assumptions is that the study of water governance is not the purview of any single approach or field of inquiry. Water is so deeply embedded within nearly every aspect of social and biophysical existence that understanding its scientific, political, economic and cultural dimensions demands an ever-widening reach of methodologies and proficiencies. These knowledges and aptitudes are not the exclusive domain of academics or transnational networks of water professionals. Individuals and communities throughout the world are engaged in a range of activities to advocate for, and contribute to, more equitable and sustainable systems of water use. This is part of our rationale for directly including activist and civil society voices as our commentaries to the different sections of this volume. It is imperative, we suggest, to produce new knowledge, but also to engage in discussion to query the relevance and uptake of that knowledge in different realms.

Avoiding the simplistic binaries that structure altogether too much writing and analysis of the global South or ideals of 'good governance', ours is an inquiry around hegemonic discourses and how these have, or have not, penetrated into diverse spaces of the global South. We consider that key issues such as the deployment of ideas of crisis and scarcity, the marketization of water, and the notion of participation require nuanced and critical attention—to be neither adopted nor cast off in simplistic terms, but to be better understood, critically engaged and brought to task for the diverse effects and consequences these discourses and practices have for many regions, peoples and ecosystems. The chapters in this volume take up the important notion of variegation; what makes different places and times dissimilar, and in some cases unique, in how water governance is invoked and practiced?

Attention to particularisms, including the context-specific manifestations of these broad and pervasive ideas and practices, need not come at the cost of ignoring more general patterns and global trends. We are very aware that development projects and governance practices in the South are influenced by discourses that are global or trans-local in nature, and often might be positioned in other contexts and places that are quite far geographically from the sites of implementation. As such, global or regional ideas and discourses are often blended, comfortably or less so, into the everyday contexts of local sites. We are also very much aware that the boundaries between global South and North are not hermetic. As ideas and practices locate and dislocate, they become lodged within global discourses and are infused with new meanings – losing their original sense of place or, for that matter, any singular essence as they settle within different circumstances and realities.

This is certainly the case with the dimensions of water governance we examine here, wherein new meanings and context-specific pathways become enmeshed with notions of scarcity, practices of marketization and ideals of participation. All of these ideas and practices scatter, are renegotiated, and give rise to new forms of resistance, politics or acquiescence. While analytics such as these may read as truisms for those engaged in critical development studies, we expect this language and the associated insights to be less familiar to those who are active in water policy worlds, and particularly those in engineering or the biophysical sciences. Part of our purpose in this volume is to think across these worlds, and also to put an accent on the types of understandings that accompany these critical perspectives, thus providing insights for all engaged in water governance across the global South.

An internet search for the word governance yields 45,300,000 hits, of which 17,000,000 are for 'good governance', a theme tightly connected to words such as democracy, accountability and transparency. Indeed at several recent high-profile water meetings and in several key publications, the water community has increasingly emphasized that the global water crisis is centrally a crisis of governance. Consider the first key message from the final report of the Marseille World Water Forum from 2012:

> the 'water crisis' the world community faces today is largely a governance crisis. Securing water for all, especially for vulnerable populations, is often not only a question of hydrology (water quantity, quality, supply, demand) and financing, but equally a matter of good governance. Managing water scarcity and water-related risks (floods, natural disasters etc.) requires resilient institutions, collaborative efforts and sound capacity at all levels.
>
> (WWF, 2012: 5)

Even with the growing engagement with ideas of governance – and good governance – we find that these are not often well linked with critical investigations of the broader hegemonic discourses from which they draw. With respect to our own engagement with the theme of governance, our interest is, as we have highlighted above, in three distinct yet interconnected focal themes that infuse the contemporary world of water in general and governance in particular: (1) scarcity and crisis (2) marketization and privatization, and (3) participation. We chose these as organizing themes of the book, and as lenses through which to investigate hegemonies of water governance for several reasons. First, all are prominent within current debates over how to best use, conserve, manage and provide access to water. A burgeoning literature on the linkages between water scarcity and potential crises in water-stressed regions (e.g. Gleick and Palaniappan, 2010; Schmidt, 2012), debates over the use of privatization and other market mechanisms to efficiently allocate water (e.g. Haughton, 2002; Robbins, 2003; Budds, 2004; Bauer, 2004; McDonald and Ruiters, 2005; Bakker, 2010), and the search for more participatory means of decision-making in water management (e.g. Sneddon and Fox, 2007; Sultana, 2009; Harris, 2009; Goldin,

2010; Jones, 2011) all signal the growing significance of water governance in high-level governmental, professional, non-governmental and academic circles. Although these are each in themselves dominant and definable discourses, they also blur and hinge on each another.

To be clear, our identification of scarcity as a hegemonic concept does not deny that water shortages are persistent and consequential for many of the planet's people and places; rather, our goal is to highlight how such scarcities are co-constructed by both material conditions and power relations that define the boundaries of water control and access (see Mahayni, Chapter 4). Our focus on marketization is similarly not one-sided, and does not endeavor to highlight only the negative dimensions of marketization or privatization schemes. As research on Chile's water reforms, enacted in the early 1980s, has shown, water markets have been a mixed bag in terms of achieving their stated goal of efficient water use, while also contributing to the inequitable distribution of water in some regions (Bauer, 2004; Budds, 2004; Harris, Chapter 10). Similarly, our focus on participation is not to simply cast these practices as good/beneficial, or bad/ damaging, but rather to consider the specific practices and effects of the notion of participation as it manifests in particular contexts such as Egypt, Ghana or Turkey. Indeed, our purpose throughout the volume, as Sneddon so aptly describes in the chapter that follows, is to consider the complex ambiguities that necessarily work in and through these discourses and practices. Part of what hegemony allows, analytically, is to highlight and attend to tensions, contradictions and complex bundles of acceptance/imposition or good/bad associated with particular governance regimes and practices.

Recognizing the strong linkages across our chosen themes, we have taken considerable care to highlight how these elements are interwoven. For this reason, whilst presenting these ideas in three distinct sections, we also emphasize and understand these discourses and practices as necessarily linked. Each of the empirical chapters in the sections that follow explores the specificities of these concepts and processes, and also attend to the linkages to other concepts and trends. Our aim is thus to both specify how these discourses and practices are similar and shared (i.e. linked through hegemonic actors or ideals) as well as how they are taken up differently, modified, rejected or embellished in particular settings.

We suggest that all three of these ideas and practices must be analyzed as 'hegemonic', although we also recognize limitations of this concept and associated analytical strategies (see Sneddon, Chapter 2; Bakker, Chapter 15). Part of our challenge in this volume is to specifically query the utility and timeliness of the notion of hegemony in opening up key avenues of analysis and investigation. While we think that this analytic tool is useful, and even central, it is insufficient to uncover the key issues and tensions at stake in contemporary water governance in any comprehensive sense. Nonetheless, we demonstrate throughout this contribution that it is a key lens through which to understand and analyze contemporary trends, and it does offer some crucial insights, specifically in forging connections across the spaces and times of the practices we interrogate.

All the chapter authors were asked to consider how the three themes intersect in relation to their particular case and to highlight and emphasize, as far as possible, connections across the book's thematic elements. We are interested in how, for example, scarcity and participation fit into marketization schemes and how participatory processes are thought to help overcome both biophysical and governance crises. Take for instance the idea of social movements. As we see from several of the responses, activist engagements and social movements are often born out of real or imagined scarcities and crises. Neither can be understood without considering the linkages between these processes. One of the central premises of 'hegemonies', we contend, is to break down or isolate issues, making the 'answer' to a particular isolated issue or problem appear to be self-evident. As such, one of the offerings of our volume is to respond to some of these conundrums and to precisely demonstrate the oversimplification of complex issues that can be found in government announcements, global water forum pronouncements and water industry media—whether related to the looming water crisis, the imperative to privatize the water sector or the drive for a participatory reform process. One of many critical tasks, as we see it, is to piece together the interconnections across sites and themes, while at the same time giving full recognition to the importance of specific historically and geographically contingent phenomena.

Related to these ideas of connection and diversity, we ask: do varied and linked hegemonies articulate in similar ways in different contexts? How might different engagements with ideas regarding water governance connect or vary across sites? Do hegemonic ideas take similar forms everywhere, or do they play out in singular ways across particular space and time? These questions hold true across the subthemes that concern this volume. We do not claim to find easy answers to these questions, yet we hope that the pages offered will provide fertile ground for exploration and progress on these questions.

The chapters that follow have all been written by authors who were invited to reflect on these theoretical ideas, while remaining focused on empirical evidence regarding water–society relations in particular locales, notably highlighting contexts in Africa, the Middle East and Western Asia. In this way, the authors each add their contextual expertise to evaluate the how and why of hegemonic discourses as they play out in different parts of the globe. We have focused on those sites that match the specific expertise of the authors, yet we expect that similarly rich insights would come from extending examinations of this type to other areas, whether Latin America or other parts of Asia. Despite the omission of these regions, we contend that our contribution is highly relevant for the global South generally. While the sites we focus on are not the only sites of interest, they are certainly sites of great relevance, particularly from a water governance perspective. We await future contributions that will engage with these ideas and fill any gaps to extend the analysis and questions opened up here.

Sneddon's contribution (Chapter 2) posits that concepts that have received certain hegemonic status—so as to constitute a nearly unassailable veracity—generate and restructure power relations in clear ways. The idea of hegemony allows us to consider the power and ubiquity of the interlinked notions of scarcity and crisis, marketization, and participation: their endurance and fitness, while also attending to their mutability, across space and time, particularly in the face of opposition. With Sneddon's framing chapter, we are invited to consider carefully how hegemonic concepts related to water governance come into being, and we are invited to question which political agents define what is, or is not, acceptable to debate in water governance. Ultimately, a focus on hegemonic ideas within water governance helps illuminate how certain approaches to water use and management are perpetuated, regardless of their effects, their efficacy or socio-ecological impacts. In addition, these ideas often leave a trail of engagements from seemingly 'global' forums and institutions, frequently but not exclusively generated in the global North, across a multitude of locales in the global South. Tracing these engagements thus comprises a fundamental task for the rest of the chapters.

In Part II, Mahayni (Chapter 4) establishes the broad contours of debates over water scarcity in his framing chapter, noting in particular how water scarcity is almost always accompanied by narratives of crisis. For Mahayni, scarcity becomes a hegemonic idea within water scarcity discussions when it is uncritically applied by policy-makers and water experts in a way that prioritizes biophysical conditions above all other explanations. This in effect neutralizes and even disguises other factors—such as inequitable access to water in 'crisis' regions—that are vitally important in explaining and addressing water shortages. Subsequent chapters explore the discourses and associated practices of water scarcity in quite different locales, and interrogate how the hegemonic impulses of the scarcity narrative influence these sites in distinct ways.

In Chapter 5, Mahayni makes a strong case for investigating the multiple pathways through which scarcity narratives are brought in to, and embedded within, the political dynamics of the city of Damascus and within national policy circles of Syria more broadly. Damascus' recent 'water crisis' is thus more robustly interpreted as an outcome of national-level agricultural and water management policies (themselves highly politicized) and increasingly arid environmental conditions in the region. Whereas narratives of crisis and scarcity are relatively recent arrivals in discussions of water governance in Damascus, such narratives have a much longer history in other regions.

Similar themes are echoed in the case of small hydropower plants (SHPs) in Turkey (Chapter 6), where Erensu scrutinizes the complex and oftentimes obscure confluence of initiatives related to privatization initiatives, renewable energy, sustainable development and water scarcity characterizing recent state and civil society debates over water governance. Erensu sees scarcity discourses as central to a modernist interpretation of water as radically separate from the social, cultural and environmental networks that define its material and ideological importance to planetary life. In Turkey, this modernist paradigm is being reworked and challenged by state and non-state actors in novel ways, exemplified by recent controversies over the development of ostensibly 'sustainable' SHPs in the northern regions of the country. This section concludes with Musemwa's (Chapter 7) incisive history of western Matabeleland, where he argues that the British colonial state of Southern Rhodesia effectively downplayed efforts by water users to draw attention to the harmful impacts of a destructive drought in the early 1960s. The rise of water scarcity as a hegemonic construct, in this instance, was blunted and manipulated by the colonial regime to further its own ends. Musemwa's important conclusion is that we should be wary of automatically conferring hegemonic status on common water governance discourses when the historical record shows their persuasive power can ebb and flow over time and space.

Moving to Part III, Harris poses a central question in her framing chapter (Chapter 10): is it helpful to suggest that ideas related to market instruments, or privatization, have become hegemonic? If yes, in what instances would the hegemony of these ideas affect the world and practice of water governance? The follow-on chapter also by Harris (Chapter 11) highlights general issues of variegation with respect to these practices, highlighting both the importance of recognizing connections globally and regionally, while also attending to context specificities in terms of how these practices and discourses play out in specific locales. This is followed by two cases: the history of water marketization and privatization in Zambia (Waters, Chapter 12), and that of privatization of water provision in urban Kenya, with specific attention to equity and poverty concerns (K'Akumu, Chapter 13). Both of these cases offer strong empirical evidence for the uneven and consequential ways that marketization and privatization of water is implemented and experienced. Focused on earlier periods in Zambia, Waters shows that marketization of water, including payment schemes, has been applied selectively. Indeed, ideas about payment applied to those using water for domestic uses, but did not apply to mining and other related water-pollution activities. Furthermore, the contemporary crisis in terms of a lack of access to water for drinking in urban areas is directly linked to practices to accommodate mining companies and certain types of economic and urban growth during the colonial period (connecting markets and market activities in a broader sense to contemporary water governance challenges in this context). Focused on the case of water privatization in Kenya, K'Akumu directly addresses the concern related to impoverished populations that often accompanies privatization schemes, with particular attention to the types of steps that can be taken to diffuse these concerns and reduce potential negative impacts for those populations.

Turning to Part IV, Goldin's framing piece (Chapter 16) on participation claims that there is imprecision about what participation means and that it means different things to different people. She isolates 'four fatal flaws' (FFFs) related to connections with ideas of decentralization and devolution, the linkages to supply drivers, vagueness about what participation means, and the impulse to isomorphism with its focus on form rather than substance. Following on this, the chapter authors in this section show how hegemonic discourses manifest themselves in real rather than idealized spaces. Barnes takes us to Egypt (Chapter 17) where power and politics determine the who and the how of inclusion in participatory water governance. Barnes sets the tone for our interrogation of participation by detailing the gender dimensions of participatory practices related to water user associations, particularly in querying the (gendered) terms through which these associations were established. The consequences are varied, from segmenting women's participation to the domestic realm, rather than to irrigation, water uses that serve to stabilize male power linked to categories of irrigators, and the prioritization schemes that flow from these associations through the water user groups. Moving to Turkey, Kadirbeyoglu and Kurtic (Chapter 18) query participatory instances both with respect to irrigation management and also small hydroelectric projects, considering the ways that both inflect power hegemonies with respect to legitimate uses and management practices. In the case of small hydroelectric production, in particular, rural communities directly challenge these trends, forcing open new spaces of participation to resist hegemonic modalities of water governance. The chapter on 'Participation's limits' (Chapter 19) by Morinville and Harris takes place in Accra, Ghana, and has a focus on the local water boards as one particular form of participation that has been promoted by governmental organizations and development agencies. The work queries hegemonies by detailing the types of participation that are counted, whilst others are not, as being in itself an enactment of hegemony, with potential for determining both the effects of community participation and access to water.

In addition to these substantive contributions from the theoretical and empirical discussions, we are also particularly pleased about the 'commentaries' that offer an innovative twist to this volume. We have asked in each section both for a practitioner/activist and an academic response (again, of course, not reifying these categories as entirely distinct and recognizing that such terms are themselves loaded with ideological influence). Here, we offer an opportunity for engagement, and discussion, in terms of how the arguments of the book resonate, travel or hold potential salience across these different worlds. Part of our purpose in doing so is based on our commitment to both academic and practitioner worlds (and thus wanting to include both in our conversation), but also to challenge and open up spaces and opportunities for knowledge production in ways that we deem to be consistent with the querying of hegemonies. We recognize too that knowledge production too often supports other linked hegemonies, and feel it is important, if not critical, to enable spaces and opportunities for other voices and expressions. We are grateful to Routledge and the reviewers for the willingness to include this innovative element, and hope that the readers will appreciate, alongside the other words of this text, the insights contained within these pieces. It is by broadening our geographic scope, by bringing different places, regions and voices into conversations, that critical reflection of and challenge to diverse hegemonies of contemporary water governance, can move forward, and flourish.

References

Bakker, K. 2010. *Privatizing Water: Governance Failure and the World's Urban Water Crisis,* Ithaca, NY: Cornell University Press.

Bauer, C. 2004. *Siren Song: Chilean Water Law as a Model for International Reform,* Washington, DC: Resources for the Future.

Budds, J. 2004. Power, nature and neoliberalism: the political ecology of water in Chile. *Singapore Journal of Tropical Geography*, 25(3), 322–42.

Gleick, P., and Palaniappan, M. 2010. Peak water limits to freshwater withdrawal and used. *Proceedings of the National Academy of Sciences*, 107(25), 11155–62.

Goldin, J. A. 2010. Water policy in South Africa: trust and knowledge as obstacles to reform. *Review of Radical Political Economics,* 42(2), 195–212.

Harris, L. M. 2009. Gender and emergent water governance: comparative overview of neoliberalized natures and gender dimensions of privatization, devolution and marketization. *Gender, Place and Culture: A Journal of Feminist Geography,* 16(4), 387–408.

Haughton, Graham. 2002. Market making: Internationalisation and global water markets. *Environment and Planning A* 34, 791-807.

Jones, S. 2011. Participation as citizenship or payment? A case study of rural drinking water governance in Mali. *Water Alternatives,* 4(1), 54-71.

McDonald, D. A., and Ruiters, G. 2005. *The Age of Commodity: Water Privatization in Southern Africa,* London: Earthscan.

Robbins, P. 2003. Transnational corporations and the discourse of water privatization. *Journal of International Development*, 15, 1073–82.

Schmidt, J. 2012. Scarce or insecure? The right to water and the ethics of global water governance. In F. Sultana and A. Loftus (eds), *The Right to Water: Politics, Governance and Social Struggles*, pp. 94–109, Abingdon: Routledge.

Sneddon, C., and Fox, C. 2007. Power, development and institutional change: participatory governance in the Lower Mekong Basin. *World Development,* 35(12), 2161–81.

Sultana, F. 2009. Community and participation in water resources management: gendering and naturing development debates from Bangladesh. *Transactions of the Institute of British Geographers*, 34, 346–63.

World Water Forum (WWF) 2012. Key message and outcomes, conditions for success, good governance. 6th World Water Forum. Marseille, 12–17 March 2012. Organization for Economic Co-operation and Development (OECD). Available at: http://www.oecd.org/gov/6th%20WWF%20water%20governance%20report%20-%2022%20May.pdf (accessed Nov. 2012).

Part I
Integrating hegemony

Social and biophysical perspectives

2 Water, governance and hegemony

Christopher Sneddon

Hegemony is like a pillow: it absorbs blows and sooner or later the would-be assailant will find it comfortable to rest upon.

(Cox, 1983: 173)

Water governance is of central concern to a range of actors within governments, corporations and civil society organizations. It also encompasses an exceedingly complex set of discourses and actions that include water policy, water management and water politics. This chapter examines the rise in recent years of a variety of concepts that have assumed hegemonic status within discourses and practices associated with water governance. The notion of hegemony, while associated most closely with the writings of the Italian political philosopher and activist Antonio Gramsci, has come to refer to a wide variety of practices and ideologies associated with the power to influence decisions and patterns of thought. More specifically, hegemony is identified with the capabilities of some dominant collective within a given society to exercise influence in such as way to have its interests appear to be the interests of society as a whole. In effect, hegemony is about the wilful creation of power relations – the 'pillow' as noted above in Robert Cox's (1983) epigram – that serve the goals and desires of a specific set of actors, although a much wider set of actors create and maintain those goals and desires. In the sphere of water governance, management and development, these actors and institutions often seem to establish and disseminate hegemonic concepts at a global level, and, indeed, one of the important critiques of water governance is that a global 'water mafia' exercises undue influence over how societies interact with and govern water (Petrella, 2001; IRN, 2003). However, one of the key themes of the present volume is that hegemony manifests and is reshaped at multiple scales and levels, from global to national as well as in local settings.

My aim here is two-fold: to establish a common frame of reference for how the subsequent chapters engage the notion of hegemony; and to briefly highlight the rise of the three hegemonic concepts specific to water governance – scarcity, marketization and participation. These concepts provide the core themes investigated in our book. While the tone of this chapter is theoretical, its aims are eminently practical. The basic water needs of millions of people around the world – whether oriented towards survival and household uses, sanitation, agriculture or other dimensions – are not being effectively addressed (UNDP, 2011). Moreover, historical efforts to meet the human needs for water have too often come at the expense of aquatic ecosystems (e.g. rivers, lakes, wetlands) that have been left in a degraded state. We argue that 'the main causes for this unacceptable state of affairs are neither technical nor "natural" but rather are, broadly speaking, of a social and political nature' (Castro, 2007: 98). It is precisely through the exercise of hegemonic concepts that many of the causes (and solutions) to lack of access to water come to be identified as sitting exclusively within technical, institutional or natural domains.

I proceed to a discussion of the concept of water governance and a framework that highlights the theoretical underpinnings of hegemony and hegemonic concepts. I then examine the three dimensions of water governance – scarcity and crisis; markets and privatization; and participatory water governance – that have emerged in recent years as hegemonic, providing the foci taken up in the present volume. This sets the stage for later 'framing' chapters by Mahayni, Harris and Goldin that examine each of these dimensions in greater detail. Short examples demonstrate the complicated ways in which hegemonic concepts guide and influence policy decisions and political dynamics in water management and development. I conclude by highlighting the advantages of thinking about water governance in a way that foregrounds hegemony and hegemonic concepts.

Water governance and hegemony

In recent years, scholars and practitioners have increasingly directed attention towards a wide range of issues in an effort to understand the complex ways that human societies modify, exploit, adapt and consume water resources. These processes come together under the rubric of water governance. Geographer Karen Bakker defines resource or environmental governance more generally as the process by which organizations ('collective social entities that govern resource use') execute and enact management institutions ('the laws, policies, rules, norms, and customs by which resources are governed'); more simply, governance is 'the process by which ... we construct and administer the exploitation of resources' (2007: 434). Governance, however, has also come to encompass additional meanings. For example, one of the key architects of global approaches to water governance, the Global Water Partnership (GWP), offers the following description:

> Governance looks at the *balance of power* and the balance of actions at *different levels of authority*. It translates into political systems, laws, regulations, institutions, financial mechanisms and civil society development and consumer rights – essentially the rules of the game.
>
> (emphasis in original; GWP, 2003: 2)[1]

This definition is interesting for several reasons, but perhaps none so more than its attention to power and authority, both key concerns of an understanding of hegemony. Moreover, the notion of governance transcends a narrow focus on how states exercise power to include a host of potential agents across private and public spheres. In this same sense, concerns over greater levels of participation within water–society relations have led to the idea of distributed governance. This 'describes a system where many different parties have roles and responsibilities – government, civil society, private sector, individuals – with the State no longer acting alone to solve societal problems' (GWP, 2003: 6). In another vein, governance can encompass both instrumental (*how* water is shared and exploited via administrative and technical tools) and process-oriented conceptions (the setting of water use goals and priorities prior to implementation). These distinctive modes of water governance can lead to vast differences in how agents understand and experience governance as a set of processes. For example, mainstream and more casual uses of water governance – in policy reports, websites and global forums – often mask deep divisions among irreconcilable intellectual and political frameworks and the policy decisions that flow from these frameworks (Castro, 2007).

These evolving understandings of water governance raise a number of critical questions: how precisely do non-state actors (e.g. multinational corporations, water-related NGOs) engage in water governance, and has their increasing presence resulted in more effective social or ecological outcomes? How are such outcomes of water governance defined as 'effective' or otherwise assessed? Responses to these questions are highly contingent on who 'sets the terms' for water governance in the first instance, and what passes for expertise, knowledge and 'best practices' in the world of water policy and management. Such concerns are both political and pragmatic – the technical and management decisions made by water planners in the context of urban supply systems or construction of water infrastructure, for example, are directly shaped by the broader understandings of water's 'appropriate' use within society (see Baker, Chapter 3). The arenas for defining such uses are of course characterized by power relations among different agents; while the invocation of 'stakeholders' is nearly ubiquitous in the policy documents associated with water governance, those actors with a larger stake, often financially or politically, are frequently in a position to alter the governance process to meet their own objectives. For these and other reasons, the concept of hegemony can facilitate a more incisive understanding of how these power relations in the water realm are shaped and contested.

In recent years, the phrase hegemony has been used to describe a wide range of discourses and practices within the sphere of water–society relations. At the level of world politics, hegemony connotes a condition in international relations whereby one state is able to enrol 'others in the exercise of [its] power by convincing, cajoling and coercing them that they should want what you want' (Agnew, 2005: 1–2). Under this rubric, hydro-hegemony occurs when one state within, for example, a shared river basin is able to assert its power over upstream flows or persuade other riparian states its uses of the basin's water resources (via abstraction, dam development and so on) will be of benefit to all (Zeitoun and Warner, 2006). At other levels, hegemony indicates a particularly potent idea or policy that readily lends itself to widespread adoption across diverse societal contexts. Michael Goldman (2007), for example, traces how the bundle of policies and management interventions carried out under the World Bank's 'Water for All' initiative in the 1990s and 2000s – emphasizing among other things the need to see water as a economic good and the mobilization of the private sector to enhance drinking water services for the poor – circulated through transnational policy networks to become a globally dominant approach to water governance. However, the concept of hegemony as deployed originally by Gramsci (1971: 12–14) and more recently by contemporary work in the social sciences (see Birkenholz, 2009; Loftus, 2009; Mann, 2009; Perkins, 2011) also directs attention to the everyday processes whereby individuals and groups internalize certain concepts and act in a way that may be inimical to their broader interests within society. In a compelling account of the state's efforts to manage competing claims over drinking water access and infrastructure in Bangalore (India), Ranganathan (2010) uses a Gramscian framework to highlight the multiple relations of power that mobilize different social groups and help define their stance towards the water projects in question.

Cox's (1983) work on the Gramscian understanding of hegemony as applied to geopolitics offers a useful way to link the notion of hegemonic concepts across spatial scales. One of Cox's key insights, drawn from Gramsci, is that hegemonic power that operates at a global scale in the sphere of international affairs is constituted by and reflective of hegemonies of social classes within particular nation-states. Hegemony in world politics is 'in its beginnings an outward expansion of the internal (national) hegemony established by a dominant social class', and (eventually) the 'economic and social institutions, the culture, the technology associated with this national hegemony become patterns for emulation abroad' (Cox, 1983: 171). Setting aside the numerous critiques and extensions of Cox's interpretations (see e.g. Cox, 1999), this line of reasoning implies that hegemonic concepts such as those examined within the contours of water governance – whether linked to markets and privatization, scarcity and crisis, or participation at national or local levels – are tangibly connected to mechanisms of world hegemony such as international organizations, which (among other functions) legitimize certain norms that serve specific interests and co-opt the elites of dependent countries. From our perspective, it is more fruitful to think of multiple hegemonies, or hegemonic projects, that privilege certain ideas about water governance and disseminate those ideas in specific ways. This reflects a more nuanced view of how hegemony actually operates in a given society, as 'consent' to be governed (or govern oneself) in a fashion that sustains the hegemonic position of others is 'constantly being rearticulated' in unexpected ways (Birkenholz, 2009: 211). We are also mindful that debates over the hegemonic properties of the neoliberal project (see below) are highly contested and remain far from settled in theoretical terms (see Barnett, 2005; Perkins, 2011).

As we employ the term, a hegemonic *concept* refers to certain ideas that become dominant within a society and hence mold and structure how individuals and groups perceive and interpret certain phenomena (Trottier, 2003: 1). Such ideas limit the terms of debate, create little space for conflicting ideas and, when applied to societal ills, tend to become the dominant frame of reference for crafting solutions. Applied to water governance, hegemonic concepts are presented by their proponents so frequently and authoritatively that they exude an aura of unassailable objectivity in the quest for more effective water policies and management practices. In Gramsci's terms, they exude 'common sense', which forms the 'ideology or conception by which people validate their day-to-day, functional position in any given political, economic, and cultural system' (Perkins, 2011: 559). We would extend the ideological sphere of hegemonic concepts in water governance to include not only individuals, but also the state agencies, international development programs and community organizations that guide and implement water interventions. Historically, state agents and their allies in the business and developmental spheres have adopted a 'hydraulic mission' to appropriate freshwater resources for human use (Molle *et al.,* 2009), underscoring the centrality of the state in creating and sustaining hegemonic ideas.

We certainly start from the assumption that ideas and approaches to human interventions within ecological systems – whether under the umbrellas of 'development', 'resource management' or 'water governance' – further the interests of political and economic elites within a given society, often at the expense of disenfranchised and marginalized social actors. These ideas circulate throughout society abetted by a variety of media – international conferences, special reports, educational forums, the internet – in such a way as to come to seem 'common-sense' approaches to dealing with societal problems. For example, Molle (2008), who examines how hegemonic concepts in water governance come packaged in 'storylines', demonstrates how the narrative of 'free water' and its solution, water pricing, flourished in the 1990s amongst the development community amidst concerns over how to decrease mismanagement and inefficiencies within irrigation systems. In this and other cases, the epistemic community forged around price-based incentives in irrigation 'largely extended from mainstream economics departments in universities and international organizations ... and eventually extended down to national water laws' (Molle, 2008: 137). We utilize hegemony in water–society relations in a similar fashion to critically investigate how certain concepts – clustered around the themes of crisis/scarcity, privatization/markets and participation – within water governance have come to be perceived by governments, international financial institutions, international NGOs and scholars as almost universally applicable to the water-related challenges of the 21st century. It is not enough, however, to simply identify and explain the emergence of such concepts. It is vital to follow such concepts as they are passed from institutional context to become implemented in specific locales.

It would be a mistake to see hegemonic concepts as rigid and unassailable. Gramsci's ideas about how to confront hegemonic ideas and the institutions that maintain and disseminate them speak to contemporary debates about whether to reform approaches to water governance via achieving some measure of control over governance mechanisms (war of maneuver) or, alternatively, undertake more difficult political and institutional changes – associated with a 'war of position' – that foment 'the long-term construction of self-conscious social groups into a concerted emancipatory bloc' within a given society (Cox, 1999: 15–16; see also Trottier, 2003). As chapters in this volume demonstrate, counterhegemonic projects seeking to challenge state- or market-oriented reforms in the water and related sectors – whether over drinking water in urban areas (Mahayni, Chapter 5; K'Akumu, Chapter 13), small scale hydropower development (Erensu, Chapter 6), or water user associations (Barnes, Chapter 17; Kadirbeyoglu and Kurtic, Chapter 18) – struggle with how to best confront the economic, ideological and political power of dominant actors.

This is of course a gross simplification of the process through which different ideas regarding water governance become hegemonic. These ideas are almost always linked to broader and oftentimes older ideas and practices regarding human–environment relations. The hegemony of the discourse surrounding water scarcity and crisis, for example, frequently adopts the language of environmental determinism and neo-Malthusianism. The emphasis on privatization of water supply systems and embracing of a market-oriented approach to water use are intimately linked to the rise of neoliberalism (Bakker, 2010). Finally, participatory water management reflects nearly three decades of critiques of mainstream approaches to economic development and governance for being the exclusive domain of government officials and affiliated experts. In recent years, calls for participatory water governance have sought to redress this bias towards top–down approaches, but the concept of participation remains hotly contested. Despite its ostensible attention to grassroots involvement, participation as a decision-making technique has at times downplayed questions of representation within communities and has often amounted to mere rhetoric in the face of long-standing power imbalances, such as those between state agencies and non-state stakeholders (Cooke and Kothari, 2001). Boiled down, we simply point out that hegemonic concepts do not operate in isolation from other forms of power, as expressed through, at one scale, North–South political-economic relations, geopolitics and economic development strategies and, at other levels, gender dynamics and intra-community struggles (Barnes, Chapter 17). Nor is it a simple matter to clearly identify and articulate how hegemonic concepts travel from distant conference sites and academic chambers to water control facilities on the outskirts of cities and irrigation weirs in rural areas. One of our goals then is to begin to trace these connections, and demonstrate how ideas regarding water governance are generated, transformed and resisted across space and time.

The rise of hegemonic concepts in water governance

With respect to the organizing themes of this volume – scarcity/crisis; privatization/ markets and participation – we understand each to be hegemonic concepts within water governance, but as hegemonic in quite specific ways (see below). However, our sense is that hegemonic concepts, no matter how potent they seem, are simultaneously more omnipresent and rigid than often presented by the architects of global water governance *and* more variegated and fungible than often presented by the water justice movement and the water activist community.

For the architects of global water governance – a group that includes the World Water Council (WWC), the Global Water Partnership (GWP), the World Bank's water team, and a host of affiliated researchers and practitioners – the observation that many parts of the world are facing an ongoing or impending crisis of water scarcity is beyond question. Scarcity in this way of thinking, and the state of 'crisis' it induces, is almost inevitably an outcome of population growth, expanded demands on water resources due to economic growth and mismanagement of existing water resources. States, territories and regions are categorized according to the level of water scarcity or stress they are experiencing, and solutions to scarcity tend to focus on dramatic increases in financial resources for expanded water supply infrastructure mediated through technological innovations (e.g. Jury and Vaux, 2007). In response, both academics and international organizations have stressed the ways that narratives oriented towards scarcity and crisis obscure questions of equity and power relations at multiple scales (see UNDP, 2006; Castro, 2007).

In recent decades, a growing chorus of scholars, water development professionals and activists have debated the societal benefits and costs of classifying water as an economic good. Translated into governance and management mechanisms, this has meant that numerous countries have adopted market-based mechanisms (e.g. water markets, privatization) in the hopes of achieving more efficient distribution of water to competing uses and different social groups. Put succinctly, the 'international pressures for the adoption of market-inspired reforms have induced a homogenization of water policies around the world, despite major social, cultural, and economic difference between countries' (Ioris, 2010: 232). Indeed, private sector involvement in the water sector has evolved quite rapidly over the past several decades, with a pronounced trend towards privatization in the developing world since the mid-1980s (Bakker, 2010), although there are more recent indications that investments of private capital in the water sector (broadly construed) are being superseded by renewed interest in public financing of water resource development and hybrid public–private partnerships (PPPs) (Hall *et al.*, 2005; Hall and Lobina, 2010; de Gouvello and Scott, 2012). In contrast to scarcity, which refers to biophysical conditions, the hegemony of market-based ideas concerning water governance is linked more directly to mechanisms of water management and distribution. The marketization of water is also linked to questions of participation (see Harris, Chapter 10), our third theme, in ways that shed light on the specific and often opaque manner in which hegemony operates within water governance.

The GWP notes that over the past fifteen years '"participation" has been a successful and powerful instrument in various fields of water management' and 'has helped identify pragmatic directions, has allowed drawing on large pools of creativity and local knowledge, helped build up commitment and create the capacity to implement changes' (GWP, 2003: 17). To be certain, participatory water governance has become a fashionable topic amongst international organizations responsible for water governance and their state-level counterparts, yet there remain a host of problematic questions regarding whether efforts to decentralize water governance – in a variety of contexts – genuinely challenge state power or other hegemonic interests (Wilder and Lankao, 2006; Sneddon and Fox, 2007). As Harris (2009) has shown, what might at first seem like progressive approaches to water governance and management – through state-sponsored and IFI-funded initiatives to, for example, devolve water control decision-making to local communities, encourage participation by women and individualize water rights – can have the perverse effect of further embedding peripheral locales within the circuits of neoliberal approaches to economic development and resource exploitation. What is notable for our purposes is that participatory water governance was first proposed as palliative to top–down approaches – for example, state- or market-directed initiatives – and can thus be seen as, initially, counter-hegemonic (see Goldin, Chapter 16). Yet, this is also suggestive of the specific pathways through which 'acceptance' of particular modes of governance occurs, in this case through the unification of diverse strategies, discourses and goals (participation for greater equity, to counter top–down imposition, and in sync with neoliberal devolution processes). It thus serves as a warning to avoid simplified understandings of how hegemonic ideas are appropriated and transformed in unexpected ways, at times marrying complex interests and actors.

Taken together, these three hegemonic concepts within water governance raise a host of challenging questions:

- How do the hegemonic concepts built around our three themes – scarcity/ crisis, privatization/markets and participation – facilitate specific approaches to water governance? What paths of governance and practice are facilitated, and which paths are cut short? Whose interests do these concepts serve and how are they articulated?
- How do these concepts travel? Through what mechanisms and networks does a concept come to be hegemonic in a specific place and time? Do they always move unilaterally from global-level actors and institutions towards local communities? How are they molded and modified in specific circumstances and locales?
- What are the tangible impacts of hegemonic concepts in water governance? How do they affect technical decisions regarding water distribution or infrastructure development?
- Given the omnipresence of these concepts within water governance, what are the alternatives? Is the most effective strategy for achieving, for example, greater levels of equity in access to clean drinking water to be found in rejecting these concepts outright, or recalibrating their meaning and application?

Responses to these questions require a transdisciplinary mindset. They demand attention to the biophysical, technological, cultural and political-economic processes and networks through which water is manipulated and consumed. A critical examination of water governance and the predominant ideas that define its application in diverse locales must be grounded in an understanding of hydrology and the rationale behind the technical decisions made by, for example urban planners and water managers (see Baker, Chapter 3). Conversely, it is equally important for water professionals to grapple with the ideological baggage that has historically delimited the range of options available after systems of water resource and management have been generated, often in ways that reflect the interests of certain social groups over others. It is in this latter arena that analyses of hegemonic concepts in water governance become particularly helpful.

Conclusions

A consideration of hegemonic concepts as applied within the sphere of water governance offers several advantages to those concerned about the future of water–society relations, whether couched in terms of ecological resilience, economic development or social justice. First and foremost, an examination of hegemonic concepts arising from recent trends in the application of water governance edicts around the globe helps clarify the role that power – in its multiple dimensions – exercises in creating and perpetuating certain practices related to water (Ekers and Loftus, 2008). As the following chapters make clear, water governance as applied at the 'ground level' through the provision of water services, through projects designed to enhance water supply and through (supposedly) community-led water management programs is often predicated on sets of power relationships far removed from the sites of actual program implementation. A focus on the hegemony of certain ideas within water governance can clarify these power relationships and the potential ecological and social consequences they foment.

Second, hegemony can help us sort out the pathways by which seemingly 'global' ideas – hatched in the forums of powerful transnational actors and organizations – become applied across a range of spatial scales. Once proposed and implemented at regional, national and local levels, hegemonic approaches to water management and development can have profound impacts on specific locales. Conversely, 'local' resistance on the part of water planners, communities and non-governmental actors can multiply and diffuse across space and time, linking seemingly unconnected movements through a common cause.

Finally, as alluded to above, a focus on hegemonic concepts allows us to think through the possibilities of counter-hegemonic projects within the framework of water governance. Whether couched in terms of a 'water manifesto' for the world's disenfranchised (Petrella, 2001), a global 'water justice movement' (Davidson-Harden *et al.,* 2007), or a general democratization of water governance (Castro, 2007; Mirosa and Harris, 2012), there are now a growing number of alternative visions for recalibrating social and ecological relations that human beings construct through and with water. Such alternatives clarify the subtle operation of hegemonic concepts via the narratives and practices of water governance, and in doing so can harden Cox's hegemonic 'pillow' and make its effects more visible.

We do not wish to overemphasize the importance of hegemony when thinking about water governance. For many practitioners and activists struggling on the frontlines of water provision and access, such theoretical concerns can seem at best esoteric and at worst a waste of time and thought. Yet the contributors to this book project see genuine value in thinking carefully about the oftentimes hidden paths whereby 'global' – in both its material and ideological sense – ideas and practices become universally applied. It is in keeping with the spirit of Gramsci's life and work to analyze one's social (and ecological) conditions in order to uncover the most effective means of changing them when they are characterized by inequities and, in our case, misuse of critical resources.

Notes

1   The Global Water Partnership was created in 1996 to promote integrated water resources management (IWRM) as the most effective way to coordinate water resource development. The GWP consists of government agencies of both developed and developing countries, UN agencies, NGOs, bilateral and multilateral development banks, professional associations and researchers (GWP, 2003).

References

Agnew, J. 2005. *Hegemony: The New Shape of Global Power,* Philadelphia: Temple University Press.

Bakker, K. 2007. The 'commons' versus the 'commodity': alter-globalization, anti-privatization and human right to water in the global South. *Antipode*, 39(3), 430–55.

Bakker, K. 2010. *Privatizing Water: Governance Failure and the World's Urban Water Crisis,* Ithaca, NY: Cornell University Press.

Barnett, C. 2005. The consolations of 'neoliberalism'. *Geoforum*, 36(1), 7–12.

Birkenholz, T. 2009. Groundwater governmentality: hegemony and technologies of resistance in Rajasthan's (India) groundwater governance. *Geographical Journal,* 175(3), 208–20.

Castro, J. E. 2007. Water governance in the twenty-first century. *Ambiente ed Sociedade,* 10(2), 97–118.

Cooke, B., and Kothari, U. 2001. The case for participation as tyranny. In B. Cooke and U. Kothari (eds), *Participation: The New Tyranny?*, pp. 1–15, London: Zed Books.

Cox, R. 1983. Gramsci, hegemony and international relations: an essay in method. *Millennium: Journal of International Studies,* 12(2), 162–75.

Cox, R. 1999. Civil society at the turn of the millennium: prospects for an alternative world order. *Review of International Studies,* 25, 3–28.

Davidson-Harden, A., Naidoo, A., and Harden, A. 2007. The geopolitics of the water justice movement. *Peace Conflict and Development,* 11, 1–34. Available at: html://www.peacestudiesjournal.org.uk (accessed Nov. 2011).

de Gouvello, B., and Scott, C. 2012. Has water privatization peaked? The future of public water governance. *Water International,* 37(2), 87–90.

Ekers, M., and Loftus, A. 2008. The power of water: developing dialogues between Foucault and Gramsci. *Environment and Planning D: Society and Space,* 26, 698–718.

Global Water Partnership (GWP). 2003. *Effective Water Governance: Learning from the Dialogues,* status report prepared for the 3rd World Water Forum, Kyoto, Stockholm: Global Water Partnership.

Goldman, M. 2007. How 'water for all!' policy became hegemonic: the power of the World Bank and its transnational policy networks. *Geoforum,* 38, 786–800.

Gramsci, A. 1971. *Selections from the Prison Notebooks,* New York: International Publishers Co.

Hall, D., and Lobina, E. 2010. The past, present and future of finance for investment in water systems. Presented at IRC 2010 Symposium: Pumps, Pipes and Promises: Costs, Finances and Accountability for Sustainable WASH Services, The Hague, 16–18 Nov. Available at: www.psiru.org (accessed Nov. 2012).

Hall, D., Lobina, E., and de la Motte, R. 2005. Public resistance to privatization in water and energy. *Development in Practice,* 15(3–4), 286–301.

Harris, L. M. 2009. Gender and emergent water governance: comparative overview of neoliberalized natures and gender dimensions of privatization, devolution and marketization. *Gender, Place and Culture: A Journal of Feminist Geography,* 16(4), 387–408.

International Rivers Network (IRN). 2003. *Who's Behind the World Water Forums? A Brief Guide to the World Water Mafia,* Berkeley, CA: IRN.

Ioris, A. A. R. 2010. The political nexus between water and economics in Brazil: a critique of recent policy reforms. *Review of Radical Political Economics,* 42(2), 231–50.

Jury, W. A., and Vaux Jr., H. J. 2007. The emerging global water crisis: managing scarcity and conflict between users. *Advances in Agronomy,* 95, 1–76.

Loftus, A. 2009. Intervening in the environment of the everyday. *Geoforum,* 40(3), 326–34.

Mann, G. 2009. Should political ecology be Marxist? A case for Gramsci's historical materialism. *Geoforum,* 40(3), 335–44.

Mirosa, O., and Harris, L. M. 2012. The human right to water: contemporary challenges and contours of a global debate. *Antipode,* 44(3), 932–49.

Molle, F. 2008. Nirvana concepts, narratives and policy models: insights from the water sector. *Water Alternatives,* 1(1), 131–56.

Molle, F., Mollinga, P., and Wester, P. 2009. Hydraulic bureaucracies and the hydraulic mission: flows of water, flows of power. *Water Alternatives,* 2(3), 328–49.

Perkins, H. 2011. Gramsci in green: neoliberal hegemony through urban forestry and the potential for a political ecology of praxis. *Geoforum,* 42, 558–66.

Petrella, R. 2001. *The Water Manifesto: Arguments for a World Water Contract,* London: Zed Books.

Ranganathan, M. 2010. Fluid hegemony: a political ecology of water, market rule, and insurgence at Bangalore's frontier. Ph.D. University of California, Berkeley.

Sneddon, C., and Fox, C. 2007. Power, development and institutional change: participatory governance in the Lower Mekong Basin. *World Development,* 35(12), 2161–81.

Trottier, J. 2003. *Water Wars: The Rise of a Hegemonic Concept. Exploring the Making of the Water War and Water Peace Belief within the Israeli–Palestinian Conflict,* Paris: UNESCO International Hydrological Programme.

United Nations Development Program (UNDP). 2006. *Beyond Scarcity: Power, Poverty and the Global Water Crisis (Human Development Report 2006),* New York: United Nations.

United Nations Development Program (UNDP). 2011. *Sustainability and Equity: A Better Future for All (Human Development Report 2011),* New York: United Nations.

Wilder, M., and Lankao, P. R. 2006. Paradoxes of decentralization: water reform and social implications in Mexico. *World Development,* 34(11), 1977–95.

Zeitoun, M., and Warner, J. 2006. Hydro-hegemony: a framework for analysis of transboundary water conflicts. *Water Policy,* 8, 435–60.

3 Hegemonic concepts and water governance from a scientific-engineering perspective

Lawrence A. Baker

Other authors of this book analyze core concepts important for water governance through the lenses of human geography, sociology, anthropology, history, and related social sciences. In this section, I examine the role of technology and the technocrats who often play a role, typically a lead part, in water governance. This is important because while a more inclusive culture of governance evolves, technocrats will not only play traditional roles such as construction of infrastructure, but also new roles, such as developing information technologies that can advance broader participation within water governance decisions.

In Chapter 2, Sneddon examines the concept of hegemony, focusing on power relations among countries, including the dominance of wealthier countries over poorer countries, accomplished historically through colonialism and in the present, through ongoing development efforts. Expanding on this discussion, an additional dimension of hegemony is the dominance of engineering practice in world water development. In other words, technical solutions to water-related problems through the application of engineering knowledge have achieved hegemonic status as a way to govern and manage water for human benefit.

Engineering has played an important part in water development for thousands of years – complex water engineering projects have been integral to human settlements across the globe. However, it was modern industrialization, fueled first by coal and later by oil that allowed exponential population growth in European and US cities and created huge problems for water management. During the early years of industrial urbanization, engineers were often called upon to solve emerging water problems quickly, often with disastrous results. The problem of engineering hegemony in water management is illustrated by the conflict between engineers and public health officials in the US regarding sewage disposal during the late 19th century (Tarr, 1996). At this time, towns and cities were developing public water supplies, but officials and the general citizenry debated the question of sewage disposal. By this time, use of the 'water closet' was expanding throughout US cities, resulting in overflowing cesspools and latrines, which had been designed for human wastes only, not large volumes of water. Disposal of sewage could have been dealt with in two ways: by constructing new 'sanitary' sewers that would be used exclusively for human wastes, separate from storm sewers ('separate sewers') or by connecting household sewers to existing storm sewers, which had been designed for urban drainage, creating what came to be known as 'combined sewers'.

Linked to this debate was the decision of whether to treat sewage before it was discharged to rivers, or to discharge untreated sewage. In the latter scheme, it was expected that the 'self-purification' process of rivers would cleanse the water. Downstream cities that withdrew the cleansed river water would treat it further (at that time, mainly through filtration), making it safe to drink. Treatment before discharge was feasible only for the smaller volumes of water conveyed by sanitary sewers, not for the much larger flows conveyed by combined sewers.

Public health officials argued for separate sewers and treatment before discharge. Engineers promoted the development of combined sewers, with no sewage treatment, arguing that it was a cheaper option for downstream cities to treat municipal water at the point of withdrawal. In most US cities, the engineers prevailed, but the tragic outcome was the spread of typhoid and other waterborne diseases downstream. Epidemics of typhoid and other waterborne diseases ended only when the technology of chlorination was adopted for water treatment (first in 1908), which combined with water filtration, nearly eliminated typhoid by the 1940s. Yet the legacy of combined sewers persisted: when it became necessary to treat sewage, upon passage of the Clean Water Act in 1972, hundreds of US cities were compelled to separate their combined sewers into separate sanitary and storm sewers, costing tens of billions of dollars. As of 2001, combined sewer overflows remained in more than 700 communities and continued to pollute surface waters during storm events, a legacy of hegemonic decision-making by engineers more than 100 years ago (EPA, 2001).

I do not mean to castigate engineers: any profession left to its own devices will tend to develop 'siloed' thinking, and all professions will argue for the supremacy of their own brand of thinking. In the US, many hegemonic mistakes made by engineering could be overcome by the wealth of the nation – society could afford to fix most errors of short-sightedness because water infrastructure costs represent only about 1 percent of GDP (CBO, 2002). By contrast, countries in Sub-Saharan Africa will need an investment of 4 percent of GDP (on average) to meet water-related Millennium Development Goals (Banerjee and Morella, 2011) and can hardly afford to repeat the mistakes of industrialized countries.

A related cultural hegemonic idea in our early US history was the premise that nature was to be conquered by technology (Adas, 2006). Water development in the western US had religious overtones, the idea of 'reclaiming' desert 'wasteland' into gardens of Eden (Reisner, 1986). In a stunning photographic narrative of the construction of the Hoover Dam, the largest engineering project of its time, Arrigo (2010) presents headlines 'boosting' the dam prior to its construction: 'Mammoth dam at Boulder Canyon promises vast wealth and unrivaled electric power for Los Angeles' (*Los Angeles Examiner*, 1921); a map of the dam site in *Popular Mechanics* (1932) was labeled 'White Gold! Harnessing a River to Reclaim a Desert.' At the onset of construction, a set of photos in the *San Francisco Examiner* (1931) was titled 'Men move mountains, make way for greatest U.S. project.' Total dam storage in the US increased rapidly from the

1930s to the 1970s. Construction of major dams in the US virtually ceased by 1980, largely due to pressure from the growing environmental movement (Graf, 1999), but large dams continue to be built in developing countries, often with negative consequences (World Commission on Dams, 2000). This development-above-all mindset persists: Erensu (Chapter 6) quotes a Turkish Minister of Water and Forestry who said, in 2012, 'my job is to build dams'. The historical lesson is that hegemonic ideas of disciplinary supremacy, on one hand, or a blind ideology of human mastery over nature, on the other, have led to many ill-conceived water development projects.

The need for expanded participation in water governance is especially important in the context of extreme events such as drought. Engineers and hydrologists have traditionally thought of drought as an entirely hydrologic phenomenon, defined, for example, on the basis of the percentage of precipitation within a given time period in relation to the long-term average. This narrow definition can contribute to a sense that these problems must be solved with engineering/hydrologic solutions, such as building more dams to store water or reducing leakage in municipal water systems. Recently, water experts have started to think of drought as a socio-ecological phenomenon, a product of both hydrologic conditions and the social system (Kallis, 2008). In this view, human systems are either more or less vulnerable to drought based on a host of political and economic factors. At one extreme, scarcity might be thought of as a human-induced drought caused by overuse of water, even in the absence of a meteorological drought. Mahayni (Chapter 5) illustrates this phenomenon for Damascus, presenting evidence of diminished flows in springs and dried-up rivers caused by overuse of groundwater. An important component of the crisis in this case was the inability of governance mechanisms in Syria to respond to overuse.

In a parallel development, ecologists have developed the concept of 'resilience', referring to the capacity of an ecosystem (human and otherwise) to respond, by adaptation, to perturbations (Gunderson and Holling, 2002). The essence of resilience is that *feedback* (for example, in a human system, collection of data and synthesis into useable information) is used to guide an *adaptive response*. A theory of drought resilience would predict that two cities facing identical hydrologic droughts might have very different outcomes: the less resilient city (with ineffective governance) would collapse or at least become severely weakened, whereas the city with effective governance would recover quickly (Baker, forthcoming). There is some evidence for this hypothesis from the archeological literature. Historical settlements that have collapsed during periods of climate extremes (drought, often interspersed with flooding) include the Hohokum settlements in what is now Arizona (Bayman, 2001), the Mayan cities of Mexico (Haug *et al.*, 2003), the Akkadian Empire of the Middle East (Cullen and deMenocal, 2000), and Ankor, Cambodia (Buckley *et al.*, 2010). The consensus of these authors is that collapse of settlements during periods of extreme hydrologic variability (droughts and flood) is often caused by the failure of sclerotic governments to respond effectively. In this view, droughts and flooding creates a tipping point for an already weakened social system.

Developing a theory of water resilience (resilience to both droughts and flooding) is important because such a theory would give us the capacity to *anticipate and react to* potential tipping points caused by hydrologic stress. This is a critical need, because droughts are likely to become more devastating in the future. Drivers include (1) climate change, which will likely produce hotter, drier, more variable climate regimes in areas of the world that are already hot; (2) rapid growth in the world's urbanized population, and especially in unorganized peri-urban areas; (3) pollution of groundwater; and (4) increasing per capita water use, paralleling increasing prosperity (Baker, forthcoming).

The discussion of resilience leads directly to the theme of participation in water governance (Goldin, Chaper 16). A key aspect of resilience is the ability to adapt on the basis of feedback. For the case of incipient drought, this feedback might include measurements of groundwater levels, reservoir storage, leakage losses in water systems, and household water use – information that could be used to adapt to changing conditions and thereby avoid the impact of a drought. For example, feedback on leakage from water pipes (sometimes 50 percent in developing countries) might lead to the adaptive measure of fixing the pipes, thereby conserving water, well before a drought occurs.

Broad participation – in this case multiple paths of information flow whereby citizens can communicate with each other and with decision-makers at various levels of government – is therefore critical with regard to the development of resilient water systems. Some elements of participation that would influence resilience to droughts and floods include incorporation of indigenous/local knowledge, the acquisition of hydrologic data for decision-making, transparency and accessibility of this data, and the ability of citizens to communicate through both formal and informal networks. The case study of drought in Southern Rhodesia presented by Musemwa (Chapter 7) illustrates how decision-making in an earlier era (the 1960s) was severely hampered by lack of hydrologic data: even the notion of scarcity, in the middle of an extreme drought, was contested! In today's information age, we have the ability to develop regional water balances based on multiple sources of data, and the ability to communicate this information to citizens. Questions about how to appropriately engage citizens remain open for debate, as several authors in this volume appropriately query. What the previous examples suggest is that resilience is a characteristic of social-ecological systems that cannot be engineered exclusively through technological innovation; rather, attention to institutions and power relations is equally important in promoting resilience.

Today, information technologies can play a huge role in increasing participation in water management. Our ability to acquire, store, manipulate and disseminate data has increased exponentially over several decades, and the cost of using this technology has decreased. Ten years ago, a gigabyte of storage on a desktop was state of the art; today's computers often have a terabyte of storage – a thousand times more. This means that digital operations – such as manipulation of geographic information system (GIS) files, which in the past could be done only on centralized computer systems located at universities and corporations, can now be done by a small non-governmental organization on a personal computer, and the outcomes can be transmitted via the internet to a cell phone in a remote village. A creative 'app' could readily allow a rural villager with a mobile phone to upload information on the depth of her well; this information, along with information compiled by neighbors, could be processed and transmitted back to her in the form of a map of groundwater depths in her region. Ordinary people can now be empowered with hydrologic information; moreover, through analysis by governments and informal networks, this information can be used to develop actionable knowledge regarding water resources. Added to this is the capacity of first world satellites, which enable detailed mapping (< 1 m^2 resolution), in multiple spectra, of crops, forests, and cities, anywhere in the world, which can also be readily shared to increase local knowledge.

While information technologies have the potential to increase participation, this potential will not be realizable unless the information is made both transparent and accessible to the population. By accessibility I mean that the relevant data must be offered in a way that ordinary citizens can acquire it. For example, mapped information must be provided in ways that don't require expensive GIS software or specialized GIS training. Moreover, governments and water development agencies must be committed to the idea that local knowledge of water resources can be a valid and crucial input point for decisions regarding water governance.

A personal experience illustrates these ideas. A few years ago, at the depth of the US recession (*c*.2009), a major power company proposed to build a very large power plant in east–central Minnesota. At the time, I was chair of an informal watershed group that was fighting the proposal. Because the type of power plant being proposed would have used large quantities of water, I dug into a technical database on water consumption in the US, developed by the US Geological Survey. As a water expert, I quickly concluded that the power plant would consume as much water as all other uses of water in the county combined (which included several small cities). This kernel of knowledge, combined with the indigenous knowledge that many nearby residents who had private wells were already experiencing water shortages, resulted in widespread concern, even among boosters of the plant. The county board, although bent on approval of the idea, inserted a condition in the development agreement that prohibited the withdrawal of groundwater for cooling, effectively preventing the plant from being built (at least until they figure out another way to cool it!). The point here is that, although hundreds of people would have benefited from this information, I was the only one in a position to access and interpret the data. The data were tansparent in that anyone could download the information for free, yet it was not readily accessible, given that almost no one could find it, and even if they did, it would have been difficult to understand and interpret. For participation to be effective, legal and technical accessibility is not sufficient: hydrologic data must also be transparent for meaningful engagement to occur. Public officials and citizens need be no more than a few 'clicks' away from the information they need for decision-making. How to get that information and what to do with it are key for constructive and engaged dialog and participation on a host of water management issues.

An excellent example of where information technologies have been used to provide sophisticated tools to local populations is the Arizona Meteorological Network (AZMET). AZMET is a meteorological network that collects data and processes this information using a model of crop water requirements to make week-by-week irrigation recommendations, on how to efficiently use water for various crops and at various locations throughout the state, available to farmers via the internet (AZMET, 2012). Importantly, the state shares not only raw data, but also processes data into recommended irrigation rates, in inches per week. Such technological advances can help to overcome some of the challenges of meaningful local participation (e.g. Kadirbeyoglu and Kurtic, Chapter 18). With technological tools in their hands, local farmers, even if not well educated, can become efficient irrigators. They also will be able to engage, or even challenge, governmental or other institutions to make the case for other water uses, as they deem appropriate.

Information technologies are rapidly spreading, increasing the potential for utilizing them to improve participation in water governance. Even in Sub-Saharan Africa, one of the poorest regions of the world, information technologies have arrived: among 17 countries, 57 percent of respondents had a mobile phone and 14 percent had both mobile phone and internet access (Tortora and Rheault, 2011). Participation via the internet has the potential to counteract all four 'flaws' proposed by Goldin (Chapter 16): it defies rigidity of government structures and is genuinely 'authentic'; it is always demand driven; it tends to reduce the 'vagueness' of participation, and it defies isomorphism, the tendency to become 'cemented in form'. Of course, the potential benefits of information technology can only be realized if governments, citizens, and other entities embrace their use, or at least, do not actively seek to limit them.

With respect to the third theme of this book, privatization and markets (Harris, Chapter 10), research in the US has shown no consistent gain in efficiency resulting from privatization of water or wastewater operations (Wolff and Hallstein, 2005). Some of the engineering and finance issues associated with privatization include: loss of control of a public service, little recourse if a privatization contract does not work, loss of transparency when a utility is turned over to a private operator, potential for loss of jobs, the need to prepare very detailed contracts, including a detailed inventory of infrastructure assets (Jacobs and How, 2005). In Atlanta, a privatization scheme failed in part over a dispute on the condition of the subterranean water infrastructure; in the end, both sides agreed to cancel a long-term contract. Because of these concerns, in 1997 only about 10 percent of the US population was served by privately operated water systems, and only 6 percent was served by privately operated wastewater systems. Van der Berg (1997) found that nine years after privatization in England and Wales it was still too early to determine whether the privatized system was more efficient than the prior public system.

Extrapolating to poorer countries, the technical and engineering problems of privatization would seem to be overwhelming. Effective privatization requires extensive engineering and management expertise in the public sector in order to maintain oversight, transparent accounting, and fair contracting processes, all of which are likely to be problematic. In her discussion of water privatization in Zambia, Waters (Chapter 12) notes that the simple task of water metering – essential for billing – could not be accomplished. Inserting the technological issues into debates about privatization is essential for understanding why privatization might succeed in some situations and fail in others.

A final point: developing new theories of water governance will require substantial transdisciplinary research efforts, that is, research that requires 'mutual interpenetration of disciplinary epistemologies' (Gibbons *et al.,* 1994). This research cannot be dominated by any one discipline: engineers, political scientists, hydrologists, geographers, sociologists, historians, anthropologists, economists, and others must be involved. Working in such highly interdisciplinary teams presents formidable obstacles (Baker, 2006) that need to be interrogated and overcome. Tools such as intergroup dialog (to allow researchers to understand each other's cultures), a common set of heuristics (Nicholson *et al.,* 2002), and modeling approaches that help to integrate findings from various disciplines, such as systems dynamics modeling (Sterman, 2001; Welling, 2011) are steps that can be taken to allow researchers from disparate disciplines to work together.

In summary, while the technocratic hegemony has failed the developing world in many ways, the problem is not the technology itself, but the way it was used. Hence, castigating the technocrats is not the solution. Instead, those seeking to improve water governance in the developing world should embrace the potential of technology to support their efforts, guided by broader social considerations.

References

Adas, M. 2006. *Dominance by Design: Technological Imperatives and America's Civilizing Mission*, Cambridge, MA: Belknap Press.

Arrigo, A. 2010. Imagining the dam: the visual rhetoric of Hoover (Boulder) dam in popular and public print media, 1920–1975. Ph.D. University of Minnesota.

Arizona Meteorological Network (AZMET). 2012. Available at: http://ag.arizona.edu/azmet (accessed Nov. 2012).

Baker, L. A. 2006. Perils and pleasures of multidisciplinary research. *Urban Ecosystems*, 9, 45–7.

Baker, L. A. (forthcoming). Urban drought resilience, in situating sustainability. In A. Rademacher (ed.), *An Unequal World,* New York: NYU Press.

Banerjee, S. G., and Morella, E. E. 2011. *Africa's Water and Sanitation Infrastructure Access, Affordability, and Alternatives,* Washington, DC: World Bank.

Bayman, J. M. 2001. The Hohokam of Southwest North America. *Journal of World Prehistory*, 15(3), 257–311.

Buckley, B. M., Anchukaitis, K. J., Penny, D., Fletcher, R., Cook, E. R., Sano, M., Nam, L. C., Wichienkeeo, A., Minh, T. T., and Hong, T.M., 2010. Climate as a contributing factor in the demise of Angkor, Cambodia. *Proceedings of the National Academy of Sciences of the United States of America*, 107(15), 6748–52.

Congressional Budget Office (CBO). 2002. *Future Investment in Drinking Water and Wastewater Infrastructure,* Washington, DC: Congressional Budget Office.

Cullen, H. M., and deMenocal, P. B. 2000. Climate change and the collapse of the Akkadian Empire: evidence from the deep sea. *Geology*, 28(4), 379–82.

Environment Protection Agency (EPA). 2001. *Report to Congress: Implementation and Enforcement of the Combined Sewer Overflow Control Policy,* Washington, DC: US Environmental Protection Agency.

Gibbons, M., Limoges, C., Nowotny, H., Schwartzman, S., Scott, P., and Trow, M. 1994. *The New Production of Knowledge: The Dynamics of Science and Research in Contemporary Societies,* London: Sage.

Graf, W. L. 1999. Dam nation: a geographic census of American dams and their large-scale hydrologic impacts. *Water Resources Research*, 35(4), 1305–11.

Gunderson, L. H., and Holling, C. S. 2002. *Panarchy: Understanding Transformations in Human and Natural Systems,* Washington, DC: Island Press.

Haug, G. H., Günther, D., Peterson, L. C., Sigman, D. M., Hughen, K. A., and Aeschlimann, B. 2003. Climate and the collapse of Maya civilization. *Science*, 299(5613), 1731–5.

Jacobs, L., and Howe, C. W. 2005. Key issues and experience in U.S. water services privitization. *Water Resources Development*, 21, 89–98.

Kallis, G. 2008. Droughts. *Annual Review of Environment and Resources,* 33(1), 85–118.

Los Angles Examiner. 1921. Mammoth dam at Boulder Canyon promises vast wealth and unrivaled electric power for Los Angeles. 24 July.

Nicholson, C. R., Starfield, A., Kofinas, G., and Kruse, J. 2002. Ten heuristics for interdisciplinary modeling projects. *Ecosystems*, 5, 376–84.

Popular Mechanics, 1932. Area affected by Hoover Dam project. June.

Reisner, M. 1986. *Cadillac Desert: The American West and its Disapearing Water,* New York: Viking Penguin.

San Francisco Examiner. 1931. Men move mountains, make way for greatest U.S. project. 9 June.

Sterman, J. D. 2001. System dynamics modeling: tools for learning in a complex world. *Calilfornia Management Review*, 43(1), 8–25.

Tarr, J. A. 1996. *The Search for the Ultimate Sink: Urban Pollution in Historical Perspective,* Akron, OH: University of Akron Press.

Tortora, B., and Rheault, M. 2011. Mobile phone access varies widely in Sub-Saharan Africa: average phone owner is more likely to be male, educated, and urban. *Gallup World,* 16 Sept. Available at: http://www.gallup.com/poll/149519/mobile-phone-access-varies-widely-sub-saharan-africa.aspx (accessed Nov. 2012).

van der Berg, C. 1997. *Water Privatization and Regulation in England and Wales: Public Policy for the Private Sector,* Washington, DC: World Bank.

Welling, K. N. 2011. *Modeling the Water Consumption of Singapore Using System Dynamics,* Boston, MA: Massachusetts Institute of Technology.

Wolff, G., and Hallstein, E. 2005. *Beyond Privatization: Restructuring Water Systems to Improve Performance,* Oakland, CA: Pacific Institute.

World Commission on Dams. 2000. *Dams and Development: A New Framework for Decision-Making.* London and Sterling, VA: Earthscan. Available at: http://www.internationalrivers.org/files/attached-files/world_commission_on_dams_final_report.pdf (accessed 5 February 2013).

Part II
Crisis and scarcity

4 Producing crisis

Hegemonic debates, mediations and representations of water scarcity

Basil Mahayni

Introduction

The global crisis of water scarcity is upon us – or so we are told. Major studies drawing on a combination of consumption trends, demographic data, complex hydrological models and local knowledge suggest that we are on the brink of a global hydrological crisis (Gleick *et al.,* 2009; UNESCO, 2009, 2006, 2003; UNDP, 2006). These are common characterizations of the global water crisis shared amongst academics, scientists and policy-makers involved in water governance. Yet these characterizations are often discordant with local experiences, perceptions and histories. This framing chapter seeks to examine the tensions between the hegemonic representations of water scarcity and the uneven material realities experienced in particular localities. It begins with a synthesis of some of the debates and dialogs in global policy circles around the definitions and manifestations of water scarcity. The chapter also synthesizes critiques of these debates in political ecology, critical development studies and other social science disciplines. The main argument of the chapter is that the conceptualization of water scarcity is a function of the political choices that define which variables matter when representing and deciphering water scarcity.

Mainstream debates about water focus primarily on the biophysical degradation of water systems and the effects of climate change. Scientists and policy-makers increasingly highlight the potential benefits of resilience planning and adaptation as crisis mitigation strategies. Social scientists argue that privileging the biophysical dimensions of water scarcity in policy and research results in managerial and engineering solutions that are technical in form and substance (Linton, 2010; Mehta, 2005). The problem with this, they argue, is that there is a high risk of failure because social relationships, political and economic interests, and local knowledge play an important part in the social and biophysical dynamics of hydrological systems. A singular emphasis on technical and engineering solutions can obscure power dynamics across multiple scales and ignore complex social, economic and political realities that condition distribution, access and use of water. The intent of this chapter, therefore, is to trace the ways that mainstream water scarcity discourse travels within broader political and economic networks, and how such networks inform particular policies by universalizing water scarcity and, conversely, obscuring uneven water access and distribution. This chapter also sets the stage for further exploration of these issues in the individual chapters that follow.

The following section of the chapter synthesizes the prominent ways of conceptualizing water scarcity, paying particular attention to the changing ways scientists and policy-makers have framed and studied water scarcity. This first section offers a discussion of key, though not exhaustive, drivers of water scarcity. The second section examines water scarcity beyond the lens of the biophysical by putting forward arguments by scholars interested in the process of scarcity production, mediation and the effects of representations of scarcity (particularly at the global level). The chapter concludes with a series of questions that frame and guides the chapters in this section.

Hegemonic frames of water scarcity

Sandra Postel (1999: 3) wrote, 'When it comes to water, nature has dealt a difficult hand.' Statistics about the state of the world's freshwater make it difficult to disagree. It is estimated that only 2.5 percent of the world's water resources is fresh and usable for myriad human needs and ecosystem services. Of this limited freshwater, 70 percent is locked away in the form of ice and permanent snow cover. Groundwater constitutes 97 percent of the accessible freshwater resources and surface water in rivers and lakes is 3 percent (Gleick *et al.*, 2009). Yet these statistics can be misleading because they overlook substantial geographical differences in freshwater supply, access and perception (Linton, 2010; Mehta, 2005). Consequently, scholars have attempted to define and categorize water scarcity. These typically fall into two categories. First order scarcity refers to declining water resources, whereas second order scarcity addresses the relative distribution of water between states, communities, competing uses and human versus ecological needs. Water scarcity also inspires a range of different definitions about what it represents. Most common among these are measurements of availability per capita (Falkenmark, 1989), with considerations of economic, technological and political adaptations (Ohlsson, 2000; Rijsberman, 2006).

Malin Falkenmark's (1989) Water Scarcity Index (WSI) demarcates levels of water scarcity into three thresholds: (1) water stress – 1,000 m^3 to 1,700 m^3 of freshwater per capita, (2) water scarcity – 500 m^3 to 1,000 m^3 of freshwater per capita and (3) severe water scarcity – less than 500 m^3 of freshwater per capita. While the Water Scarcity Index attempts to introduce nuance into water scarcity analyses, it does not account for institutional, social or political-economic variations that affect the societal capacity to respond to water scarcity. In an effort to extend the WSI, Ohlsson (2000) incorporates the UNDP's Human Development Index as a proxy measure of adaptive capacity into the water scarcity index calculations. This Social Water Scarcity Index (SWSI) seeks to account for fluctuations in first order scarcity and the capacity for dealing with second order scarcity and entails assessments of the capacity to respond to relative scarcity, distributional inequalities and ecosystem services. These scarcity indices generated new insights into the degree of water scarcity and the coping strategies for water crises within different country contexts.

Indeed, the indices reflect the critical tensions between human welfare, ecosystem services and hydrological systems and between existing supplies and demands. Such works also offer insights into commonly accepted baseline measurements, such as the UN recommendation of 40–50 liters per day proposed as a sufficient quantity for drinking, cooking and sanitation – a quantity that has not yet been universally met. Yet the Water Scarcity Index and the SWSI offer inherently generalized accounts and do not reflect spatial and temporal variability in water availability or differences in demand, access, distribution, and use of water. Most people lack access to water not because of water shortages but because of poor water infrastructure and service delivery (Rijsberman, 2006). Furthermore, water demand is dependent and contingent on use. For example, agriculture requires approximately 3,500 liters per person per day and although this too is dependent upon the particularly livestock or crop, the WSI and the SWSI are not designed to reflect these variations. Additionally, they do not reflect the ways that water cycles through social and economic systems. For example, the majority of water for domestic purposes is recycled, while most of the water (40–90 percent) provided to agriculture is evapotranspired in the food production process. Water scarcity can also be relative as competing users value water differently, which exposes access to and use of water to various power dynamics (Rijsberman, 2006). Consequently, water security has been offered as a means of refining the blunter notion of scarcity and conceptualizing the complex dynamics of water systems.

Yet definitions of water security also vary. Cook and Bakker (2012) offer a dynamic analysis of the ways that analyses and definitions of water security have evolved according to disciplines and geography. Like integrated water management, they argue that generality is strength in water security as it can be operationalized in particular ways to improve water governance (Cook and Bakker, 2012). One commonly cited definition of water security is 'an acceptable quantity and quality of water for health, livelihoods, ecosystems, production, coupled with an acceptable level of water-related risks to people, environments and economies' (Grey and Sadoff, 2007: 547–8). The concept of water security encapsulates the mismatch between demand and supply, and the tensions between response capacity and shortages or, inversely, inundation. More specifically, the conceptual framework of water security helps clarify the likelihood of conflict when communities and/or institutions are unable to respond to problems of relative scarcity or inundation, and to the distributional inequalities in water access and control that may result from these situations (Grey and Sadoff, 2007). One factor that might contribute to conflict is the variable investment capacity and water infrastructure across communities. The International Water Management Institute (IWMI) has characterized places as economically 'water scarce' based on the availability of water resources in relation to investment capacity and infrastructural development (see Rijsberman, 2006), while the Water Poverty

Index disaggregates this measurement to household and community levels (Sullivan, 2002; Sullivan *et al.*, 2003).

Hegemonic debates about water scarcity also tend to privilege surface and groundwater resources, or 'blue water', while overlooking water embedded in soil profiles and plants, also referred to as 'green water' (Allan, 2001). Most scientific studies of water scarcity neglect 'green water', the primary source of water in agriculture, despite the disproportionate influence of agriculture on regional and global water deficits. The concept of 'virtual water' attempts to redress the limitations in existing water scarcity studies by calculating comparative advantage in use of 'blue' and 'green water' in commodity production (Allan, 2001). Additionally, Allan (2006) also distinguishes between 'big water' and 'small water' scarcity. 'Big water' scarcity unfolds when agriculture and food production are affected by limited water supplies. Water deficits can, in theory, be overcome by acknowledging the localized comparative advantage (or lack thereof) in food production and thus water use. This comparative advantage is reflected in the amount of water utilized and embedded in crops and crop production, and in turn, traded in commodities. The problem remains, however, that food policies are often enmeshed in geopolitical relations across nation-states and food distribution in general can be highly politicized (Johnston *et al.*, 2010).

'Small water' scarcity reflects the water shortages faced by society and industry. This water is always blue water, and primarily affects the poor, as they are more likely to struggle to access potable water and sanitation. For Allan (2006), the key to making the most effective use of scarce water supplies is to diversify economies away from water-intensive activities by importing these commodities, including food, and in turn, making sure that sufficient volumes of 'blue water' are made available for immediate needs of human consumption and industry. Countries that are unable to deal with small water crises are at risk, while those facing 'big water' crises can likely manage this through trade of agricultural commodities. The challenge remains, however, that water scarcity, whether 'big' or 'small', is conditioned by a host of other factors that transcend simplistic governance choices or technical interventions. For the most part, the water scarcity indices, water security and 'virtual water' all concern quantity. For some, the emphasis on water quantity is misplaced. Rather, water *quality* should be prioritized because of the widespread implications for public health, livelihoods and ecosystem services (Biswas and Tortajada, 2011; see also UNESCO, 2009, 2006, 2003). Policy-makers, planners and public health experts stress that poor water quality and dilapidated infrastructure intensify public health crises in the global South, particularly in urban areas. According to the UN World Water Development Report (UNESCO, 2009), one to two million people, 90 percent of whom are children, die each year from preventable diseases caused by contaminated water, limited access to sanitation and poor hygienic conditions. In addition, many of these communities face structural barriers such as inadequate housing and sanitation, and limited livelihood opportunities that constrain their options for water access and use.

Aside from, but related to quantity and quality debates, global climate change and hydrological variability have engendered a new urgency in water governance debates, which pose enormous challenges. This is particularly the case as water governance faces the increasing likelihood of expanding and shifting water scarcity conditions across the planet (see Tortajada, 2010a, 2010b). Climate change and changing hydrological cycles affect storage capacity and the replenishment of surface and groundwater (UNDP, 2006). Scientists and policy-makers now advocate for localized assessments of water scarcity (Gleick *et al.,* 2009) by scaling down regional and global hydrological models (UNDP, 2006). There is a related push to move away from static hydrological baseline studies that underlie many water policies (Gleick *et al.,* 2009). In order to incorporate greater flexibility into water governance and respond to changing ecosystems affected by climate change, the Intergovernmental Panel on Climate Change (2007) has pressed for greater adaptive planning, defined by 'initiatives and measures to reduce the vulnerability of natural and human systems against actual and expected climate change efforts'. Despite the important contributions of the growing body of scholarship focused on water governance, the biophysical dimensions of water scarcity continue to take precedence in research.

As evidenced above, policy-makers and water engineers are trying to integrate climate change studies with research on projected socio-economic trends to inform various supply and demand adaptation strategies (Gleick *et al.,* 2009). An interdisciplinary approach that combines social and biophysical interactions as a way addressing water scarcity is, however, easier said than done due to scale differences in analyses, inconsistencies in definitions and geographical variability in social and biophysical dynamics (see Cook and Bakker, 2012; Bakker, 2012). For example, the call for adaptive governance is predicated on assessments of quantitative water scarcity and it does not necessarily account for relative water scarcity, water quality or how different individuals and communities experience water in both material and social senses. It is therefore important to examine the ways that the discourse of scarcity is constructed and how a sense of crisis is generated, through this discourse, as an impetus for reform. In many governance circles, there is too often a linear path from scarcity to impending crisis to market-based reforms, and consideration of alternative means of confronting water–society dilemmas is sidelined (see Parts III and IV of this volume). In many cities throughout the global South, popular protests and social movements have contested water reform projects because the hegemonic assumptions of water governance often do not adequately reflect daily realities, particularly distributional inequalities (these themes are picked up by all of our activist respondents in this volume).

Mediations, productions and representations of scarcity

Sandra Postel's (1999) assertion that the 'era of water scarcity' is upon us carries a double meaning. First, it suggests that available freshwater supplies are biophysically constrained. Second, it reflects the ways that hegemonic debates about water resources prioritize water scarcity as an object of analysis and concern. These two definitions characterize why and how mainstream debates tend to reflect and circulate hegemonic assumptions about water scarcity. Water scarcity is not solely reducible to diminished supplies, overuse or contamination. This is because numerous processes (e.g. nation-building, state development policies, urban planning and investment priorities), at first glance far removed from water resource issues, have shaped urban and rural landscapes, contemporary water scarcity, distribution and access, as well as water reform and governance efforts.

As an example, historical processes related to early settlements, colonial planning and state-building policies and practices mediate water scarcity in its various forms throughout the world (Gandy, 2006). Consequently, cities in the global South have pockets of both formal and informal access to water (Bakker, 2003) with distributional inequalities that are likely to grow with ongoing deterioration of infrastructure (Gandy, 2006), irrespective of available supplies of freshwater. Simply extending connections to poor neighborhoods is unlikely to create the conditions for equitable access because the reasons behind the (re)production of access inequalities are neglected. Reducing access disparities in engineering and policy senses risks failure without examining context and history (see Swyngedouw, 2004).

Prescriptive public policies packaged as a series of 'best practices' assumed to be universal in their application is one consequence of normalizing (unequal) access to water (Goldman, 2007). Yet these often fail due to the political and economic priorities of vested stakeholders. For example, the response of the Yorkshire Water Services (YWS) during the 1995 summer drought in the West Yorkshire region of England was shaped by the profit imperatives in the water utility. The devastating effects of the drought were produced and conditioned by the privatization of the water system in 1989, profit incentives, inadequate meteorological modeling and ineffective demand forecasting (Bakker, 2004, 2000). Such water crises, however, are not unique to formal institutions and, as Bakker (2010) argues, informal institutions, especially in cities of the global South, also shape the dynamics of water scarcity. Thus, while governance reforms are regularly regarded as technical interventions in various aspects of formal water systems, a multitude of political, historical, economic and social interests also shape the experience and the production of water crises (Bakker, 2010; Loftus, 2006).

Knowledge production of formal and informal water systems by institutions such as the World Bank, among others, are also shaped by power interests that guide research goals, frameworks and the dissemination of findings (Goldman, 2005). Social scientists have also critiqued scientific assumptions that underlie water resource development and human–environment interactions (Mitchell, 2002). More broadly, water research and policy shape, and has been shaped by, an evolution of hydrological science, through complex models of water systems, that situates nearly all water issues within a framework of scarcity (Linton, 2010).

One of the common assumptions of the progenitors of global water governance is that scarcity necessarily begets crisis. Mehta (2005) speaks directly to the interest of this chapter by arguing that discourses of water crises often obscure underlying inequalities in water use and access.

> The water 'crisis' is, thus, also a crisis of unequal power relations and skewed control over a finite resource. Blanket statements of scarcity often fail to address the relational and distributional aspects of water scarcity and their links with prevailing social and power relations, which have a tremendous bearing on how water is used or abused.
>
> (Mehta, 2005: 4)

Elsewhere, Mehta (2010) argues that the assumptions behind models should be analyzed alongside contested meanings and experiences of scarcities across space and time. Indeed, some communities might perceive scarcity despite the abundance of water (Mehta, 2005). It is important to keep in mind that a critique of these ideas does not only ask whether or not scarcity exists, but investigates how assumptions and ideas forge a body of thought related to scarcity into a singularizing problematic (Luks, 2010). Luks (2010: 99) asserts that:

> There are undeniable facts 'out there', but social dealing with these facts is a completely different issue ... yes, the world *is* limited, resources *are* used, we *can* measure environmental change – but when we talk about scarcity, we do not talk about these developments out there but refer to something that is fundamentally socially constructed.

Thus, the representation of water scarcity and the material complexities of scarcity are in constant tension, and if this tension is neglected it may increase access and distribution inequalities and further compound biophysical degradation of water resources. One way of bridging the tension between discourse and material realities is by examining diverse knowledge claims and experiences, as well as the reasons and contextual pathways through which particular dimensions of water scarcity exist (Mehta, 2005). One starting point is the definition of scarcity and the imperatives of water research (Mehta, 2010).

The various definitions of water scarcity discussed above speak directly to the commonly accepted linear relationships between variable hydrological systems and climate patterns, pollution, population growth and haphazard urbanization on freshwater resources (Linton, 2010). This, in turn, has guided policies such as market-based governance (Mehta, 2010; Harris, Chapter 10), which proved disastrous for the urban poor throughout Asia (see Shiva, 2002), Africa (see McDonald and Ruiters, 2005; Waters, Chapter 12; K'Akumu, Chapter 13) and Latin America (see Perreault, 2006). Discourses of water scarcity can also deepen the political power that states exercise relative to other states and towards their citizens in the pursuit of strategic policy goals. Alatout (2009, 2007) demonstrates the ways that perception and representation of water resources were interjected into political actions of the Israeli state in his analysis of Zionist immigration and Israeli state security in the early to mid-1900s. Yet the policy choices pursued by states and international development institutions to mitigate resource scarcities can also produce the conditions for social unrest. Activists contesting World Water Forums where hegemonic policies are debated, and infrastructural development projects, such as dams or water diversions, highlight the severe disjuncture between the debates in the boardrooms and the daily experiences of those most marginalized when it comes to water policy and water scarcity (Khagram, 2004; Mehta, 2010; Shiva, 2002).

Conclusion

A serious evaluation of water scarcity must go beyond studies of how to bring supply and demand into balance. This framing chapter underscores a theme across this literature that crises of water scarcity are also manifestations of unequal access and distribution. Crises are as much biophysical as they are a product of mismanagement that produces the conditions under which drought (or flooding) is more acutely experienced. Perpetuating discourses about water scarcity is politically charged as various institutes and policy networks become invested in reinforcing particular assumptions and policy ideas. It is important to understand the root causes that underlie the production of water scarcities, the dynamics of access and distribution that create conditions of scarcity for some and abundance for others, and to interrogate the analytical and policy frameworks designed to alleviate water scarcity crises (see in particular, Mahayni, Chapter 5).

This brings us back to the core question: is the crisis of water scarcity upon us? It is undeniable that millions of people around the world do not have access to clean, potable water or sanitation infrastructure. Others only have sporadic access to water because of dilapidated infrastructure or incompetent management. Declining water tables, dried riverbeds or months of drought have displaced millions of others. Although alleviating these conditions should be a priority, there are important questions linked to these conditions that too often go unanswered. How do we overcome the tension between biophysical realities and social inequalities? In what ways does history shape urban and rural waterscapes and how does this influence or shape the possibilities for reform? How do local experiences and perceptions refract against global water governance and policy debates? I do not mean to suggest that biophysical scarcity is somehow unimportant in the lives of millions of people in the global South. Yet for future research – as represented in part by the chapters that follow – it is imperative to chart new ways of examining the intersections between biophysical changes and the political-economic factors that produce water scarcity, and, in doing so, paying attention to the ways in which water scarcity is just as much a struggle of ideas, as it is a struggle over hydrologic realities and effects.

References

Alatout, S. 2007. State-ing natural resources through law: the codification and articulation of water scarcity and citizenship in Israel. *Arab World Geographer*, 10(1), 16–37.

Alatout, S. 2009. Bringing abundance into environmental politics: constructing a Zionist network of water abundance, immigration, and colonization. *Social Studies of Science*, 39(3), 363–94.

Allan, T. 2001. *The Middle East Water Question: Hydropolitics and the Global Economy,* New York: I. B. Taurus & Co.

Allan, T. 2006. Virtual water: part of an invisible synergy that ameliorates water scarcity. In P. Rogers, M. Ramon and L. Martinez-Cortina (eds), *Water Crisis: Myth or Reality?*, pp. 131–50, Leiden: Taylor & Francis.

Bakker, K. 2000. Privatizing water, producing scarcity: the Yorkshire drought of 1995. *Economic Geography*, 76(1), 4–27.

Bakker, K. 2003. Archipelagos and networks: urbanization and water privatization in the South. *Geographical Journal*, 169(4), 328–41.

Bakker, K. 2004. *An Uncooperative Commodity,* New York: Oxford University Press.

Bakker, K. 2010. *Privatizing Water: Governance Failure and the World's Urban Water Crisis*, Ithaca, NY: Cornell University Press.

Bakker, K. 2012. Water security: research challenges and opportunities. *Science*, 337(6097), 914–15.

Biswas, A., and Tortajada, C. 2011. Water quality management: an introductory framework. *Water Resources Development*, 27(1), 5–11.

Cook, C., and Bakker, K. 2012. Water security: debating an emerging paradigm. *Global Environmental Change*, 22(1), 94–102.

Falkenmark, M. 1989. The massive water scarcity now threatening Africa: why isn't it being addressed? *Ambio*, 18(2), 112–18.

Gandy, M. 2006. Planning, anti-planning and the infrastructure crisis facing metropolitan Lagos. *Urban Studies*, 43(2), 371–96.

Gleick, P., Cooley, H., Cohen, M. J., Morikawa, M., Morrison, J., and Palaniappan, M. 2009. *The World's Water 2008–2009: The Biennial Report on Freshwater Resources,* Washington, DC: Island Press.

Goldman, M. 2005. *Imperial Nature: The World Bank and Struggles for Social Justice in the Age of Globalization,* New Haven, CT: Yale University Press.

Goldman, M. 2007. How 'water for all!' policy became hegemonic: the power of the World Bank and its transnational policy networks. *Geoforum*, 38(5), 786–800.

Grey, D., and. Sadoff, C. W. 2007. Sink or swim? Water security for growth and development. *Water Policy*, 9(6), 545–71.

Intergovernmental Panel on Climate Change (IPCC). 2007, *Glossary A-D: Climate Change 2007: Synthesis Report,* Geneva: IPCC. Available at: http://www.ipcc.ch/publications_ and_data/ar4/syr/en/annexessglossary-a-d.html.

Johnston, R. M., Lacombe, G., Hoanh, C. T., Noble, A. D., Pavelic, P., Smakhtin, V., Suhardiman, D., Kam, S. P., and Choo, P. S. 2010. *Climate Change, Water and Agriculture in the Greater Mekong Subregion,* Colombo: International Water Management Institute.

Khagram, S. 2004. *Dams and Development: Transnational Struggles for Water and Power,* Ithaca, NY: Cornell University Press.

Linton, J. 2010. *What is Water? The History of a Modern Abstraction*, Vancouver: UBC Press.

Loftus, A. 2006. Reification and the dictatorship of the water meter. *Antipode*, 38(5), 1023–44.

Luks, F. 2010. Deconstructing economic interpretations of sustainable development: limits, scarcity, and abundance. In L. Mehta (ed.), *The Limits to Scarcity: Contesting the Politics of Allocation*, pp. 93–108, Washington, DC: Earthscan.

McDonald, D. A., and Ruiters, G. 2005. *The Age of Commodity: Water Privatization in Southern Africa*, London: Earthscan.

Mehta, L. 2005. *The Politics and Poetics of Water: Naturalising Scarcity in Western India*, New Delhi: Orient Longman.

Mehta, L. 2010. The scare, naturalization, and politicization of scarcity. In L. Mehta (ed.), *The Limits to Scarcity: Contesting the Politics of Allocation*, pp. 13–30, Washington, DC: Earthscan.

Mitchell, T. 2002. *Rule of Experts: Egypt, Techno-Politics, Modernity*, Berkeley, CA: University of California Press.

Ohlsson, L. 2000. Water conflicts and social resource scarcity, *Physics and Chemistry of the Earth, Part B: Hydrology, Oceans, and Atmosphere*, 25(3), 213–20.

Perreault, T. 2006. From the Guerra Del Agua to the Guerra Del Gas: resource governance, neoliberalism, and popular protest in Bolivia. *Antipode*, 38(1), 150–72.

Postel, S. 1999. *Pillar of Sand: Can the Irrigation Miracle Last?* New York: Worldwatch Institute.

Rijsberman, F. R. 2006. Water scarcity: fact or fiction? *Agricultural Water Management*, 80, 5–22.

Shiva, V. 2002. *Water Wars: Privatization, Pollution, and Profit*, London: Pluto Press.

Sullivan, C. 2002. Calculating a water poverty index, *World Development*, 30(7), 1195–1210.

Sullivan, C. A., Meigh, J. R., Giacomello, A. M., Fediw, T., Lawrence, P., Samad, M., Mlote, S., Huton, C., Allan, J. A., Schulze, R. E., Dlamini, D. J. M., Cosgrove, W. J., Delli Prisocli, J., Gleick, P., Smout, I., Cobbing, J., Calow, R., Hunt, C., Hussain, A., Acreman, M. C., King, J., Malomo, S., Tate, E. L., O'Regan, D., Milner, S., and Steyl. I. 2003. The water poverty index: development and application at the community scale. *Natural Resource Forum*, 27, 189–99.

Swyngedouw, E. 2004. *Social Power and the Urbanization of Water*, New York: Oxford University Press.

Tortajada, C. 2010a. Water governance: some critical issues. *International Journal of Water Resources Development*, 26(2), 297–307.

Tortajada, C. 2010b. Water governance: a research agenda. *International Journal of Water Resources Development*, 26(2), 309–16.

United Nations Development Programme (UNDP). 2006. *Human Development Report 2006: Beyond Scarcity – Power, Poverty, and the Global Water Crisis*, New York: Palgrave Macmillan.

United Nations Educational, Scientific, and Cultural Organization (UNESCO). 2003. *Water for People, Water for Life*, United Nations World Water Development Report, New York: Berghan Books and UNESCO Publishing.

United Nations Educational, Scientific, and Cultural Organization (UNESCO). 2006. *Water: A Shared Responsibility*, United Nations World Water Development Report 2, New York: Berghan Books and UNESCO Publishing.

United Nations Educational, Scientific, and Cultural Organization (UNESCO), 2009. *Water in a Changing World*, United Nations World Water Development Report 3, New York: Earthscan and UNESCO Publishing.

5 Tensions in narratives and lived realities of water crisis in Damascus

Basil Mahayni

Introduction

Ibn Jubayr, a 12th-century Moorish traveler, wrote of Damascus:

> Its ground is sickened with superfluity of water so that *[Damascus] yearns even for a drought*. To the east, its green Ghuta stretches as far as the eye can see, and wherever you look its ripe fruits hold the gaze. By Allah, they spoke truth who said: 'If paradise is on earth then Damascus without a doubt is in it'.
>
> (de Chatel, 2008a)

Seven centuries later, Mark Twain similarly depicted the city where they say time stands still:

> With her forest of foliage and her abundance of water, Damascus must be a wonder of wonders to the Bedouin from the deserts. Damascus is simply an oasis – that is what it is. For four thousand years its waters have not gone dry or its fertility failed. Now we can understand why the city has existed for so long. It could not die. So long as its waters remain to it away out there in the midst of that howling desert, so long will Damascus live to bless the sight of the tired and thirsty wayfarer.
>
> (Twain, 1899: 201)

Today, Ibn Jubayr and Twain would not recognize Damascus. The Barada River no longer snakes through the city, watering apricot orchards and old Damascene homes alike. The Ghuta, once a lush oasis, is ecologically devastated. In recent years, water experts have expressed fear that Damascus faces an imminent crisis. Mufak Khalouf, the head of the Damascus Water Supply and Sewerage Authority, asserted at a 2009 water conference that 'If we don't do something fast, we'll be facing a catastrophe we have not witnessed for the past 50 years' (Bergstein, 2009). According to a critical report on the state of water resources in the Middle East (see El-Ashry *et al.*, 2010), the crisis has arrived. Damascus no longer yearns for drought.

Water scarcity in the Middle East heightens the prospect of humanitarian crises, threatens economic development and elevates the risk of conflict in an already strife-ridden region (El-Ashry *et al.*, 2010). This prognosis takes on new meanings as ceaseless violence grips Syria. In order to stave off the threat of water scarcity, regional water experts call for greater market-valuation of water and commercialization of water resources and utilities, because 'free water is wasted water' (El-Ashry *et al.,* 2010). The impetus for reform in the Syrian water sector is compelled by a water scarcity crisis that is driven by a combination of climate change, unsustainable water use in urban and rural areas, and haphazard urbanization and population growth (El-Ashry *et al.,* 2010; GTZ, 2009; SARPC, 2006; Rogers, 1994). In Damascus, a multitude of market-based governance reforms have been introduced in the last ten years in order to stem a continuing decline in quality and quantity of freshwater resources.

These reforms are part of a new wave of economic restructuring introduced under the leadership of President Bashar al-Assad. While President Assad's father, Hafez, oversaw the implementation of significant economic liberalization, or *infitah*, policies throughout the 1970s, 1980s, and 1990s (Hinnebusch, 1997; Sukkar, 1994), it was only in 2005 when the Syrian government announced the 10th Five Year Plan, which called for a transition to a social market economy, that Syria experienced a more serious and rapid reform process (Haddad, 2012; SARPC, 2006). Modelled after the Chinese experience of single-party rule and economic liberalization, the Syrian government renewed attention to reforming public institutions and governance policies in several sectors of the economy (Haddad, 2012), including water. One example of these reforms is the Modernization Program of the Syrian Water Sector (MPSWS), a cooperative agreement with the German Technical Development Corporation (GTZ) to implement managerial and institutional reforms in the Damascus water sector.

While the narratives of water scarcity in Damascus resonate with daily realities, there are critical silences with respect to how we understand the history and production of this water scarcity. More specifically, and noticeably absent in mainstream reports and analyses of water scarcity in Damascus and Syria, are the effects of state development policies on the production of water scarcity and the associated socio-economic effects. Additionally, scientists and policy-makers often isolate Damascus from a broader set of conditions unfolding across time throughout Syria that make the articulation of a perceived and real water crisis in Damascus possible. This chapter argues that there is a need to consider long-term and multi-scalar effects of Ba'athist agricultural policies and state subsidization schemes across Syria and the ways that these link to the emergence of contemporary 'water crisis' in urban Damascus.

Water scarcity crises are geographical, as the effects of drought and mismanagement lead to collapsed livelihoods, and in turn intensified migration from agricultural regions in Syria towards urban centers. Yet local and national water management reform policies may inadequately reflect the dynamic processes that create water scarcity crises. Framing water scarcity without understanding the far-reaching effects of government policies on communities facing distinct yet interconnected crises risks legitimating certain types of reforms that may ultimately become hegemonic – such as market-based governance (see Sneddon, Chapter 2; Mahayni, Chapter 4; Harris, Chapter 10). There are new opportunities to develop more effective responses to the very real concerns of drought, livelihood and displacement as we deepen our understanding of water scarcity and crises as interlinked geographical concerns.

In this chapter, I first review literature on development and modernization in urban and rural water governance in order to explain why the critical silences on state development policy matter. As this discussion suggests, the literature has yet to effectively address geographical dimensions of water scarcity and crises. Second, I examine policy documents, statements by experts and reform projects from Damascus and Syria to understand the contemporary mainstream framing of the water crisis. Third, I discuss how these problems tie geographically unique places and people together through an analysis of Syrian government policies over the past half-century, suggesting that these have been central to the contemporary production of water scarcity. Last, I conclude with a brief synthesis of my argument that water scarcity crises imbricate a diffuse set of factors that create dynamic problems, meriting dynamic solutions that go beyond marketization of the water sector.

State-making and formation: politics of modernization and water resources

The effects of state development and modernization on water management and irrigation (Baker, 2005; Gelles, 2000; Lansing, 1991; Wittfogel, 1981; Worster, 1992) and on the development of urban water infrastructures (Kaika, 2005; Joyce, 2003) have been well documented. Urban water scholars note that the extent and conditions of water infrastructures, access and use reveal the residual effects of colonial and post-colonial urban planning, changing economic interests and power differences in society (Gandy, 2008, 2006a, 2006b; Kooy and Bakker, 2008; Swyngedouw, 2004). Similarly, local customs, practices and beliefs, state development policy and ideological imperatives, as well as transnational development norms have shaped, and continue to shape, rural water governance and irrigation practices in a myriad of ways (Baker, 2005; Gelles, 2000; Haines, 2011; Harris, 2008). Scholarship about urban and rural water systems and governance suggests that water policy and infrastructural development are often politically charged processes, inflected with power differences in decision-making and policy implementation. This chapter builds on this scholarship by investigating the ways that urban and rural water governance and crises become interlinked and mutually imbricated.

One key factor is development planning and the modernization of water systems, which have been important processes in state-making and formation (Baker, 2005), particularly, but not only, in the Middle East and other arid regions (see Alatout, 2009, 2007; Harris and Alatout, 2010).[1] These development policies have been shaped by ideological imperatives that have motivated and guided elites in colonial and post-independence eras (Gelles, 2000; Mosse, 2003; Swyngedouw, 2007, 2004, 1999). Following from these insights, this chapter argues that Syria's development policies and recent reforms, which have been central to the consolidation and emergence of Syrian state institutions and political regimes, produced the conditions for water crises in Damascus and Syria's rural communities. In addition they created deep and imbricated links between urban and rural communities in Syria. While there are many factors that are responsible for the production of water scarcity crises in Damascus, there has been little attention to the ways that crises elsewhere have reinforced the concerns and conditions in the capital city.

Tracing the argument in this way builds on the sense that water is a critical focal point in state planning and modernization, and also is central to dynamic struggles over access and distribution across different spaces and times (Linton, 2010). Consider the following example from another context: following colonial decline in the late 1800s and early 1900s, Spanish bureaucrats believed that hydrological science and engineering coupled with deepened alliances with peasant communities could reduce regional water deficits and revolutionize the productive potential of the Spanish countryside (Swyngedouw, 2007, 1999). Similarly, in another case, Pakistani authorities sustained a series of British modernization irrigation schemes in the Sindh province, which marked the 'arrival' of a modern Pakistani state and society (Haines, 2011). These projects, however, were not universally implemented in rural areas throughout colonial or post-colonial eras and spaces, and their design and management inevitably overlapped with pre-colonial, colonial and post-colonial water governance practices and ideologies (Mosse, 2003). Indeed, differentiated planning was a key feature of modern urban water systems, just as it was with techno-scientific planning and engineering in colonial and post-colonial eras (Kaika, 2005). In other examples that trace these dynamics, these practices demarcated elite from non-elite neighborhoods, producing inequalities in access and distribution that continue to affect cities such as Bombay and Jakarta today (Gandy, 2006a, 2006b; Kooy and Bakker, 2008; McFarlane, 2008).

Thus while modernization successfully enhanced agricultural and energy production in many contexts, and also frequently extended access to potable water and sanitation in urban and rural areas, there have also been negative consequences, including increased environmental degradation, depleted water resources, and the production and reinforcing of socio-economic inequalities. As noted in the framing chapter for this section (Mahayni, Chapter 4), these crises are often depicted through techno-scientific lenses while ignoring the politics and policies that produce water scarcity and degradation (see also Hardiman, 2007). Yet drivers and perceptions of water scarcity are shaped by struggles over access and distribution and by the ability to respond to the effects of drought, declining water tables or poor water quality (Bakker, 2000; Mehta, 2008, 2005). The case of Syria demonstrates, however, that the production of water scarcity and its effects in urban and rural water systems are not simply geographically isolated phenomena. Instead, water crises in urban and rural areas are interlinked and deeply entangled, as state development policies and reforms have shaped water use practices and coping strategies across space and time. Nevertheless, as the next section highlights, mainstream analyses have tended to neglect these factors, instead treating the crisis in Damascus as an isolated concern.

Producing crisis in Damascus

At a dinner party in Damascus in the summer of 2010, the host, taking an interest in my research on water scarcity and development in Syria, expressed to me: 'Please help us restore our water.' The fact that Damascus, the oldest continuously inhabited city in the world, is seemingly running out of water poses difficult questions for residents and policy-makers alike. The Barada River, which originates in the Anti-Lebanon Mountains and historically sustained the municipal and agricultural needs of Damascus, is now a waste-filled remnant of its past. The flow rate of the 'Ain al-Fijeh spring, the primary source of drinking water in Damascus, has declined over the last decade, and the Barada and Awaj basin regularly experiences annual negative recharge rates. Table 5.1 shows the extent of the falling flow rates, in millions of cubic meters, for the eleven largest freshwater springs on the Barada and Awaj basin over the last thirteen years. The extent of this change, especially for the 'Ain al-Fijeh spring, is concerning because demand for water on the Barada and Awaj basin is growing and changing.

Scientists and policy-makers argue that declining water quantity and the degradation of the Damascus's water resources are worsened by unchecked urbanization, inefficient water use and climate change (GTZ, 2009; SARPC, 2006). Proliferating informal urban settlements in Damascus lack basic amenities, including access to water and sanitation (SARMSEA, 2003). This has resulted in as many as 35,000 unlicensed wells in operation, in addition to 10,000 officially licensed wells (SAROPMCBS, 2011). The high rates of non-revenue water (NRW) are accentuated by the state's limited regulation of well construction in the rural Damascus governorate (Salman and Mualla, 2003) and by deteriorating pipes and illegal taps in the city of Damascus, which alone produce 27 percent water loss in the municipal system (Smets, 2009). Consequently, there are increasing calls for inter-basin transfers from the coastal areas to meet the city's growing water demand (Mourad and Berndtsson, 2012; Salman and Mualla, 2003; Smets, 2009) in addition to a growing emphasis on wastewater treatment plants in order to restore freshwater resources (de Chatel, 2010).

Officials in both public and private sectors have openly expressed concern about the water crisis in Damascus and Syria. Wael Mualla, a professor in water engineering at the University of Damascus, told an English-language weekly in Syria: 'Syria has crossed the "water poverty" threshold of 1,000 cubic meters of renewable water resources per year. It is not a situation of severe stress like in other countries in the region such as Jordan or the Gulf countries, but we must nevertheless manage our supplies carefully' (de Chatel, 2008b). Similarly, Abdullah Droubi, Director of the Water Resources Department at the Arab Center for the Studies of Arid Zones and Dry Lands (ACSAD), stated:

Table 5.1 Flow rates for freshwater springs on Barada and Awaj Basin

Spring	98	99	00	01	02	03	04	05	06	07	08	09	10	%Chg
Ain Al- Fijeh	6850	3870	4360	4000	6528	11088	8499	8195	5247	3715	6400	5424	4801	−29
Ain Mneen	31	–	0	2	0	319	344	133	0	0	0	–		−100
Ain Al-Baradeh	145	65	78	71	79	197	98	116	63	0	37	37		−100
Ain Al-Khadra	168	106	73	67	83	173	167	153	88	65	32	35	85	−49
Al Tbebia	536	269	210	204	254	545	486	521	344	237	78	115	189	−65
Barada	1915	740	381	307	380	3241	2682	2521	1336	683	221	354	526	−72
Beit-jen	1080	690	754	590	675	2052	615	906	692	636	470	497	490	−54
Jerjanieh	11	9	7	5	5	16	20	14	11	6	0	10	7	−36
Katane	235	46	105	77	135	522	416	563	104	0	67	57	114	−51
Ye'four	270	127	44	–	–									−100
Tamasiat	728	590	561	494	632	777	678	528	534	410	361	362	497	−31

Source: SAROPMCBS, 2011

Most people don't realize the complexity of the situation. They are still carrying on like they did 20 years ago, squandering water without further thought. We can no longer permit ourselves to have this attitude. We have to value the resource at its true worth and think of future generations. Syria has a very high growth rate and this will have serious impact on water resources.

(de Chatel, 2008b)

Wael Seif, a Syrian water engineer, also expressed his concern, stating:

Syria is late in this. For too long, the sector has focused on technical issues such as building more dams and reclaiming more land. Many in the water sector still do not thoroughly appreciate the value of water; that the resources are under pressure. Available fresh water is really limited nowadays.

(de Chatel, 2010)

These claims and reports reiterate the narrative that population growth and unchecked urbanization, inefficient water use by farmers and urban users who do not understand the value of water, in addition to climate change, all drive the deterioration of water quality and declining water quantity.

The water scarcity crisis is hardly unique to Damascus, as scientists estimate that freshwater resources for Syria on the whole halved in the past decade (Worth, 2010). The Ministry of Irrigation estimated that between 1998 and 2007 the national water balance deficit was on average three billion cubic meters, an overuse of almost of 20 percent (Smets, 2009). A baseline report of Syria's freshwater resources jointly published by GTZ and the Syrian Ministry of Housing and Construction notes that:

Syria, like most other countries in the Middle East and North Africa region, cannot meet its current water demand. With a changing economic structure and a high population growth rate, demands for irrigation and water supply services will change accordingly. Shifting rainfall patterns due to climate change and the relatively high dependence on internationally shared water resources are further challenging water resources management in Syria. In 2000–2007, Syria's available water resources for use were on average of 800 m^3 per capita, while the actual renewable water resources were on average 1250 m^3 per capita, clearly indicating the situation of unsustainable water use.

(Smets, 2009: xii)

According to the Arab Forum for Environment and Development (see El-Ashry *et al.*, 2010), the per capita volume of water for Syria in 2006 was estimated at 865 m^3 and is expected to drop to 650 m^3 by 2015 and to 550 m^3 by 2025, approaching the level of severe water scarcity.

It is important to keep in mind, however, that policy reports about Damascus specifically or Syria generally often overlook or understate the variable

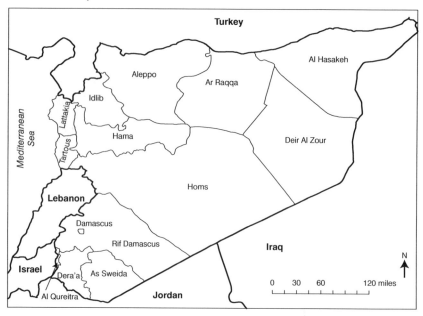

Figure 5.1 Map of Syria (cartography by Basil Mahayni 2012)

geographies of these water crises and their complex linkages across space and time. For example, though the dynamics of the water crisis in Damascus is substantially different than the devastating drought in between 2008 and 2010 in eastern Syria, a key agricultural region, the crises are interlinked. This drought affected 1.3 million residents (Worth, 2010) and observers estimate that 65,000 families left their villages (Ababsa, 2011; International Red Cross, 2011; Worth, 2010). Though the drought was most acutely felt in the governorates of Al Hasakeh, Deir al Zour and Ar Raqqa, its effects reverberated throughout the country as thousands migrated to Damascus and Aleppo (International Red Cross, 2011). Figure 5.1 highlights the distance between urban Damascus and the rural Damascus governorates, and drought-ridden areas in eastern Syria.

Thus, the framing the crisis in Damascus as an urban problem, driven by population pressures stemming from rural-to-urban migration, as well as war refugees from Iraq, and climate change, is only part of the picture. There is critical silence about the ways that concerns in Damascus are related to the rural water crises elsewhere in Syria. More specifically, the production of water scarcity in Damascus is not an isolated phenomenon but is also interwoven in the diffuse and dynamic effects of state policies that have shaped the nature of agricultural livelihoods and later livelihood collapse in eastern Syria. I provide further detail on these processes below.

Revisiting urban water scarcity: Damascus and Syria's agricultural modernization

The Syrian state's political relationship to the agriculturalist classes (see Hinnebusch, 1989; Wedeen, 1999) and the importance of agriculture to its modernization project has been elaborated elsewhere in the literature, but generally neglected in the mainstream policy and scientific reports of water scarcity (Barnes, 2009). Syria's long tradition of centralized development planning and economic policymaking (Haddad, 2012) includes the modernization of the agricultural sector under Ba'ath Party rule since the early 1960s (Hinnebusch, 2011). One of the key political commitments of the Ba'ath Party when it came to power in 1963 was a socialist agricultural sector based on state-led development, state farms and peasant co-operatives (Hinnebusch, 2011). These policies intensified when a new class of officers from rural Syria, including Hafez al-Assad, replaced the urban-based party elites in the mid-1960s (Batatu, 1999). In 50 years of Ba'ath Party rule, the Syrian government's agricultural development goals and land reforms reinforced a critical political alliance between the state and the peasant classes (Hinnebusch, 1989; Wedeen, 1999). Yet such reforms did not come easily.

The Syrian government struggled to overcome land ownership inequalities due to residual civil code inconsistencies from the period of Ottoman rule and the French mandate, compounded by regular political instability in the 1950s and 1960s (Warriner, 1962). The Agrarian Reform Law No. 161 in 1958 accelerated the redistribution of land but these policies were rolled back following the collapse of the Egypt–Syria merger, after which land and political power were restored to large landholders in Syria. In 1963, the Ba'ath Party seized power and issued Decree No. 88, which cancelled the actions of the previous regime, restored the policies of Agrarian Reform Law No. 161 and reduced the maximum area of land that could be owned privately (Batatu, 1999). While these policies reduced the political power of traditional landholding families, the government struggled to keep agricultural production economically viable and sustainable. By the mid-1970s, the government faced new challenges as the West's potential use of the 'food weapon' against the Arab oil embargo threatened to create food shortages. This resulted in a policy of food self-sufficiency (Hinnebusch, 2011), which shifted crop production towards wheat instead of cotton and reformed pricing policies. By 1977, prices paid to Syrian farmers were substantially higher than those paid to American farmers for wheat (more than 100 percent more), soybeans and sugar beet (LOC, 1987).

Facing serious budget crises, the Syrian government introduced a series of liberalization measures throughout the 1980s, 1990s and 2000s, which freed up land for private ownership and enabled greater private investment in the agricultural sector (El Hindi, 2011). These changes came against the backdrop of greater *infitah* policies that opened the economy to more private-sector participation and investment generally (Kienle, 1994). In addition, the state agricultural pricing board opted to do away with controlled pricing in favor of price supports and subsidies that corresponded to production costs and global market prices (El Hindi, 2011). In 2005, the Syrian government introduced the notion of the 'social market economy' in the 10th Five Year Plan (SARPC, 2006), which confronted the deep economic crisis of the late 1990s and early 2000s through intensified liberalization.

In the agricultural sector, Decision No. 83 in December 2000 ended 43 years of collectivist land reform experiments and land was parcelled out with 'right of use', rather than ownership, in shares of three hectares for irrigated land and eight hectares for non-irrigated land. But this process was hardly tension-free as former landowners, farm workers and state employees scrambled to claim land-use rights, often resulting in less than equitable land access. Many complained about these reforms, including rare revolt in the village of Disbi Afnan in the province of Ar Raqqa in December 2002 (Ababsa, 2011). Additionally, rather than benefiting poor farmers, Syrians with close relations with the state and the Ba'ath Party, which included traditional landholding families, often received more land and increased their wealth, while their traditional constituency was marginalized. Later, economic liberalization policies and the government's relaxation of fuel subsidies in 2005 (described below) increased the effects of drought and declining water tables (IRIN, 2005) and reinforced the inequalities that emerged from land reforms, culminating in the forced migration of these peasants towards Damascus and other urban areas by 2010 (Ababsa, 2011).

After decades of state support, a substantial decline in domestic production from a peak of 604,000 barrels per day in 1996 to 470,000 barrels per day in 2008 constrained the state's ability to subsidize diesel fuel. As of 2005, the Syrian government purchased diesel at a rate of 30–35 Syrian pounds per liter (about $0.60) but sold the fuel at 7 Syrian pounds per liter ($0.14), culminating in total state subsidy expenditures of $1 to $1.5 billion per year over the span of five years (IRIN, 2005). In May 2008, the government reduced the subsidy, which increased the price of fuel by 250 percent from 7 Syrian pounds per liter ($0.14) to 25 Syrian pounds per liter ($0.52) (Lennert, 2009).[2] The Syrian government also faced difficulties importing fuel due to rising global oil prices, and struggled to prevent illegal smuggling to Turkey and Lebanon where consumers were willing to pay more for cheap diesel. Though the effects of the subsidy reductions are felt most acutely among the poor, for some economists, the cash-strapped Syrian state left policy-makers no other choice. Abdul Kader Husrieh, a Syrian economist, stated: 'Abolishing the subsidies will lead to inflation and a drastic increase in living costs, however given the current unbearable cost of subsidies, their gradual abolishment seems to be the only option' (IRIN, 2005).

Farmers relying on subsidized fuel are more likely to feel the effects of subsidy reforms. Salim Zahouch, an assistant representative for the FAO in Syria, observed that some farmers in north-eastern Syria stopped irrigating their wheat crop two to three weeks before the scheduled harvest because of fuel cost increases (Lennert, 2009). For certain farmers, the high cost of fuel prevented them from transporting their harvests to the urban centers, and some fed their crops to livestock (Lennert, 2009). One farmer from Ar-Raqqa governorate told a journalist with *Syria Today* that he stopped farming because he could no longer afford the fuel to irrigate his crops, as costs reached as high as 5,000 Syrian pounds, or $105, per day (Lennert, 2009). A water engineer based in Damascus told me that the rising fuel costs cut many farmers out of the agricultural market and, when coupled with drought, prevented the farmers from accessing already declining groundwater resources, though he was unsure whether any systematic studies on the effects of these fuel policies existed.

The modernization of Syria's agricultural industry and the subsequent production of water scarcity in eastern Syria, however, is not a phenomenon that affects only rural areas. One subsistence farmer from Damascus whose plot of land is approximately a half hour from the center of the city explained to me that the declining water table has affected his ability to irrigate his cropland. Speaking against a backdrop of growing informal settlements encroaching upon his property, he explained that the commonly attributed drivers of water scarcity are slightly misleading. Though the number of residents neighboring his plot of land has increased, there has not been a correlative increase in competition for water. Instead, his access has been primarily affected by the government's changing fuel subsidization policies. His motorized diesel-fuelled pump, which enhanced his ability to irrigate, produced a sudden drop in the water table and undermined his ability to access water. He subsequently dismantled the pump, which needed repairs, and instead transfers freshwater from the local water network into a converted pool before using it for flood irrigation. He sought to reutilize the well as the water table continued to drop, but explained that he was unable to do so because he could not afford the repairs or the rising cost of fuel. Consequently, he supplements the freshwater with wastewater runoff and has helped organize a water rationing system with neighboring farmers to rotate wastewater and freshwater, based on community-agreed conventions and governmental agreements. The case of this farmer highlights how technology intensified pressure on the groundwater resources, with poor farmers more likely to confront the constraints of a declining water table, whereas wealthy farmers can afford newer technologies or absorb the cost of reduced production by other means (Hardiman, 2007; Mehta, 2008). But his story also reflects the effects of state subsidies tied to agricultural development goals that shaped the ability of the farmers in Syria to access water in significant volumes.

Policy experts also lament the disproportionate attention to water quantity in the analyses of water scarcity in Damascus. Local industries, textile manufacturing and agriculture have polluted freshwater springs through unregulated chemical disposal and fertilizer runoff (SARMSEA, 2003), leading to high levels of e-coli bacteria from the percolation of sewage in the groundwater and nitrate levels that exceed World Health Organization standards (Smets, 2009). Damascus has only one water treatment plant operating at capacity (SARMSEA, 2003). In addition, many farmers make use of the wastewater before it reaches the wastewater treatment plant, resulting in ecological and health implications. That the water crises involve poor water quality and water quantity concerns are indicative of their multifaceted nature. Yet hegemonic discourses often either privilege water quantity over quality, or separate them out into distinct problems. Indeed, even these debates over water quality and quantity remain silent about the factors that shaped and reshape water management practices across multiple scales and mediate the effects of drought today.

Thus framing water scarcity in Damascus as a problem of population, inefficient use of water and urbanization ignores the ways these variables are posed as concerns to be resolved without questioning who benefits from thinking about water scarcity in these ways, in addition to foreclosing other ways of analyzing the water crises. Additionally, policy documents that address the crisis of agriculture and irrigation in Syria (see Miski and Shawaf, 2003; SARMSEA, 2003; Smets, 2009) tend to universalize the condition of water scarcity for entire regions (e.g. El-Ashry *et al.*, 2010) or overlook important differences between water basins and within water basins (e.g. GTZ, 2009). They also underplay the intimate relationship between water quantity and water quality. Thus, to suggest that the arrival of the eco-refugees, among other groups, is a population problem overlooks the ways in which water scarcity crises in Damascus and eastern Syria are interlinked to the state's fuel subsidy policies. The crisis in Damascus is a product of imbricated communities, water governance practices and use, and the effects of development policies across different water basins. The resettled migrants and refugees from within and outside of Syria in largely informal suburbs of Damascus (Ababsa, 2011) are victims of crises that are largely beyond their control in their home communities, yet they are treated as outsiders and blamed for accentuating the water crisis in Damascus through theft and illegal access, as they try to meet their household and livelihood needs (Smets, 2009). These displaced residents have been affected by economic reforms and reduced state subsidies that accentuated the effects of drought and increasingly variable water access. Residents in Damascus are not exempt from these crises, while the resettled eco-refugees (i.e. from agricultural areas) likely experienced new forms of marginalization (see Worth, 2010). The state's neglect of poor rural and urban Syrians most affected by changing water availability and changing economies helps explain why most of the popular protests throughout 2011 and 2012 started in marginalized communities, particularly in rural areas and low-income suburbs of Damascus.

Conclusion

In my examination of policy documents and my interviews with policy-makers to better understand the contours of Damascus's 'water crisis', an underlying emphasis on the value of water was clearly apparent. Experts and professional reports painted a picture of consumers of water – farmers and urban residents alike – who seemingly did not understand the value of the water on the Barada and Awaj basin. The widespread pollution and illegal pumping were depleting an already fragile basin beset by problems of intensifying drought cycles, unchecked urbanization and significant demographic shifts.

What is missed in these narratives, however, is that water scarcity in Damascus and Syria is deeply imbricated in the politics of the state's modernization and development policies since the 1960s, ultimately producing similar and linked crises throughout the country. The identification of the drivers of water scarcity and the crisis narratives produce and reproduce a particular hegemonic social and environmental order that feeds into market-based reforms. The problem, however, is that these hegemonic discourses are often oversimplified and foreclose other analyses that can inform more dynamic policy initiatives that will take into account the complexities of water management and the production of water scarcity. It is important to acknowledge the uneven effects of water scarcity and the deep entanglements between state policies and ideology, as well as the socio-natural relationships and practices within and between water basins. The crisis in Damascus is not isolated to the city, but the dynamics of water scarcity and crisis are geographical and temporal, combining a set of dynamic and diffuse factors in different parts of the country linked by their political relationship to the state vis-à-vis development policies, subsidies and reforms.

Notes

1 State-making involves the negotiated arrangements between state agents and local elites that hinge upon compliance and commitment whereas state formation encompasses the creation of institutions and knowledge that systematize practices and the creation of the state as a sanctioned authority recognized as legitimate by citizens (Baker, 2005). These two processes underlie the development imperative by invoking the state's ability to (1) create the conditions for development and (2) reproduce these conditions (Scott, 1998).
2 The Syrian government did introduce welfare support by increasing price supports for crops and they distributed special coupons for subsidized fuel to the poorest families to ensure that the diesel fuel was accessible (Lennert, 2009). In 2011, the government reintroduced the fuel subsidies following the ouster of Tunisian President Zine El-Abidine bin Ali (Oweiss, 2011).

References

Ababsa, M. 2011. Agrarian counter reform in Syria (2000–2010). In R. Hinnebusch, A. El Hindi, M. Khaddam and M. Ababsa (eds), *Agriculture and Reform in Syria*, ch. 4, Fife: Lynne Rienner Publishers.

Alatout, S. 2007. State-ing natural resources through law: the codification and articulation of water scarcity and citizenship in Israel. *Arab World Geographer*, 10(1), 16–37.

Alatout, S. 2009. Bringing abundance into environmental politics: constructing a Zionist network of water abundance, immigration, and colonization. *Social Studies of Science*, 39(3), 363–94.

Baker, J. M. 2005. *The Kuhls of Kangra: Community-Manager Irrigation in the Western Himalaya,* Seattle, WA: University of Washington Press.

Bakker, K. 2000. Privatizing water, producing scarcity: the Yorkshire drought of 1995. *Economic Geography,* 76(1), 4–27.

Barnes, J. 2009. Managing the waters of bath country: the politics of water scarcity in Syria. *Geopolitics*, 14(3), 510–30.

Batatu, H. 1999. *Syria's Peasantry, the Descendants of its Lesser Rural Notables, and their Politics,* Princeton, NJ: Princeton University Press.

Bergstein, R. 2009. Syria suffers water shortage: more news on Middle Eastern drought. *Green Prophet.* Available at: http://www.greenprophet.com/2009/02/drought-in-syria (accessed Jan. 2011).

de Chatel, F. 2008a. A drought in Eden. *Syria Today.* Available at: http://www.syria-today.com/index.php/january-2008/485-focus/4251-a-drought-in-eden (accessed Jan. 2011).

de Chatel, F. 2008b. Running dry. *Syria Today.* Available at: http://www.syria-today.com/index.php/august-2008/243-focus/645-running-dry (accessed Jan. 2011).

de Chatel, F. 2010. Murky waters. *Syria Today.* Available at: http://www.syria-today.com/index.php/january-2010/500-focus/5262-murky-waters (accessed Jan. 2011).

El-Ashry, M., Saab, N., and Zeitoon, B., eds. 2010. *Water: Sustainable Management of a Scarce Resource,* Beirut: Arab Forum for Environment and Development.

El Hindi, A. 2011. Syria's agricultural sector: situation, role, challenges, and prospects. In R. Hinnebusch, A. El Hindi, M. Khaddam and M. Ababsa (eds), *Agriculture and Reform in Syria,* ch. 2, Fife: Lynne Rienner Publishers.

Gandy, M. 2006a. Planning, anti-planning, and the infrastructure crisis facing metropolitan Lagos. *Urban Studies,* 43(2), 371–96.

Gandy, M. 2006b. *Water, Sanitation, and the Modern City: Colonial and Post-Colonial Experiences in Lagos and Mumbai,* UNDP Human Development Report Office Occasional Paper, New York: United Nations Development Programme. Available at: http://hdr.undp.org/en/reports/global/hdr2006/papers/gandy%20matthew.pdf (accessed June 2011).

Gandy, M. 2008. Landscapes of disaster: water, modernity, and urban fragmentation in Mumbai. *Environment and Planning A,* 40(1), 108–30.

Gelles, P. 2000. *Water and Power in Highland Peru: The Cultural Politics of Irrigation and Development,* New Brunswick, NJ: Rutgers University Press.

German Technical Development Corporation (GTZ). 2009. *Modernisation Programme for the Syrian Water Sector,* Damascus: German Technical Development Corporation. Available at: http://www.water.co.sy/index.php?m=179 (accessed May 2011).

Haddad, B. 2012. *Business Networks in Syria: The Political Economy of Authoritarian Resilience,* Stanford, CA: Stanford University Press.

Haines, D. 2011. Concrete 'progress': irrigation, development and modernity in mid-twentieth century Sind. *Modern Asian Studies,* 45(1), 179–200.

Hardiman, D. 2007. The politics of water scarcity in Gujarat. In A. Baviskar (ed.), *Waterscapes: The Cultural Politics of a Natural Resource,* ch. 2, New Delhi: Permanent Black.

Harris, L. M. 2008. Modernizing the nation: postcolonialism, postdevelopmentalism, and ambivalent spaces of difference in southeastern Turkey. *Geoforum,* 39(5), 1698–1708.

Harris, L. M., and Alatout, S. 2010. Negotiating hydro-scales, forging states: comparison of the upper Tigris/Euphrates and Jordan River Basins. *Political Geography,* 29(3), 148–56.

Hinnebusch, R. 1989. *Peasant and Bureaucracy in Ba'thist Syria: The Political Economy of Rural Development,* Boulder, CO: Westview Press.

Hinnebusch, R. 1997. Syria: the politics of economic liberalization. *Third World Quarterly,* 18(2), 249–65.

Hinnebusch, R. 2011. The Baath's agrarian revolution (1963–2000). In R. Hinnebusch, A. El Hindi, M. Khaddam and M. Ababsa (eds), *Agriculture and Reform in Syria,* ch. 1, Fife: Lynne Rienner Publishers.

International Federation of Red Cross and Red Crescent Societies (Red Cross). 2011. *Syria: Drought Final Report,* Damascus: Red Cross. Available at: http://reliefweb.int/sites/

reliefweb.int/files/resources/9D9B233E271B4D45C125786000301C47-Full_Report. pdf (accessed May 2012).

IRIN. 2005. Syria: People queue for fuel as subsidies cuts are announced. Available at: http://www.irinnews.org/Report/25628/SYRIA-People-queue-for-fuel-as-subsidies-cuts-are-announced (accessed March 2012).

Joyce, P. 2003. *The Rule of Freedom: Liberalism and the Modern City,* London and New York: Verso.

Kaika, M. 2005. *City of Flows,* London: Routledge.

Kienle, E. 1994. The return of politics? Scenarios for Syria's second *infitah*. In E. Kienle (ed.), *Contemporary Syria: Liberalization between Cold War and Cold Peace,* pp. 114–31, London: Academic Press.

Kooy, M., and Bakker, K. 2008. Splintered networks: the colonial and contemporary waters of Jakarta. *Geoforum*, 39(6), 1843–58.

Lansing, S. 1991. *Priests and Programmers: Technologies of Power in the Engineered Landscape of Bali,* Princeton, NJ: Princeton University Press.

Lennert, J. 2009. Tough times. *Syria Today.* Available at: http://www.syria-today.com/index.php/may-2009/303-focus/1432-tough-times (accessed Jan. 2011).

Library of Congress (LOC). 1987. Syria: role of government in agriculture. *Library of Congress Country Studies,* Washington, DC: Library of Congress. Available at: http://lcweb2.loc.gov/cgi-bin/query/r?frd/cstdy:@field(DOCID+sy0068) (accessed Aug. 2012).

Linton, J. 2010. *What is Water? The History of a Modern Abstraction,* Vancouver: UBC Press.

McFarlane, C. 2008. Governing the contaminated city: infrastructure and sanitation in colonial and post-colonial Bombay. *International Journal of Urban and Regional Research*, 32(2), 415–35.

Mehta, L. 2005. *The Politics and Poetics of Water: Naturalising Scarcity in Western India,* New Delhi: Orient Longman.

Mehta, L. 2008. Contexts and constructions of scarcity. In A. Baviskar (ed.), *Contested Grounds: Essays on Nature, Culture, and Power*, ch. 2, New Delhi: Oxford University Press.

Miski, A. F., and Shawaf, S. 2003. *Protection and Sustainable Use of Groundwater and Soil Resources in the Arab Region,* Damascus: ACSAD-German Technical Cooperation Project. Available at: http://www.bgr.bund.de/EN/Themen/Wasser/Projekte/abgeschlossen/TZ/Acsad/Vol_6_fb_pdf.pdf?__blob=publicationFile&v=2 (accessed June 2011).

Mosse, D. 2003. *The Rule of Water,* Delhi: Oxford University Press.

Mourad, K., and Berndtsson, R. 2012. Water status in the Syrian Water Basins. *Open Journal of Modern Hydrology*, 2(1), 15–20.

Oweiss, K. Y. 2011. Syria hikes key price subsidy after Tunisia events. Reuters Africa. Available at: http://af.reuters.com/article/tunisiaNews/idAFLDE70F0DH20110116 (accessed Jan. 2011).

Rogers, P. 1994. The agenda for the next thirty years. In P. Rogers and P. Lydon (eds), *Water in the Arab World: Perspectives and Prognoses,* Cambridge, MA: Harvard University Press.

Salman, M., and Mualla, W. 2003. The utilization of water resources for agriculture in Syria: analysis of current situation and future challenges. In Ettore Majorana Foundation and Centre for Scientific Culture, Erice International Seminars Planetary Emergencies,

Aug., Erice, Italy. Available from: ftp://ftp.fao.org/agl/iptrid/conf_egypt_03.pdf (accessed May 2011).

Scott, J. 1998. *Seeing like a State: How Certain Schemes to Improve the Human Condition have Failed,* New Haven, CT: Yale University Press.

Smets, S. 2009. *Baseline Water Sector Report for GTZ Modernization of the Syrian Water Sector Support to Sector Planning and Coordination,* Damascus: State Planning Commission and German Technical Development Corporation.

Sukkar, N. 1994. The crisis of 1986 and Syria's plan for reform. In E. Kienle (ed.), *Contemporary Syria: Liberalization Between Cold War and Cold Peace,* pp. 26–43, London: Academic Press.

Swyngedouw, E. 1999. Modernity and hybridity: nature, *regeneracionismo,* and the production of the Spanish waterscape, 1890–1930. *Annals of the Association of American Geographers,* 89(3), 443–65.

Swyngedouw, E. 2004. *Social Power and the Urbanization of Water,* New York: Oxford University Press.

Swyngedouw, E. 2007. Technonatural revolutions: the scalar politics of Franco's hydro-social dream for Spain, 1939–1975. *Transactions of the Institute of British Geographers,* 32(1), 9–28.

Syrian Arab Republic Office of the Prime Minister Central Bureau of Statistics (SAROPMCBS). 2011. *Statistical Abstract 2011,* Damascus: Central Bureau of Statistics.

Syrian Arab Republic State Planning Commission (SARPC). 2006. *The Five Year Plan 2006-2010,* Damascus: Syrian Arab Republic State Planning Commission. Available at: http://www.planning.gov.sy/index.php?page_id=24 (accessed Aug. 2009).

Syrian Arab Republic Ministry of State for Environmental Affairs (SARMSEA). 2003. *Strategy and National Environmental Action Plan for the Syrian Arab Republic,* Damascus: Syrian Arab Republic Ministry of State for Environmental Affairs.

Twain, M. 1899. *The Innocents Abroad or the New Pilgrims' Progress: Being Some Account of the Steamship Quaker City's Pleasure Exclusion to Europe and the Holy Land,* New York: Harper & Brothers Publishers.

Warriner, D. 1962. *Land Reform and Development in the Middle East,* New York: Oxford University Press.

Wedeen, L. 1999. *Ambiguities of Domination: Politics, Rhetoric, and Symbols in Contemporary Syria,* Chicago: University of Chicago Press.

Wittfogel, K. 1981. *Oriental Despotism: A Comparative Study of Total Power,* New Haven, CT: Yale University Press.

Worster, R. 1992. *Rivers of Empire: Water, Aridity, and the Growth of the American West,* New York: Oxford University Press.

Worth, R. F. 2010. Earth is parched where Syrian farms thrived. *New York Times.* Available at: http://www.nytimes.com/2010/10/14/world/middleeast/14syria.html?_r=1&emc=eta1 (accessed Dec. 2010).

6 Abundance and scarcity amidst the crisis of 'modern water'

The changing water–energy nexus in Turkey

Sinan Erensu

[With small hydropower plants] we have been replacing the age-old 'river flows, Turk just stares' mentality with 'river flows, Turk builds' motto … Those who call themselves environmentalists claim that we are selling these streams out. It is simply not true! The law we passed only transfers the right of usage … We all benefit from this [in form of electricity] … Nature was entrusted to us, we protect it properly!

(Recep Tayyip Erdogan, Turkish Prime Minister: NTVMSNBC, 2009[1])

Introduction

The Turkish hydropower scene has been undergoing a considerable transformation in the last decade. Large-scale, state-owned dam projects receded to the background in the face of emerging 'environmentally friendly', privately owned, small-size hydropower plants (SHPs). This new way of converting water into energy has also provoked unprecedented resistance from local communities and activists, eager to protect their control of and access to rivers. Today, there are approximately 2,000 licensed SHP projects, more than half of which are under construction, or under planning, in the mountainous Black Sea coastal region of northern Turkey. SHPs are presented by investors as well as by the government as cornerstone 'green' components of Turkey's 'great leap forward' (Gibbons and Moore, 2011). In what follows, I discuss what this transformation means for the idea and governance of water in Turkey, as well as what it signals for new parameters of a global and a national water–energy nexus.

The transformation of the water–energy nexus in Turkey maps onto worldwide developments in energy production and environmental governance. Pressing concerns over climate change as well as depletion of fossil fuels have created a sense of crisis around energy production. The consequent push for carbon control has paved the way for new regulatory mechanisms, new market tools such as carbon trade and an intense search for diverse low-carbon energy sources. Carbon-control mechanisms certainly hold some prospect as a new and tighter form of environmental regulation, yet operating under existing market premises they also produce highly uneven social and spatial outcomes at every scale (Baldwin, 2009; Bumpus and Liverman, 2008; While *et al.,* 2010).

Under these circumstances, water has been rediscovered as a low-carbon energy alternative. This rediscovery has implications for the way changes in water governance are unfolding. These changes were driven forward since the early 1990s by extensive depletion and pollution of water resources, and increasing problems in water distribution. Persistent environmental and distributional demands over water exceeded existing water governance paradigms, characterized by technical expertise and state monopoly, and triggered a market-based, decentralized restructuring. Challenging the technical understanding of water that dominated the 20th century, the emergent crisis in water governance also allowed local water-users to express alternative understandings of, and cultural and social attachments to, water (Linton, 2010). The Cochabamba water wars and global anti-large-dam campaigns are among such democratizing consequences of the crisis, in so far as they overturn and influence policy decisions and render local participation a must (see Part IV below).

The changes in these two domains, energy production and water governance, interact with each other in ways that complicate how we understand, use and fight for water. This chapter sheds light on the limits as well as the possibilities of this moment of dual crisis – of water and energy – and discusses the ruptures as well as the continuities it sustains. I propose that the emerging carbon-control era does not weaken the hegemony of notions of scarcity and abundance, and the powerful rationales of political and technical intervention that go with them – rather, it attributes new meanings to these notions. Green energy developments, such as the contested SHP projects in Turkey (see also Kadirbeyoglu and Kurtic, Chapter 18), simultaneously introduce mechanisms of environmental protection and produce new definitions of scarcity and abundance, generating new geographies of value and establishing new hegemonies over nature and water.

The chapter has six sections. Following a brief introduction I proceed by discussing what the crisis of modern water governance entails as well as its relevance for the emergence of SHPs. In the third section, I introduce concepts of scarcity, abundance and waste. The following two sections, respectively, focus on the ruptures and continuities SHPs present for water governance. The fourth section centers around the scarcity/abundance relation surrounding SHP projects, pointing out how certain scarcities call for patriotic responses and citizen responsibility, while certain abundances legitimize state and market powers to override local livelihoods. In the fifth section, I ask how changing state–market relations, as well as increased reliance on entrepreneurialism and construction as means of development, bear upon water governance, and this is followed by the conclusion.

Modern water in transition

In his evocative text geographer Jamie Linton argues that what has come to be identified as *water crisis* from 1990s onwards is actually the *crisis of modern water*, that is, the crisis of 'the dominant … way of knowing and relating to water' (2010: 14). In other words, the crisis has more to do with the hegemonic water discourse and practice than lack of water *per se*. The hegemonic discourse on modern water, which dominated governance of water throughout the 20th century on a global scale, relies on 'the presumption that any and all waters can be and should be considered apart from their social and ecological relations and reduced to an abstract quantity' (ibid.). Modern water aims at, and for a long while succeeded at, rendering water manageable, homogeneous and universal by efficaciously keeping ecological, cultural or political factors at a distance (ibid., p. 8). The end result has been a spectacular accomplishment; modern water has left its mark on numerous infrastructures we now take for granted, such as tap water, irrigations systems, flood control mechanisms and hydroelectric systems. This was only possible by reducing water to a single identity, confining its scope to a narrow matter of technical expertise, treating it as merely a national/economic resource and abstracting it from its socio-natural complexity. Yet this powerful discourse, Linton argues, can no longer be maintained and modern water has entered a 'critical phase' wherein water can no longer be understood as abstract – independent from its ecological, cultural, and political contexts (2010: 19). What precipitated the crisis of modern water? For certain, water's material shortage was an important factor: state institutions were unable to provide continuous clean tap water to all and they frequently mismanaged droughts (see Musemwa, Chapter 7; K'Akumu, Chapter 13). As various indigenous movements and urban activists fought for the right to water, their concerns merged with a strengthening environmentalism that targeted pollution of water basins and climate change-related water cycle shifts (see also Varghese, Chapter 14). The restlessness went beyond physical scarcity of water, and initiated a more fundamental crisis at the discursive level. It challenged not only existing ways of administering water, but also how water is understood and known.

Linton's strong emphasis on the crisis of modern water is informed by, among others, Karen Bakker's (2004, 2010) work, which traces what she calls a paradigmatic shift in water governance systems taking place since the 1990s. The conventional water governance that dominated much of the 20th century was the product of a state (municipal) hydraulic paradigm that relied on public ownership of modern hydraulic technologies and infrastructures, with a commitment to 'social equity and universal provision', as well as to meeting the needs of burgeoning national economies (Bakker, 2004: 31–5). Towards the end of the century, the rising sense of state failure engulfed the state hydraulic paradigm. Contamination and deficiency of urban water delivery systems led to the emergence of a new market-oriented environmental paradigm that championed conservation through private mechanisms. This transformation was built upon privatization and commercialization of water supply, but as Bakker reminds us, stretched over institutional, socio-economical as well as technical dimensions. What Bakker describes as the paradigmatic shift and what Linton defines as the crisis of modern water correspond to the same historical conjuncture wherein practical/administrative and discursive collapse of the conventional water regimes left a void in which different solutions, including increased privatization and marketization (see Harris, Chapter 10), could emerge.

If the modern water discourse is at a critical conjuncture, then what are some of its more concrete indications? Both Linton (2010: 52–4) and Bakker (2010: 54–9) rightfully point to the changing cultural status of large dams as one of the most visible and emblematic symptoms of the diminishing hegemony of the modern water discourse. Large dams have been the ultimate symbols of development, prosperity and modernity throughout the 20th century. As large-scale state-sponsored development projects, they have not only pushed the limits of national achievement and pride, but also represented the triumph of mankind and technology over nature. Nevertheless, beginning from late 1960s, large dams were increasingly subjects of heavy criticism due to the immense damage they did to the surrounding ecosystems and neighboring human settlements (Goldsmith and Hildyard, 1984). In the late 1980s and 1990s, local anti-dam campaigns in the global South managed to bring many projects to a halt (McCully, 2001), forcing the World Bank, the main financier of such projects, to reconsider its entire research and project evaluation practices and rebuild its image through a new focus on environmentalism (Goldman, 2005). Persistent anti-dam campaigns culminated in the publication of the World Commission on Dams (WCD) report in 2000 (Sneddon and Fox, 2008).[2] Against this background, Linton, Bakker and others have argued that the era of large dams is over; its fall initiates and signals a paradigm shift in water governance.

SHPs appeared at this juncture as a response to criticisms of large-scale projects. There is widely shared consensus that SHPs avoid replicating many of the problems of large dams by offering environmentally friendly and minimally intrusive structures that are also faster to build and easier to finance (Greenpeace, 2010: 178; International Energy Agency, 2006; Rivers International, 2010). The most important feature that makes SHPs more sustainable compared to large dams is that most SHPs are run-of-the-river and require neither damming nor a reservoir to hold large amounts of water. This minimizes the problem of flooding, as well as sedimentation capture, among the most pronounced physical impacts of large dams. Instead of relying on the kinetic power of stored reservoir water, SHPs exploit the 'head', the vertical distance between a higher area (which becomes the intake weir) and a lower area (which becomes the plant where the turbines are located), features often available on mountain streams (see Figure 6.1). Along the head, the stream is diverted into a channel or a tunnel system that follows the contour of a hillside, then left to flow inside a penstock pipe, and is finally released to the riverbed after going through the turbines inside a powerhouse. Despite being one of the basic methods of energy creation, SHPs have actually become popular in the last decade, alongside wind and solar farms, growing in installed capacity by 75 percent globally between 2004 and 2010 (Greenpeace, 2010). Given their small size and relative affordability, SHPs do not have to be centralized state undertakings; merging interest in green energy with marketization trends – it is often private entrepreneurs who are able to build and run them.

Finally, concerns over climate change and growing interest in energy renewables constitute another emerging component of the critical conjuncture of a transforming modern water discourse. Unlike large dams, SHPs are eligible for

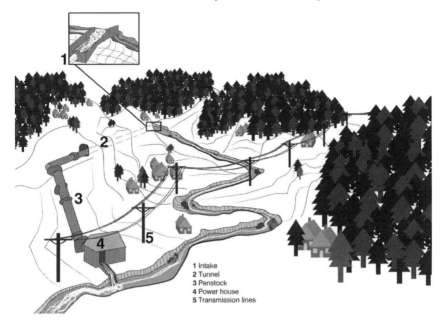

1 Intake
2 Tunnel
3 Penstock
4 Power house
5 Transmission lines

Figure 6.1 A typical SHP layout (created by Deniz Erk and Bertan Kiliccioglu)

various national and global incentives designed to promote investment in green technologies. So far, the World Bank's Clean Technology Fund has allocated a total of $1.1 billion for Turkey's renewable energy initiatives, most of which has been channelled to SHP developments (*Hydroworld*, 2011). These funds are managed and distributed by the Industrial Development Bank of Turkey, the country's major development agency, and provide an important attraction for private green energy companies. While the state provides incentives such as land appropriation for construction, purchase guarantees and feed-in tariffs, these funds act as liquid incentives. Another significant incentive at global level is the opportunity to participate in carbon trade markets.[3]

In the light of the above, SHPs respond to changing parameters of the water–energy nexus and comply with the WCD's call for 'decentralized small-scale options based on renewable sources' (2000: p. xxxii).[4] Yet, since their first appearance in 2008, SHP projects have been heavily contested in Turkey, especially along the water-rich Black Sea Coast that will host more than half of the total planned projects. Contrary to what one might expect, the country's notorious history with large dams[5] did not cause SHPs to be welcomed as the new eco-friendly alternative. Protesters' objections revolve around claims ranging from the negative impact on water quality from the construction phase to negative consequences for local flora and fauna; reduced access to water for livelihoods; and repercussions for agriculture, fisheries and recreation. Additionally, concerns also include the effects of power transmission lines for human and livestock health. However, apart from all of these possible reasons, protesters agree on the fundamental sense that SHP construction threatens their living space and that SHP developments are the beginning of a process of rural transformation that is bound to culminate in mass out-migration from what many consider as ancestral homeland (*baba topragi*).

The fact that individual anti-SHP campaigns have matured into a nationwide movement[6] around notions of environmental justice, local control over natural resources and alternative environmental imaginaries challenges SHPs' environmentally friendly and low-impact image, and forces us to reconsider the limits, as well as potential, of the change in the modern water paradigm. In what follows, I explain how the ideas and practices of SHP management in Turkey are supported by both new and old water paradigms. The greening of energy production does not do away with perceptions of water scarcity and the need to act on such out of concern for national security. Similarly, despite privatization of energy production, the state continues to be heavily involved (see Islar, 2012b). Nonetheless, the current norms, mechanisms and institutions of carbon control that SHPs are a part of include, and even depend on, ideas of water as a technical object to be managed. These suggest that the crisis of modern water could unfold and revitalize an old notion – as much as it could enable alternative imaginaries.

Scarcity, abundance and waste: the water–energy nexus

Much has been written in the last decade that deconstructs the notion of scarcity (see Mahayni, Chapter 4; Sneddon, Chapter 2). For example, studies on the deregulation of water governance illustrate how the state of emergency surrounding water scarcity is as much a construction at the discursive level as a consequence of material realities (Bakker, 2004; Kaika, 2003). This 'produced' or 'constructed' aspect of scarcity, it has been argued, legitimizes a particular economics-oriented approach to resource management, naturalizes scarcity as a perpetual state of being (Luks, 2010), and successfully depoliticizes otherwise highly political distributional decisions (Swyngedouw, 2011).

While the recognition of both material and constructed aspects of scarcity is most welcome, its power is limited in the absence of its 'elusive twin' – abundance (Mehta, 2010: 14; see also Xenos, 1989: 35). Abundance is rarely dealt with in the literature, as Samer Alatout (2009) expounds, although abundance is as socially constructed as scarcity and frequently similarly utilized for political ends.[7] Abundance and scarcity are co-constitutive, each fulfilling its meaning through the image of the other. Mainstream economics, for example, rests on the promise of the possibility of abundance as long as scarce resources are managed properly and not wasted. Yet their relationship is rarely stable; resources and commodities once deemed abundant might be reframed as scarce depending on changing production regimes as well as social and cultural norms. Governmental interventions in the water realm often are based on assumptions of scarcity, but also act on the assumption of its resolvability. In the case of energy politics, discourses of scarcity rely on abundance of wasted natural resources and set into motion processes of securitization of energy.

In the narrative of many early modern hydrologists in North America, water was abundant and to be used in energy creation, yet it was simultaneously defined as 'capable of scarcity' unless used properly (Linton, 2006: 15). Such delicate definitions demarcated water as matter only knowable by experts and gave rise to the discipline of 'hydro-economics' in which 'the prefix conveys the idea of water and is followed by the conception of its efficient employment, of utility or of thrift' (Newell, 1920: 31, cited in Linton, 2006: 16; see also discussion of the hegemonic role of engineers in water governance in Baker, Chapter 3). If the water–energy nexus and the reduction of water to merely an economic resource were constructed in and through the discourse of abundance and scarcity, starting a century ago, then we might ask, in the light of more recent paradigmatic changes in water governance, what is the contemporary role of scarcity/abundance discourse in defining water? To what extent do improved environmental regulations, and the advent of eco-friendly technologies open possibilities for, as Linton expects, 'disestablishing water's resource identity' (Linton, 2006)? The emergent SHP regime in Turkey might help us query what gets transformed and what stays intact in the changing water governance paradigm.

Discovering the abundance of renewables: a rupture?

In 2010 Turkey launched an ambitious green energy program that pledged to increase the share of renewable energy sources in total power generation from 20 percent up to 30 percent by the year 2023, the centennial of the Turkish Republic (ETKB, 2010). SHPs constitute an important part of this new drive. They are expected to contribute to the program by bringing an additional 20,000 MW installed capacity in the next 15 years, alongside 19,200 MW from wind power, and 600 MW from geothermal (Baris and Kucukali, 2012: 9). The program was unveiled following a boom in green energy investments in Turkey. The country's clean energy investment growth rate in the 2004–9 period is the highest among the G20 nations, raising $1.9 billion in 2009 alone. Despite these ever increasing figures and ambitious projections, Turkey's energy dependency is at a record high of 78 percent (Yildiz, 2010) and state agencies still predict a severe energy crisis by 2016, given ever increasing demand (TEIAS, 2009).[8]

Energy insecurity and outages are not new for Turkey. The last wave of electricity shortage, which hit the country at the turn of the millennium, was so widespread that even the President at the time, Suleyman Demirel, complained: 'We just cannot run any industries in this situation' (*Milliyet*, 1999). Panic over this outage forced the government to import 3.5 billion KW/h of electricity from Bulgaria in 2000 (*Milliyet*, 2000) and to sign a natural gas import agreement with the Russian Federation under notoriously unfavorable conditions (Kaygusuz and Arsel, 2005). Another long-lasting repercussion of the outage was that it kick-started a comprehensive energy market reform that included liberalization of energy production and distribution, privatization of existing facilities and institutional restructuring of the sector. The reform had long been on the table as an IMF loan package condition, as well as part of integration with the European

Union (Erdogdu, 2007), yet the outage crisis heightened its urgency. What is more, in 2001, the biggest economic crisis in the Republic's history hit the country, strengthening the perception that the state was incapable of efficiently and successfully managing energy provision. Thus, in such a context of vulnerability, liberalization and growing privatization of the energy sector surfaced as the answer to the problems.

Together with liberalization and privatization, the other solution was to look for and create new energy sources. Having negligble oil and natural gas, Turkey had always been considered poor in energy resources. It was in this context and around this time that universities, and research and development units at private companies, developed an increased interest in renewable energy. This was followed by a plethora of academic publications by a group of Turkish engineers calculating the possible economic value of renewables in Turkey, and arguing how long-time neglected natural resources of the country could remedy its energy scarcity (Kaygusuz, 1999, 2002; Oguzata, 2007; Balat, 2008). As the knowledge creation on its renewable energy sources accumulated, it became evident that Turkey was indeed extremely abundant in wind, hydro, solar and geothermal energy potentials, ranking in the top tier globally almost in every category.

This radically changed the energy map of the country – responding to energy scarcities by designating new geographies of untapped abundance. By the year 2000, having dammed most of its major rivers, especially those in the Tigris and Euphrates basins in Southeastern Anatolia, Turkey was already the fifth richest country in hydroelectricity generation in Europe. Yet, with growing interest in renewable energy, it soon was realized by State Hydraulic Works and investors that the country had overlooked its small hydro potential altogether. In 2006, the European Small Hydro Association (ESHA) calculated that Turkey had the second largest small hydro potential in Europe after Norway, yet the country had tapped only 3 percent of it (ESHA, 2004: 24). The bulk of this potential was to be found along the water-rich Black Sea Coast which had not as yet been integral to Turkey's earlier hydroelectricity investments. Turkey's representation as a country suffering from energy scarcity changed to a country that is 'blessed with an abundance of clean energy resources' (PwC, 2009: 3).

The Black Sea Coastal Region offers an ideal environment for SHPs due to a unique combination of high precipitation[9] and sloped valleys with hundreds of streams and rapids only exploitable by SHPs. Six provinces in the Eastern Black Sea Region[10] occupy only 4.5 percent of the total land surface, yet they are expected to host a total of 533 SHPs, that is equal to 27 percent of all SHP licenses in the country (TMMOB, 2011) (see Figure 6.2).

It might be misleading however to liken the discovery of the Black Sea Coast as a water-rich region to the discovery of a new oil reserve trapped under the earth's surface. While the latter is literally a discovery of a resource, existence of which had been unknown, the former is rather a conjunctural valorization of something that had been already known. Turkey's hydro potential maps were drawn almost 60 years ago, including every stream and rapid in every region. The realization of this potential, however, requires the coalescence of different factors under new

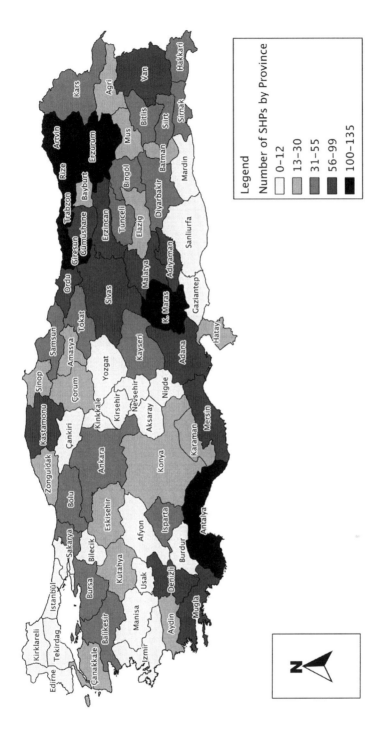

Figure 6.2 Distribution of small hydropower plants (SHPs), including those in operation, under construction and planned, in Turkey by province.
Source: TMMOB (2010). Cartography by Basil Mahayni (2012)

Table 6.1 Co-evolution of privatization and greening of energy production in Turkey

Year	Law #	Law Title	SHP-related Objective
2001	4628	Electricity Market Law	Establishes Electricity Market Regulatory Authority (EMRA), enables private entrepreneurs to build, own, and operate power plants with licenses provided from EMRA.
2003	25318	Revision of Environmental Impact Assessment (EIA) Bylaw	Defines when EIA is necessary by installed capacity: 0-0.5 MW: EIA not required (required since 2011) 0.5-25 MW: Ministry of Environment decides if EIA is required 25 MW & up: EIA is required.
2003	25150	Water Usage Rights Bylaw	Enables private entrepreneurs to rent out river sections for 49 years for the purpose of hydroelectricity production. Defines can suyu (lifeline water), the minimum amount of water that must be left in the riverbed along the penstock, as 30%.
2005	5346	Renewable Energy Law	Guarantees to provide feed-in tariffs for private electricity producers with renewable energy source certificates, offers up to 85% discount to rent out forest land for green energy projects.
2008	5784	Revision of Electricity Market Law	Public and private entities need not apply for license to generate electricity in facilities with capacities 500 KW and under; government guarantees to buy excess electricity

Source: Baris and Kucukali (2012), Kucukali and Baris (2009), Ocak and Gedik (2011), and TMOBB (2011).

hegemonic ideas (see Sneddon, Chapter 2). In the case of SHPs, it was the energy crisis of late 1990s and its construction as a fundamental yet solvable scarcity that merged together the movement away from large-scale efforts (towards small-scale more participatory projects, see Goldin, Chapter 16) with environmental and marketization/privatization imperatives of the past several decades (Harris, Chapter 10), including increasing focus on climate change and 'green energy'. Thus, SHPs became the hegemonic alternative that replaced the state hydraulic paradigm and modern water that was now in crisis. A quick overview of regulations of the early 2000s demonstrates the mutuality between these trends, particularly showing that the renewable energy drive in the country was enmeshed with a paradigm of liberalization of the sector.

The transformation of the Turkish water–energy nexus demonstrates how global carbon control trends interplay with a certain discourse of crisis and scarcity to bear on how water is used and governed. Discourses of crisis and scarcity and environmental sensitivities fuel each other, legitimizing and popularizing green projects. On the other hand, what shapes water is not a particular material scarcity of water *per se*, but a sense of scarcity triggered by the fear that the country lacks the sufficient energy to realize its developmental goals. It is the promise of future abundance that creates the current crisis and the perception of underutilized nature as wasteful and, thus, legitimizes political projects such as liberalization/ privatization in the energy sector in the name of efficiency. Accordingly, market environmentalism emerges as the hegemonic mode of converting water into energy. Yet the Turkish state has been critical in disseminating discourses of crisis and scarcity, as well as determining how market environmentalism plays out on the ground. Its continuing role is also visible in how it presents this transformation of the Turkish water–energy nexus as development – the subject of the next section.

Water and development: a continuity?

In the opening vignette, I quoted the Turkish Prime Minister criticizing the 'river flows, Turk just stares' mentality. This phrase is now a prime-ministerial trademark, underlining unutilized water flow as wasteful. The argument of waste is certainly based on the assumption that there is an abundance of water that local communities are unable to make efficient use of. This binary established between scarce energy and abundant water attempts to single-handedly reorder the relationship between water and society, valuing certain uses of water while devaluing other uses and relationships to the rivers. With respect to opposition to the SHPs, any protest is rendered irrational and backward through rhetorical questions such as 'Are you not using electricity in your homes? Do you not want development?' (Kara *et al.*, 2010). Opposition is also branded as unpatriotic, and its origins are cynically sought outside (of the country) as governing officials express bafflement at the ingratitude shown by protesters to this great service, cast as a developmental leap forward (Kozok, 2012). It is the promise of further growth and development that is expected to produce consent for SHPs. To be sure, development has always been in the Turkish state's ideological repertoire as a key modernizing tool (Harris, 2008, 2011). Rather than reiterating this, I turn to the consideration of how development mobilizes implementation of green solutions by bringing ever-present concepts, such as scarcity and abundance, into contact with new models of governance.

Water governance, in many parts of the world, has highlighted symbols of development, for instance, through the building of large dams.[11] Turkey is no exception. The Southeastern Anatolia Project (GAP is the Turkish acronym) is perhaps the best example of modern water in Turkish development history. Located in the basins of Euphrates and Tigris and extending over nine provinces, GAP is one of the world's largest centralized project endeavors, hosting 22 dams and 19 large hydropower plants and providing a quarter of the country's power supply. As a technical-bureaucratic intervention, GAP was planned as part of the state hydraulic paradigm that aimed to develop national industry as well as an impoverished region through the management of water.[12]

One would expect SHPs to disrupt this version of modern developmentalism since they are decentralized, private and ostensibly eco-sensitive. Yet none of these characteristics means that the state is disappearing from water governance and hydropower. For one, the state elite is present at almost all SHP opening ceremonies. When there are demonstrations, the gendarmerie frequently intervenes to suppress opposition, creating the perception that they are siding with investors. As for ministers, the current Minister of Water and Forestry recently declared that his job was to create dams (*Hurriyet Daily News*, 2010). Beyond its ceremonial appearance, ideological role and security provision, the state's involvement is integral to the realization of SHPs to the extent that the developments require transfer of land and water rights from local users to private companies (see Islar, 2012b).

While the state considers SHP investments as part of a state developmental project, SHPs are nonetheless strikingly different from GAP in that they do not include any social or cultural development dimensions.[13] What developmental goals, if any, are SHPs expected to accomplish? Apart from achieving energy independence, SHP developments overlap with the contemporary trends in urban and regional governance in terms of channeling national and international financial instruments to infrastructure investments with the hope of boosting growth and of unearthing untapped resources, whether it be capital available in urban land, rural natures or somewhere in between (Goldman, 2011). Construction, thus, becomes the major political tool not only to sustain a growth-led development model but also to harbor a local bourgeoisie that is indebted to the government through mechanisms of privatization, marketization and transfer of property rights.[14] SHP developments in Turkey are not only undertaken by a handful of national and international conglomerates that already operate in the energy sector. Thanks to the availability of international green funds and national incentives, many small and mid-sized local companies have also seen SHPs as an investment opportunity and managed to enter the lucrative green energy sector. Today, among the companies involved in green energy, one can find denim producers (Bianet, 2011) as well as professional football clubs (Sabah, 2012). On the other hand, the SHP construction process enables and requires involvement of local subcontractors and middlemen. In this manner, not only are economic growth targets approximated, through boosting the construction sector, but also a chain of numerous actors, who are tied to the government in one way or another, is produced. It is perhaps these opportunities and outsourcing networks that widen SHPs' influence and increase their power. Another way to think about this, then, is to consider that SHP constructions are sustained both by a perceived abundance of water and a produced abundance of small entrepreneurs and contractors.

The SHP development model also concerns the delegation of social services to construction companies. Companies spend a fraction of investment costs on services such as school renovation, mosque repair and village road asphalting in order to appease and co-opt any possible resistance by the local population. Yet, since there is no state mandate for such service provision, it is the individual companies, and the resistance they expect to see from the local population, that determines what and how much will be done.

At first sight, this new development model appears to be fully dependent on the private sector. However, Bakker (2010) reminds us that the shift in water governance from state control to market domination should not be perceived as a total shift wherein state and market are conceptualized as mutually exclusive, even opposing poles. Not only are there multiple intermediate orders between the two systems (Bakker, 2010: 5), it is also not necessarily true that there is a relationship of competition and conflicting interests between the actor that we call state and those that we associate with the market. In this case, it is the Turkish state that enables and encourages private-sector involvement in energy production by way of connecting global financiers to local capital, publicly defending the SHP projects, guaranteeing the purchase of excess electricity from private plants, issuing permits and licenses, and diffusing hope that the public can all benefit from these projects by participating either as investors, subcontractors or construction workers.

Concluding remarks

I started this chapter with Linton's argument that the changes in water governance in the last decade are symptoms of a crisis in the modern construction of water. The question at stake is whether this crisis can abolish the modern objectification of water and open up new ways of imagining and relating to water. My aim throughout the chapter has been to understand SHPs from this vantage point. Showing how green energy policies and practices are prone to be captured by discourses of scarcity, crisis and development, I have argued that this effectively erodes their potential to offer alternative socio-environmental futures and to avoid pitfalls of 'carbon democracy' (Mitchell, 2011).

Especially in comparison to large dams, SHPs echo worldwide changes in water governance in the aftermath of crisis; on the surface, they are small, private and eco-friendly. Yet a closer look shows that this might be illusory. One of the key mechanisms of objectifying water, i.e. the discourse of scarcity/abundance, still occupies a central place in contemporary water governance. Moreover, widely celebrated global carbon-control mechanisms add new layers of meaning and a renewed sense of urgency to the notions of abundance and scarcity; and, perhaps inadvertently, contribute to the depoliticization of key public policy decisions. Likewise, the roles of development and the state are not disappearing; on the contrary, the objectification of water remains, albeit with new faces.

Gramsci contends that the crisis of hegemony can go two ways: it can lead to hegemony's collapse or it can cause hegemony to recreate and reproduce itself (Sneddon, Chapter 2). I find Gramsci's warning salient, and believe that the conditions under which SHPs exist in Turkey allow us to argue for such a two-way exit out of a crisis. Yet this two-way process is not politics-free; in fact, local and national resistance to SHPs makes all the difference in the direction of the transformation. Oppositional acts, from bare protest to appropriation of environmental impact assessments, disrupt and extend imaginations and uses of water. It is in the realm of politics more than in the realm of governance that water's objectification remains most unsettled.

Notes

1 The twist of the proverb has been rearticulated multiple times by the Prime Minister and his Ministers in different occasions. Ozesmi, 2011, too, drew attention to its centrality for contemporary SHP campaigns.
2 The report acknowledges the 'dams have made an important and significant contribution to human development,' yet argues that 'in too many cases an unacceptable, and often unnecessary and high price has been paid to secure those benefits, especially in social and environmental terms, by people displaced, by community' (WCD, 2000: 310).
3 For a discussion on SHPs' eligibility for carbon trade mechanisms see the World Bank's Carbon Finance Unit's web page, available on <http://wbcarbonfinance.org/ Router.cfm?Page=FAQ&ItemID=24677>.
4 See Rivers International (2010) for an evaluation of SHP projects as 'best practices' on a review published for the ten-year anniversary of WCD report.
5 In 2000, Turkey was ranked eight in the list of countries with the highest number of large dams by the WCD report (McCully, 2001: p. xxvii).
6 Although a very important component of the changing water–energy nexus in Turkey, the anti-SHP movement is outside the scope of this chapter and will be mentioned only tangentially. Emerging works on the struggle employ different perspectives and provide valuable insights. For a 'recognition vs. redistribution' perspective, see Islar (2012a); for a social ecology point of view, see Eryilmaz (2012); and for a rich journalistic account, see Hamsici (2011). See also Kadirbeyoglu and Kurtic, Chapter 18.
7 Environmental history of colonial expansion is one of few literatures that take abundance seriously. Westward expansion in the US exemplifies such transformation of perceived abundance to perceived scarcity as the frontier wilderness gets transformed from a plethora of raw materials to natural resources that are in need of conservation (Cronon, 1994).
8 Turkey imports crude oil from its Middle Eastern neighbors and natural gas from Russia, Iran and Azerbaijan.
9 Thanks to its oceanic climate, the Black Sea Region receives twice as much rainfall as the country average (Sen, 2011) and is the only region in the entire country that does not require irrigated agriculture.
10 The newly established Eastern Black Sea Region Development Agency covers these six provinces: Artvin, Rize, Trabzon, Gumushane, Giresun and Ordu.
11 See Cummings (2009) on Brazil, Hathaway and Pottinger (2009) on South Africa and Khagram (2004) on India.
12 Like many other high-modernist projects, GAP too has been heavily criticized for causing social, cultural, ecological and environmental problems. Alongside forced displacements and despoliation of the local ecosystem, some serious concerns have been voiced regarding inundation of sites of cultural and historical importance, and the project was accused of having a secret security agenda of controlling the predominantly Kurdish region (KHRP, 2005). Over time, however, GAP aimed at transforming its negative image and tried to adopt a more nuanced approach by embracing premises of 'sustainability' and reformulating itself as a 'multi-sector and integrated regional development effort' (Carkoglu and Eder, 2005; Harris, 2008).
13 It is worth noting that GAP's social and cultural dimensions were not initially integral to the development but were added later at the urging of international entities and as projects began to fail in the absence of local involvement (Carkoglu and Eder, 2005; Harris, 2008; 2011). SHPs, on the other hand, seem not to follow such a trajectory.
14 For a set of articles on the ideological role of a construction-fuelled development model of Turkish conservative liberalism, see Balaban (2011), Bora (2011) and Gulhan (2011).

References

Alatout, S. 2009. Bringing abundance back into environmental politics: constructing a Zionist network of abundance, immigration, and colonization 1918–1948. *Social Studies of Science*, 39(3), 363–94.

Bakker, K. 2004. *An Uncooperative Commodity,* New York: Oxford University Press.

Bakker, K. 2010. *Privatizing Water: Governance Failure and the World's Urban Water Crisis,* Ithaca, NY: Cornell University Press.

Balaban, O. 2011. Insaat sektoru neyin lokomotifi? *Birikim*, 270, 19–26.

Balat, H. 2008. Contribution of green energy sources to electrical power production of Turkey: a review. *Renewable and Sustainable Energy Reviews,* 12(6), 1652–66.

Baldwin, A. 2009. Carbon nullius: race, nature and the cultural politics of forest carbon in Canada. *Antipode*, 41(2), 231–55.

Baris, K., and Kucukali, S. 2012. Availability of renewable energy sources in Turkey: current situation, potential, government policies and the EU perspective. *Energy Policy*, 42, 377–91.

Bianet, 2011. *Hopalilardan Little Big Onunde HES Protestosu.* Available at: http://bianet. org/bianet/goc/127688-hopalilardan-little-big-onunde-hes-protestosu (accessed Feb. 2012).

Bora, T. 2011. Turk muhafazakarligi ve insaat sehveti: buyuk olsun, bizim olsun. *Birikim*, 270, 5–18.

Bumpus, A., and Liverman, D. 2008 Accumulation by decarbonization and the governance of the carbon offsets. *Economic Geography*, 84(2), 127–55.

Carkoglu, A., and Eder, M. 2005. Development Alla Turca: The Southeastern Anatolia Development Project (GAP). In F. Adaman and M. Arsel (eds), *Environmentalism in Turkey: Between Democracy and Development?*, pp. 167–84, Burlington, VT: Ashgate.

Cronon, W. 1994. Landscapes of abundance and scarcity. In C. A. Milner, C. A. O'Connor and M. A. Sandweiss (eds), *Oxford History of American West*, pp. 603–38, Oxford: Oxford University Press.

Cummings, B. 2009. *Dam the Rivers, Damn the People: Development and Resistance in Amazonian Brazil,* New York: Routledge.

Erdogdu, E. 2007. Regulatory reform in Turkish energy industry: an analysis. *Energy Policy*, 35(2), 984–93.

Eryilmaz, C. 2012. Social ecology challenges environmental participation: HES opposition cases in Turkey. Ph.D. Middle East Technical University.

ESHA. 2004. *Small Hydropower Situation in the New EU Member States and Candidate Countries.* Available at: http://www.esha.be/fileadmin/esha_files/documents/ publications/publications/Report_on_SHP_in_New_European_Member_States.pdf (accessed Feb. 2012).

ETKB. 2010. *Enerji ve Tabii Kaynaklar Bakanligi 2010-2014 Stratejik Plani,* Ankara: Ministry of Energy and Natural Resources. Available at: http://www.enerji.gov.tr/ yayinlar_raporlar/ETKB_2010_2014_Stratejik_Plani.pdf (accessed Feb. 2012).

Gibbons, F., and Moore, L. 2011. Turkey's great leap forward risks cultural and environmental bankruptcy. *Guardian,* 29 May. Available at: http://www.guardian.co.uk/ world/2011/may/29/turkey-nuclear-hydro-power-development (accessed Feb. 2012).

Goldman, M. 2005. *Imperial Nature: The World Bank and Struggles for Social Justice in the Age of Globalization,* New Haven, CT: Yale University Press.

Goldman, M. 2011. Speculative urbanism and the making of the next world city. *International Journal of Urban and Regional Research,* 35(3), 555–81.

Goldsmith, E., and Hildyard, N. 1984. *Social and Environmental Effects of Large Dams,* Wadebridge, UK: Wadebridge Ecological Center.

Greenpeace. 2010. *Energy [R]evolution: A Sustainable World Energy Outlook,* Greenpeace International, EREC and GWEC. Available at: http://www.greenpeace.org/international/ Global/international/publications/climate/2012/Energy%20Revolution%202012/ ER2012.pdf (accessed Nov. 2012).

Gulhan, S. 2011. Konuta hucum. *Birikim,* 270, 27–33.

Hamsici, M. 2011. *Dereler ve Isyanlar,* Istanbul: Nota Bene.

Harris, L. M. 2008. Modernizing the nation: postcolonialism, postdevelopmentalism, and ambivalent spaces of difference in southeastern Turkey. *Geoforum,* 39(5), 1698–1708.

Harris, L. M. 2011. Salts, soils, and (un)sustainabilities? Analyzing narratives of environmental change in Southeastern Anatolia. In D. K. Davis and E. Burke III (eds), *Environmental Imaginaries in the Middle East and North Africa,* Athens, OH: University of Ohio Press.

Hathaway, T., and Pottinger, L. 2008. The great hydro-rush: the privatization of Africa's rivers. In D. A. McDonald (ed.), *Electric Capitalism: Recolonising Africa on the Power Grid,* pp. 149–79, Sterling, VA: Earthscan.

Hurriyet Daily News. 2010. Turkish environment minister defends controversial dams. Available at: http://www.hurriyetdailynews.com/default.aspx?pageid=438&n=environment-minister-defends-controversial-dams-2010-10-21 (accessed Feb. 2012).

Hydroworld. 2011. World Bank funds additional turkey renewables, including hydro. Available at: http://www.hydroworld.com/articles/2011/12/world -bank-funds-additional.html (accessed Feb. 2012).

International Energy Agency. 2006. *Renewable Energy: RD&D Priorities: Insights form IEA Technology Programs,* Paris: IEA.

Islar, M. 2012a. Struggles for recognition: privatization of water use rights of Turkish rivers. *Local Environment,* 17(3), 317–29.

Islar, M. 2012b. Privatised hydropower development in Turkey: a case of water grabbing? *Water Alternatives,* 5(2), 376–91.

Kaika, M. 2003. Constructing scarcity and sensationalizing water politics: 170 days that shook Athens. *Antipode,* 35(5), 919–54.

Kara, M., Ensari, O., and Ozturk, D. 2010. HES istemeyen elektrik kullanmasin. *Hurriyet.* Available at: http://www.hurriyet.com.tr/ekonomi/15551860.asp (accessed Aug. 2012).

Kaygusuz, K. 1999. Hydro potential in Turkey. *Energy Sources,* 21(7), 581–8.

Kaygusuz, K. 2002. Renewable and sustainable energy use in Turkey: a review. *Renewable and Sustainable Energy Reviews,* 6(4), 339–66.

Kaygusuz, K., and Arsel, M. 2005. Energy politics and policy. In F. Adaman and M. Arsel (eds), *Environmentalism in Turkey: Between Democracy and Development?* Burlington, VT: Ashgate.

Khagram, S. 2004. *Dams and Development: Transnational Struggles for Water and Power,* Ithaca, NY: Cornell University Press.

KHRP. 2005. *The Cultural and Environmental Impact of Large Dams in Southeast Turkey: Fact-Finding Mission Report,* London: KHRP.

Kozok, F. 2012. Bakan'dan Cevrecilere Savas. *Cumhuriyet.* Available at: http://www. cumhuriyet.com.tr/?hn=327120 (accessed Aug. 2012).

Kucukali, S., and Baris, K. 2009. Assessment of small hydropower (SHP) development in Turkey: laws, regulations and EU policy perspective. *Energy Policy,* 37(10), 3872–9.

Linton, J. 2006. The social nature of natural resources: the case of water. *Reconstruction,* 6(3). Available at: http://reconstruction.eserver.org/063/linton.shtml (accessed 5 February 2013)

Linton, J. 2010. *What is Water? The History of a Modern Abstraction,* Vancouver: UBC Press.

Luks, F. 2010. Deconstructing economic interpretations of sustainable development: limits, scarcity and abundance. In L. Mehta (ed.), *The Limits to Scarcity: Contesting the Politics of Allocation,* pp. 93–108, Washington, DC: Earthscan.

McCully, P. 2001. *Silenced Rivers: The Ecology and Politics of Large Dams,* New York: Zed Books.

Mehta, L. 2010. Naturalization, and politicization of scarcity. In L. Mehta (ed.), *The Limits to Scarcity: Contesting the Politics of Allocation,* pp. 13–30, Washington, DC: Earthscan.

Milliyet. 1999. Demirel de kesinti magduru. 11 Nov., p. 11.

Milliyet. 2000. 2003'e kadar kesinti. 11 Oct., p. 7.

Mitchell, T. 2011. *Carbon Democracy: Political Power in the Age of Oil,* New York: Verso.

Newell, F. H. 1920. *Water Resources: Present and Future Uses,* New Haven, CT: Yale University Press.

NTVMSNBC. 2009. Erdogan: akarsular satilmiyor. Available at: http://www.ntvmsnbc. com/id/25122222 (accessed Feb. 2012).

Ocak, A. T., and Gedik, D. 2011. Dere yatagina sigmayan yalanlar: Turkiye'de HES'ler. *Guncel Hukuk,* 92(8), 12–16.

Oguzata, R. T. 2007. Potential of renewable energies in Turkey. *Journal of Energy Engineering,* 133(1), 63–8.

Ozesmi, U. 2011. Water flows, Turk watches: struggles to stop small-scale hydroelectric power plants (HES) in Turkey. Unpublished paper presented at International Research Workshop on Struggling for Water: Dams, Pipes and Urban-Rural Transformations in the Global South, University of Minnesota, Nov.

Pricewaterhouse Coopers (PwC). 2009. *On the Sunny Side of the Street: Opportunities and Challenges in the Turkish Renewable Energy Market,* Istanbul: Pricewaterhouse Coopers Turkey. Available at: http://www.lb.boell.org/downloads/renewable_energy_ turkey.pdf (accessed Feb.).

Rivers International. 2010. *Protecting Rivers and Rights: The World Commission on Dams Recommendations in Action Briefing Kit.* Berkeley, CA: Rivers International.

Sabah. 2012. *HES'ten 10 milyon dolar gelecek.* Available at: http://www.sabah.com.tr/ SabahSpor/Futbol/2012/01/10/hesten-10-milyon-dolar-gelecek (accessed Feb. 2012).

Sen, Z. 2011. Water for energy: hydropower is vital for Turkey. In A. Kibaroglu, W. Scheumann, and A. Kramer (eds), *Turkey's Water Policy: National Frameworks and International Cooperation.* Berlin: Springer.

Sneddon, C., and Fox, C. 2008. Struggles over dams as struggles for justice : The World Commission on Dams (WCD) and anti-dam campaigns in Thailand and Mozambique. *Society and Natural Resources,* 21(7), 37–41.

Swyngedouw, E. 2011. Depoliticized environments: the end of nature, climate change and the post-political condition. *Royal Institute of Philosophy Supplement,* 69, 253–74.

TEIAS. 2009. *Turkish Electrical Energy 10-Year Generation Capacity Projection 2010–2019,* Ankara: Turkish Electricity Transmission Corporation. Available at: http://www. epdk.gov.tr/documents/10157/92882607-4178-4755-91d4-9fe9b2d833d9 (accessed Feb. 2012).

TMMOB. 2010. *TMMOB Hidroelektrik Santraller Raporu,* Ankara: Union of Chambers of Turkish Engineers and Architects.

World Commission on Dams (WCD). 2000. *Dams and Development: A New Framework for Decision-Making; Report of the World Commission on Dams,* London: Earthscan.

While, A., Jonas, A. E. G., and Gibbs, D. 2010. From sustainable development to carbon control: eco-state restructuring and the politics of urban and regional development. *Transactions of the Institute of British Geographers*, 35(1), 76–93.

Xenos, N. 1989. *Scarcity and Modernity,* New York: Routledge.

Yildiz, T. 2010. Turkey's energy economy and future energy vision. *Hurriyet Daily News*, 22 Oct., pp. 1–3.

7 Water scarcity and the colonial state

The emergence of a hydraulic bureaucracy in south-western Matabeleland, Zimbabwe, 1964–1972

Muchaparara Musemwa

Introduction

Once perceived to be an abundant resource, water is becoming progressively and more acutely scarce in many parts of the world. Nonetheless, global analyses and engagements on the notion of 'water scarcity', led for example by the Global Water Partnership, the World Water Council, and the Social Charter for Water, continue, as Mehta has argued, to 'draw on rather vague political, economic or theoretical assumptions rather than on empirically grounded facts and realities' (2000: 1). Mehta further posits that, because of their abstract nature, these analyses are inclined to be 'apolitical', 'ahistorical' and far removed from socio-political materialities. Moreover, global discourses often construct and cast 'water scarcity' in universal terms and obfuscate underlying connections with power dynamics, as well as ecological, socio-political, temporal and anthropogenic aspects across diverse scales (Mahayni, Chapter 4; Mehta, 2000). Consequently, such accounts of water scarcity or 'crises' conceal questions about struggles over control and access to water. What is required, as a number of scholars on the production of 'water scarcity' have stressed (Bakker, 2000; Mehta, 2000; Swyngedouw, 1999; Worster, 1985), is a far more nuanced understanding of the manifold aspects of water and its diverse manifestations as experienced within the quotidian environments in which people eke out a living. After all, as Fontein (2008: 738) argues, water is at the center of the complexity of social and historical concerns that underpin multiple disciplines, as amply reflected in this and other chapters in this volume.

One aspect of water scarcity that has historically confronted societies is drought – a 'real' scarcity which is as much an environmental problem as it is a social problem, constituting 'biophysical and social manifestations' such as diminishing groundwater aquifers, acute water shortage and deepening inequality in access to water for multiple consumers (Johnston, 2005: 135; Mehta, 2000, 2005). But, as much as droughts are the result of biophysical and ecological conditions, water scarcity could also be, and has often been, the outcome of anthropogenic interventions, i.e. it can be 'manufactured' (Bakker, 2000; Mehta, 2005). Accordingly, global narratives referred to above attest to the emergence of 'water scarcity' as one of a number of hegemonic concepts (e.g. privatization, etc.) that have become central precepts within societies especially pertaining to water governance. Such hegemonic ideas, as Sneddon (Chapter 2) asserts, 'mold and structure how individuals and groups perceive and interpret certain phenomena'. This chapter responds to the challenges posed by earlier scholars and examines, through an empirically grounded case-study of the 1964–5 drought scourge that afflicted south-western Matabeleland, Southern Rhodesia (now Zimbabwe), how 'water scarcity' came to be established as a dominant idea in this specific locale and at this particular time. This drought was one of the most severe climate episodes in the environmental history of this country and, as such, elicits questions about the implications of water scarcity as a hegemonic concept. The chapter analyzes how water was institutionalized in south-western Matabeleland following this catastrophic drought during the colonial era. It documents how a community of local water users in south-western Matabeleland struggled to attain control over the resource on which their livelihoods depended, after experiencing the cumulative impact of serial droughts which culminated in the 1964–5 drought. This action came about only after protracted years of the colonial state's inertia in dealing with water scarcity in this region.[1] As the effects of the drought deepened and triggered a 'crisis' condition, water scarcity became a decidedly hegemonic concept and emerged as a dominant theme within this semi-arid area. A community of water users, involving white commercial farmers and African peasants, environmentalists, miners, state and municipal officials, and engineers debated and interpreted the diverse meanings and tragedies of persistent bouts of drought/water scarcity.

Looking to the state to introduce water reforms to ensure long-term solutions, many stakeholders of the region called on the state to extend its 'hydraulic mission', specifically to mobilize all surface and groundwater resources by building large-scale water reservoirs. This prompted the formation of a new hydraulic authority, the Matabeleland Development Council (MDC) in 1965. The pressures brought to bear on the state by the collective inter-sectoral interests in this region ended its historic and systemic inability to provide solutions to the endemic scourge of water scarcity. The chapter ends in 1972 when yet another severe drought struck, leading the colonial state to finally acknowledge the failure of past water development policies and practices, and compelling it to launch, in the same year, a broader investigation into the hydro- and agro-economic conditions of south-western Matabeleland.

This case-study demonstrates how the struggles and demands of these water users accentuated the supremacy of the colonial state in producing and nurturing the hegemonic notion of water scarcity in this context. The study also provides a textured expression of the tensions between the hegemonic depictions of water scarcity and the unequal substantive realities in specific milieux. It therefore suggests an alternative way of thinking about the animosity that this rise to state hydro-hegemony had to contend with and the manner in which water scarcity as a hegemonic idea only came to the fore in relation to specific politics and institutional pathways. The chapter unravels the relationships between different local water users and how they comprehended water scarcity and cooperated in such critical times of adverse resource scarcity. Finally, the chapter underscores the notion that 'change is greatly facilitated by crisis' (Richards, 2002: 17) as the water users' appeals emanating from this dramatic climate event helped to delegitimize the state's arguments for maintaining the status quo.

In thinking about the implications of the absence of water, various scholars (Molle *et al.*, 2009; Sneddon, Chapter 2; Mahayni, Chapter 4; Swyngedouw, 1999; Turton and Ohlsson, 1999; Worster, 1985) have argued that water scarcity, in and of itself, is not the primary question. The concern, rather, is whether a society has the capacity to adapt in order to cope with the challenges it presents. These scholars contend that two fundamental shifts take place as water is utilized to fulfil human needs. The first one is the transformation of water from a state of abundance to a state of shortage as a result of extraction. The second is the shift from a state of water shortage to a state of overexploitation of water resources to the point of diminishing returns. The first shift involves the laying down of substantial hydraulic infrastructure (often by the state) to tap into more water. This resource expansion is often referred to as the 'hydraulic mission', referring to a central government agency driven largely by hydraulic engineers (Reisner, 1986; Swyngedouw, 1999; Turton and Meissner, 2002; Wester, 2009; Worster, 1985; see also Baker, Chapter 3; Erensu, Chapter 6). The state takes the lead, controls water, and contributes to the emergence of hydraulic bureaucracies whose main task is developing water resources. Despite the more recent emphasis on decentralization and devolution of control over water, the state continues to play a central role in determining the responses to and control of water resources. Despite such reforms, local control and management have continued to play an important role in many contexts, including in colonial Zimbabwe, and throughout the developing world.

Throughout the 20th century, the role of the state in water resource development was 'an emergent, and frequently intentional, political strategy for controlling space, water and people in many countries' (Wester *et al.*, 2009: 395). This produced hydrocracies that were bent on, among other things, managing the flow of rivers, and 'green(ing) the desert' by expanding water resources for the sake of modernity and the advancement of people's welfare (Bakker, 2002; Kaika, 2006). Although such developments date back to the second half of the 19th century, by the beginning of the 20th century there was 'a general craze for irrigation development', even as some of the presumed advantages were fervently contested, particularly during drought periods (Molle *et al.*, 2009: 395). Irrigation projects widely became symbols of hegemonic control, modernity and civilization (Wester *et al.*, 2009). For much of the second half of the 19th century, irrigation development was often done through private enterprise, with notable exceptions in Egypt and India and elsewhere (Beinart and Hughes, 2007). However, this was to change at the beginning of the 20th century when public investments in irrigation became widespread, resulting in the formation of state water bureaucracies. The same debates and discourses went on to inform the establishment of a water authority to undertake and coordinate water development in the drought-prone region of south-western Matabeleland.

Figure 7.1 Agro-economic survey of south-western Matabeleland: report by the Agricultural Development Authority, Salisbury, Rhodesia, August 1972.

Physical location and geographical features of south-western Matabeleland

South-western Matabeleland is marked by a boundary in the north that runs along the main watershed, i.e. adjacent to the Plumtree–Bulawayo railway line; in the south by the Shashi and Limpopo rivers; in the west by the Ramaquabane river; and finally in the east by the eastern watershed of the Umzingwane river (ADA, 1972: 1). (See Figure 7.1.) In the mid-1890s, the region consisted of approximately 4.201 million hectares of overall land area, divided along racial lines such that 2.298 million hectares was European Land, 1.731 million hectares was Tribal Trust Land (TTL) for African peasants, 0.085 million hectares was for African Purchase areas, and the remainder, 0.085 million hectares, was National Land and Parks and Wild Life Land (ADA, 1972: 1). African reserves were carved out of these TTLs. These reserves were the least endowed with reliable water supplies (Palmer, 1977).

The climate of this region is notable for its relatively short, erratic and variable rainy seasons, as well as long dry winter periods. Annual rainfall tends to diminish from about 600 mm from the north along the Zambezi–Limpopo watershed to 350 mm in the south. The effects of the decrease in rainfall are compounded by the rise of mean annual temperature from 18.5°C in Bulawayo to 23°C at Beitbridge. The entire area is within the medium to low hydrological zones of colonial Zimbabwe (Shinn, 1974). The main drainage system comprises seven major rivers (Ramaquabane, on the western border, Ingqwesi, Sansukwe, Simukwe, Shashani, Tuli and Umzingwane). The rivers flow south towards the Shashi and Limpopo rivers (ADA, 1972: 3–4). These rivers are historically prone to drying up in the long dry season (April–October inclusively). A mean annual total of some 185,000 million gallons of runoff is lost to this region, as most of it flows to the sea.

The population of the countryside at the time of the 1964–5 drought was approximately 250,000, the majority of whom were Africans. Both Africans and Europeans practiced cattle farming, making beef production the anchor of south-western Matabeleland's economy. The cattle population in the TTL was approximately 407,000 in January 1960. Despite the semi-aridity of south-western Matabeleland, extensive investment had been made in the area. Mining, meat processing and canning, among other industries, were well established. Against this semi-arid climatic and topographical setting, the lack of water storage facilities, and therefore the loss of water as runoff during the rainy season, meant populations and livelihoods in this region were vulnerable to drought. If this region went for just one season without copious rains (as often occurred), the livelihoods of its inhabitants (ranchers, commercial farmers and African peasants) were threatened; the City of Bulawayo also depended for its domestic consumption and industrial use on water drawn from this hinterland.

The 1964–1965 drought in south-western Matabeleland: its antecedents and impact

The drought of 1964–5 represents the culmination of a series of consecutive droughts that severely hit south-western Matabeleland in particular and Southern Rhodesia in general. Three years (1959, 1960 and 1963) of failed rains had dire consequences for farmers throughout the region. The social and economic basis of their livelihoods was severely undermined by the shortage of water and a limited range of alternatives.[2] This was not the first time that droughts had afflicted this region. In fact, drought in south-western Matabeleland has been part of much of the region's history, dating back as far as the 1840s when the Ndebele under Mzilikazi first settled in Matabeleland (Iliffe, 1990). Before the 1964–5 drought, there had been a number of droughts recorded by missionaries, notably in 1867, 1872, 1882, 1884, 1887 and 1889 (Iliffe, 1990). The last major drought before 1964–5 was in 1947 and it was considered to be devastating.[3] This was followed by the 1960–3 dry spell when rainfall was extremely erratic, followed by the complete failure of the rains in early 1964 through to 1965. All in all, this was shattering for the local African and European farmers, despite the fact that the overall impact was not uniform. Water engineers in the Ministry of Water Development readily admitted the Department's incapability to deal with the immense impact of the water crisis, especially for Africans living and farming in the region. L. R. Wynn, a water engineer in the Ministry of Water Development responsible for the Bulawayo Province, was candid in his assessment of the situation:

The year under review is probably one of the worst drought years to be recorded. There was nothing much this Ministry could do to relieve the situation as the effect was widespread. From the Ramaquabane River in the West to the Beitbridge area in the East, few if any crops survived to maturity and the inhabitants had to find work wherever possible to buy food ... It is estimated that up to 100,000 cattle were lost due to drought. Not all the deaths were due to water shortage by any means. There was just as acute a shortage of grazing. This serves to highlight the fact that development plans for the south-western Lowveld must include fodder crops under irrigation.[4]

In view of the seasonal variations and the physiographic features of south-western Matabeleland, it is clear that drought was a recurrent feature. Following the 1964–5 drought there were further extended dry spells in rapid succession in 1965–6 and 1967–8.[5] This situation was formally acknowledged in May 1965 when the state founded the Matabeleland Development Council (MDC) to advise the state on water development and implementation of related development projects (including dams and irrigation schemes). The formation of the MDC was a result of growing pressures from a wide spectrum of concerned water users largely based in south-western Matabeleland.

A flashback to 1961 and 1962 reveals that the rainy seasons were relatively good. On the other hand, the 1964–5 drought was hailed as more severe than the three years of scant rains that had preceded it. Approximately 100,000 cattle, belonging to both white commercial farmers and African peasants, died in 1964.[6] Water scarcity swiftly transmuted into grazing scarcity. The impact of the drought varied and different levels of scarcity had ramifications for some people more than others. Overall, these scarcities produced desperate conditions for humans, animals and the environment. To eke out a living farmers and ranchers resorted to short-term solutions that at times made them even more vulnerable. As the Secretary of Agriculture observes, cattle producers in south-western Matabeleland resorted to selling their cattle off the veld 'at lower weights and grades than is normally possible'.[7] African farmers suffered more than their European counterparts. Most Africans living in the TTLs were subsistence farmers who relied, for the most part, on erratic rainfall. To realize a better yield, they ploughed significant areas of dry-land annually with the expectation that they would harvest enough grain to meet their families' food needs (ADA, 1972: 36). Without recourse to other alternatives, the scarcity of rainfall could spell disaster such as the calamities reported in the Matopos area where the drought led to pervasive crop failure as well as a loss of 12,000 of their cattle (*Chronicle*, 1965a). In the absence of relief from the state, options for some African farmers were few and far-between. Selling their stock at depressed prices was one such option (ibid.). In order to cope with the effects of the drought on their cattle, some farmers were obliged to graze their cattle on nearby European farms, where some grazing was still available. Many left their cattle to graze in the Matopos National Park even though this was illegal. At one time, a total of 2,000 cattle owned by Africans were found grazing on European farms where there was still some pasture owing to the existence of irrigation schemes, while an estimated 5,000 were found grazing in the Matopos National Park (ibid.). An informant, VaMadumeja, also highlighted that some people sent their cattle to other regions less affected by drought such as Kafusi, Gobatema and Malambapeli.[8] The drought also ravaged three African reserves – Sansukwe, Mphoengs and Kwene – where people were reportedly starving. A Member of Parliament, Benny Goldstein of the Rhodesia Party, was stunned by the anguish of both cattle and humans in parts of the drought-stricken south-western Matabeleland: 'The cattle could hardly stand. Women were walking miles through the bush for a small tin of water to bring a little relief to their families' (*Chronicle*, 1965b). The elderly people I interviewed at Chief Nhlamba's homestead in Ntepe village, Gwanda South, testified that the drought presented grave challenges for many people. Several people were forced to eat a type of porridge that was made from the dried and ground roots of the *umthopi* tree to survive. Others ate *shomwe* (amarula seed) that was filling for a couple of hours before one started feeling hungry again. Yet others, especially the elderly, went in desperation to the Njelele Shrine in Matopos to pray to Mwali/Mlimo for the rains.[9]

The relentless drought inevitably affected the cattle market. P. J. Creiff, owner of the 19,000-acre Broken Wheel Ranch, told a *Chronicle* newspaper reporter that the impact of the drought was so grave that he had to sell 'more than 200 cattle because there was no grazing for them' (*Chronicle*, 1965b). The lack of grazing halted the sale at auctioneers and the over-supply of cattle depressed prices at official sales points in Bulawayo. The quality and condition of cattle steadily worsened, putting pressure on the ranchers to sell. Some, however, refused to sell at a discounted price.[10] On 18 February 1965, a defiant rancher withheld his 100 head of breeding-stock in Bulawayo, refusing to sell his cows and heifers 'at rock bottom prices' (*Chronicle*, 1965c). Plummeting milk production also compelled some farmers to nourish their cows with 'expensive milled proteins' (ibid.).

The effects of this drought illustrate only too well how water scarcity can be life-threatening and how, as Sneddon (Chapter 2), Mahayni (Chapter 4), Erensu (Chapter 6), and Varghese (Chapter 14) argue, the basic water requirements of people locally and globally often are not being realistically tackled. With cases of extreme water scarcity as portrayed above, the lack of adequate long-term water resource planning on the part of the colonial state was a significant shortcoming. The poor rainy seasons preceding the 1964–5 drought event all illustrate the lack of institutional response to the consequences and mitigation of drought, as one official attested: 'Many farmers have lost faith that there will be "normal" rainfall in Matabeleland and for them, the only hope of salvation lies in us placing all our resources into the construction of major dams.'[11]

The discourse that evolved over the institutionalization of water resources proved, as Mosse has argued, 'to be a complex and contested task: one that is never just about water as an economic resource; but about water as a symbol of identity, power and citizenship' (2008: 948). Mosse concludes in his analysis of water systems that droughts are 'as much about the state as they are about communities of users, and the wider-political-administrative systems within which struggles over rights and responsibilities take place' (ibid.). It is to the south-western Matabeleland 'communities of users' that we now turn.

Reactions to the impact of the 1964–1965 drought and its aftermath

The ravages of drought and the extent of its impact on south-western Matabeleland stimulated varied responses. A mix of politicians, European farmers and ranchers, provincial water engineers, City of Bulawayo senior executives and councillors, conservationists, businessmen, mining industry representatives and citizens (mostly white) were, despite their competing uses of water, brought together because of a shared experience of water scarcity. Together they initiated consultative meetings, conferences and calls for action to address the devastation of drought. Civil society rallied against the failures of the colonial state that for far too long had done little to solve the water crisis that afflicted this cattle-producing region. For many, the drought in south-western Matabeleland was a veritable sign of this region's state of neglect and underdevelopment. The attention paid to the drought of 1965 by these different interest groups produced variegated and multiple meanings and perceptions of 'drought' and questions about what sort of 'relief' was the most suitable for the region. The relationship between power and technology was interrogated, with drought and relief emerging as among the most pressing national issues at the time. Because of the severity of the drought, the Legislative Assembly was also forced to debate how to respond.

As the effects of water scarcity intensified in the months of February and March 1965, the *Chronicle* aired numerous letters reflecting concerns from ordinary white farmers and townsmen from the city of Bulawayo. Reflections from two writers are illustrative of these concerns. A farmer, simply referred to as Giles, urged the authorities to introduce a robust soil conservation program to 'stop erosion in Matabeleland catchment areas' where about 25 dam projects were to be implemented (*Chronicle*, 1965d). Similarly, E. E. Macpherson expressed anxiety about the possibility of the wretched ecological conditions transforming south-western Matabeleland into a desert. He feared that 'the sands of the desert will engulf Bulawayo' unless a solution was found. He envisioned an Armageddon of sorts:

> Our city will be known no more and everybody – but everybody – butchers, bakers, newspaper editors and reporters, lawyers, and doctors, can pack their kit and get out if they are still strong enough to tramp through the surrounding sand drifts. (Ibid.)

Many more influential people, such as S. Rabinovitz, the President of the Bulawayo Chamber of Commerce, contested the transitory nature of drought relief measures (*Chronicle*, 1965e).

In effect, diverse groupings of concerned water users pressed the state to intervene. A small subcommittee produced a set of proposals for the development of water resources for south-western Matabeleland in October 1964.[12] It included two senior officials of the Bulawayo City Council (BCC), the Chairman of the BCC Water and Electricity Committee, and both the City Engineer and his Deputy. The content of the proposals isolate the significance and meaning of the absence of water to humans, businesses, industries and the City of Bulawayo. To this end, Johnston has argued that water scarcity does not only manifest the important dimensions of 'supply (the conditions and actions that affect quantity and quality) and demand (intended and projected use), but also the relative aspects of how water is valued (the cultural meanings and economic values)' (2005: 135).

Throughout this process, including the documentation of the negative effects of the drought, as well as arguments as to what should be done about it, it was clear that there were multiple interests, users and uses of water at play. Some insisted that the Irrigation Department had constructed only a few isolated dams to please elites, demanding a lasting solution that would more systematically deal with water security. Industries also expressed their opinion, those with interests in gold, chrome and asbestos; meat processing and canning plants; a big cement factory at Colleen Bawn; and many others similarly felt threatened by inadequate water resources.[13] For the gold mining industry, more water meant that it would be able to resuscitate old mines in Gwanda, Tuli River, Colleen Bawn and Filabusi that had been closed partly due to water scarcity. Similarly, the United Portland Cement Company (Pvt.) Limited, fully endorsed the proposed water development scheme for the south-western Matabeleland region as it would enhance productivity in the cement industry[14] (see intersections with analysis of mining in colonial Zambia by Waters, Chapter 12).

Concerns about water scarcity reinforced the enduring rural–urban links between the City of Bulawayo and its rural hinterland (south-western Matabeleland), epitomizing what Kaika has called the continuing 'dialectics between the production of nature and the production of cities' (2006: 276). For its part, the City of Bulawayo was in dire need of water security. The City had by 1965 constructed three dams in south-western Matabeleland, namely, Lower Ncema (1943), Mzingwane (1956), and Inyankuni (1965) (Musemwa, 2006). On numerous occasions, when the south-western Matabeleland catchment experienced low rainfall, the water levels in the dams fell, threatening water supplies to the city. There was no shortage of arguments in support of an integrated and lasting solution, which inevitably pointed to large-scale water development schemes.

Some members of the Southern Rhodesia Legislature were similarly not persuaded by the efficacy of short-term solutions to the drought emergency. Concerned about the perilous position of the cattle and agricultural industries in Matabeleland, the House of Assembly passed a motion calling upon the Government to urgently establish large-scale coordinated water schemes in south-western Matabeleland.[15] Not every parliamentarian was in favor of large-scale water development schemes. The lengthy debate in the Legislative Assembly was also taken up by environmental organizations such as the Natural Resources Board, the Intensive Area committees, farmers and ranchers in south-western Matabeleland who were convinced of the futility of drought relief measures for long-term purposes. Thus, while they all appreciated short-to-medium-term mitigation from the state, they pressed for long-term solutions such as dam-building as guarantors against future droughts. The diverse concerns raised above were all to be repeated and bolstered in a much more organized way as a call to decisive action was made on the state at a conference on how to respond to water scarcity.

Conference on water supplies in south-western Matabeleland

This section discusses how the local water users, based on their experience of the vagaries of water scarcity in this region, perceived and interpreted their own and the state's understanding of this phenomenon of drought and the resultant water crisis. It explores the tensions that marked the rise of water scarcity as a hegemonic concept in this locale. These tensions were quite evident at a conference organized to consider solutions to the crisis. As the impact of the 1964–5 drought deepened, 21 Intensive Conservation Areas (ICA) committees, located in the districts of south-western Matabeleland under the aegis of the Natural Resources Board (NRB), convened a conference on 21 April 1965, to discuss the drought.[16] Together with local multiple water users bound by a common cause – water scarcity – the conservation committees enjoined the state to end the water crisis, once and for all. At this conference, held in Bulawayo, Rhodesia's second largest city after Salisbury (now Harare), a number of intertwined themes that hone our grasp of the diverse nature of water scarcity as a hegemonic idea materialized. Different conceptualizations of water scarcity between the diverse users and the state surfaced. Notably, as a common scourge confronted the different water users in the region, consensus on how it was to be addressed was quick to develop. But the solution to the water scarcity problem proposed by these water users was clearly at variance with that of the state. While the state went for quick-fix, short-term solutions, such as immediate drought relief measures, the different delegates were vehemently opposed to it and pushed for a long-term solution, namely dam-building. Some also believed that, because of the existence of groundwater, which was largely untapped, water resources were in fact abundant.

The chairperson of the NRB set the tone of the conference by placing water firmly at the center of the region's survival and stressed its critical role to all the economic constituent parts of south-western Matabeleland: 'Water is the life-blood of Matabeleland and whether it be European or African agriculture, industry, mining, the Railways or the Municipalities and T. M. B.'s [Tobacco Marketing Boards] all are equally involved. Matabeleland's water resources cannot be dealt with in isolation.'[17] He berated the Government for not doing much to develop the region's water resources. The conference's theme focusing on 'long term water development' simply undercut the state's short-term relief measures, which it systematically introduced every time a drought visited this region.[18] The Government's offer of £3 million as part of the immediate relief measures was deemed a niggardly offer, best seen as a 'short-term rescue operation' rather than a serious signal of the state's intention to make a radical intervention.[19] In an era of large-scale hydraulic projects across the world, water users at the conference were already convinced that large dams were the sole enduring guarantors against water scarcity. The state was censured for its hegemonic practice of building dams supposedly for a privileged few. For example, a Filabusi district farmer reproached 'official thinking' which sanctioned the haphazard construction of 'various schemes, some good, some rather hair-brained'. In his view, the state had failed to produce a holistic plan to guard against those who inconsiderately got their individual 'pet schemes' on track without fear of any government restrictions. If such a practice was allowed to continue it would severely affect the water table in the long run. The state was further reproached for not having any conceivable water development plan for this region. Yet it had, in 1965, constructed a mega-water project in the adjacent territory of the south-east Lowveld, the Sabi-Limpopo Authority. They questioned why an area that had never been occupied could have received such top priority at the expense of a region renowned as the country's leading beef-producing province. Established in 1965 under the provisions of the Sabi-Limpopo Authority Act of 1964, the authority was a regional planning and development body whose role was 'to exploit, conserve and utilize the water resources of the area, with the object of facilitating and expediting the economic development of the area in the national interest' (Pollock, 1968: 76; see also Stanbridge, 1969; Wolmer, 2007). The Filabusi farmer spoke for many at the conference when he urged the state to extend its 'hydraulic mission' so that a 'similar face lift ... (could) be given to this part of the country',[20] by appropriating all surface and groundwater resources. To sensitize the state, the farmer tersely warned: 'the only alternative left to us is for us all to seriously consider packing our bags and follow our drought stricken cattle to pastures new with the utmost speed'.[21]

Reference was also made to the region's untapped groundwater and runoff at the conference. Although the 1964–5 drought resulted in limited water supplies in this region, the conference grappled with the question about whether this natural and biophysical event made water scarce in absolute ways. The arguments presented were that, whilst such water had not yet been fully exploited, it was always going to be difficult to make the claim that south-western Matabeleland suffered from resource scarcity: 'The province has the water resources available if it likes to make proper use of them,' argued the conference chairperson.[22] He was supported by a retired member of the NRB: 'There are dams underground, we do not have to spend more money, we just have to take the water out – it is artesian water, plenty of it.'[23] Thus, participants at the conference contested the hegemonic idea of water scarcity as a mere biophysical condition and argued that it could be averted if the state made creative interventions in the region because, among other issues, it had abundant groundwater which could be tapped.

Competing versions of how the water scarcity problem in south-western Matabeleland was to be solved were advanced at the conference. A consensus emerged over the need to have a single water authority to appropriate and manage all the water for the region's use. However, the structure the authority would adopt did not go uncontested. Some preferred it to be a replica of the just-completed (1965) complex and autonomous Sabi-Limpopo Authority (which itself was patterned along the Tennessee Valley Authority (TVA) in the US) in the south-eastern Lowveld (Wolmer, 2007). Yet others sharply opposed a wholesale super-imposition of the Sabi-Limpopo Authority structure on south-western Matabeleland for fear that the central focus of what they were proposing – namely the development of water resources – would be lost because the focus of the former's responsibilities went beyond simple water development.[24] In the final analysis, the delegates adopted a resolution endorsing the 'immediate establishment of an authority for the development of the water resources of Matabeleland'. They proposed the appointment of a broad-based council, comprising representatives from bodies critical and specific to the economy of the region, namely: 'the Intensive Conservation Area committees, Tribal Trust Land, City Council of Bulawayo, Chambers of Commerce and Industry, Chamber of Mines and the Institute of Bankers'.[25] The most significant result of the conference was the birth of the Matabeleland Development Council (MDC) – a 'hydraulic bureaucracy' readily welcomed but, more importantly, uncontested by the state. The state perceived this new authority as a structure it could manage without committing the same financial outlay of millions of pounds it had spent on the creation of the Sabi-Limpopo Authority. Following the appointment of the first office-bearers of the MDC on 20 May 1965, within a short space of time, the MDC turned south-western Matabeleland into a hive of activity as engineers went about testing the availability of underground water at designated dam sites, or embarked on exploratory drilling to test the foundations of possible dams, or surveying future potential sites for irrigation development, and so on (*Chronicle*, 1965f). By September 1966, the MDC had constructed a number of water schemes that included the Tuli-Makwe Dam and the irrigation scheme in Gwanda, among others (*Chronicle*, 1966).

The conviction that large dam schemes were the panacea for alleviating the perennial water problems faced by the drought-prone region seemed to hold promise for a few years to come. However, for all the MDC's acclaimed successes in alleviating the impact of water scarcity and food insecurity, towards the end of 1968, news that numerous dam schemes that had been proposed by the public water utility council had been cancelled 'for economic reasons' hit the headlines (*Chronicle*, 1968). This situation was compounded by the 1967–8 drought spell which the Secretary for Agriculture said 'dealt the industry a most grievous blow'.[26] Thus, the poor agricultural performance in areas such as south-western Matabeleland compelled the state to search for other alternatives. In 1972, the government commissioned the Agricultural Development Authority (ADA) to conduct an agro-economic survey of south-western Matabeleland. Unlike the pressures exerted on it by the diverse community of water users in 1965, this time around the state was in firm control of the situation and was the first to order ADA to investigate long-term plans for the harnessing of water to ensure that 'rational' allocation of these limited water resources were drawn up to safeguard sound future development. While the *Report on the Agro-Economic Survey of South-Western Matabeleland* was released, it was never implemented as Rhodesia was plunged into a guerrilla-armed struggle led by the two nationalist parties, ZANU (PF) and PF-ZAPU.

Conclusion

Contemporary global debates and analyses of hegemonic concepts such as water scarcity have tended to be abstract, ahistorical and apolitical. There is a dire need for such discourses to be evaluated and considered in relation to specific historical, political, ecological and quotidian settings in order to capture the questions about struggles over water control and underlying anthropogenic power dynamics. This chapter has attempted to locate 'water scarcity' – one of the emerging and powerful hegemonic concepts in water governance – within a specific historical and ecological setting to explore how it came to be constituted as a hegemonic idea in south-western Matabeleland in the mid-1960s. The chapter has examined how the severe drought of 1964–5 produced deleterious consequences for the diverse classes of water users. It explored how this diverse community of water users experienced water scarcity and how they reacted to avoid the recurrence of this scourge. Despite the disparateness of this group, they came together and severely reprimanded the Southern Rhodesian colonial state for not having proactively attempted to find enduring solutions to a water scarcity problem that was as old as the colony itself, especially in this region. They unanimously invoked the state to introduce water reforms that guaranteed long-lasting solutions by inducing it to extend its 'hydraulic mission' to their part of the country. This specified demand underscores the extent to which diverse hegemonies can mutually reinforce each other. Indeed, the nexus between water scarcity as a hegemonic concept and the consolidation of the hegemonic 'hydraulic mission' concept and related practices is amply underscored by the case-study presented in this chapter (see also Sneddon, Chapter 2; Baker, Chapter 3; Erensu, Chapter 6). This resulted in the state succumbing to the demands of the water users and readily adopting their proposal. The state also agreed to establish the Matabeleland Development Council (MDC) to oversee water development and governance issues. Thus the escalating tensions between water users and the colonial state entrenched 'water scarcity' as a dominant idea that was to find concrete expression in the creation of a state-controlled hydraulic structure to mobilize surface and groundwater through engineering technologies designed to reduce the impact of water scarcity and droughts. As the conference deliberations attest, the variegated community of water users, miners, farmers, municipal officials, current and retired engineers and conservationists, 'set the terms' for water governance in south-western Matabeleland in the first place – an agenda the state was surprisingly all too willing to adopt. This case-study suggests that the state, powerful as it maybe, does not hold the sole, absolute and ultimate prerogative to shape and influence how hegemonic concepts operate on the 'ground level', as this is also contingent on other actors.

Acknowledgements

I would like to thank the Transformation Office at the University of the Witwatersrand, Johannesburg, South Africa, for awarding me the Carnegie Large Research Grant which made the research for this chapter possible. I would also like to thank the archivists at the Bulawayo National Archives, especially Mr Michael Kwesu, for their assistance in accessing archival materials; Mr Jackson Ndlovu, Librarian of the Edward Ndlovu.Memorial Library, Gwanda and Chief Nhlamba of Ntepe Village and all my interviewees in Gwanda South.

Notes

1 For more information on this, see Mufema (2005).
2 Southern Rhodesia, *Report of the Director of the Division of Irrigation for the year ended 31 Dec. 1960*, 18.
3 *Southern Rhodesia: Legislative Assembly Debates, First Session – Sixth Parliament*, 19 Feb. 1947, 2709.
4 Provincial Water Engineer, Bulawayo, *Annual Report for the year ended 31 Dec. 1964* (Salisbury, Rhodesia: Ministry of Water Development, 1965).
5 *Report of the Secretary for Agriculture for the period 1 Oct., 1970 to 30 Sept., 1971* (Salisbury, Rhodesia: Ministry of Agriculture, [1971]), 3.
6 Bulawayo National Archives (BNA), ICA/4/14: Proposals for the Development of the Water Resources of South-west Matabeleland, Bulawayo, Oct. 1964, p. 7.
7 *Report of the Secretary for Agriculture for the period 1 Oct., 1965 to 30 Sept. 1966* (Salisbury, Rhodesia: Ministry of Agriculture, [1966]), 1.
8 Interview with Mr D. Madumeja (87 years old) of Ntepe Village, Gwanda South, 21 Nov. 2011, at Joshua M. Nkomo Polytechnic, Gwanda Town, Matabeleland South, Zimbabwe.
9 Interviews with Chief Nhlamba, Mrs Mathe and Old Man Ndlovu, on 22 Nov. 2011, at Chief Nhlamba's homestead in Ntepe Village, Gwanda South.
10 BNA: Location 25/5/7R: Box No.: 6722 – Ministry of Water development: Annual report for the year ended 31 Dec. 1965, Provincial Water Engineer, Bulawayo Province.
11 Ibid.
12 Bulawayo City Council (BCC) Minutes. (NB: These minutes are located at the Bulawayo Townhall): 'Development of the Water Resources of South-West Matabeleland', Annexure to City of Bulawayo Council Meeting held 18 Nov. 1964.
13 BCC Minutes: 'Development of the Water resources of South-West Matabeleland'.
14 BNA ICA/4/14: Proposals for the Development of the Water Resources of South-west Matabeleland.
15 *Southern Rhodesia: Legislative Assembly Debates*, 60 (1965), 1042.
16 BNA ICA/4/14: Verbatim Record of a Conference on Water Supplies in Matabeleland held in the Museum, Bulawayo, Wednesday, 21 April 1965, p. 1.
17 Ibid.
18 Ibid.
19 Ibid.
20 Ibid., p. 14.
21 Ibid., p. 16.
22 Ibid., p. 2.
23 Ibid., p. 18.
24 Ibid., p. 25.
25 Ibid., p. 39.
26 *Report of the Secretary for Agriculture … 1 Oct. 1970 to 30 Sept. 1971.*

References

Agricultural Development Authority (ADA). 1972. *Agro-Economic Survey of South-Western Matabeleland*, Salisbury, Rhodesia: ADA.

Bakker, K. 2000. Privatizing water, producing scarcity: the Yorkshire drought of 1995. *Economic Geography*, 76(1), 4–27.

Bakker, K. 2002. From state to market? Water mercantilization in Spain. *Environment and Planning A*, 34(5), 767–90.

Beinart, W., and Hughes, L. 2007. *Environment and Empire,* Oxford: Oxford University Press.

Chronicle, 1965a. African farmers hit by drought. 15 Jan.

Chronicle, 1965b. Drought brings starvation: costly farm relief predicted for stricken areas. 26 Feb.

Chronicle, 1965c. 100 head of stock unsold as rancher refuses low prices. 19 Feb.

Chronicle, 1965d. Stop erosion in Matabeleland catchment areas. 6 March.

Chronicle, 1965e. Think big on drought. 1 April.

Chronicle, 1965f. Nine for development council: Matabeleland's 'team' named. 21 May.

Chronicle, 1966. Bill up to £2m. 21 Sept.

Chronicle, 1968. Plans for new dams shelved. 6 Sept.

Fontein, J. 2008. The power of water: landscape, water and the state in southern and eastern Africa: an introduction. *Journal of Southern African Studies*, 34(4), 737–56.

Iliffe, J. 1990. *Famine in Zimbabwe, 1890–1960,* Gweru: Mambo Press.

Johnston, B. R. 2005. The commodification of water and the human dimensions of manufactured scarcity. In L. Whiteford and S. Whiteford (eds), *Globalization, Water, and Health: Resource Management in Times of Scarcity,* Oxford: James Currey.

Kaika, M. 2006. Dams as symbols of modernization: the urbanization of nature between geographical imagination and materiality. *Annals of the Association of American Geographers*, 96(2), 276–301.

Mehta, L. 2000. *Water for the Twenty-First Century: Challenges and Misconceptions*, IDS Working Paper, 111, Brighton: Institute of Development Studies. Available at: https:// entwicklungspolitik.uni-hohenheim.de/uploads/media/Water_for_the_Twenty-First_Century-ids-workingpaper_111_04.pdf (accessed Nov. 2012).

Mehta, L., 2005. *The Politics and Poetics of Water: Naturalizing Scarcity in Western India,* New Dehli: Orient Longman.

Molle, F., Mollinga, P. P., and Wester, P. 2009. Hydraulic bureaucracies and hydraulic mission: flows of water, flows of power. *Water Alternatives*, 2(3), 328–49.

Mosse, D. 2008. Epilogue: the cultural politics of water – a comparative perspective. *Journal of Southern African Studies*, 34(4), 939–48.

Mufema, E. 2005. The role and significance of Zimbabwe's Water Resources Commission, 1953–54. In J. W. N. Tempelhoff (ed.), *African Water Histories: Transdisciplinary Discourses*, pp.15–34, Vanderbijlpark: North-West University.

Musemwa, M. 2006. A tale of two cities: the evolution of the city of Bulawayo and Makokoba township under conditions of water scarcity, 1894–1953. *South African Historical Journal*, 55(1), 186–209.

Palmer, R. 1977. *Land and Racial Domination in Rhodesia*, London: Heinemann.

Pollock, N. C. 1968. Irrigation in the Rhodesian low-veld, *Geographical Journal*, 134(1), 70–7.

Reisner, M. 1986. *Cadillac Desert: The American West and its Disappearing Water,* New York: Penguin.

Richards, A. 2002. *Coping with Water Scarcity: The Governance Challenge*, Policy Paper, 54, Berkeley, CA: Institute on Global Conflict and Cooperation, UC Berkeley.

Shinn, A. 1974. The early European settlement of the south western districts of Southern Rhodesia. *Rhodesiana*, 30, 13–33.

Stanbridge, P. J. 1969. Long range planning in under-developed countries, *Long Range Planning*, 2(2), 38–45.

Swyngedouw, E. 1999. Modernity and hybridity: nature, *regeneracionismo*, and the production of the Spanish waterscape, 1890–1930. *Annals of the Association of American Geographers.* 89(3), 443–65.

Turton, A. R., and Meissner, R. 2002. The hydrosocial contract and its manifestation in society: a South African case study. In A. R. Turton and R. Henwood (eds), *Hydropolitics in the Developing World: A Southern African Perspective*, pp. 37–60, Pretoria: African Water Issues Research Unit, Centre for International Political Studies, University of Pretoria.

Turton, A. R., and Olhsson, L. 1999. *Water Scarcity and Social Stability: Towards a Deeper Understanding of the Key Concepts Needed to Manage Scarcity in Developing Countries,* Occasional Paper, 17, London: Water Issues Study Group, School of Oriental and African Studies, University of London.

Wester, P. 2009. Capturing the waters: the hydraulic mission in the Lerma-Chapala Basin (1876–1976). *Water History*, 1(1), 9–29.

Wester, P., Rap, E., and Vargas-Velázquez, S. 2009. The hydraulic mission and the Mexican hydrocracy: regulating and reforming the flows of water and power. *Water Alternatives*, 2(3), 395–415.

Wolmer, W. 2007. *From Wilderness Vision to Farm Invasions: Conservation and Development in Zimbabwe's South-East Lowveld,* Oxford: James Currey.

Worster, D. 1985. *Rivers of Empire: Water, Aridity, and the Growth of the American West,* Oxford: Oxford University Press.

8   Water

Life? An agent of political space and protest? An instrument of hegemony?

Uygar Özesmi

The planet in general, and many nation-states in particular, are undergoing huge transformations. We have reached the limits for many aspects of nature beyond the human realm. Our atmospheric chemistry and the ability of the hydrosphere to nurture life on Earth are facing critical challenge. The social and political transformation that is ongoing will lead us in different directions, with the possibilities including a range of extremes. At one level, we might end up with a context of scarcity, and with it control, exclusion and oppression. This dystopian future might rely on relatively few pockets of freedom. In a more utopian sense, we could work to create a society that is relatively abundant, free and egalitarian. Of course, where we will actually end up is likely to be somewhere in the middle, given the complex geography of our world. Nonetheless, many of us are in a position to strive for the latter scenario. The key issue here is to think through the ways that abundance is often linked with freedom and equality, while scarcity is often related to control, exclusion and oppression. A typical example is the situation that contributed to the recent revolution in Egypt (Piper, 2012) or the effects of the famines in North Korea (Woo-Cumings, n.d.). These processes, as several of the chapters in this volume suggest, are mutually reinforcing. Thus, contributing to these debates as an activist involved in diverse environmental struggles, it is quite apparent that any reference to scarcity of water or water problems in general needs to make the necessary connections with the broader socio-political environment. The current moment indeed has characteristics of a state of crisis, yet also signals moments of transformation and clear opportunities for social change. Some refer to these breaking points as a 'crisitunity' (opportunity arising from crisis). Ideas along these lines are implicit in several chapters of this section, yet are not openly and bluntly stated. In all chapters in this section water governance and 'scarcity' are looked at through two main lenses: modernization and (closely related) hegemony.

As stated in the chapters, irrigation and energy projects around the use of water have become symbols of hegemonic control, modernity and civilization, mostly because they are about iconic structures of dams and pipes, and the taming of water as one of the largest forces in nature. However, the central themes of modernization and hegemony that the chapters deal with sadly are not ones that the civil society worker or the local activist will readily relate to directly. The project of modernization is certainly present in the minds of some politicians and state bureaucrats, but the project has dramatically shifted to one of economic growth *über alles*, above all and most important. The notion of hegemony can be more readily challenged, if it has a strong aspect of economic influence and power, the more subtle version of normalized and everyday forms of hegemony are far more sinister and need strong wake-up calls, or 'mind bombs' in Greenpeace terminology. The villagers of the mountains of North-East Anatolia or of South-West Taurides would have been completely forgotten – not necessarily a bad thing – if not for the government's aims regarding economic exploitation of water to fuel the growth of the Turkish economy. In Turkey and most of the global South – with the exclusion of Bhutan – modernizing aspects are a strong discourse, but often remain only that. The modernist projects do not always translate into direct benefits. Simply put, state or corporate hydraulic energy projects of any size often bring no or little economic or other benefit, but instead may actually harm the livelihoods of local populations through negative environmental impacts. The local benefits don't move beyond the empty promises of hegemonic ideas of modernization. What is sold to locals is a dream of prosperity – of modernity. It is the failing of that dream which has been a wake-up call for many, to begin to challenge individual projects or the overall sense of what sort of benefits they may bring (see the chapters on HEP resistance, Erensu, Chapter 6; Kadirbeyoglu and Kurtic, Chapter 18).

In line with the accumulation of economic power, today water remains generally instrumentalized as a 'resource' in the hands of the state, companies and so-called entrepreneurs and investors. Investment banks, some largely resourced by pension funds, extend their force and infrastructure, and drive ever more exploitation of water. Extending from this, anyone who holds any financial savings or 'security' is implicated. Therefore the true force behind many modernist water or other environmental changes we observe in the current conceptualization is 'capitalism'. Even if you use another term, what I am referring to here is the model of economic growth that so many societies are locked into. This bind exists because of a monetary system that depends on creating more debt. When money is printed this money is given against some service or good. So for the economy to grow there is a need for use of labor and material resources. Essentially this debt then can only be covered by exploiting nature and peoples' time and labor. There is no other true 'capital'. Today if any value is to be created in monetary capital, this can only be covered if 'paid back' from nature's exploitation (cf. Wainwright and Mann, 2012). If we want to create real value, then this value or capital accumulation needs to come from nature's production or human production that mimics nature's ways operating within the space of nature's resilience. In essence, current economic growth must necessarily be subsidized from exploitation either of labor, or of nature. The logic of exploitation is what many activists reference, as they rally in places from Wall Street in New York to Peri Suyu in Munzur, Turkey. Unfortunately, despite the linkages that appear clear to many activists, the political economy of water is not addressed much in the chapters of this section. This may be read as a form of alienation of people from the water about which they write.

In another perspective, it is hard to imagine people and water as disconnected. People are of course beings of water – beings of flowing water that connects us to other beings, human and more than human alike.

There might be even a related and larger danger. I wonder if in the chapters in this section, water is recreated as a 'resource' or at least as something that has value. We are forced to consider if water is a vehicle of power in the eyes of students, of academics or of some bureaucrats or politicians or even of civil society workers. What does it mean if these texts do not reach the civil society workers and others beyond the academic circle? The activist perspective provides a clear contrast to this. Many of us tend to think of beings as flowing water, or water as a being itself rather than as a resource. Indeed, for some civil society workers or activists the central theme is the contestation of the very notion of water as a 'resource' to start with. As such, we can think of yet other ways the hegemonies of water recirculate in the types of stories we tell about water. To give a bit more attention to this idea that water is not a 'resource' but a 'being', consider that many argue that water is what makes life possible. It is an (or the) essential ingredient of life. Our bodies consist of 70 percent water, hence we are beings of water. We can live without food for weeks, but can't survive beyond a few days without water. In the chapters, water cycles through social and economic systems. Indeed, they do a good job of showing those connections. Yet there is very little sense or notion of how water cycles through our bodies and through the planet's life support systems.

Following on this alternative conceptualization of water, it becomes more clear how and why the marketization or commercialization of water is currently a major point of resistance for activists (see Part III, particularly Varghese, Chapter 14). What is resisted here is not modernity, but the capitalist conception of economy, and the economical structures of capitalist society. Hegemony, if we are to define it from the viewpoint of many activists, would be not over people but over people *and* water as interlinked beings of water, as interconnected forces of life. The central argument for many activists is quite simply that life has no price. Water is beyond value and has an intrinsic value, which is not for sale. Therefore the logic that calls for market valuation of water and commercialization of water resources and utilities because 'free water is wasted water' is precisely what activists are resisting. This is the case not only in Turkey (e.g. against hydraulic projects) but in the example of FAME (Alternative World Water Forum) or among farmer groups such as La Via Campesina or for Friends of the Earth. For many activists, water, if anything else, is a *right*. An inanimate 'being' that every living being has a right to. As water is a component of life on Earth the limit to water rights is based on basic needs. No one has a right beyond that, especially the government (or state). Further, the right to access water in a given region can only be exercised by those who live there – whether plants, animals or humans. By this logic, one should not be allowed to store and use water for the benefit of those outside that watershed. Water may be a global commons, but insofar as it is a commons, it should reasonably only be used locally. Water, when used locally for urban or industrial uses, should be recycled, given back only once it has been treated to a quality where nature can reabsorb it. This cycling could also be thought through to include consideration of the embedded (or virtual) water that may be exported with the agricultural or manufacturing goods that are shipped across watersheds and countries. In brief, any disruptive interference with the water cycle outside of natural processes is seen from many activist perspectives as a crime against nature. Transferring of water from one basin to another, or storing it or diverting it is essentially stealing water. Hence the modernist dream of controlling water and using water for human benefit only through 'projects' is at the center of resistance. The utopian imagination is that of a society which lives within the natural resilience of an ecosystem. As such, natural and social processes operate effectively within the constraints and opportunities of nature's resilience.

While the logic of such an eco-centric view may appear simple (or even unreasonable), we also have to consider the complexity of ever-increasing population and consumption. Thus, any possible alternative ideals face an onslaught of ideological hegemonies, where these ideas come to appear less and less possible, or increasingly out of step. Thus, even a 'pure' ethical position that seeks to respect life and nature cannot escape the multiple hegemonies which it faces. For example, the left political movements in Turkey have seen the rapid economic exploitation of rural riverine communities and have started to use the space for political organizing around local resistance (also explored in Kadirbeyoglu and Kurtic, Chapter 18; and Erensu, Chapter 6). The villagers living close to small-size hydropower plants (SHPs) in the Black Sea region were traditionally opposed to state policies and interventions in the region. In general, many felt as though they had long been neglected – not getting any share of the larger economic development of the country. The SHPs were a vehicle to transfer the region's 'richness' of water to the broader economy and country – in the form of electricity. Yet this longer history of resistance meant that they were ripe for organizing. Emigration was prevalent, with a large diaspora in Istanbul. This diaspora developed a strong romanticism around the notion of a pristine green homeland, where their elders lived in harmony with nature. The elders with their local wisdom were treated as many indigenous peoples are – with a sense of a focused and inherent knowledge of nature (cf. Slater, 1995). Many émigrés held up these communities, and especially the elders, as 'custodians of the land' and the 'holders of tradition'. The local political arms of leftist movements have organized in this created space using watch posts, sit-ins, resistance to entry of construction companies and monkey-wrenching of construction machinery. The diaspora in the urban areas, although not generally aligned with the leftist organizations, acted as amplifiers and loudspeakers for this growing movement. The resistance against the small-size hydropower plants (SHPs) quickly became a hot topic in the country, but had little or no effect on government policy. Indeed, even as the resistance grew, the populace of the region continued to vote for the conservative ruling party (AKP). The resistance had a large resonance, an echo, but not a strong rural population ready also to shift their voting patterns. The alliances the leftist movements created were vocal, yet remained largely local and relatively insignificant in terms of votes. In other words, in these examples water had a loud voice, but no political power. This is the case despite the fact that this has been one of the few issues in Turkey where there has been strong and legitimate resistance to state and governmental policies (environmental or otherwise). One could say that developmentalist notions had established a hegemony over larger populations. The rural populations were dwindling despite the echo in the cities.

For the leftist movements this area was also one of the few remaining areas to act with leveraged local support due to water being 'stolen'. As the state was instrumentalizing water for economic growth, these movements likewise instrumentalized water for political power. The instrumentalization by leftist movements was very apparent and clear, as they aggressively excluded more apolitical, non-ideological environmental organizations from becoming part of the struggle. The movement that emerged was comprised of political and ideological organizations together with apolitical and relatively weak ideological actors who essentially shared the same values and were striving for the same outcome. They all agreed that water is a 'being' that cannot be commodified. Yet for the leftists among the movement, water was a commodity of a different type – power. In the face of the continuing onslaught by the government and companies, water provided a clear resource – a reserve of power – through which diverse factions could organize against a clear enemy or target. This is the sense in which I suggest that water has further been instrumentalized. This reality of course does not make the effects of the instrumentalization the same. The activists are not the same as those politicians who strive for power through opening up policies for small-size hydropower plants (SHPs), for instance lifting the Environmental Impact Assessment (EIA) requirements. The activists are also quite distinct from the contractors, companies and investment banks that line up to make profits so that they can grow and stay alive in a constant debt environment. This shared treatment of water as instrumentalized rather shows that civil society and activists do not only speak the language of hegemony – they are in fact living it every day. This is part of the reality of their struggle, whether it be against larger forces of the capitalist economic system, or the struggles among themselves as they jockey to gain more power and visibility for their specific organizations or causes.

Let's say the obvious. Where there is oppression there will be resistance. Hegemony holds true whether there is acceptance or not, and whether power is noticed or not. Indeed, hegemony is often most adept at naming and recognizing power where it is least obvious – when there is compliance, consent and lack of recognition. One of the important reasons to attend to activism and politics is precisely the ways that activism forces open realization and recognition of power dynamics. Realization is often directly linked to struggle. Part of what activists often strive for is the awareness of issues that comes only with the struggle and growth of a movement. Therefore, for an activist, power is something one challenges at every turn. First is the need to recognize and challenge power in oneself. An activist needs to be constantly aware of his or her own power, and attend to its effects. Secondarily, activists also must be aware of power in others, including in allied organizations and movements. As Lord Acton wrote: 'Power tends to corrupt, and absolute power corrupts absolutely. Great men are almost always bad men' (1887). Therefore the struggle to keep water from being commodified and to recognize and resist other forms of hegemonies must be first and foremost about different relations of power. If a struggle is to be a just and ethical struggle, ultimately we must be alive to the struggle for salvation as beings of water. Even as we focus on different uses of water, we in the end have to come to terms with the fact that for many uses of water, the ends don't justify the means. For water in particular, there is no limit and no end. Water cycles through all of us.

References

Lord Acton. 1887. Letter to Bishop Mandell Creighton, 3 April. In *The Life and Letters of Mandell Creighton*, ed. L. Creighton, vol. 1, ch. 13, London and New York: Longmans, Green, 1904.

Piper, K. 2012. *Revolution of the Thirsty*. Available at: http://places.designobserver.com/feature/egypt-revolution-of-the-thirsty/34318 (accessed Nov. 2012).

Slater, C. 1995. Amazonia as edenic narrative. In W. Cronon (ed.), *Uncommon Ground: Rethinking the Human Place in Nature,* pp. 114–31, New York: W. W. Norton & Co.

Wainwright, J., and Mann, G. 2012. Climate Leviathan. *Antipode*, 45(1), 1–22. Available at: http://onlinelibrary.wiley.com/doi/10.1111/j.1467-8330.2012.01018.x/abstract (accessed Nov. 2012)].

Woo-Cumings, M. n.d., *The Political Ecology of Famine: The North Korean Catastrophe and its Lessons*. Available at: http://personal.lse.ac.uk/SIDEL/images/WooFamine.pdf (accessed Nov. 2012).

9 Commentary: water scarcity in late modernity

Samer Alatout

Water scarcity has long been an idiom of the biophysical and positivist social sciences; and, historically, has most often been used to describe local and regional conditions. In the past three decades, however, water scarcity jumped the geographic scale to become a global phenomenon. Even when seen through local and regional prisms, water scarcity has been increasingly perceived as a global problem that demands global responses (see Taylor and Buttel, 1992). It has also become the concern of global institutions like the World Bank, multiple United Nations organizations and international aid groups. In addition to biophysical sciences and engineering, positivist social sciences were also engaged in efforts to find solutions to water scarcity, defined as a central environmental problem. However, around the same time that it jumped scales and became a dominant discourse in policy circles, critical social sciences also began interrogating the issue of water scarcity (e.g. Alatout, 2008; Mehta, 2005; Bakker, 2000). This has been especially true since the emergence of both social constructionist and discursive frameworks as influential traditions for discussing social and biophysical problems alike in the 1980s and 1990s. Basil Mahayni's framing chapter (Chapter 4) provides an excellent critical engagement with such contributions.

Many authors have recently focused on the neoliberal turn in governance of water resources. This makes good sense since neoliberal accounts of nature, society and the economy have been dominant in recent shifts in governmental rationalities associated with late modernity.[1] For example, all three empirical pieces (Mahayni, Chapter 5; Erensu, Chapter 6; and Musemwa, Chapter 7) and one review piece (Mahayni, Chapter 4) in this section interrogate neoliberalist shifts in water governance in one way or another. The most common indications of this shift of governmental rationality have been calls for commodifying, privatizing, decentralizing and marketizing water resources (Bakker, 2010, 2000; see Part III). In general, the changes in principles of water governance go hand in hand with calls for the freeing of trade, opening national markets and allowing market mechanisms to work free from governmental interventions – all familiar to us from the project of globalization (McMichael, 2008). Under neoliberalism, solving the problem of water scarcity is therefore hinged on unleashing different types of freedoms (economic in particular, but also political). I take these accounts as my point of departure precisely because I am interested in the tensions between the freedoms unleashed by the neoliberal project and the unfreedoms propagated by that same project or, what Mahayni (Chapter 4) describes as the tension 'between the hegemonic representation of water scarcity and the uneven material realities experienced in particular localities' (Mahayni, Chapter 4).

So much of the literature on water resources scarcity and management, however, seems to underscore the fact that neoliberal responses constitute a historical rupture with the most recent paradigm of water governance under the nation-state developmental model, from circa 1940s to the 1980s (Linton, 2010; Bakker, 2004; Mehta, 2005; for an excellent contrast that traces continuities rather than ruptures, see Erensu, Chapter 6).[2] Within that model, governmental intervention in the management of water resources has often been taken for granted. The state was entrusted with controlling those resources for the benefit of national security, economy, progress and modernization. When compared to nation-statism and the dominance of the nation-state system in international politics, neoliberal governmental rationality indeed seems like a rupture. Instead of territorial enclosure, protectionism and discipline, neoliberalism ushers in multiple freedoms including those of trade and, more importantly, from governmental interventions – at least that is the focus of neoliberal discourse. But if we are to investigate further, we find traces of the ways neoliberalism governs water scarcity in European governmental challenges of the 17th century and in colonialism. Historical genealogical work, which traces modalities of the past in the present, does not only qualify the sense of rupture implied in many arguments regarding water management and governance, it also directs our attention to continuities; it opens up the historical process by which structures of global inequalities have been inscribed in the governance of water scarcity (for more on the genealogical method of history, see Foucault, 1984).[3] This is necessary for our understanding of the management of water scarcity under neoliberal governmental rationality and the inequalities that multiply within the neoliberal discursive framework of freedom.

Hence, I propose a genealogical approach that traces back the origin of water scarcity and proposals to govern it, like commodification, privatization, decentralization and freedom of trade, to that of the scarcity of grain and its governance in 17th-century Europe as discussed by Michel Foucault (2007: 29–53). In addition, I provide a political-geographic correction to Foucault's account by turning attention to the colonial encounter. I can only sketch these approaches here, given the required scope, but I argue these tasks are well worth pursuing in the future.

Water scarcity: from a crisis to a condition of possibility

In one of his lectures explaining the new, emerging governmental rationality in France during the 17th century, Michel Foucault (2007: 29–53; see also Burchell *et al.*, 1991) points to the dissimilar ways that different rationalities of government conceived of the scarcity of grain (a major concern in Europe during the 17th century). Here, Foucault differentiates two levels of scarcity of grain, which are at the heart of the shift of technologies of government from what Foucault calls disciplinary to security apparatuses of government: scarcity-scourge and scarcity-dearness. Scarcity-dearness refers to the conditions of scarcity long before a moment of crisis takes place and includes long periods of drought, lower productivity, rising prices, difficult access to grain and so on. Scarcity-scourge is the moment of a general crisis of access that might result in revolts and is thus a threat to social stability and peace, to the system of government as such.

Disciplinary governmental rationality was obsessed with the moment of crisis because of the threat of the ultimate revolt and hence the threat to the sovereign or the administrative state. Governmental practice was one of discipline prior to the 1750s: enclosure, prohibition and surveillance. Trade of grain was prohibited, at times even within the state itself. Everything about grain was under state surveillance and control. The mid-1700s, however, were years of change. Under pressure from a group of influential economists called the physiocrats, predating classical economists of the early 18th century, legal structures were set up to 'free' grain from dominant disciplinary arrangements.[4] Freedom was not only an economic technique of trade and exchange; it was, for Foucault, and even for the physiocrats, a technology of government.

Protection against a crisis, the physiocratic argument went, should not be carried out through the prohibition of trade or through more governmental intervention; it should rather be guaranteed by freeing the grain from such controls. They argued in very similar fashion to recent neoliberal arguments: crises do not take place in a sudden turn of events, they take time to develop.[5] If for any reason there was a prolonged scarcity of grain, scarcity-dearness in Foucault's terms, then market mechanisms, through freedom as a technology of government, would be more than capable of dealing with scarcity before it became a crisis: rise in prices, migration, increased trade, etc. In other words, rather than controlling life to prevent a moment of crisis, government should be concerned with securing freedom (specifically of trade) as the only dependable defense against a crisis. This is precisely the origin of neoliberal freedoms.

However, Foucault ignored what I think is the very condition of these freedoms: the unfreedoms engendered by colonialism (for a similar correction of Foucault's treatment of sexuality, see Stoler, 1995; for a general geographic correction of Foucault's theories of power and governmentality, see Elden, 2007; Alatout, 2006). A political-geographic correction to Foucault underscores the central role of the colonial encounter in shifting European governmental rationality. It turns our attention to the unfreedoms produced in conjunction with and as the condition of possibility of those freedoms. In other words, freedom as a technology of government was predicated on unfreedom as a technology of coloniality. Freedom and unfreedom created and distributed their own subjects in geographies of inequality: colonizer and colonized.

I do not have enough space to discuss the intermediate stage between colonialism and neoliberalism, from the mid-20th century to the 1980s, but I should at least mention that postcoloniality, dominated by a concern for international development, engendered a new political geography, structured by the colonial encounter: that of the developed world and the underdeveloped world. Freedom and unfreedom functioned through multiple ideological (nationalism and nation-statism), economic (capitalism and socialism) and institutional (World Bank and the International Monetary Fund) controls in the international system of states. Here, postcolonial relations created their own geographically distributed subjects: developed and underdeveloped. Since postcoloniality is understood through the prism of development and underdevelopment as the specific governmental rationality that neoliberalism is responding to, I would like to offer a brief description of how water scarcity and, I would speculate, scarcities of energy and food as well, has been imagined and governed (see Mahayni, Chapter 5 for the relationship between water scarcity and food; Erensu, Chapter 6 for the relationship between water scarcity and energy).[6] Water scarcity as a crisis for the underdeveloped, postcolonial, world (and here I might be overgeneralizing by quite a distance) was an existential threat that had to be prevented at all costs and that meant the need for managing every drop of water and making it count. As I mentioned at the beginning, fearful of their standing within the international system of states, the governmental rationality of what I call here nation-statism increasingly focused energies on preventing water scarcity through the centralization of water's legal, institutional and technical apparatuses. Efforts were meant to utilize water in the process of making the nation-state more secure, independent, competitive, wealthy and resilient. An example from my own work on the Israeli state during the 1950s (Alatout, 2008) would make the point. Centralization of water governance and management in Israel was made possible by establishing national institutions for water planning and centralizing water governance within them (like Tahal), writing a legal code (1959) that nationalized every drop of water within state boundaries, building the National Water Carrier that technically centralized the extraction and distribution of water resources, installing water meters for the purposes of surveillance and control, and even going to war over shared water bodies like the Jordan River.[7] Israel's response to water scarcity in an interventionist framework might be stark, but it is definitely not unique. So much of the literature on water management between the 1950s and 1980s, including the empirical cases in this section, emphasizes similar techniques of government that could be described as disciplinary.

Neoliberal governmental rationality responds to water scarcity differently. The issue of water scarcity as a crisis or scarcity-scourge is not of concern, or maybe I should say that it is a major concern so long as nation-states, borders, discipline and control are the way water scarcity is managed. Opening up these borders and enclosures, freedom of trade and movement, of people and things, is the only way to manage water scarcity. Nature as freedom should be unshackled and allowed to function: then water will travel from water abundant regions to water scarce regions, in the form of liquid, food or energy.[8] If freedom of trade, exchange and movement are guaranteed, then humans will respond to different stresses: they will move, they will buy, they will increase or decrease the prices and they will create new technologies. Freedom as a technology of government again points to the peculiarity of water scarcity: water might be scarce in any region under any climate for whatever reasons, but that scarcity will only be temporary if people and things are free. It will never turn into scarcity-scourge because of the multiple responses that any stresses will enable.

So, in this sense, water scarcity-dearness is not only a possibility, it is as a matter of fact, the very condition of life in late modernity. For that reason, the very management of water scarcity in neoliberalism is predicated on a specific understanding of nature, human and otherwise, and on allowing that nature to function freely. Water scarcity-dearness will result in multiple responses that will prevent scarcity-scourge from taking place. The only guarantee against a crisis is freedom.

However, neoliberal freedoms are the products of history and they are subject to the political geographies that already structured and continue to structure life in the world.[9] Colonialism and postcolonialism left their traces in how neoliberal governmental rationality functions with its own geographies of inequity: global North and global South. It also creates its own subjects: now, probably more so than any time in history, the free and the unfree. The historical patterns of freedom and unfreedom are produced and reproduced in institutional structures that continue to consolidate wealth and freedoms in the historic metropoles, developed nations and the global North; they also continue to consolidate poverty and unfreedoms in the colonies, underdeveloped world and the global South.

It is this historical and political-geographic structuring of neoliberal response to water scarcity, traced back to the colonial encounter, that is at once productive and prohibitive. Productive in the sense that water scarcity is increasingly the concern of local, national and international institutions; it is productive in the sense that everybody is invited and prodded to talk about and research it; it is productive in the sense that it is a natural condition of life that should be studied and responded to; and it is productive in the sense that it calls for the expansion of human freedoms. It is prohibitive in the sense that it hides inequities behind the generic language of freedom; it naturalizes structured systems of dominance and differentiation; it makes the answer to every question 'more freedom' while at the same time following the historical, political-geographic pattern set three centuries ago.

Notes

1 I use late modernity here, instead of postmodernity, to emphasize my belief that contemporary transitions since the 1970s have strong continuities with modernity. This will become clear in my argument for a genealogical approach to water scarcity, emphasizing historical traces rather than ruptures. Seminal works debating the legitimacy of different uses of the term modernity include Baudrillard, 1995; Beck *et al.*, 1994; Latour, 1993; Beck, 1992; Lyotard, 1979.

2 To be more precise and fair, the sense of rupture that Bakker (2000) and Mehta (2005) speak about is rather limited. So, they emphasize shifts in the economic and technical instruments used to govern water resources. Neither subscribes to the notion e.g. that the nation-state is a dead institution under globalization and neoliberalism. In that sense, their arguments are more in line with what Peck and Tickell (2002) describe as the rolling out of new state projects rather than the rolling back of state altogether.

3 Bakker (2012: 620) calls for a similar 'historical-geographical' approach, following Swyngedouw (1999).
4 Francois Quesnay (2004 [1758]) is not only considered to be the first work to describe physiocratic economic thought, but also to be the first monograph to introduce systematic economic analysis in the modern period (Vardi, 2012). Foucault (2007: 50) references a number of the physiocrats, but especially a Quesnay piece that was published in 1757 under the title of 'Grain'.
5 There are of course clear differences between the physiocrats and classical and neoliberal economists, if only their emphasis on land as the source of all wealth and agriculture as main human activity (Vardi, 2012).
6 Jessica Barnes (2009) makes a similar argument to that of Mahayni (Chapter 5). She demonstrates how water scarcity in Syria was tied to the Ba'ath's Party agricultural and food policies.
7 This should not be taken to say that I consider Israel to be a postcolonial state. Israel is fraught with peculiarities, itself occupying multiple positionalities as a colonial state on the one hand, but one that is masquerading and imagining itself as postcolonial. While the particularities of Israel deserve greater investigation, I bring it up here only as an example for the dominance of nation-statism during the postcolonial period that was also obsessed with questions of economic development.
8 Tony Allan (2001) is famous for commenting on, but also championing, water trade in the form of food trade (virtual water). In this case, water travels from abundant regions to water poor regions in the form of food. Freedom of trade is the best protection against water scarcity-scourge or crisis. For a critical response, see Mahayni (Chapter 4). Mahayni makes an excellent point in this discussion about the fact that international food policies and trade are riddled with unequal geopolitical relations.
9 In a somewhat similar fashion, Leila Harris (Chapter 11) builds on Brenner *et al.* (2010) to emphasize how varied has the rolling out of the neoliberal project been across the world. However, she acknowledges that those variegations are nevertheless politically and geographically patterned, which might create political geographies like North and South. Harris focuses on differences and similarities in the neoliberal project and makes that her research focus. On the other hand, I underscore the historical-geographic suturing together of the world in structures of inequality that guarantee differential distribution of advantages and disadvantages.

References

Alatout, S. 2006. Towards a bio-territorial conception of power: territory, population, and environmental narratives in Palestine and Israel. *Political Geography,* 25, 601–21.
Alatout, S. 2008. 'States' of scarcity: water, space, and identity politics in Israel, 1948–59. *Environment and Planning D: Society and Space,* 26(6), 959–82.
Allan, T. 2001. *The Middle East Water Question: Hydropolitics and the Global Economy,* New York: I. B. Taurus & Co.
Bakker, K. 2000. Privatizing water, producing scarcity: the Yorkshire drought of 1995. *Economic Geography,* 76(1), 4–27.
Bakker, K. 2004. *An Uncooperative Commodity,* New York: Oxford University Press.
Bakker, K. 2010. *Privatizing Water: Governance Failure and the World's Urban Water Crisis,* Ithaca, NY: Cornell University Press.
Bakker, K. 2012. Water: political, biopolitical, material. *Social Studies of Science,* 42(4), 616–23.
Barnes, J. 2009. Managing the waters of Bath Country: the politics of water scarcity in Syria. *Geopolitics,* 14(3), 510–30.

Baudrillard, J. 1995. *Simulacra and Simulation*, Ann Arbor, MI: University of Michigan Press.

Beck, U. 1992. *Risk Society: Towards a New Modernity*, London: Sage Publications.

Beck, U., Giddens, A., and Lash, S., 1994. *Reflexive Modernization: Politics, Tradition and Aesthetics in the Modern Social Order*, Stanford, CA: Stanford University Press.

Brenner, N., Peck, J., and Theodore, N., 2010. Variegated neoliberalization: geographies, modalities, pathways. *Global Networks,* 10(2), 182–222.

Burchell, G., Gordon, C., and Miller, P., eds. 1991. *The Foucault Effect: Studies in Governmentality*, Chicago, IL: University of Chicago Press.

Elden, S. 2007. Governmentality, calculation, territory. *Environment and Planning D: Society and Space,* 25(3), 562–80.

Foucault, M. 1984. Nietzsche, genealogy, history. In P. Rabinow (ed.), *The Foucault Reader*, pp. 76–100, New York: Pantheon.

Foucault, M. 2007. *Security, Territory, Population: Lectures at the College de France, 1977–1978,* New York: Palgrave Macmillan.

Latour, B. 1993. *We have Never Been Modern*, Cambridge, MA: Harvard University Press.

Linton, J. 2010. *What is Water? The History of a Modern Abstraction*, Vancouver: UBC Press.

Lyotard, J. 1979. *The Postmodern Condition: A Report on Knowledge*, Minneapolis, MN: University of Minnesota Press.

McMichael, P. 2008. *Development and Social Change: A Global Perspective*, Thousand Oaks, CA: Pine Forge Press.

Mehta, L. 2005. *The Politics and Poetics of Water: Naturalising Scarcity in Western India*, New Delhi: Orient Longman.

Peck, J., and Tickell, A. 2002. Neoliberalizing space. *Antipode*, 34(3), 380–404.

Quesnay, F. 2004 [1758]. *The Economic Table*, Honolulu, HI: University Press of the Pacific.

Stoler, A. 1995. *Race and the Education of Desire*, Durham, NC: Duke University Press.

Swyngedouw, E. 1999. Modernity and hybridity: nature, regeneracionismo, and the production of the Spanish waterscape, 1890–1930. *Annals of the Association of American Geographers*, 89(3), 443–65.

Taylor, P. J., and Buttel, F. 1992. How do we know we have global environmental problems? Science and the globalization of environmental discourse. *Geoforum,* 23(3), 405–23.

Vardi, L. 2012. *The Physiocrats and the World of the Enlightenment*, New York: Cambridge University Press.

Part III
Marketization and privatization

10 Framing the debate on water marketization

Leila M. Harris

Is it helpful to suggest that ideas related to market instruments, or privatization, have become hegemonic in the water governance realm? And if yes, how does the hegemony of these ideas affect water governance, particularly as it plays out in varied locales? Does the notion of hegemony enable us to appropriately account for differences regarding these practices in space and time? The answers to these questions are anything but simple.

The chapters in this part of the book explore these complexities, with particular attention to historical and geographical variability; how marketization, privatization or similar processes come to be; and how these concepts and practices play out in diverse locales. However, we do not conclude from the diversity of experiences with these 'hybrid neoliberal forms' (Peck, 2004) that these processes are wholly different from place to place. Indeed, we suggest that these diverse practices are connected, mutually imbricated and co-constitutive (cf. Martin, 2005).

This is precisely why we find the idea of hegemonic constructions, or those dominant norms with respect to water governance, so useful for analyzing these processes. For example, the role of the International Financial Institutions (IFIs) is particularly important for considering the how and why of privatization and marketization as these unfold across the global South, particularly as these institutions have increasingly required these changes as part of loan conditions. Yet these changes are also taking hold in other sites through, for instance, 'best practice' models promoted by the World Bank, International Monetary Fund and other institutions (e.g. Goldman, 2007; see Smith, 2004, for the example of South Africa). With respect to Northern locales, these are also some of the sites with the fastest uptake of marketization and privatization, although absent from direct IFI influence in the same way. This speaks to the hegemony of these ideas in terms of their ideological hold and capacity to transform water governance in diverse sites, even as they face very different water conditions and governance challenges (see Chapter 11 that follows for more discussion).

Part of the task at hand is precisely to attend to the varied pathways through which ideas and practices related to marketization, privatization or commodification of water have become hegemonic. We therefore need to begin an investigation of these concepts and practices with an understanding of whether they are gaining ground through recommendations or influence of IFIs (e.g. as in Ghana and

Indonesia), or as part of more general political-economic neoliberalization shifts whereby economic instruments are being promoted in environmental governance more generally (Heynen *et al.*, 2007; Mansfield, 2007).

It is worth first providing some basic definitions of the terms we are interrogating. In these pages we are most concerned with privatization, commodification and marketization of water – linked, albeit distinct, processes. *Privatization* refers to a role for private companies in water provision and management, and as such typically involves transferring some or all assets from public to private hands. In an absolute sense, this would involve full ownership and operation by the private sector. However, full privatization models of this type remain relatively rare. Much more common is a hybrid model, leaving ownership unaffected, yet transferring some responsibilities to the private sector. Increasingly we see this occur through public–private partnerships (PPPs), or short-term contracts more akin to outsourcing models (Bakker, 2010, for full discussion of the range of associated terms). *Commodification*, somewhat distinct, is the process of converting a good or service formerly subject to non-market social rules into one subjected to market rules. Very closely connected, *marketization* refers to the construction of markets for trading and selling, e.g. for water rights. Even though these different terms are often problematically conflated, marketization or commodification could certainly occur under the auspices of a public entity, perhaps involving the use of pricing instruments, the establishment of markets or similar mechanisms.

Indeed, the conflation of these somewhat distinct processes leads to quite a bit of conceptual confusion in water governance debates. The pairing of these distinct ideas (I refer to this here as bundling) has also contributed to accelerated promotion of privatization on the grounds that this is the only mechanism that might engage pricing or other market instruments to ensure efficiency or more conservation-oriented water uses (Harris, Chapter 11; Bakker, 2007). In analyzing the rising 'hegemony' of water privatization in global water policy circles (see Goldman, 2007), an important initial step is to unbundle these processes and concepts. Rather than accepting the notion that only private entities might be suitable to engage and manage markets, or realize efficiencies of the type commonly associated with commodified water, it is more helpful to delink these as separable concepts and approaches. Indeed, one of the only ways to understand the hegemonic rise of water privatization from the establishment of the Dublin Principles (1992) onwards is to consider the ways that these concepts and approaches have been bundled and taken as indivisible. In fact Dublin's call for treatment of water as an 'economic good' has frequently (and in practice) been taken to mean that it should be privatized. Clearly these should be understood as distinct concepts, each with their own hegemonic status and influence.

As the agenda of marketized water unfolds, a very clear feature is the considerable interest and controversy this has stirred up, particularly in the form of resistance to privatization in many developing contexts. Critiques of privatization come in many forms, based either on 'outcomes' or on ethical grounds. Market-based instruments, although similarly the target of critics (e.g. for promoting 'most productive' uses of water over basic needs), tend to be seen as somewhat more benign and are promoted in diverse circles, including among conservation practitioners and environmentalists. Privatization is often portrayed as key to promoting 'efficiency' and making effective use of technological know-how and the business savvy of large water purveyors. Commodification is more typically seen as effective given associated pricing and market incentives that are believed to encourage efficiencies and conservation-oriented behaviors (e.g. to reduce over-use or to grow certain crops that might be higher value or more suitable to particular landscape conditions). It is clear then that, even with considerable anti-privatization resistance, other dimensions of linked concepts remain somewhat more accepted in diverse circles. With key assumptions related to the utility of these practices and concepts in place, yet often not explicitly evaluated, there is a clear need to investigate the performance of governance mechanisms related to these concepts, as they function as delinked and also as bundled concepts, as well as to interrogate some of the implicit and explicit ideas that underpin them.

Along these lines, analysts have suggested that privatization is not necessarily more efficient for water provision. Further, it has also been suggested that there is likely to be considerable public support and involvement required for improvements to water provision systems (Braadbaart, 2002; Bayliss, 2001). Nonetheless, these associations persist (e.g. privatization as linked with efficiency), underscoring the need to pay more attention precisely to the notion of hegemony. Hegemony as a concept is useful to call attention to what mechanisms give an idea force or staying power, despite the uncertainty related to empirical evidence in support of such positions. We also find that nuanced and intersectional analysis is needed, particularly to move away from an overly simplified public versus private debate that has dominated water policy and governance circles over the past several decades, often leading to sidestepping of other key issues (Bakker, 2010; Budds and McGranahan, 2003).

Considering other parts and themes of this book, it is clear that oftentimes ideas of scarcity accelerate privatization and commodification shifts (Bakker, 2003). With respect to participation, one of the primary concerns is that these marketized and privatized approaches might disenfranchise community participation in water governance, in addition to aggravating the situation with respect to other equity and environmental concerns (Heynen *et al.*, 2007; Harris, 2009). There is a need to interrogate connections between these different governance shifts and processes, as well as to disentangle them and to be specific about which processes are in fact at stake. Such specification is undoubtedly more helpful than grouping all concurrent processes under the banner of privatization or neoliberalization (see Gleick *et al.*, 2002–3; Bakker, 2007, 2010, for further discussion of these concepts and their key differences). To be sure, critics have suggested that social equity (e.g. gender, poverty and other key themes that strongly relate to participatory water governance) and environmental outcomes are the primary 'losses' associated with water privatization and marketization (see Harris, 2009). While there is certainly evidence of this from diverse contexts, and also a sense that theoretically associated goals are likely to be inconsistent (e.g. profit imperatives versus affordability or equity concerns), there remains a clear need to further investigate and substantiate such claims, particularly to be able to generalize or scale up across sites.

Taking a genealogical approach consistent with our focus on the 'hegemony' of particular governance concepts and practices, it is also important to understand more fully how these models for water governance have emerged as dominant in the contemporary moment. What are the intellectual, institutional or political genealogies of these practices? In highlighting these questions, we are particularly interested in the 'why now' question – why are we seeing such dramatic shifts in the practice of water governance globally, regionally, and locally at this particular historical moment? The chapters in this part provide critical genealogies of marketization, privatization and commodification of water across various locales. These are distinct stories, shaped by particular histories and geographies. Yet it is noteworthy how similar some of these trajectories are. In the case of privatization in Kenya, we see some formal provisions that could enable consideration of impoverished populations, but this is not necessarily carried through in practice. In particular, informal settlements and those at the outskirts of the city remain underserved in the context of privatization and pricing imperatives associated with those governance mechanisms (K'Akumu, Chapter 13). For the historical example from Zambia, water is fundamentally transformed to serve the interest of private mining companies, with considerable quality implications. Interestingly, marketized logics in the water realm are also applied very unevenly, as private companies are not asked to pay for pollution of waters in a way that might correspond with 'payment for water' by other consumers. Waters also picks up the idea of bundling discussed here to examine the complex ways that logics are bundled and unbundled, to diverse effect (Waters, Chapter 12). Finally in the broad comparative analysis offered in Chapter 11, we see a tracing of ways that different regions and locales have followed similar and different trajectories, with consideration of what this diversity or 'variegation' might mean to be able to trace, understand and analyze these practices. For instance, while marketization and privatization occur differently and for different reasons in different times and places, Harris suggests that we nonetheless need to attend to broad correspondences and differences across locales and realms. It is only in this way that we can consider the complex effects and pathways of water marketization, privatization and commodification in the contemporary moment.

While we consider it is important to document and analyze broad trends, we also recognize the difficulty of tracing these shifts precisely. Nonetheless, there is considerable evidence that the uptake of these governance modalities has been on the rise in the water realm in the past several decades. Goldman (2007: 786) suggests that the number of people of the global South who received water from Northern-based private firms grew to over 400 million in 2000, and that this may be as high as 1.2 billion by 2015. Specifically, since the 1990s, there has been an 800 percent increase in African, Asian and Latin American water users purchasing water from European owned private firms (2007: 788). Although our interest in this volume is more squarely on the global South, water privatization and commodification has also risen considerably in industrialized and Northern contexts. As explored in the next chapter, this varied temporality and spatiality, from North to South and over time, are crucial for how we theorize ideas of water privatization, marketization or commodification. The notion of 'hegemony' may appear to suggest a homogeneous, top–down model for water governance, yet we find clear evidence that this is not the case in any absolute or linear sense. Nor is this the Gramscian sense of how hegemony operated within specific societies (see Sneddon, Chapter 2). Instead, the complexities of specific places (including indebtedness, local political conflict or institutional failure) are all central to how and why these processes unfold as they do. In multi-scalar senses as well, these processes cannot be understood without situating particular locales (whether Accra, Ghana or urban Kenya) within other histories and geographies that reflect the trajectories of uneven trade relations, colonialism or global debt.

Rather than telling this story as if there is a top–down singular pathway for privatization and marketization of water, our case studies seek to advance discussions that delineate both the general patterns in evidence (e.g. the rise of privatization in many corners of the globe) as well as the issues that differentiate these patterns (e.g. the different forms and varied effects that privatization or marketization may take). A look at the history of water privatization will, for instance, reflect distinctive geographies and considerable variability with respect to the uptake and effects of these practices.

From a perspective that takes seriously ideas of hegemony, it is also notable that, while ideas of privatization and marketization were diffusing rapidly over several recent decades, there has been somewhat of a slowdown over the past decade (Bakker, 2012). Many transnational companies have reduced interest in investing in Southern contexts, suggesting yet another evolving pattern in terms of how these governance practices change in the contemporary moment (ibid.). Despite such notable shifts, marketization and commodification remain predominant governance approaches in the water realm. What might serve to challenge, upset or possibly retrench particular 'hegemonies?' How can we theorize 'counter-hegemonies' in the water realm? This is another consideration we are interested in inviting through our theoretical and empirical analyses.

While discussions along these lines interrogate the pathways and effects of increasing privatization and commodification of water, there is very little available literature directly considering why and how these governance instruments travel, including how to account for their uptake and dissemination across diverse locales. Goldman's (2007) work is among the closest offerings in this regard. His analysis provides us with a starting point from which to interrogate the particular role of institutions, particularly the IFIs, in disseminating ideas and practices in the water governance realm. This is a key part of the puzzle, particularly with respect to the institutional genealogies at stake providing a way into deciphering and analyzing these shifts (see also Bakker, 2013). Our volume complements such a discussion by offering a sense of the specific uptake and dissemination of these ideas in diverse times and places (with particular focus on the Middle East and Africa). With respect to Goldman's contribution, his work focuses in on the role of the World Bank in promoting particular water governance strategies, the Bank's role in dispersal of ideas, and ways that the Bank was central to networking water professionals and 'training' them so that they became central instruments in the spread of privatization and similar practices. Tracing the ideas of privatization, marketization and the concept of 'water for all' over time and in relation to several important water governance milestones, Goldman highlights the increasing visibility of these ideas at the Johannesburg World Summit on Sustainable Development in 2002. As he suggests, the final outcome read very much like a World Bank policy paper, suggesting that 'water privatization is the best policy to tackle the global South's poverty and water delivery problems' (2007: 787). Relevant to our focus in this volume, he asks why such a diverse set of actors reached consensus around this idea? Part of the explanation, he suggests, lies with the role of the World Bank and IMF in generating these ideas, and spreading them throughout the global South, whether through conditions on loans requiring governments to embrace neoliberal policy recommendations or training institutes centered on similar policy prescriptions.

Besides these general themes, other questions we speak to (and invite consideration of) include the following:

- How is geo-institutional *variegation* (Brenner *et al.*, 2010) systematically produced, and accentuated and in what ways is it key to the neoliberalization of water, and specific practices related to privatization, commodification or marketization?
- How do broader discourses or practices, such as those associated with neoliberalism, facilitate the marketization or privatization of water?
- How does biophysical variability, or crises related to water and water scarcities, serve to cement or upset the privatization or marketization of water?
- How does the context of crisis that leads to the implementation of these schemes play into the diverse causes and outcomes of these shifts (particularly as often financial and governance crisis paves the way for these shifts)?
- What are the ecological or social equity outcomes related to these shifts, specifically as they also relate to possibilities for participation?
- How does water marketization or privatization articulate with discourses around 'water for all'/human rights to water, or other concurrent trends in water policy and governance?

As suggested by the questions above, whenever possible, we also attend to the intersection of issues regarding privatization, marketization and commodification with our other focal themes of scarcity/crisis, and participation. We do so because these themes and practices are never totally isolatable or distinct from other key governance ideas, in the water realm or more generally. Indeed, one of the broader points of this volume is that there are multiple hegemonies at play in the arena of water governance, and they inevitably reinforce or otherwise influence one another in ways that demand analysis and attention.

References

Bakker, K. 2003. Political ecology of water privatization. *Studies in Political Economy*, 70, 35–58.

Bakker, K. 2007. The commons versus the commodity: after globalization, anti-privatization and the human right to water in the Global South. *Antipode*, 39(3), 430–55.

Bakker, K. 2010. *Privatizing Water: Governance Failure and the World's Urban Water Crisis*, Ithaca, NY, and London: Cornell University Press.

Bakker, K. 2012. Water privatization, urbanization and development. American Association for the Advancement of Science Annual Meeting, Vancouver, 16–20 Feb.

Bakker, K. 2013. Constructing 'public' water: the world bank, urban water supply, and the biopolitics of development. *Environment and Planning D: Society and Space*, 31.

Bayliss, K. 2001. Water privatization in Africa: how successful is it? Public Services International Research Unit, University of Greenwich. Available at: www.eldis.org (accessed Jan. 2009).

Braadbaart, O. 2002. Private versus public provision of water services, does ownership matter for utility efficiency? *Journal of Water Supply Research and Technology*, 51(7), 375–88.

Brenner, N., Peck, J., and Theodore, N. 2010. Variegated neoliberalization: geographies, modalities, pathways. *Global Networks,* 10(2), 182–222.

Budds, J., and McGranahan, G. 2003. Are the debates on water privatization missing the point? Experiences from Africa, Asia and Latin America. *Environment and Urbanization,* 15(2), 87–114.

Dublin Principles. 1992. *The Dublin Statement on Water and Sustainable Development*. Available at: www.wmo.int/pages/prog/hwrp/documents/english/icwedece.html (accessed July 2012).

Gleick, P., Wolff, E., Chalecki, E. L., and Reyes, R. 2002–3. The privatization of water and water systems. In P. Gleick (ed.), *The World's Water: Biennial Report of Freshwater Resources*, pp. 57–85, Washington, DC: Island Press.

Goldman, M. 2007. How 'water for all!' policy became hegemonic: the power of the World Bank and its transnational policy networks. *Geoforum,* 38(5), 786–800.

Harris, L. M. 2009. Gender and emergent water governance: comparative overview of neoliberalized natures and gender dimensions of privatization, devolution, and marketization. *Gender, Place, and Culture,* 16(4), 387–408.

Heynen, N., McCarthy, J., Prudham, S., and Robbins, P., eds. 2007. *Neoliberal Environments: False Promises and Unnatural Consequences*, New York: Routledge.

Mansfield, B. 2007. Privatization: property and the remaking of nature–society relations. Introduction to the special issue. *Antipode,* 39(3), 393–405.

Martin, P. 2005. Comparative topographies of neoliberalism in Mexico. *Environment and Planning A*, 37(2), 203–20.

Peck, J. 2004. Geography and public policy: constructions of neoliberalism. *Progress in Human Geography,* 28(3), 392–405.

Smith, L. 2004. The murky waters of the second wave of neoliberalism: corporatization as a service delivery model in Cape Town. *Geoforum*, 35(3), 375–93.

11 Variable histories and geographies of marketization and privatization

Leila M. Harris

Introduction

We often discuss marketization and privatization of water as if the processes that are implied by these terms are uniform and well understood. The aim of this chapter is to make the case that historically and geographically there have been, and continue to be, diverse pathways of marketization and privatization, even as we might nonetheless characterize some regional or global trends. Linked to this, there are also diverse effects of these processes as they unfold in various places and times. While this volume is generally concerned with the linked processes of privatization, marketization, corporatization and other aspects of hegemonic water governance (see Harris, Chapter 10; or discussion in Bakker, 2010a, 2010b, for definitions and typologies relevant to understand these linked processes), here I focus primarily on privatization of water governance (shifting from public to private management, either partially or *in toto*), with some discussion of marketization (engaging market instruments for water provision, pricing, and determination of appropriate use).[1]

The chapter begins with a brief discussion of some of the major contours of privatization and marketization of water, drawing on histories of these governance trends in Europe and North America. The next section documents major shifts of the past several decades, often termed as an era of neoliberal water governance. I then connect these to recent discussions of *variegation* before moving on to address other shifts that might be considered 'resistant' to these trends, characterizing these shifts again as variegated, yet also with decipherable patterns and trends. Finally, the chapter closes with a discussion of what an enriched understanding of these variable histories and geographies offers for water governance debates.

Before proceeding, it is worth briefly reviewing the concept of neoliberalism and the idea of *variegation*. Neoliberalism refers to policies and practices that emphasize market orientation – the 'politically guided intensification of market rule and commodification' (Brenner *et al.*, 2010). A large literature on 'neoliberal natures' has considered the importance and socio-ecological effects of the use of market instruments, including privatization and commodification of water (Heynen *et al.*, 2007; Bakker, 2010b; Harris, 2009a). Recent work from theorists of neoliberalism has emphasized the concept of *variegation*, referring to the uneven or varied character of neoliberalization (Brenner *et al.*, 2010). Following this conceptualization, key questions are foregrounded to highlight how neoliberalization reinforces geo-spatial and institutional differences across countries and regions, including: what are the spatio-temporal contours and parameters of unevenness in the context of neoliberalization, and indeed, how does neoliberalization require, and also reinforce, such geo-institutional differentiation? In what ways does neoliberalization unfold differently across space and time, particularly in relation to uneven landscapes, socio-natures, economics and institutions (cf. Bakker, 2010b)? Further, to what extent are regulatory and geo-institutional differences exploited, intensified or reworked through neoliberalization processes?

In the water realm, this begs questions related to the ways that what we term 'neoliberal water governance', including diverse practices such as devolution, marketization and privatization (see Harris, 2009a; Goldman, 2007; Bakker, 2007; J. E. Castro, 2008), rely on, exploit or exaggerate key geo-historical and institutional differences across countries, regions or locales. As in the discussion in Bakker (2010b), we can also consider the ways that specific biophysical attributes of socio-natures in the water realm may also be accented or exaggerated through these processes. Further, these discussions open up the need to attend to the specific cross-scalar forms of power in which neoliberalization trends are embedded, including the ways that neoliberalization shifts rely on, or exaggerate, uneven relations of power with respect to regional formations, nationalisms or local politics. As Bakker (2010b) argues with respect to the importance of variegation for studies of neoliberal natures, local experiences of the neoliberalization of nature reflect the interplay of inherited institutional lineages, policy landscapes, local economic and political dynamics, and the multi-scalar dynamics of regulatory restructuring. In light of this formulation of variegation, the problem with a case-study approach (specifically, site- and resource-specific studies of neoliberalization) is that it enables differentiation to be empirically documented, but foregoes an analysis of the systematic production of geo-institutional differentiation, insofar as it neglects to articulate local cases with translocal neoliberalization processes (Bakker, 2010b: 721).

Here, the effort is to highlight contextual and historical specificities, but also to contribute to a theorization of trans-local and regional connections and patterns. Consider for instance, the suggestion by Brenner *et al.* that actually existing neoliberal forms meld with 'crisis ridden geographies of Keynesian state failure' (2010: 35). Here they are suggesting that 'state failure' serves to establish the fields of opportunity and spaces of realization for the first rounds of neoliberalization. Highlighting connections of this type, the variegation concept opens up lines of inquiry related to the more general themes of interest for this volume: crisis/scarcity, privatization/marketization and participation, all of which may be pushed forward as a consequence of, and also constituted in relation to, 'state failure' or other dimensions of social, institutional and biophysical difference. Consider Goldin's discussion of the ways that popular participation is linked with ideas of inefficient or ineffective state bureaucracies (Chapter 16), or the fact that privatization and marketization have also been pursued based on the ideas that states have often failed regarding service provision in the water realm (Bakker, 2010a, 2013).

History matters: from privatization to public provision and back again

One of the most interesting aspects of water governance debates has been the ways that crises (biophysical or governance) are invoked to justify the need to privatize water sources, or to engage market instruments more fully (Bakker, 2010a). Indeed, ideas of biophysical scarcity, or crises of mismanagement, are often central to the discourse and debate that ushers in privatization – cast as an obvious pathway for improvement. In brief, the argument is often made that private water provision will be more efficient, will promote conservation or will produce costs savings that will make the water system more sustainable over the long term. These ideas are familiar to anyone interested in contemporary water governance (see Muller, 2003; Franceys and Nickson, 2003; J. P. Castro, 2008, for other discussions on potential benefits of privatization or public–private partnerships, hereafter PPPs). Consideration of ideas of water crisis and scarcity as central to justifying water privatization and marketization also helps to make clear the complex linkages between the different 'hegemonic' concepts and the practices that structure this volume.

However, investigating these issues historically, it is clear that the connection between crisis and privatization trajectories has not always been uniform or one-way. As Gleick *et al.* (2002–3) describe, in the United States over a century ago water provision was primarily the purview of private firms. Citing widespread failures, including high incidence of typhoid among African American populations, among other issues, the case was made that water systems should be made public (in Boston, Chicago and elsewhere). The argument that was proffered was that private companies did not have the appropriate incentives for long-term investment in the system, nor could they provide water to lower income communities. Especially since water is a social good – society as a whole benefits if all people have access to clean and safe water – it was cast as imperative to hand over the water systems to public control, particularly to ensure that long-term infrastructural investments were made and that poorer segments of society were served.

Interestingly, and important for the theoretical contribution of this chapter, the exact same rationale was used in France and other locations in Europe around the same time period (also near the turn of the 19th century, late 1800s to early 1900s), to argue that water provision should be privatized. In brief, governance failure was similarly invoked as a motive for change, but in this case it was to argue for the opposite: the need to turn from public to private provision (or partial privatization in some cases). From this comparison, it is clear that the current trend, whereby we see a virtual repeat of the earlier debate as it played out in

Europe (i.e. the need to switch from public to private provision), has not always been the case historically.

If you look at the historical record for both public and private provision, clear evidence of the 'success' or 'failure' of both can be found. For instance, evidence suggests that privatization in Argentina in the 1980s led to improvements in public health, while similar improvements were documented with the switch to public provision in the US example (Palaniappan *et al.*, 2004–5: 47). In broad senses, regardless of whether provision is public or private, the history of water provision generally is one of governance 'failure' (Bakker, 2010a). In recent decades, by focusing so much attention on whether or not provision should be public or private, we have failed to attend to the more general issue of improving water governance, irrespective of the specific forms it takes (Bakker, 2010a; Harris, 2009b). Given our focus in this volume, it is worth querying to what degree the narrowing of the debate is linked to hegemonic water governance understandings, as a key aspect of hegemonies is to close the terms of debate and limit discussion of alternatives (see Sneddon, Chapter 2). The examples above are also suggestive of the need to explore more fully the importance and implications of historic and geographic variability in these debates, in terms of how and why governance changes unfold in various locales and to what effect. This is precisely the focus of the remainder of this chapter, aimed at considering more recent privatization and marketization governance shifts, including their uneven implementation and effects across regions and locales.

Patterns of shifting water governance: Europe and North America

To begin, I provide a quick review of the two contexts already mentioned – Europe and North America. Of course, even as part of the purpose of this discussion is to recognize regional trends and shifts, there is considerable variation within these regional contexts, as well as within some of the national contexts noted. In Europe, we can find evidence for a strong history of private water provision, as well as the use of market instruments, even as there have also been considerable state subsidies and support. State support in the water realm might include direct subsidies for low-income communities, cross-subsidization through taxation or pricing of water, or investment in public infrastructure. France is a paradigmatic example in this regard. It is home to the giant water entities Suez (following a 1997 merger between Compagnie de Suez and Lyonnaise des Eaux, one of the oldest operating multinationals in the world dating back to the 1800s); and Veolia, formerly Vivendi, also with a very long history and with a sectorally and geographically diverse portfolio that includes water. Very early on, the precursor to this company was the Compagnie Générale des Eaux. One of the first of this type, the Compagnie was initially declared by decree of Napoleon III in 1854, operating to serve the water system of the French city of Lyon, and later obtained a 50-year concession for the capital city of Paris. In sum, key features of this model relate to the fact that, although private companies have long operated here, they often do so with significant public support, regulation and oversight. Many other leading multinationals in the water realm are also based in Europe, although most with a shorter history than their French counterparts (including Thames Water from London and Vitens Evides from the Netherlands). Across Europe, there is clear articulation of these companies, and privatization and marketization generally, with corresponding institutional and political forms, including significant social safety nets and regulatory oversight.

Our conceptual mapping of Europe and North America, with respect to water privatization and marketization, is certainly distinct (given their opposite histories of engagement with these governance forms) but also similar – to the degree that both serve as key sites of knowledge dissemination and institutional modeling in the contemporary moment. Without overstating the case, Europe and North America both serve as institutional and intellectual sites where hegemonic concepts regarding water governance are formulated and disseminated (Goldman, 2007, 2005). I am very careful not to suggest that these sites are the 'same', nor to suggest that neoliberalization merely disseminates from the North to the South in any linear sense (see Peck and Theodore, 2010; Goldman, 2005). Nonetheless, these regions appear to play important roles as strongholds of privatization and marketization, in terms of neoliberalization as an ideological and policy movement, and as important sites for the contemporary dissemination and uptake of privatization and marketization models for water and other realms.

As a point of further illustration, while not directly mapped against these geographies in any absolute sense, the International Financial Institutions (IFIs, including the International Monetary Fund, IMF, and World Bank, IBRD) are institutions where European and North American countries are particularly influential. As Michael Goldman has documented at length (2005, 2007), these institutions deserve particular attention in any discussion of water marketization and privatization. Interestingly, attention to the role of IFIs makes the role of the United States a bit more central than a mapping that only focuses on the centers of power for the various water companies: Washington, DC, is the home to both entities; the US always appoints the President of the Bank, and also carries considerable voting and veto authority (Woods, 2003, 2006).

Before turning to patterns across the global South, there are a few additional notes of interest regarding Northern water governance shifts of the past several decades, specifically in the North American context. While earlier in the 19th century the argument was made that water should return to the public realm, more recently there has been a marked shift in favor of privatization and marketization, as evidenced in both Canada and the United States (Gleick *et al.*, 2002–3; Bakker, 2007). For instance, during recent decades, North America has witnessed a rise in the privatization of water in cities such as Atlanta, GA, Detroit, MI, and Walkerton, ON, as well as the rising use of market instruments such as novel pricing instruments and markets (e.g. in Texas and elsewhere, Whited, 2010). Returning to the historic shift that occurred over a century ago, it has been estimated that, at one point in the 19th century, 94 percent of the US market for water was provided by private firms, and that this later went down to as low as 15 percent (Gleick *et al.*, 2002–3). With the recent shift back towards water privatization from the 1980s onwards, some have estimated that this percentage could increase to as much as 75 percent by the year 2015 (Goldman, 2007). However, cancelled contracts in a range of markets, including large markets such as Atlanta, suggest that this may be unlikely. Nevertheless, North America can be understood as a context where privatization and more recent PPP forms are proceeding, even if a bit more slowly than might have previously been anticipated.

While this discussion is primarily directed to marketization and privatization of water, again there is a clear relationship between these trends and the issue of participatory governance. These changes have often occurred in reaction to the perception of overly bureaucratized and unwieldy state bureaucracies. As such, privatization and marketization have often proceeded hand in hand with devolution to more local scales (e.g. municipalities), and as such, the trajectories and effects of these 'neoliberalization' processes cannot reasonably be delinked from ideas of participatory governance. At once, with devolution, municipalities were asked to manage water infrastructure and delivery. Without capacity in this regard, they might indeed be forced to turn to private contractors, even as they are also asked to increasingly open up governance process to citizen and local participation. While these processes clearly dovetail, there are also noticeable tensions between these shifts. These histories and trajectories help to expose mutual reinforcements, yet also tensions, between the water governance hegemonies that are of interest for the volume on the whole.

Part of my purpose in noting these 'Northern' pathways is based on the contention that we cannot begin to understand the situation of the South without also establishing a sense of variegated processes as they link to sites of the North. As the several brief examples provided illustrate, the diverse political or geo-institutional landscapes that articulate with these changes, as well as their uneven effects as they occur in distinct places and times, imply we need to account for this heterogeneity in our analyses and interpretations. This is an issue I return to below.

Patterns and pathways of shifting water governance: the global South

Even as the pathways and patterns are again not uniform or absolute, the South offers a somewhat distinct set of processes and considerations. Again, the IFIs are important to this story, providing institutional and political economic pathways that clearly connect the North and South. Others have focused on the role of these institutions in fostering political economic shifts in the South, for instance analyzing the 'impulse to lend' and its role in exacerbating the debt crisis, notably in the 1970s and 1980s (Woods, 2006; Goldman, 2005). Here, I briefly review some considerations of importance with respect to the IFIs, then trace specific patterns that can be deciphered regionally, specifically for sites in Latin America and Africa.

The rapid expansion in lending during the 1970s and 1980s (following the post-Second World War boom) had implications for the type of development projects that were funded and also for the distinct IFI 'bail-out loans' provided to heavily indebted economies. Often these loans were coupled with austerity measures that were believed to best enable these countries to pay back these loans (i.e. by reducing overall indebtedness, making these economies more favorable for international investors and so forth). Bakker (2013) has recently analyzed the importance of the ability to repay for 'development' project loans at the World Bank (somewhat distinct from the Bank's 'crisis' lending practices). As she argues, the focus on repayment ability was central to prioritization of projects for funding. In the water sector, this meant that large infrastructure projects were viewed as more favorable (e.g. dams and similar projects that often engaged Northern firms for know-how and construction), and relatively fewer loans were provided for water delivery systems that would serve, for example, fast-growing urban areas. According to Bakker, the IFI lending preferences are key to understanding the types of infrastructure (or lack thereof) that currently exist around the globe. While large dams and reservoirs had clear benefits for industry and had better possibilities for loan repayment, basic services were generally less 'profitable' and as such were not prioritized for lending. This analysis forces us to connect how the lending preferences of IFIs have served in part to structure the current 'water crisis', whereby over one billion of the world's population still do not have access to sufficient water and sanitation (see also Bakker, 2010a, for general discussion of water governance failure).

With respect to bail-out loans for countries that face heavy indebtedness or economic crisis, this facet of Bank lending has also been critical to conditioning the particular geographies and pathways of water governance changes in the South. Indeed, in recent years the privatization of water systems has become a primary loan conditionality for the IMF and World Bank. As Goldman (2007) explains, as of 1990, a small population in the global South received water from US or European water firms. By 2000, over 400 million people did – a number that could be as high as 1.2 billion by 2015. Goldman's explanation of this rapid rise is again tightly linked to the practices of the IFIs. In many cases privatization has been explicitly required as part of loan conditionalities, particularly for the most indebted of countries. This was precisely the case with Ghana's loan deal that was brokered at the end of the 1990s, with the IMF's emergency post-conflict policy loan to Guinea Bissau, as well as with Tanzania's acceptance of poverty reduction loans. It is also notable that in 2001, all eleven of the World Bank's water and sanitation loans carried conditionalities that required either privatization or significant changes to these services to increase cost recovery. In the same year, all $20 billion of water-related loans from the Bank had specific cost-recovery mandates (Goldman, 2007). Even when loan conditionalities are not required or imposed in this way, the World Bank has nonetheless been influential in promoting these shifts through 'best practice models' and training institutes (ibid., see also Smith, 2008, 2004). As such, the IFIs and their practices are clearly key players in water governance reforms of the past several decades, helping to consolidate hegemonies related to water privatization and marketization.

While I am claiming that there are key patterns and trends in evidence across the global South, again we have to attend to the variegated character of these shifts. Without oversimplifying, we can document somewhat distinct patterns that can be characterized regionally, for instance, with respect to Africa and Latin America – among the locations with the most rapid uptake of privatization and marketization. As Goldman (2007) estimates, from the 1990s, there has been an 800 percent increase in African, Asian, Latin American water users purchasing water from European and North American-owned private firms. In the discussion below, I consider these regional trajectories (focusing on Africa and Latin America, but not Asia), arguing that while they are not uniform, there are nonetheless some decipherable 'trajectories' and outcomes linked to these hegemonic water governance norms.

Beginning with Latin America, in general terms, the first 'wave' of water privatization and marketization has often been traced to the 'Chilean model', and has been extensively analyzed through the work of Carl Bauer (e.g. 1997, 1998, 2005). In brief, in the early 1980s, Chile embraced a 'wholesale neoliberalization' strategy in the water sector, coinciding with a number of reforms (including a New Water Law in 1980) associated with Pinochet's authoritarian rule. Chile's experience with these neoliberal reforms was eventually hailed as a success and backed by the IFIs as a model to be replicated elsewhere. Given that the IFIs were heavily involved in structural adjustment throughout Latin America, this helped set the stage for dissemination, for instance to Mexico and Argentina. Again, providing a point of intersection with our interest in participation, SAPs often also followed on the heels of, and were directly linked to, democratization reforms following authoritarian rule in many of these contexts (see Goldin, Chapter 16).

Mexico is one example worth considering. In the 1980s, indebtedness led Mexico to enter into new loan agreements and to take on significant restructuring with guidance from the IFIs. Reduction and privatization of services and reformulation of the Mexican water law (in 1992) were part of these reforms (see Ahlers, 2005; Ennis-McMillan, 2005, for discussion of the Mexico case; and Bennett *et al.*, 2005, for discussion of neoliberal water reforms across Latin America). The quick adoption of water marketization and privatization is reflective of some of the general patterns already discussed – heavy indebtedness and influence of the IFIs. These cases also clearly connect water governance reforms to broader political instabilities and 'crisis ridden geographies', specifically those arising from post-authoritarian legacies and democratic transition (Sader, 2009, Harris and Roa, forthcoming for discussion).

Similar, yet different, trajectories can be traced in several African contexts. Similarities include the fragile political and economic conditions particularly associated with colonialism and independence. Many states were established as late as the 1960s after long and intense struggles for independence following the colonial era. There were also considerable challenges associated with weak economic bases often reliant on a handful of export commodities, reflective of nondiversified economies (Porter and Sheppard, 1998), as well as political challenges associated with (post)-authoritarianism and violence. It was in this context that the IFIs intervened. These institutions provided loans intended to stabilize heavily indebted countries, as well as development funding for infrastructure projects. It was in such a context that Ghana was forced to privatize the water system for its capital city, Accra (Amenga-Etego and Grusky, 2005; see also Morinville and Harris, Chapter 19). All told, by 2002, more than eighteen water privatization contracts had been signed between European firms and African governments (Goldman, 2007).

South Africa is particularly interesting example to highlight as part of this discussion, in that some of its water systems have been privatized (e.g. Johannesburg and Durban), albeit this was not forced through loan conditionalities. This example speaks directly to Goldman's point about the role of the IFIs in training key actors, and in promoting privatization and marketization through 'best practice' models (see also Smith, 2004). With devolution, and increasing roles for municipalities with respect to water provision in South Africa, there are highly variegated experiences with these changes across the country. Each municipality is charged with implementing water governance, even as they all must meet national constitutional expectations and guidelines including the constitutional right to water and the Free Basic Minimum Water Allocation. The City of Cape Town's system has not been privatized, but has been corporatized in line with IFI guidance, adopting general discourses regarding government failure, private-sector efficiencies and the need to 'get prices right' (Goldman, 2007; Smith, 2008). Cote d'Ivoire is yet another interesting example, in that the water in capital city Abijian has been privatized for several decades and is generally considered to be 'successful' (Hall and Lobina, 2006). With respect to another important point about variegation across the South, as J. E. Castro (2008) explains, even though a major argument for private-sector involvement has been to extend services to the underserved, between 1990 and 2005, private-sector investment in the water sector was concentrated in Latin America, East Asia, the Caribbean and the Pacific (89 percent). Areas including the Middle East, North Africa, South Asia and Sub-Saharan Africa received scant or no investment during this period, although these areas were amongst those where the lack of access to water and sanitation is among the most notable. This author concludes that private-sector participation and neoliberal policies have therefore contributed to reinforcing and deepening inequalities (J. E. Castro, 2008: 67). These examples illustrate that, even though the ideas and practices associated with privatization of water provision services may have achieved hegemonic status, the effects are diverse, and the actual implementation remains highly uneven. As the examples below also suggest, this implementation has also been importantly contested.

These changes are clearly unfolding very differently across the South. A point of emphasis here is the way in which the history and geography of colonialism (or apartheid in the case of South Africa), authoritarianism, and associated economic disarticulation and indebtedness, are central to the story of how and why privatization and marketization of water has taken hold in various contexts.

We also see distinct 'effects' of these shifts, whether mediated by local politics, or specific policy and governance landscapes (e.g. as with South Africa's constitution and water policies). Clearly, there are key differences between these sites, yet also connections between them regarding IFI influence, loan conditionalities or general political and economic fragility (or crisis). With such considerations in mind, we can begin to understand the fairly sharp distinctions between the pathways and effects of marketization and privatization of water in both global North and South. I now move on to a brief discussion of 'resistance' to these shifts as this also unfolds across these sites, before returning to the broader theoretical and conceptual issues in the conclusion.

Resistance, counter-movements and responses to marketization and privatization

Particularly in the past decade, we have witnessed some very clear counter-movements to these shifts, some of which can be understood as direct responses to the influence of the IFIs, water pricing and tariff increases, or similar issues discussed above. Among them, a collection of social movements has clustered around the concept of global water justice and has leveraged significant pressure to promote justice and equity considerations. These movements counter the hegemonic discourses and logics that have promoted profit, efficiency and other goals over ideas of universal access, justice or affordability of water. The movement to promote a 'human right to water', culminating in the adoption of this right by the UN general assembly in 2010 is a significant element of this resistance (Mirosa and Harris, 2012; Sultana and Loftus, 2011).

In many of the specific contexts mentioned above, there have also been considerable on-the-ground protest movements, with protests occurring in sites such as Tucuman, Argentina; Cochabamba, Boliva; Accra, Ghana; as well as in South Africa, Thailand and the Philippines (Bennett *et al.*, 2005; Amenga-Etego and Grusky, 2005). These protests and resistance movements have slowed and even reversed the pace and extent of privatization, leading to cancelled contracts (e.g. Tucuman and Cochabamba), or slowing the pace of privatization, as with the case of Accra (in 2011: see Morinville and Harris, Chapter 19).

Another very notable recent shift has gained in force over the past five or six years, particularly in Latin America. As explored elsewhere (see Harris and Roa, forthcoming) several countries (e.g. Bolivia, Ecuador and Uruguay) have adopted constitutional reforms to endorse the Human Right to Water and to specifically outlaw the marketization and privatization of water. Consider the language of Bolivia's new constitution, suggesting that water cannot be considered an economic good, and that rights of people and nature need to be prioritized above economic needs. Those authors suggest that constitutional reform, in particular, may be an important resistance tool for these countries, providing one clear point of leverage where they might be in a stronger position to oppose imposition by the IFIs. The pattern of constitutional reforms is also suggestive for the broader discussion of variegation. While there may be resistance to water privatization in

North America, these resistance movements may occur more at the local realm (e.g. in Atlanta at the municipal scale where reforms are ongoing). By contrast, constitutional reform in several Latin American countries at the national level might be reflective of the specific geo-institutional differences these countries face – particularly the common pathway of IFI influence and imposition that makes these contexts quite distinct from Northern counterparts. The scale of response makes sense both in terms of political economic instabilities that have led to repeated constitutional reforms in these contexts (there have been many constitutional reforms over the past several decades), as well as with respect to the imperative to 'scale' up and formalize protest as one of the only ways to minimize the role of the IFIs in forcing further shifts along these lines in the future (ibid).

Conclusion: revisiting variegation and its importance in the context of water marketization and privatization

While I have tried not to oversimplify the trends as they are manifest in different locations, whether in Africa or Latin America, I have nonetheless argued that recognizing and tracing some of these general patterns is crucial to any discussion of what water marketization and privatization might mean, particularly in the global South. Precisely through recognition of variegation, I have suggested that we can recognize some discernible patterns that are important for how and why the privatization and marketization of water have unfolded over the recent decades. For the South, it is clear that these shifts are linked to vulnerabilities associated with legacies of colonialism, post-authoritarianism, or uneven trading possibilities and indebtedness. The distinct pathways of change, as well as the role for IFIs, also suggest outcomes that are distinct from those in the North. Returning to variegation, one of the key questions posed relates to ways that geo-institutional differences and histories can be exploited or exaggerated in the context of neoliberalization shifts. With respect to water privatization and marketization, I offer several potential insights in this regard as a conclusion to this discussion.

For North America, prior to the recent marketization and privatization shifts, many sites had already made significant public investments to build dams and other large-scale infrastructure associated with the state hydraulic paradigm of the previous half-century (Worster, 1985; Sneddon and Fox, 2011). With significant infrastructure and with most cities already enjoying near-universal coverage, it is clear that a shift towards privatization or full cost recovery means something quite different in these sites. Focusing in on full cost recovery specifically, we can imagine that these practices will have very different implications depending on the relative degree of infrastructural investment required (likely to be significantly more in Southern sites, even as much of the infrastructure in the North America or Europe is ageing and is in need of repair). For the more recent era of neoliberalization and cost recovery in the North, not only has much of the heavy lifting occurred in terms of public infrastructural investment, but customers in those areas may also be more able or willing to accept the price hikes that often accompany privatization or marketization. Municipalities may also be more likely to provide continuing subsidies or backstop financing should a system face cost overruns. By contrast, in many Southern sites, where similar investments have not previously been made, customers may be less able to absorb price increases and governments also may be unable to provide subsidies or other support.

Recalling the IFIs' structuring loan conditions for heavily indebted contexts (e.g. Ghana), or vulnerabilities following on authoritarian legacies (e.g. Chile), it is clear that geo-institutional variegation is key to understanding what sets the stage for these governance shifts. Variegation also highlights important differences between North and South that are central for any analysis of these shifts, confounding any idea that we might understand these varied engagements with 'marketization' or 'privatization' as a singular set of processes (cf. Bakker, 2010b). Variegation is clearly suggestive of uneven relations of power. But what of the ways that uneven power dynamics might be further exaggerated through shifting water governance? As one illustration for such a claim, consider that indebtedness and democratization challenges in Ghana paved the way for structural adjustment and IFI loans requiring water privatization in the capital. Commentators including Yeboah (2006) have argued that the foreign interference in forcing Accra's privatization has had a de-democratizing effect. Here we see the linkage between the way in which shifts occur and how variegated histories and geographies may also aggravate those patterns.

Returning to other themes of interest for this volume, it is worth returning to the intersections of privatization and marketization with notions of crisis and scarcity. Again, in a relatively straightforward sense, these processes have often been coupled, as ideas of biophysical scarcity or state crisis are often cited to promote privatization and marketization of water. As such, in order to contest the ongoing privatization of water, there may be 'good reason to challenge the "global water scarcity" and "crisis" discourses of the transnational water policy network, and to examine the very real political-economic interests that lie behind [them]' (Goldman, 2007: 795).

Goldman and Bakker, two theorists who have been very vocal and influential in these debates, also offer intriguing examples of ways that marketization and privatization shifts may also reinforce or even forge new types of biophysical and institutional crises. Recall the earlier discussion of Bakker (2013) who suggests that preferences for repayment of loans undercut possibilities to fund public-works projects to provide water to the urban poor, contributing to the contemporary water crisis throughout the South. Similarly, Goldman (2007) notes that the privatization of water and installation of meters in Johannesburg led to a situation in which those unable to pay for this water source were forced to rely on unsafe water. In the case of KwaZulu Natal in 2000, inability of residents to pay for connection fees for newly installed meters contributed to such a situation, and a widespread cholera outbreak that followed (Pauw, 2003; Bond, 2001). Further still, Hall and Lobina (2006) suggest that the privatization push drastically reduced the amount of aid funding available for water and sanitation activities in the South. These examples speak directly to the complex ways that privatization or marketization of water are linked to other 'crises', as well as the ways that crises not only pave the way for these shifts, but also may be aggravated as an outcome of these changes.

Indeed, one of the most difficult things about the privatization and marketization 'push' is the lack of attention to specific pathways of governance, infrastructural differences or biophysical dimensions of water. Context specificities are often overlooked, and instead a one-size-fits-all solution is promoted as 'the answer' to diverse crises and vulnerabilities. As I have shown here, we need to think more carefully about historical and geographic variegation and difference, as crucial to better understanding both how and why these processes unfold, and what effects they have in specific sites. Variegation is key to understanding the foundation on which neoliberalized water governance unfolds (e.g. debt crisis, postcolonial and authoritarian legacies). To the degree that marketization or privatization enhance governance or financial vulnerabilities, or indeed, contribute to de-democratization, variegation itself can also be understood as a product and outcome of these changes. As such, water governance provides a clear example of broader neoliberalization processes, but given its importance for life and livelihoods, it may also represent an important 'frontier' or limit to nature's ongoing neoliberalization (cf. Harris, 2009b). Indeed, water has been one of the domains that have been characterized by significant protest and resistance. As such, the water governance patterns as explored in this chapter, and throughout this book, might be understood as representing a particularly controversial and perhaps consequential 'limit' to neoliberalization and associated political economic changes. Conceptually, politically and ethically, there is evidence that the water governance domain is one where dominant and hegemonic conceptions (including privatization, marketization and broader linked concepts associated with neoliberalization) might be challenged and called to account.

Note

1   Some prefer the language of marketization as a broad umbrella term, particularly as pure privatization remains a relatively rare form among this broader set of practices, with the potential to also obscure the diversity of forms that private sector involvement takes in the water sector (J. E. Castro, 2008).

References

Ahlers, R. 2005. Empowering or disempowering: gender dimensions of neoliberal water policy in Mexico and Bolivia. In V. Bennett, S. Davila-Poblete and M. Nieves Rico (eds), *Opposing Currents: The Politics of Water and Gender in Latin America*, pp. 53–71, Pittsburgh, PA: University of Pittsburgh Press.

Amenga-Etego, R. N., and Grusky, S. 2005. The new face of conditionalities: the World Bank and water privatization in Ghana. In D. A. McDonald and G. Ruiters (eds), *The Age of Commodity: Water Privatization in Southern Africa*, pp. 275–90, London and Sterling, VA: Earthscan.

Bakker, K. 2007. The commons versus the commodity: after globalization, anti-privatization and the human right to water in the Global South. *Antipode*, 39(3), 430–55.

Bakker, K. 2010a. *Privatizing Water: Governance Failure and the World's Urban Water Crisis,* Ithaca, NY, and London: Cornell University Press.

Bakker, K. 2010b. The limits of 'neoliberal natures': debating green neoliberalism. *Progress in Human Geography*, 34(6), 715–35.

Bakker, K. 2013. Constructing 'public' water: the World Bank, urban water supply, and the biopolitics of development. *Environment and Planning D: Society and Space*, 31.

Bauer, C. J. 1997. Bringing water markets down to earth: the political economy of water rights in Chile, 1976–1995. *World Development*, 25(5), 639–56.

Bauer, C. J. 1998. *Against the Current: Privatization, Water Markets, and the State in Chile,* Boston, MA: Kluwer Academic Publishers.

Bauer, C. J. 2005. In the image of the market: the Chilean model of water resources management. *International Journal of Water*, 3(2), 146–65.

Bennett, V., Davila-Poblete, S., and Nieves Rico, M., eds. 2005. *Opposing Currents: The Politics of Water and Gender in Latin America,* Pittsburgh, PA: University of Pittsburgh Press.

Brenner, N., Peck, J., and Theodore, N., 2010. Variegated neoliberalization: geographies, modalities, pathways. *Global Networks,* 10(2), 182–222.

Bond, P. 2001. The World Bank in the time of cholera, *Z Space*. Available at: http://www.zcommunications.org/the-world-bank-in-the-time-of-cholera-by-patrick-bond (accessed July 2012).

Castro, J. P. 2008. Water services in Latin America: experiences with public–private partnerships. *International Journal of Water,* 4(3), 235–57.

Castro, J. E. 2008. Neoliberal water and sanitation policies as a failed development strategy: lessons from developing countries. *Progress in Development Studies,* 8(1), 63–83.

Ennis-McMillan, M. 2005. La vida del pueblo: women, equity, and household water management in the valley of Mexico. In V. Bennett, S. Davila-Poblete and M. Nieves Rico (eds), *Opposing Currents: The Politics of Water and Gender in Latin America*, pp. 137–53, Pittsburgh, PA: Pittsburgh University Press.

Franceys, R., and Nickson, A. 2003. *Tapping the Market: The Challenge of Institutional Reform in the Urban Water Sector,* Basingstoke: Palgrave Macmillan Press.

Gleick, P., Wolff, G., Chalecki, E., and Reyes, R. 2002–3. The privatization of water and water systems. In P. Gleick (ed.), *The World's Water 2002–2003: The Biennial Report of Freshwater Resources,* Washington, DC: Island Press.

Goldman, M. 2005. *Imperial Nature: the World Bank and Struggles for Social Justice in the Age of Globalization,* New Haven, CT: Yale University Press.

Goldman, M. 2007. How 'water for all!' policy became hegemonic: the power of the World Bank and its transnational policy networks. *Geoforum*, 38(5), 786–800.

Hall, D., and Lobina, E. 2006. *Pipe Dreams: The Failure of the Private Sector to Invest in Water Services in Developing Countries,* London: World Development Movement, PSIR Unit.

Harris, L. M. 2009a. Gender and emergent water governance: comparative overview of neoliberalized natures and gender dimensions of privatization, devolution, and marketization. *Gender, Place and Culture*, 16(4), 387–408.

Harris, L. M. 2009b. Review of *Neoliberal Environments* (N. Heynen, et al., 2007). *Annals of the Association of American Geographers*, 99(1), 209–13.

Harris, L. M., and Roa, C., forthcoming. Recent waves of water governance: constitutional reform and resistance to neoliberalization (1990–2010).

Heynen, N., McCarthy, J., Prudham, S., and Robbins, P., eds. 2007. *Neoliberal Environments: False Promises and Unnatural Consequences,* New York: Routledge.

Mirosa, O., and Harris, L. M. 2012. The human right to water: contemporary challenges and contours of a global debate. *Antipode*, 44(3), 932–49.

Muller, M. 2003. Public–private partnerships in water: a South African perspective on the global debate. *Journal of International Development,* 15(8), 1115–25.

Palaniappan, M., Gleick, P., Hunt, C., and Srinivasan, V. 2004–5. Water privatization: principles and practices. In P. Gleick (ed.), *The World's Water: The Biennial Report on Freshwater Resources*, pp. 45–78, Washington, DC: Island Press.

Pauw, J. 2003. The politics of underdevelopment: metered to death: how a water experiment caused riots and a cholera epidemic. *International Journal of Health Services*, 33(4), 819–30.

Peck, J., and Theodore, N. 2010. Mobilizing policy: models, methods, and mutations. *Geoforum,* 41(2), 169–74.

Porter, P., and Sheppard, E. 1998. *A World of Difference,* London: Guilford Press.

Sader, E. 2009. Postneoliberalism in Latin America. *Development Dialogue*, 51, 171–9.

Smith, L. 2004. The murky waters of the second wave of neoliberalism: corporatization as a service delivery model in Cape Town. *Geoforum*, 35(3), 375–93.

Smith, L. 2008. Power and the hierarchy of knowledge: a review of a decade of the World Bank's relationship with South Africa. *Geoforum*, 39(1), 236–51.

Sneddon, C., and Fox, C. 2011. The Cold War, the US Bureau of Reclamation and the technopolitics of river basin development, 1950–1970. *Political Geography*, 30(8), 450–60.

Sultana, F., and Loftus, A., eds. 2011. *The Right to Water: Politics, Governance and Social Struggles,* Abingdon: Taylor & Francis.

Whited, M. 2010. Economic impacts of irrigation water transfers on Uvalde County, Texas. *Journal of Regional Analysis and Policy*, 40(2), 65–75.

Woods, N. 2003. The United States and international financial institutions: power and influence within the World Bank and IMF. In R. Foot, S. N. McFarlane and M. Mastanduno (eds), *US Hegemony and International Organizations*, pp. 92–114, Oxford: Oxford University Press.

Woods, N. 2006. *The Globalizers: The IMF, the World Bank, and their Borrowers,* Ithaca, NY: Cornell University Press.

Worster, D. 1985. *Rivers of Empire: Water, Aridity and the Growth of the American West,* New York: Pantheon.

Yeboah, I. 2006. Subaltern strategies and development practice: urban water privatization in Ghana. *Geographical Journal*, 172(1), 50–65.

12 (Dis)connecting the flow, steering the waters

Building hegemonies and 'private water' in Zambia, 1930s to the present

Hillary Waters

> Everything is dependent on what the World Bank and [International Monetary Fund] say. They just throw decisions down our throats – take [our advice] or you die …
>
> (Resident Development Committees (RDCs), 2007)

> Clearly people do not understand the value of water and they expect it to fall from the sky and not cost anything.
>
> (Spillet, 2002)

In the 1930s, the Roan Antelope Mine in Zambia, owned by the London-based Selection Trust Group, followed the expert advice of London's Ross Institute for Tropical Diseases to 'cure' Zambia's landscape of malaria by quickening the Luanshya river and filling nearby marshes, *damboes*, with toxic mining tailings (Watson, 1953: 54). By focusing public health efforts on malaria, which disproportionately infected European miners, the Roan Mine created the image of the town of Luanshya being a 'garden-city' of 'healthfulness' and beauty despite its toxic re-engineered waters (Watson, 1953: 54). Couching their justifications in hegemonic discourses of public health and engineering, the Ross Institute's solutions appeared objective and scientific[1] despite this 'conquest of the wetlands' being less about curing malaria than 'employ[ing] water] in highly controlled ways' that held clear benefits for mining operations (Schumaker, 2008: 835).

In recent years, the hegemonic concepts governing water have shifted both in Zambia and globally. Nonetheless, the ways hegemony operates are substantially similar. Utilizing rhetoric of crisis and failure (Mahayni, Chapter 4), market-based neoliberal solutions are now posited as objectively and undeniably the best solutions for urban water provision – scientific, efficient and effective. Even when critiqued, the underlying premises supporting privatization, corporatization and commodification continue to frame the debate by focusing on poor urban residents, pitting efficiency against equality and emphasizing domestic water rights (McDonald and Ruiters, 2005; Swyngedouw, 2007; Bakker, 2010).

At the same time, these hegemonic framings leave out some uses of water. Water is categorized into types, each with its 'objective' or 'rational' purpose and way to manage it. For example, immense amounts of water are consumed, controlled and polluted by companies and industries who can pay (though often do not pay much), yet funding to remediate industrial pollution is often seen as an environmental problem and public responsibility despite the many private actors involved. That is, there are many ways to use water, and pay for it, yet it appears market logics are only required for some of these ways (domestic drinking) and not others (industrial pollution). 'Market principles' operate when water is taken or consumed, but not when it is made 'unconsumable'. In Zambia at present, the way neoliberal water policies are enacted – and who benefits from them – demands closer consideration. Zambia's social, economic, political and material pasts have come together to condition how these contemporary policies work (or do not work) on the ground.

If hegemony is indeed experienced locally through the bundling of diverse ideologies, knowledges, institutions and historical moments (Harris, Chapter 10), here, I consider the case of water and mining in Zambia to argue that water is melded together with certain ideals, and cleaved apart from others. That is, hegemony is a dual process: it is produced and made powerful through bundling. Bundling indivisibly links certain concepts, approaches and powerful actors. And then, unbundling makes certain connections invisible through abstracting water from its socio-material relationships. This abstraction enables hegemonic ideas to 'exude an aura of unassailable objectivity' (Sneddon, Chapter 2).

As I explore below, apparent objectivity is often created through the use of technical, scientific or 'expert' language that *unbundles* or *abstracts* water from its socio-political context. Jamie Linton (2008, 2010), in particular, has forcefully argued that modern science represents water in a way that 'abstracts' water, meaning it considers water as merely molecules to be managed through technology and science rather than an intricate player in social, political and economic networks. In brief, following Linton, *abstraction* makes the techniques we employ to manipulate, control, dam, divert, use or pollute water appear like 'natural' or 'objective' solutions.

For example, at the Roan Mine in Zambia, global public health rhetoric, modernist engineering expertise and the socio-political waterscape were bundled together to restructure the Zambian landscape. *Abstraction* allowed public health experts and engineers to obscure the economic and political players and beneficiaries of this re-engineered waterscape, as the private interests of mining companies became less visible and the detrimental impacts of these changes to Africans were largely ignored. Significantly, abstraction 'make[s] invisible the expert discourses, the interests, the winners and the losers that might be entailed in … apparently innocuous [practices of water governance]' (Linton, 2008: 187). I argue hegemony works, in part, through abstraction. Together, hegemony and abstraction enable powerful networks, including industrial polluters, to hide involvement in water management despite being central players in water processes.

In this chapter, I build on Sneddon's and Harris's assertions in this volume that when hegemonic discourses are deployed they tend to oversimplify the variegated ways privatization is experienced locally. I draw on four colonial and postcolonial moments in Zambia, emplacing hegemonic concepts around water governance within the Zambian socio-waterscape. The moments I trace include: engineering for urban malaria control in the 1930s, the building of the Kariba Dam in the 1950s, and urban domestic water services in both colonial and neo-liberal eras. In each of these, I ask: how do hegemonic concepts about water travel to Zambia? How is the implementation and bundling of hegemonic concepts shaped by local context? And finally, how might hegemony work with abstraction to render invisible those with the power to 'mold and structure' (Sneddon, Chapter 2) the Zambian waterscape?

The Zambian waterscape

It is no secret that water management has been crucial for building colonial control and state power across the globe (Gilmartin, 1994; Swyngedouw, 2004; Mosse, 2008; Schumaker, 2008; Gibbs, 2009). But how this is done and towards what ends vary between places. Zambia (formerly Northern Rhodesia) is located in central southern Africa and hosts much of the mineral-rich Copperbelt. The origins of the Zambezi and Kafue rivers, which supply water to 40 percent of Sub-Saharan Africa, are in the region (Figure 12.1). Here, the legacy of corporate rule and Westerners' exclusive interest in mining natural resources is crucial for understanding the history, morphology and power of the waterscape.

Colonization began under the British South Africa Company (BSAC), which administered and developed the territory until 1924 and even afterwards

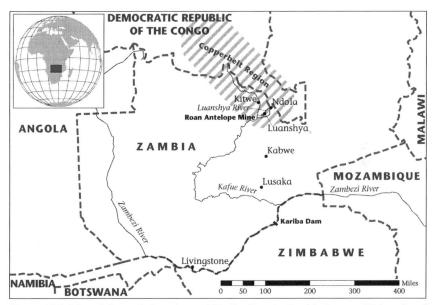

Figure 12.1 Map of Copperbelt region and Kariba Dam in Zambia (source: University of Minnesota Cartography Lab)

powerfully reshaped the landscape for profit. Roads, pipes and workers' housing were constructed across the region to support mining operations (Slinn, 1971). When administrative control passed to the Colonial Office, the BSAC retained unlimited rights to mineral resources in exchange for a 20 percent tariff, effectively cementing the prioritization of mining (Slinn, 1971: 379).

These next two stories pivot around two themes. The first is the concept of private water. I argue that private water is not new, even as we talk about the neoliberal ideology of water privatization gaining force in the contemporary era. In fact, it may be useful to view privatization more broadly than companies owning or selling water services and consider the myriad ways private interests are served when corporations are not held responsible for potentially negative effects of their water (mis)use. The second builds on the notions of bundling and abstraction to highlight how hegemony works. In both of these stories, networks of people, water and institutions bundle distinct ideologies such as public health expertise, modernist engineering, liberal economics and colonial racism. This reveals how global concepts acquire the power to shape local waterscapes in ways that are potentially both ecologically and socially harmful. Then, by abstracting water from its social and political relations, certain ways of controlling water appear rational and objective.

Malaria control

By 1930, high malarial rates in the Copperbelt made it infamous for sickness and death (Watson, 1953; Schumaker, 2008). Once this notoriety impeded mining operations, the Roan Mine hired the Ross Institute to re-engineer the waterscape for malaria prevention. Malcolm Watson and his colleagues applied a technique they developed in Malaysia: rather than targeting malaria itself they sought to control the vectors of the disease, mosquitoes (Watson, 1953).

Surveying the land, they found stagnant and slow-moving water ideal for mosquito spawning. Despite the fact that mining activities, including dams and pit lakes, were a significant cause of increased malarial rates in Copperbelt towns, they blamed the marshy *damboes* and the sinuosity of the river (Schumaker, 2008). Overlooking the role of the meandering river and its *damboes* in local agriculture, the Ross Institute proposed to 'cure' the river through channeling, eliminating vegetation along the banks and filling *damboes* (Watson, 1953: 54).

Roan Mine engineers were reluctant to take on such a large task. They agreed to the plan after the Institute emphasized two direct benefits to mining operations (Schumaker, 2008). First, draining the land lowered the water table, allowing copper to be mined via the cheaper method of sinking for open-pit mining rather than drilling deep-pit shafts. Second, *damboes* could be filled with excess tailings – often toxic wastes resulting from the froth floatation process, which separates the copper from rock using water and copper sulfide.

To quicken the river's flow, it was first channeled and straightened. Since vegetation slows the flow of water and provides a habitat for spawning, upwards of 1,000 gallons of oil were sprayed along these engineered riverbanks and in marshy areas to eliminate growth (Watson, 1953: 55). At various times this mixture included crude oil from the mine, paraffin, solar oil, Tarakon oil and kerosene, before it was replaced by DDT in 1945 (Watson, 1953: 45–141). Additionally, *damboes* and flood-prone areas were filled with tailings and urban refuse (Watson, 1953: 54).

The results of this vast hydrological, mechanical and chemical undertaking were rapid. Despite a few setbacks, by the second year of the project they had largely succeeded in controlling the local water. In 1931, Watson commented that, 'in spite of the flooded loops and fresh seepages, the valley even during the worst weather could hardly be compared with the same place a year before. Instead of being a swamp … it was for the most part dry' (Watson, 1953: 47–8). With the straightened channels clear of riverbank vegetation and *damboes*, the Luanshya valley now drained within 24 hours of rainfall, where previously the rainwater would irrigate the landscape for months (Watson, 1953: 55). Soon, extra measures were taken to 'irrigate the grass' in the dry season and mitigate flash floods during heavy rains (Watson, 1953: 55).

Apart from the ecological harms, the agricultural impacts of these practices increased African workers' food insecurity and malnutrition rates among African children (Schumaker, 2008). African mine workers and their families could not grow (as much) in their gardens due to both the groundwater pollution and the Ross Institute's assumption that African practices of water use, including irrigation via *damboes*, allowed 'life-giving water to run to waste' (Watson, 1953: p. xiv; Schumaker, 2008). The Ross Institute asserted that their 'modern scientific methods' (Watson, 1953: 19) and 'special knowledge and skill' (Watson, 1953: 61) produced the most objective, efficient and healthy project plan. While Watson himself said that the project was done so 'all could live healthy lives [and] enjoy life as if they had been in a temperate climate', he focused on the health issues disproportionately impacting Europeans (1953: 59).

This focus on malaria to the exclusion of other health considerations is probably not surprising given the Ross Institute was contracted to decrease the prevalence of malaria. What is important, however, is the way certain global hegemonic concepts – the public health expertise of the Ross Institute, the engineering expertise of the West, the racism of colonialism – bundled together in the Copperbelt's unique social, economic and ecological context with the effect of furthering the interests of some at the expense of others. Although there was no system for the Roan Mine to quantify or pay for the water they controlled and polluted through this process, they used the water by sending it downstream or making it ill-suited for other needs. Without even commodifying water, they engineered the waterscape to further private business interests.

Perhaps most significantly, the solution was offered under the guise of objective science and technical knowledge and expertise. Local cultural and agricultural uses of water were deemed irrelevant to the river and its function, as were the complex ecological 'uses' of the river (for fish habitat, vegetation and so forth). Engineering provided a way to view water as 'bounded, knowable and separate from society' (Mosse, 2008: 940).

The Ross Institute considered their system of maximizing flow and minimizing retention the most 'efficient' way to manage water in Central Africa (Watson, 1953: 60). The Roan Mine project was lauded internationally for its effectiveness and mimicked throughout the Copperbelt (Watson, 1953: 155). Nearby, the Nkana Mine bragged that the local river was 'harmless' due to being 'now under 30 feet of slimes' (ibid.). Watson 'made a deep impression on South Africans' and was invited to meet with leaders of the sugar industry (Watson, 1953: 60). Watson writes, 'England, too, was watching' (ibid.). Their solution traveled beyond Luanshya as an abstract expertise, free of its ecological and economic context at Roan Mine.

Damming water

Merely 20 years later, another major engineering project – the construction of the Kariba Dam – again threatened African livelihoods and served to privilege European interests. Finished in 1958, the dam displaced over 60,000 residents and 'marked the debut of the World Bank's controversial role in [large] dam financing' (Hathaway and Pottinger, 2009: 152). Here, I am not going to discuss the dam's impact, as there is a large literature on the negative social and hydrological effects of dams (see Colson, 1971; McCully, 2001). Instead, I focus on why a large dam was built on the Zambezi river at Kariba when the Federation originally approved a smaller, regional dam on the Kafue river (McGregor, 2009: 107).

While the immediate impetus for building the Kariba Dam came from Lord Malvern, the Federal Prime Minister of the Federation of Rhodesia and Nyasaland, it was motivated by years of corporate colonial control in Northern and Southern Rhodesia. The Federation of Rhodesia and Nyasaland (now Zambia, Zimbabwe and Malawi) was established in 1953 to empower the British in Central Africa and weaken the regional strength of the Union of South Africa's apartheid government (McGregor, 2009). In their quest for power, the Federation developed proposals for constructing an electricity-generating dam to supply the mining industry in the Copperbelt. The Federation's original plan was to dam the Kafue river, a smaller Zambezi tributary in Northern Rhodesia that would supply enough electricity for the mines (McGregor, 2009: 107). Northern Rhodesians and mining companies favored the Kafue Dam over the larger Kariba Dam, as it could be constructed faster, the electricity would not need to travel as far and it would be entirely within Northern Rhodesia (McGregor, 2009: 107).

However, Malvern, a white Southern Rhodesian, preferred the dam be located on the Zambezi river (McGregor, 2009: 106). His reasoning centered on Southern Rhodesians' scramble to retain authority in the face of political threats and racial fears. These reasons included: the sense that a physical dam between the territories would cement the weak political alliance between Northern and Southern Rhodesia; a Southern Rhodesian fear of becoming too economically dependent on the mines in the North – particularly given the potential for African rule in the region; and finally, Malvern saw great symbolism in constructing a large, modern dam on the Zambezi (McGregor, 2009: 107–8). It would be 'a monument to the white man's genius', impressive enough to 'show the world what a young colony could achieve' (cited in McGregor, 2009: 107).

In spite of Northern Rhodesian resistance, Malvern switched the dam site without a vote in the Federation by simply relabeling the Kafue Dam 'territorial' (McGregor, 2009: 109). This designation excluded World Bank financing and reinitiated the decision process. Malvern then 'commission[ed] a team of independent international consultants to review [his] decision' (McGregor, 2009: 107). The committee deemed the hydrological records for the Kafue river inadequate and their report justified the location change 'based on the best independent and up to date technical advice' (cited in McGregor, 2009: 107).

Northern Rhodesians vehemently resisted the site change and veneer of scientific expertise used to legitimize it. To them, the authoritative nature of the site change was emblematic of Southern Rhodesian's misuse of power. White Northern Rhodesians petitioned the Queen of England, saying the switch was 'indefensible' (McGregor, 2009: 107). They questioned the committee's expertise and technical knowledge, arguing (correctly) that Malvern's cost estimates were too low and his plans were based on inadequate science (McGregor, 2009: 108). While Sir John Caldicott, a Southern Rhodesian Minister, said '"there was no political motive in this whatsoever... facts and figures" decided the matter', Northern Rhodesian Chief Secretary Sir Arthur Benson 'accused the Federal government of calculated deception' (cited in McGregor, 2009: 108). Africans in Northern Rhodesia also voiced opposition, seeing the dam 'as a cynical device to extend white power' (McGregor, 2009: 108). The Tonga, displaced by the reservoir, 'regarded it as a theft of their land by powerful Europeans' (Colson, 1971: 5). The Federation's disregard for African opposition only escalated Northern Rhodesian nationalist sentiment.

Here we see a parallel process to how hegemony was bundled and abstracted under the Roan Mine's malaria prevention plan. The goal for the river was to produce electricity to benefit private interests. While this water was not overtly privatized or sold by quantity, it became 'private water' and just as susceptible to political manipulation as corporate control. Only economic costs and benefits were considered in these debates, overlooking the non-quantifiable (or unquantified) and social concerns as well as Malvern's political motivations. Southern Rhodesians argued that per-unit electricity would be cheaper with the Kariba Dam, making it the most economically efficient, while Northern Rhodesians argued that the Kafue Dam would be cheaper overall and generate electricity sooner (McGregor, 2009: 106–10). As McGregor skillfully argues, 'The decision to build [Kariba] was based on technical calculations related to the generation of energy, and the displacement of people was considered only a marginal cost rather than a social issue' (2009: 109).

In the end, while both sides used hydrologic data and economic equations, Malvern's use of technical, engineering-based language, numerical targets and global consultants with cited scientific expertise made Kariba the rational location. This abstraction of the river from its socio-political and ecological context masked the significant political maneuver Malvern made in switching the dam site.

Water privatization:[2] colonial past and hegemonic present

Just as hegemony 'molds and structures' (Sneddon, Chapter 2) the waterscape and abstraction clouds the ways politics, people and economics are dissolved within it, water itself (and the materials used to manage it) can also condition hegemony. As David Mosse argues, 'water systems are not only shaped by, but also themselves shape, social and political relations. The ecology of water ... constrains the play of social and political forces' (2008: 941). That is, water is not merely acted upon. Indeed, it plays a role in shaping how hegemonic concepts are enacted locally.

And, as Mosse later eloquently states, 'water history has a tendency to repeat itself. In the long view, parallels and paradoxes emerge' (2008: 945). Considering some of these parallels and paradoxes, I examine how social and material remnants from a past of 'private water' influence the current experience of water privatization in Zambian cities. In doing so, I argue water privatization is not that new. While we might now focus on neoliberal hegemony, the case of Zambia shows private control over urban water systems has deep historical roots. A few exceptional studies of colonial Rhodesia explore specific histories of private water systems built and controlled by mining companies (Kazimbaya-Senkwe and Guy, 2007; Musemwa, 2008). These earlier forms of private water continue to condition how calls for water privatization actually unfold – who benefits and how ideologies are experienced. Bundling is again useful to consider how historical moments and materials conjoin to structure and enable hegemony in water governance.

Colonial urban water networks

Copperbelt cities first developed under the control of and for the benefit of mining corporations. Prior to 1924, mining towns were free from the 'government interference' of the British Colonial Office and their structure 'generally promot[ed] a spirit of dependence' on their parent companies (Mutale, 2004: 102). Mining companies built houses for their African workers in a barracks style, constructed roads and operated a police force (Mutale, 2004: 104). Water networks constructed first to serve the mines were extended to nearby towns for their workers' domestic use. Later companies agreed to supply water to the rest of the town for a profit, 'on condition that the government agreed not to claim any share of available water' (Kazimbaya-Senkwe and Guy, 2007: 874). This early form of water privatization ensured that mining operations could continue even during water shortages and solidified dependence on the mines for both employees and town residents.

Further, this private water delivery system created and reinforced racial inequalities, as well as inequities between miners and non-miners. For example, in Luanshya, Asians and Europeans were allotted 210 gallons of water per person per day as opposed to the 5 gallons allotted to African workers (Kazimbaya-Senkwe and Guy, 2007: 880). European neighborhoods had metered tap water provided to individual houses with different pricing structures and quotas for mine versus non-mine workers (Mutale, 2004: 148). In neighborhoods housing African mine workers, water was obtained via communal boreholes or water pipes connected to communal water taps.

Extending water services into African neighborhoods not inhabited by mine workers was done for profit. Prior to 1929, the Durban System financed 'social welfare services' – housing, roads and water – through profits from beer (Mutale, 2004: 42). One resident protested: 'If we drink beer to give profits then one day there will be water supplied to us in taps. How much beer must I drink before my children can drink water? Do other countries make poor people drink beer to collect money for water?' (Hall 1964: 135 cited in Mutale, 2004: 42).

Despite their divided system based on quotas, beer, control and efficiency, mining companies soon learned the difficulty of profiting from domestic water service. In Luanshya, the commercial venture was 'unsuccessful because they could not attract sufficient clientele to make them economically viable' (Kazimbaya-Senkwe and Guy, 2007: 879). Partly to blame was the unreliability of domestic water services due to prioritizing mines over residents (Kazimbaya-Senkwe and Guy, 2007: 879). In the 1950s, mines limited domestic consumption to ensure the mines could operate. By 1960, the mine in Luanshya (the first urban water network in the country) disinvested from water provision (Kazimbaya-Senkwe and Guy, 2007: 876). After mines fully divested from domestic water service provision in 1974, only 58 percent of those who lived in the formerly public township areas had access to water, while 100 percent of residents in mining areas had access (Mutale, 2004: 149).

It appears private companies were able to build water networks – but not networks that led to just, dependable or efficient service for domestic consumers. Interestingly, some of the very reasons for disinvesture of water services by colonial companies have become the primary assumptions undergirding the promotion of water privatization in the present. These include efficiency, technology and the encouragement of appropriate use of water through pricing mechanisms (Harris, Chapter 10). By the early 2000s, when water privatization policies were (again) discussed in Zambia, it seems much of this history had been ignored despite its continuing significance (Kazimbaya-Senkwe and Guy, 2007).

Neoliberalism: revisiting and entrenching the past

As with many other Southern states, privatization is heavily pushed in Zambia at present, particularly through the World Bank and International Monetary Fund. Their water governance experts premise arguments on the assumption that the public sphere has failed to govern water effectively because the government's goals – strengthening the state, increasing their voting bloc through subsidies or handouts, and legitimating taxes – conflict with managing water in an economically efficient manner (McDonald and Ruiters, 2005; Bakker, 2010; Harris, Chapter 10). According to proponents, privatization would cut out inefficiencies, encourage investment in infrastructure to expand networks to poor areas, end political corruption and profit private companies who would invest in the local community (McDonald and Ruiters, 2005; Bakker, 2010; World Bank, 2011).

Despite strong evidence challenging these assumptions, the World Bank often makes water privatization a condition for receiving loans or debt relief (Goldman, 2007: 794; Harris, Chapter 10). Following the lead of major international financial institutions, international non-governmental aid organizations such as Habitat and WaterAid have taken up privatization as the solution to the urban water crisis (Goldman, 2007: 794). This speaks directly to how hegemony still travels. The World Bank's own global experts call for private control of Zambian water. International NGOs with diverse social and ecological goals utilize the hegemonic concept's underlying assumptions. The question becomes how this global hegemonic concept is bundled to achieve an aura of objectivity over local waterscapes.

To comply with World Bank and International Monetary Fund demands and attain Highly Indebted Poor Country status for debt relief, Zambia embarked on the road towards privatization. In 2000 the Zambian government privatized Zambia Consolidated Copper Mines (ZCCM). Not only did they sell for a low price, mining companies were given low tax and tariff rates and low liability for pollution due to the low global copper prices (Myers, 2005). Most of Zambia's copper resources were sold to foreign investors, including the Anglo-American Corporation, a descendant of Zambia's original colonizer: the British South African Company (Myers, 2005: 115).

Later in 2000, Zambia passed the Peri-Urban Water Supply and Sanitation Strategy as a first step in privatizing urban water utilities (Cocq, 2005: 246). While city councils remain officially responsible for water provision, the government sold water rights to private companies incorporated by local governments for ten-year contracts (Banda, 2007). This means the (mostly foreign) private water companies are regulated and hold provision rights but do not hold responsibility for the crumbling, incomplete and uneven infrastructural network (Cocq, 2005). Ian Banda, the manager of Kafubu Water and Sewerage Company in Ndola, says due to lacking financial capital their water operation is 'firefighting' (fixing leaking or broken pipes) rather than extending or improving infrastructure (2007).

Relatedly, Severn-Trent, the British company leasing Lusaka Water and Sewerage Company, recommended private companies oversee day-to-day operations while leaving the Zambian government 'with the responsibility for new capital investments' (Severn-Trent, 2002: 14.3), an increasingly common pattern globally (Harris, Chapter 10). Severn-Trent argued capital investments were too risky and they were unlikely to profit from extending the network to poor neighborhoods (Severn-Trent, 2002: 4.23). Utility companies argue the government should infuse them with capital to extend and fix infrastructure – although now mining companies are, revealingly, pitching in.

A number of issues plague contemporary water privatization in Zambian cities. First, this system adversely impacts both poor and wealthy Zambians. The number of residents with access to (safe) water remains at 56 percent in poorer, peri-urban neighborhoods (Cocq, 2005: 244). Broken and leaking infrastructure causes service interruptions in poorer and wealthier neighborhoods alike (Cocq, 2005: 244). Second, residents distrust water meters and complain about 'paying for air' (Cocq, 2005). Finally, residents feel a loss of control due to the perceived illegality of accessing water outside the private system (Mutale, 2004: 163; RDCs, 2007), All in all, most residents agree privatization has done little to improve or extend water service (Cocq, 2005; RDCs, 2007).

While privatization policies are presented as objective, rational or universal solutions, the effects of their implementation are highly conditioned by Zambia's socio-political and material history. Here, both the infrastructure and colonial patterns of inequality remain. The continued disparity between neighborhoods built around communal wells and tap water may be the most obvious remains of the water system privatized in an earlier era, but there are also more subtle reminders. Cross-subsidies follow from the exclusionary spaces in colonial urban planning rather than being primarily based on income or wealth. At times, wealthy residents have greater subsidies than poor residents as water is subsidized in neighborhoods with standpipes, while 'metered consumption wherever it occurs (low-, medium-, or high-cost areas) is not' (Mutale, 2004: 163). And when wealthy residents build houses at the urban periphery they, too, may not have access to the city water network (RDCs, 2007).

Other tensions can be observed as global notions of neoliberal water governance articulate with local realities. One such tension is designating the role of 'expert' – those who mediate how hegemonies are instantiated. Privatization is justified via notions of expertise whereby transnational companies with technical and scientific capacity are necessary to improve water access and quality. However, in Zambia, representatives from all sides claim the role of expert and few, if any, the providers of investment capital. From business executives, engineers and government officials to non-governmental community advocates and local religious leaders, *who* can legitimize themselves as 'the expert' is highly contested (Banda, 2007; Chabe, 2007; Mwandila, 2007).

For example, Sebastian Chabe, a member of a public–private partnership the Ndola Development Trust and the owner of Koppa Mining Services, says: 'The private sector is expected to intervene with ideas, practical ideas. The private sector knows what Ndola needs [and] defines the requirements of the community [and will then] make an appeal for the government to come in and intervene [with money]' (2007). On the other hand, many in government and non-governmental organizations – including the Ndola City Council's town clerk Mpanda Mwandila – flip these responsibilities. When delineating roles, Mwandila says the 'private part comes in with the financial muscle and [the] local government comes in with experience [expertise]' for management (2007). How – and which of – these local actors articulate with international actors, institutions and expertise will have significant bearing on the Zambian waterscape and, in turn, the hegemony of neoliberal water policy.

Hidden players: what about the mines?

Given these complex tensions related to the realities and effects of privatization, as well as this book's framing of hegemonies in water management, it is useful to ask 'why privatize?' and 'who benefits from these transformations?' These questions may reveal how hegemony works – and in whose interests. Yet, it is difficult to delineate who benefits from neoliberal water policies in Zambia. Clearly the benefit to the consumer is negligible, if existent. The other visible players in water privatization debates – the local and national government, private water companies and international financial institutions – do not appear to be faring much better. The debt relief offered for consenting to World Bank demands pales in comparison to the loss of control and potential revenue for the government. Water companies claim that, even with grants and subsidies, they don't profit and some have attempted to back out of their agreements (Cocq, 2005; Banda, 2007). Finally, the World Bank entices foreign water companies through subsidies (Cocq, 2005). Thus, their direct financial benefit is negligible, if existent, although, as Goldman has asserted, these practices help to assert the hegemony of the bank itself as 'expert' and power-broker (2007).

Given the historical significance of mines in the Zambian waterscape – and their continued significance in the Zambian economy – we must ask: is it possible that mines and other major industries benefit from water privatization in a way that structures how neoliberalism is enacted locally? One potential way industries may benefit directly is eliminating cross-subsidies from companies to government (Cocq, 2005). But notwithstanding any potential benefit in terms of direct income, the failures of the contemporary hegemonic discourse and its associated practices to include requirements that private entities pay for water pollution and alternative types of consumption should not be overlooked.

Neoliberal privatization emphasizes payment for (certain types of) use but not abuse. Rarely, if ever, is industrial water pollution considered under market logics (for a notable exception, see Budds and Hinojosa-Valencia, 2012). Instead, since water pollution is deemed an environmental problem, it demands a different type of solution. That is, polluted water is abstracted differently than domestic water and thus different solutions are considered objective, scientific and efficient. Because of this, the connections between the waters – and players involved in manipulating or managing them – are made invisible.

Although silent in the urban privatization debate, industries – and therefore 'private water' if not privatized water – remain significant players in Zambia's waterscape. By some estimates, more than 93,000 tons of industrial waste contaminate Zambian rivers each year (Blacksmith Institute, 2012). The Environmental Council of Zambia argues corporate negligence has led to ongoing water pollution of the Kafue river, with the Konkola Copper Mine (KCM) 'consistently operating outside of the [generous] limits set [in law]' (Fraser and Lungu, 2007: 38). Categorizing decontaminated water as a public good further allows polluters to obfuscate their influence in the waterscape.

Industrial water pollution becomes visible during a crisis. In 2006 and 2011, KCM released acidic mining waste directly into the Kafue river from their leaching plant (Fraser and Lungu, 2007; BBC News, 2011). In the 2006 incident, heavy metal levels significantly exceeded the acceptable levels of copper, manganese and cobalt in the Kafue river (Fraser and Lungu, 2007: 36). One resident said, 'We are scared ... We drank because we were thirsty. But the taste was bitter ... Most people are sick. Most people can't even stand up. If we try to put chlorine, the water becomes black. If we boil it, it becomes brown' (cited in Fraser and Lungu, 2007: 36). After this incident, the Chingola Town Clerk reported that KCM

> Operated for one week without adding lime to Mutimpa Slurry dam, discharging effluent of 1.5 pH. That was almost pure acid ... the pipes could not withstand [this level of acidity], and burst ... This pollution was done willfully, knowingly. Pumping slurry without lime [to balance the acidity], that's irresponsible.
>
> (Cited in Fraser and Lungu, 2007: 37)

Urban water utility companies are not financially responsible for cleaning up major industrial surface and groundwater pollution – this is regulated by the ECZ and relies mostly on grants.

But the ongoing water pollution that takes place between catastrophic events also demands consideration. Although water utilities filter and sanitize water, industries are only fined for catastrophic pollution – when it is proven to exceed the actual pollution levels of ZCCM when it was controlled by the state or colonial company (and it is questionable whether the fines are high enough). And their negligible tax rates – that even the IMF has recently agreed are too low – are highly inadequate given the true cost of ongoing water pollution.

Clearly, in Zambia, the mining industry conditioned the possibilities for contemporary water governance. Their practices are factors in determining the use, management and condition of water. By viewing water control and pollution by mining interests as an environmental problem rather than a provision problem, water is effectively abstracted according to a different type of use. This separation, as well as the concurrent bundling, helps to consolidate particular hegemonies. In isolation, each water policy – even when they have contradictory premises – appears as the objective, only adequate way to manage, control or access water for that separated domain. That is, particular hegemonies are constituted through each particular abstraction. In this case, the idea that urban water services should be privatized for efficiency is divorced from the notion that government should cover the externalized environmental costs of the mining industry. The result is not only water privatization but further entrenching of 'private water'.

Conclusion

This chapter has shown how networks of discourses, ideologies and institutions have changed not only *how* water is managed but *towards what ends*. Who has what role and why, as well as how particular types of expertise are legitimized, conditions how hegemonic concepts are bundled in a particular place and for particular debates. Concurrently, water is separated from social, political and economic relationships to make certain practices appear objective and impartial. This was seen in the 1930s when hegemonic health rhetoric and engineering expertise were bundled to re-engineer the waterscape for malaria prevention and in the 1950s when Malvern utilized economic efficiency, modern engineering and technical-institutional rhetoric to mask the deeply political nature of the decision to build a dam at Kariba.

Finally, this process is seen in contemporary neoliberal water policy. The connections between neoliberal water and 'private water' are often complex and not as novel as many theoretical debates suppose. Particular notions of privatization and payment for services are selectively applied. Together, abstraction and bundling hegemonies shape the water debate, 'restrict[ing it] to questions of *who* gets to dictate private sector-led development ... rather than *whether* private sector-led development is the correct policy option' (Cocq, 2005: 244). These histories show how, just as water is never pure, abstract or separated from social and material relationships, the production of hegemonic discourses bundles ideas of scientific expertise or public necessity with politics and desire.[3]

Notes

1 To be clear, I am not arguing that science, hydrology, or engineering is false. Instead, I posit that the ways we utilize, discuss, and acquire hydrologic scientific knowledge are not neutral – in fact, they are often deeply embedded in the ways those in power seek to relate to and control water (Gilmartin 1994; Gibbs, 2009; Linton, 2010; Sneddon, Chapter 2).

2 Privatization, here, is purposely used vaguely. As Bakker (2010) and Harris (Chapter 10) have stated, there are many different types of water policies that typically fall under the rubric of neoliberal water governance, commercialization, or privatization.

3 Special thanks are due to Leila Harris, whose brilliant editing made this chapter what it is.

References

Bakker, K. 2010. *Privatizing Water: Governance Failure and the World's Urban Water Crisis,* New York: Cornell University Press.

Banda, I. N. 2007. Discussion about Kafubu Water & Sewerage Company [conversation]. Personal communication, 7 Nov.

BBC News. 2011. Zambia KCM says power failure caused Kafue river pollution. *BBC News*, 15 Jan.

Blacksmith Institute. 2012. *Heavy Metals and Mining in Kafue River Basin.* Available at: www.blacksmithinstitute.org/projects/display/171 (accessed March 2012).

Budds, J., and Hinojosa-Valencia, L. 2012. Restructuring and rescaling water governance in mining contexts: the co-production of waterscapes in Peru. *Water Alternatives*, 5(1), 119–37.

Chabe, S. 2007. Discussion regarding Koppa Mining Services and Ndola Development Trust [conversation]. Personal communication, 15 Nov.

Cocq, K. 2005. 'There is *still* no alternative?': the beginnings of water privatization in Lusaka. In D. McDonald and G. Ruiters (eds), *The Age of Commodity: Water Privatization in Southern Africa*, pp. 240–58, London: Earthscan.

Colson, E. 1971. *The Social Consequences of Resettlement: The Impact of the Kariba Dam*, Manchester: Manchester University Press.

Fraser, A., and Lungu, J. 2007. *For Whom the Windfalls? Winners and Losers in the Privatisation of Zambia's Copper Mines*, Lusaka: Government of Zambia and Civil Society Trade Network of Zambia.

Gibbs, L. M. 2009. Just add water: colonisation, water governance, and the Australian inland. *Environment and Planning A: International Journal of Urban and Regional Research*, 41(12), 2964–83.

Gilmartin, D. 1994. Scientific empire and imperial science: colonialism and irrigation technology in the Indus Basin. *Journal of Asian Studies*, 53(4), 1127–49.

Goldman, M. 2007. How 'water for all' policy became hegemonic: the power of the World Bank and its transnational policy networks. *Geoforum*, 38(5), 786–800.

Hathaway, T., and Pottinger, L. 2009. The great hydro-rush: the privatization of Africa's rivers. In D. McDonald (ed.), *Electric Capitalism: Recolonising Africa on the Power Grid*, pp. 149–79, London: Earthscan.

Kazimbaya-Senkwe, B. M., and Guy, S. C. 2007. Back to the future? Privatization and domestication of water in the Copperbelt Province of Zambia, 1900–2000. *Geoforum*, 38(5), 869–85.

Linton, J. 2008. Is the hydrological cycle sustainable? A historical-geographical critique of a modern concept. *Annals of the Association of American Geographers*, 93(3), 630–49.

Linton, J. 2010. *What is Water? The History of a Modern Abstraction*, Vancouver: University of British Colombia Press.

McCully, P. 2001. *Silenced Rivers: The Ecology and Politics of Large Dams*, London: Zed Books.

McDonald, D., and Ruiters, G., eds. 2005. *The Age of Commodity: Water Privatization in Southern Africa*, London: Earthscan.

McGregor, J. 2009. *Crossing the Zambezi: The Politics of Landscape on a Central African Frontier*, Harare: Weaver Press.

Mosse, D. 2008. Epilogue: the cultural politics of water. A comparative perspective. *Journal of Southern African Studies*, 34(4), 939–48.

Musemwa, M. 2008. Early struggles over water: from private to public water utility in the city of Bulawayo, Zimbabwe, 1894–1924. *Journal of Southern African Studies*, 34(4), 881–98.

Mutale, E. 2004. *The Management of Urban Development in Zambia*, Burlington, VT: Ashgate.

Mwandila, M. 2007. Discussion on Ndola City Council [conversation]. Personal communication, 12 Sept.

Myers, G. 2005. *Disposable Cities: Garbage, Governance and Sustainable Development in Urban Africa*, Burlington, VT: Ashgate.

Resident Development Committees (RDCs). 2007. Discussion with several Ndola-based RDCs [conversation]. Personal communication, June–Dec.

Schumaker, L. 2008. Slimes and death-dealing dambos: water, industry and the garden city on Zambia's Copperbelt. *Journal of Southern African Studies*, 34(4), 823–40.

Severn-Trent Plc. 2002. *PSP Options for Water Services in the City of Lusaka, Zambia*, Lusaka: Severn-Trent Plc.

Slinn, P. 1971. Commercial concessions and politics during the colonial period: the role of the British South Africa Company in Northern Rhodesia 1890–1964. *African Affairs*, 71(281), 365–4.

Spillet, P. 2002. Interview by Bob Carty. CBC. Available at: http://www.cbc.ca/news/features/water/spillet.html (accessed Jan. 2011).

Swyngedouw, E. 2004. *Social Power and the Urbanization of Water: Flows of Power,* Oxford: Oxford University Press.

Swyngedouw, E. 2007. Dispossessing H20: the contested terrain of water privatization. In N. Heynen, J. McCarthy, S. Prudham, and P. Robbins (eds), *Neoliberal Environments: False Promises and Unnatural Consequences*, pp. 51–62, New York: Routledge.

Watson, M. 1953. *African Highway: The Battle for Health in Central Africa,* London: Murray.

World Bank. 2011. *Bringing Water to Where it is Needed Most: Innovative Private Sector Participation in Water and Sanitation,* Washington, DC: International Finance Corporation of the World Bank Group.

13 Privatization of the urban water supply in Kenya

Policy framework for pro-poor provision[1]

O. A. K'Akumu

Introduction

Over the decades privatization has become a predominant paradigm in the provision of water both in the global North and South (Hukka, 2003). In the context of the latter, this chapter presents Kenya as a case study where experiments with the privatization of water began way back in 1995 (see K'Akumu and Appida, 2006). Seven years down the line, in 2002, a major law was passed as a reform package to provide the enabling environment for water privatization and marketization among other things (see Republic of Kenya, 2002). Specifically, the law is divided into two main parts: Part III – dealing with Water Resources Management and Part IV – dealing with Water Supply and Sewerage services (K'Akumu, 2008). However this chapter only deals with the latter and particularly tackles privatization of the urban water supply.

The chapter proceeds in two parts. The first part deals with the issues that initially drove the privatization project. At the international level, difficulties in provision in low- and middle-income nations have been cited as the main drivers of privatization. Nevertheless, for the case of Kenya, other issues were also at play including an increasing urban population, under-served slum areas, and the outbreaks of waterborne diseases. It is also worth noting that privatization can proceed in different ways based on different models (see Harris's framing piece, Chapter 10). The Kenyan project culminated into the 'Public Limited Company' (PLC) model following the initiatives of the 'Northern-based' German development partners.

The second section deals with the implications of privatization for the urban poor. This involves critical issues of social equity and participatory water governance that are attendant to water privatization as well as the concept of 'water for all' (see Chapter 10). Since privatization of water was likely to cut off supplies to the poor who may not provide a lucrative customer base to a formal water provider in a Southern context, the chapter brings up a policy framework that could be useful in ensuring provision for the poor. Aspects of this framework include: representation in public water agencies, a water development forum, a water services trust fund, social tariffication, contractual clauses or conditionalities, and alternative water suppliers.

Finally the chapter makes conclusions on the two major issues: first, that privatization in Kenya is hegemonic in nature, i.e. influenced by Northern ideas, institutions and experiences. Secondly, the policy framework for pro-poor provision has not been effectively employed in Kenya within the paradigm of privatization.

The difficulties in improving urban water supplies

Difficulties in provision in low- and middle-income nations

In the recent past and in many contexts, an urban water supply had long been seen as being provided by a piped system managed by a government agency. But governments in most low-income and many middle-income nations, including the Government of Kenya, had failed to provide for growing urban populations (UN-Habitat, 2003; Solo, 1999; Budds and McGranahan, 2003; Hardoy *et al.*, 2001; Anton, 1993; and more recently Bakker, 2010 – these sources are referenced throughout this section on difficulties that face municipal systems across multiple contexts). Despite substantial funding and investments both from governments and from international agencies, many providers had failed to expand water supply systems – especially to serve those living outside of central districts. Their failure to manage existing supplies, including the maintenance of piped systems, all too often led to large volumes of water lost to leaks and to illegal connections. A series of other difficulties have also often manifested across a range of contexts. Provisions for collecting payments from those who were connected were often deficient, and tariffs were not increased on par with service costs (and often fell below the cost of provision). The management of public utilities was also not transparent and had been subject to political interference, which allowed for corruption at multiple levels. Management was known to recruit staff using criteria other than merit and revenues had often been diverted away from the operation, maintenance, and expansion of the system towards personal or political benefit. Overstaffing had been common at lower levels, while the technical and management levels had often faced a shortage of qualified personnel as a result of political interference and inadequate or unreliable remuneration. There had also been problems with accessing finance. Public utilities often lacked access to the capital needed for service improvement and expansion and many did not qualify for private capital. Many public service providers also accumulated large debt burdens to the point where they became financially insolvent. Most had become dependent on central government to bail them out. The result has all too often been a situation where governments and utilities have had little or no capacity to expand to areas lacking services, to replace obsolete technology, to address leaks and to ensure adequate water quality and quantity. In short – there is a situation of widespread water governance failure (cf. Bakker, 2010).

Urban water supply in Kenya

Rapidly growing urban populations have complicated the urban water supply situation in Kenya. Table 13.1 indicates that, by 1999, Kenya's urban population was close to 10 million, and included slightly more than one-third of the nation's 28,686,607 inhabitants. In 2009 the urban population was more than 12 million, representing 32 percent of the total population of 38,610,808 (Republic of Kenya, 2010b: 31). An increasing urban population implies increasing demand on urban service providers, including for water. These increasing demands take place against a backdrop of a static institutional base of dwindling revenue, in addition to problems posed by obsolete technology. As such, in the context of urban areas of Kenya, this inevitably translated into inadequate services in the water sector. Tables 13.1 and 13.2 respectively show the urban populations and main sources of drinking water in Kenya.

The 2009 population census suggested that about 24.3 percent of the population of the capital city, Nairobi, had no access to any form of piped water (Table 13.2). The rest had direct or indirect access. There were those with water directly piped into dwellings (23.4 percent) and those who accessed water from outside their dwellings (52.3 percent). Having access to piped water and having a piped connection are two different things, especially in the informal settlements in which over half of Nairobi's population lives. In these settlements, the poor rarely have piped water connections to their homes, and have to access piped water from kiosks or vendors, which is relatively expensive and often inconvenient. As such, there is a need to consider the particular situation of the most impoverished and underserved in assessment of water provision and governance, particularly to consider the effects of privatization schemes such as that which has unfolded in urban areas of Kenya over recent decades.

According to the recent estimates, only 22 percent of slum households in Nairobi have water connections, while 75 percent accesses water through water vendors (UN-Habitat, 2007). An earlier review of water and sanitation in Nairobi had shown that, in informal settlements, only 11.7 percent of households had water directly available on plot and 85.6 percent obtained water from kiosks

Table 13.1 Urban population in Kenya in 1999 and 2009

Urban Center	Census Year	
	1999	*2009*
Nairobi	2,143,254	3,133,518
Mombasa	665,018	938,131
Kisumu	322,734	409,928
Nakuru	231,262	307,990
Others	6,614,723	7,697,808
Total urban population	9,996,991	12,487,375

Source: Republic of Kenya (2001: 3-1), and Republic of Kenya (2010: 31, 194)

Table 13.2 Percentage distribution of households by main source of water according to the 2009 Census

Source	Region			
	Nairobi	*Urban Kenya*	*Rural Kenya*	*Total Kenya*
Piped	75.70	53.13	15.71	29.96
Piped into dwelling	23.42	14.39	2.26	6.88
Piped	52.28	38.74	13.45	23.08
Not piped	24.30	46.87	84.29	70.04
Rain harvested	0.05	0.49	0.95	0.78
Borehole	5.97	10.47	11.31	10.99
Protected well	0.58	6.1	8.13	7.35
Protected spring	0.36	3.28	9.25	6.97
Unprotected well	0.18	2.2	7.82	5.68
Unprotected spring	0.09	1.53	6.22	4.44
Jabias	0.12	0.21	0.37	0.31
Stream/river	0.14	7.49	30.26	21.59
Vendor	16.45	13.4	2.32	6.54
Lake	0.01	0.48	1.51	1.12
Dam	0.08	0.53	2.83	1.95
Pond	0.20	0.61	2.97	2.07
Other sources	0.07	0.08	0.35	0.25

Source: Republic of Kenya (2011: 19)

(Alder, 1995). In addition, even when piped water connections are provided, there are often water shortages and the quality of the water is in doubt. There are also problems with regard to piped water management. In Nairobi, for example, during April–May 2003, there was no water in the piped system over the course of several weeks in certain parts of the city.

In other Kenyan urban centers there were also water shortage problems. Machakos, for example, has experienced a persistent water shortage (K'Akumu, 2004). In other cities, such as Mombasa (Munga *et al.*, 2005; Mwaguni, 2002) and Kisumu, there have been several large-scale outbreaks of waterborne diseases. In Kisumu, for instance, WHO's Global Task Force on Cholera Control (2010) reported incidences of cholera outbreaks in mid-October 1997, late March 2007 and March 2008. The Kisumu City Development Strategies 2004-9 identified waterborne diseases (e.g. typhoid, diarrhea) as some of the common diseases in the city. According to the document, 'diarrhea and typhoid has been closely linked to the limited supply of piped water and poor sanitary conditions, with higher concentration in the peri-urban areas where shallow-well water and pit latrines provide alternatives to the conventional water and sanitation systems' (UN-Habitat, n.d.).

For Nairobi, it was estimated that only 50 percent of the water can be accounted for (Onjala, 2002).[2] Corruption had also been reported in the water departments. As noted by Onjala (2002: 10):

> when the water rationing had taken root in Nairobi, it was discovered that many illegal structures ... had been built on top of water lines, and their owners have been siphoning the council water in collusion with council officers to provide car wash services etc. for many years.

This author also documents rampant corruption as one of the reasons why privatization of water had to be instituted in Kenya.

This is the context against which Kenya's water privatization unfolded. In short, it was a context with clear deficiencies in both water provision and water policy. This called for reforms in the water sector that aimed to fulfill two principal goals:

- To supply water of good quality and in sufficient quantities to meet the various needs for water while ensuring safety; and
- To establish an efficient and effective institutional framework to achieve systematic development and management of the water sector.

(Donde, 1997)

The government undertook a program of reform, which included delinking its own institutions from the provision of water and sanitation; in brief, privatization.

Privatization as a reform option

Privatization of water in Kenya

Unsurprisingly, reforms in the water sector in Kenya took the path of privatization following what has become a stock response to water governance problems in the contemporary policy domain. Simply put, privatization is the process and outcome of transferring the ownership and or control of a public enterprise to private hands. In the water sector the degree of ceding of the ownership and or control of services enterprises differs from country to country or from city to city, thereby yielding different typologies and pathways of privatization, as pointed out by Harris (Chapter 11). Furthermore K'Akumu (2006) highlighted the continuum of models that privatization in the water sector may take, including: PLC, Service contract, Management contract, Affermage contract, Lease contract, Concession contract, BOT, Joint venture and Divestiture (see also Stottman, 2000; Onjala, 2002; UN-Habitat, 2003; Budds and McGranahan, 2003; Hukka, 2003; Bakker 2003, 2010).

In Kenya, the privatization process began with a pilot water privatization project initiated in 1995 by German development partners, i.e. the then German Agency for Technical Co-operation (GTZ) and the German Bank of Reconstruction (KFW) in collaboration with the Urban Water and Sanitation

Management (UWASAM) Project (K'Akumu and Appida, 2006). This pilot process adopted the 'PLC model' that sought to transform the water and sewerage departments (WSDs) of municipal councils into public limited companies (PLCs). A PLC is a company limited by shares; it can be private if the private sector holds the shares and public if the shares are held by the public sector. In general, the public entity may be tempted to incorporate a PLC in order to enhance its autonomy from public control so as to effectively compete in the market. In the Western world, the 'PLC model' is commonly found in the Netherlands and Germany (UN-Habitat, 2003). Hence its application in Kenya could have been influenced by the German development partners; an action that explains the hegemonic character of water privatization in Kenya where institutions from the global North influence water governance structures in the South. This model is technically referred to as commercialization, which UN-Habitat (1998: 44) defines as 'a form of privatization which entails establishing and registering of water and sanitation companies owned wholly by local authorities'. Similarly, Jaglin (2002) defines commercialization as a form of privatization involving the transformation of a public body into a private company with public capital.

The pilot project in Kenya involved three individual municipalities of Eldoret, Kericho, and Nyeri (UN-Habitat, 1998) who incorporated private companies to undertake water supply in their respective jurisdictions. These PLCs were standard in nature with share capital distributed as shown in Table 13.3.

In Table 13.3, the subscribers holding one share each represented their offices on the board of directors (UN-Habitat, 1998). Apart from the three shareholders, the companies were to have not more than six other directors representing other stakeholders, including the local institutions, women and consumers. The Managing Director was to be an automatic member of the board of directors, bringing the total participants to ten individuals.

Whereas this experiment happened without a comprehensive legal and policy environment for water privatization, eventually a Water Act was solidified in 2002 that created a formal framework. With this new law, the country decided to adopt the pilot model for a comprehensive nation-wide privatization of water supply in which municipal authorities formed private companies to undertake the provision of water services within their jurisdictions. It suffices to say that the pilot project

Table 13.3 The distribution of share capital for water public limited companies

Shareholders	No. of shares	%
The municipal council	4,997	99.94
The mayor	1	0.02
The town clerk	1	0.02
The town treasurer	1	0.02
Total	5,000	100.00

Source: K'Akumu and Appida (2006)

influenced the content of the legislation. For instance, the Water Act of 2002, made express provision that no water provider shall be licensed to operate unless its services are to be provided on 'a *commercial basis* and in accordance with *sound business principles*' (Republic of Kenya, 2002). Hence the law prescribed commercialization. Therefore before the Water Act of 2002 only a handful of municipal authorities provided their denizens with water through their Water and Sanitation Departments (WSDs); in the rest of the municipal jurisdictions water was provided by a national public entity – the National Water Conservation and Pipeline Corporation (NWCPC). However following the enactment of the 2002 Water Law the later municipalities formed their own water PLCs to take over the water infrastructure from NWCPC, while the former transformed their WSDs into PLCs.

Privatization is not the only option

While privatization has been pursued in many contexts, there is also a range of critiques regarding its theoretical basis, conceptual objectives, tangible goals and implementation procedures. Many critics have also suggested that the assumed benefits of privatization have been overstated, and not borne out empirically. In terms of economic theory, privatization would not necessarily present an advantage over public enterprise (Eberhard, 2001) and privatization is certainly not a pre-condition for efficient management (Bhattacharyya *et al.*, 1994). The view that privatization was intended to achieve efficiency has been contested – for instance, Kinnersley (1994) suggested that the original idea was to remove existing and prospective debt from public accounts. With regard to actual performance, many experiences with water privatization in low- and middle-income nations have proved disappointing, especially with regard to expanding provision for lower-income groups. In addition, privatization has generally failed to attract private capital, reduce corruption, reduce tariffs and protect the interests of the poor (see Harris, Chapter 10; Chapter 11). In a study involving 24 municipalities in Spain, García-Sánchez (2006) found that privatization would not necessarily lead to greater efficiency in service provision. A similar study conducted in Africa also found no evidence of better performance in private utilities compared to state-owned utilities (see Kirkpatrick *et al.*, 2006).

The process itself of privatization has also been subject to criticism. The first criticism is that it has often been rushed, without first ensuring that adequate rules and regulations have been laid down (Postel, 1997). There has been implementation within inappropriate contexts, with little consideration for equity requirements, despite the importance of equity considerations in safeguarding the interests of the poor. Jaglin (2002) contends that achieving economic efficiency has often taken precedence over other equally important aims such as equity and consumer protection.

Given these tensions, the remainder of this chapter looks at the measures that have been put in place to ensure that the needs of the poor are addressed within the context of privatization.

Implications for the urban poor

The scale of urban poverty in Kenya is significant. An estimate for 1994 suggested close to 2 million urban poor, half of them in Nairobi (Republic of Kenya, 1996). The number has certainly increased rapidly since then; an official government report suggested that 49 percent of the urban population were below the poverty line in 1997, which implied more than 4 million urban poor (Republic of Kenya, 2000).

There is a strong spatial link between water provision and poverty in the cities of the South where, in typical cases, the urban poor live on city peripheries in terms of urban and service boundaries. This is largely because the price of land near city centers, where infrastructure and services are available, is far above what they can afford. In the peripheral areas, water supply infrastructure may not have been put in place or, where it has, the pressure in the pipes may be so low that this leads to persistent shortages, as those closer to the central areas, or those 'upstream' in the piped network, may use up the available supply (Ahmed and Sohail, 2003). When the poor are not living in the periphery, they are living in inner informal settlements that are still peripheral areas in terms of the infrastructure and service network.

If not located far from the service networks, the settlements occupied by the urban poor are likely to be located on hazardous sites such as valleys, flood plains, river banks and disused quarries, and these present many engineering difficulties for infrastructure provision (Anton, 1993). Supplying these areas with water may therefore involve high unit costs. When this is combined with the limited capacity of the population to pay for water, there is often a large gap between costs and potential cost-recovery. Private enterprises, seeking to maximize profits or minimize losses, may in theory avoid these areas if they are deemed to be not profitable.

Another problem with regard to improving water provision is that most of the settlements where the urban poor live in Kenya contravene official laws and regulations. Their land tenure is not legalized, they are unplanned (and often lack access roads), and their buildings contravene the building code. They are also regarded as an eyesore by middle- and upper-income groups. They are almost entirely left out of the programs and budgets of national and local authorities. In terms of water supply, most of these areas lack a piped water network, largely because providing connections to each house plot is difficult where plot ownership is unregistered (and perhaps contested) and settlements are unplanned.

In many informal settlements, there are no public rights of way to allow pipes to be laid and it is difficult and complicated to determine who 'owns' what and with whom any service contract should be signed. Large sections of the population in the informal settlements are tenants and the housing structures are often 'owned' by absentee landlords. A private water provider is likely to avoid any provision for household connections in these settlements. Yet, the inhabitants of these settlements have a constitutional right to water services. Specifically, as part of the economic and social rights, the Kenyan constitution states that every person has the right 'to clean and safe water in adequate quantities' (Republic of Kenya, 2010a: 32).

Participatory management approaches

Goldin (in her framing piece on participation in this volume, Chapter 16) and the other authors of this volume see participation as one of the hegemonic instruments of the contemporary water governance. Hence it is not surprising that the Water Act of 2002 made provision for a participatory approach to the management of water services. Participation has been recognized and promoted in contemporary water governance with the aim to empower communities and ensure better outcomes in service provision (see also Morinville and Harris, Chapter 19). In this regard, the Water Act of 2002 (under part IV dealing with Water Supply and Sewerage) spelled out instruments and institutions that, potentially, the poor or their advocates may use to ensure that the former also get their rightful share of the water. These instruments and institutions include provisions to ensure representation in public water agencies and water development forums. This section looks briefly at these instruments and institutions that water users can engage to participate in decisions around water use and access.

Representations in public water agencies

The Water Services Regulatory Board is meant to regulate the operations of water services boards and water service providers. For instance, the slogan of the regulator is: 'Ensuring access to quality water services for all'. Currently, the provision is that the Minister in charge of water resources appoints members to the board, while the President appoints the Chair. The Water Services Board too has to be constituted by the Minister. When making appointments to these two boards, the Minister is meant to consider, among other things, 'the degree to which water users, or water users of particular kinds, are represented on the board ... at the time of appointment' (Republic of Kenya, 2002).

Although the law does not specifically refer to the poor, in this case, the poor can be considered as 'water users of a particular kind' (special interest group) or low-powered stakeholders, and therefore they have a right to be represented on these boards. In theory, therefore, the boards present the poor with a forum through which they can lobby and push for their right to access to water supply. There are various ways in which access can be achieved. Unfortunately while constituting these boards the Ministers have not given consideration to the poor's representation, thereby overlooking their potential role toward inclusive service provision (see also Goldin, Chapter 16, for problems around representation and participation).

Water development forum

The Act, under part IV dealing with Water Supply and Sewerage, also provides for another forum known as the National Water Services Strategy. This is another instrument for participatory planning in the water sector. The law requires the Minister in charge of water supplies to formulate the strategy through public consultation. This should provide the poor with the possibility to air their grievances and influence water development policy in the country. One of the objectives of the National Water Services Strategy is: 'to institute arrangements to ensure that at all times there is in every area of Kenya a person capable of providing water supply' (Republic of Kenya, 2002).

This is meant to ensure that no area is left without a water supply program. The strategy would contain details such as:

- Existing water services;
- The number and location of persons who are not being provided with basic water supply;
- A plan for the extension of water services to under-served areas;
- A time frame for the plan; and
- An investment program.

All these provisions should create some opportunity to the urban poor, who form the bulk of the under-served settlements, to be considered in water supply programs and strategies. Indeed this has been done in the first National Water Services Strategy running from 2007 to 2015. The strategy has dedicated a chapter on: Water Supply in the Settlements of the Urban Poor. In this context the strategic goal is: 'To achieve the MDG by fast tracking affordable and sustainable access to safe water in the settlements of the urban poor' (Republic of Kenya, 2007: 15).

The shortcoming of the strategy is that the law did not make any provisions to guide its implementation in the new context. A possible way of getting around this shortcoming might be to use various other water management instruments and institutions such as trust funds, social tariffication, contractual clauses and alternative water providers.

Water services trust fund

This is one of the reform institutions in the water sector, formed by a trusts deed under the Water Act of 2002. The objective of the fund is to help finance water provision in areas of Kenya that are without adequate water services (Republic of Kenya, 2002). According to the Act, the activities of the fund are financed by an 'exchequer'. Additional financing comes from donor institutions interested in the improvement of water services such as the Danish International Development Agency (Danida), German Development Agency (GTZ) and the German Development Bank (KfW), the Swedish International Development Agency

(Sida), European Union (EU), United Nations Children's Fund (UNICEF), and the African Development Bank (AfDB).

The fund has four main programs for water financing: Community Project Cycle (CPC) for rural water and sanitation projects, Urban Project Cycle (UPC) for urban and sanitation projects, Water Resources Users Association Development Cycle (WDC) for water resource projects and Output Based Aid (OBA), a micro-credit window within the World Bank and facilitated through K-Rep Bank, a local poor banking institution.

The UPC is intended to fund water and sanitation in the low-income urban areas. It has three main programs.

1   Urban Projects Concept is funded by KfW, European Union and GTZ. In 2007, the program piloted the kiosk system and on-site sanitation in three urban locations in Kenya. Depending on the success of this pilot projects, the fund avers that plans are underway for up scaling it to the poor urban countrywide. Secondly in 2009, the fund published two calls: one for proposals for Lake Victoria North Water Services Board jurisdiction and another for all jurisdictions countrywide.
2   Ecosan is a program funded by GTZ and SIDA.
3   Majidata is an information program providing pro-poor database covering all the urban low-income areas of Kenya funded by UN-Habitat, the German Development Bank (KfW), Google and GIZ. The database provides information that may assist other actors to prepare tailor-made water supply and sanitation programs for the urban slums and low-income planned areas located within their service jurisdictions. This should be logged as the greatest achievement for the fund and is in line with Baker's (Chapter 3) emphasis on information technology as a potentially empowering tool for water provision.

As can be seen, as far as concerns provision for the urban poor, the fund has little to report despite being in existence for eight years. Therefore in this context, it is underperforming its mandate. However the high concentration of hegemonic institutions supporting these programs cannot escape the discerning eye. These institutions are hegemonic in the sense that, with the exception of AfDB (if its water governance policy is any different from the rest), they are either European or globally based. Therefore water privatization agenda in Kenya should be understood, in part, as driven by hegemonic and external forces. Consistent with the broader theorization of hegemony (Sneddon, Chapter 2), this does not imply they are necessarily harmful. Yet, it is nonetheless important to identify the ways that water privatization in Kenya is driven by hegemonic forces, recognizing their external points of origin.

Lastly the National Water Services Strategy 2007–15, as part of its medium-term indicators, tasked the fund to do the following concerning water supply in the settlements of the urban poor (Republic of Kenya, 2007):

1   To finance the design of national technical and managerial standards for low-cost technologies by 2008
2   To identify by 2008 and help reduce, annually, the number of service areas supplied by providers who use raw water from non-controlled sources
3   To avail baseline data for all settlements of the urban poor by 2009
4   To publish and disseminate widely, one example of best practices for the service provision of the urban poor not later than the end of the year
5   To support water service providers to provide water to 500,000 new consumers annually from 2008

Available evidence shows that only number 3 above could have been achieved, hence based on the evaluation on the national water services strategy, the fund is not providing the expected service to the poor.

Social tariffication

Social tariffication refers to charging a 'social' rather than a 'commercial' tariff. It is a policy instrument that may be used to ensure that the poor get water in instances where charges based on full cost-recovery would be too expensive. The Water Act of 2002 created the Water Services Regulatory Board whose function, among others, is 'to develop guidelines for the fixing of tariffs for the provision of water services'. The board has since come up with a tariff guideline whose objective it says is to establish tariffs that balance commercial, social and ecological interests by ensuring access to all while allowing water providers to recover 'justified costs'. This objective engrains social tariffication.

Social tariffication may work for those poor citizens who are connected to the main water network but who may otherwise not be able to afford the market price. Particularly given that low-income households may consume low volumes of water, this policy enables the first or minimal water needs to be consumed at low cost. The 'social tariff' can price the first block of consumption (which corresponds to basic needs) cheaply, and thereafter each block of consumption becomes progressively more expensive (UN-Habitat, 1989). Again, the poor may benefit from this policy instrument, but would be more likely to do so if they could also command influence in the Water Services Regulatory Board, where tariffs would be determined.

Contractual clauses or conditionalities

When the Water Services Regulatory Board grants a license the specified tariffs become an automatic conditionality that the water provider must adhere to. Nevertheless the law allows the board a window to insert other conditionalities and this can be used for the benefit of the poor. For example, as part of its contractual obligation, the board may require that under the license a provider must extend the water network to an area which is unserved – for instance, to informal settlements or to communities living on the peripheral areas of the services boundaries. Failure to perform such conditionality would constitute a breach of contract leading to withdrawal of the license.

Again, it is important that representatives from urban poor organizations, or their advocates, sit on this board, so that they can influence policy in the way that has been suggested. If they are under-represented, the Board may ignore their plight and promote other agendas that may be detrimental to them. Being on the Board would also allow them to ensure that the licensee performs according to the conditions attached to the license.

Alternative water suppliers

Given the number of urban dwellers who get unsatisfactory or no service at all from the conventional piped water network, a number of alternative water suppliers have emerged to address these shortfalls (see Table 13.2). From the table it can be seen that their percentage contribution to urban water supply is significant; in Nairobi they supply about a quarter and in urban areas in general about half of households. The alternative water suppliers include drinking water companies that supply water in disposable bottles, which are sold in supermarkets, shops, kiosks and even by hawkers. There are also those who supply drinking water to offices using large returnable containers. Water tankers supply homes during periods of serious water shortages; however, because of transportation costs, their overall costs are bound to be higher than the standard piped provision. Therefore they may not be considered an option for the poor.

There is another group of providers who serve the poor; they include well-owners and cart-pushers. Cart-pushers provide tap water for those who are not served by taps, while well-owners provide cheaper water than the official supplier, catering for those unable to afford official rates, while also providing water for all during shortages. However, the quality of this water is less certain. Hence although the water may be affordable, it may be substandard.

Studies have revealed that alternative low-income suppliers can provide water at an acceptable standard. The studies also show that alternative suppliers hold several advantages over official suppliers where providing water for the poor is concerned. These advantages may include efficiency, cost-effectiveness, good customer relations and lower rates (Solo, 1999; Collignon and Vezina, 2000).

There is a potential for alternative providers to cater to the needs of the occupants of informal settlements and other low-income groups. The role of the informal economy is recognized in other sectors; for example, in the petroleum subsector of the energy sector, when it was being liberalized, the informal sector in the form of independent dealers was recognized. The formal water companies, including foreign ones with sophisticated technology and management systems, can only be relevant to economies or societies that are 'formal' in nature. They are not appropriate for those living in informal settlements, many of whom do not even have a billing address.

Carpenter has suggested that the future of privatization of water in low-income countries lies with the small-scale provider, and that its success will measure up to the performance of their counterparts in the liberalization of the telecommunications digital/wireless industry: 'Why not look to household point-of-use purification of water as a viable alternative to massive new infrastructure, particularly in rural areas and in urban slums, which will not see that infrastructure for years, even decades' (Carpenter, 2003: 101).

Unfortunately, the Water Act of 2002 did not recognize the alternative water suppliers despite the role they play in providing services to the under-served. Instead, the Act even tightened the rules for their operations. In section 56, it stipulates that:

> No person shall, within the limits of supply of a licensee [formal water supplier] provide water services to more than 20 households; or supply more than 25,000 liters of water a day for domestic purposes, or more than 100,000 liters of water a day for any purpose, except under the authority of a license.
>
> (Republic of Kenya, 2002)

This authority is in the form of a supply contract. Applying for a water supply license is much more difficult and complicated than applying for a street vendor's license from City Hall. An alternative water provider cannot apply for direct licensing by the regulatory board. They can only supply water by contract through the Water Supply Board.

There are no overt policy arrangements to encourage alternative water suppliers, despite their importance as supplementary suppliers essential for large sections of the lower-income groups. It is possible for the poor to influence issues through the boards by licensing these alternative water providers. But the policy should encourage and support the operations of alternative water providers/ suppliers to ensure that the poor get a basic water supply in spite of 'privatization' or 'licensing'.

However, alternative suppliers should only be considered as a stopgap measure. Policy measures should seek to ensure good-quality formal provision for all, otherwise the poor are left as captive consumers of 'informal' rather than standard and more substantive services.

Conclusions

In Kenya, as in so many other low- and middle-income nations of the global South, provision of water to the urban and rural populations remains largely unsatisfactory. One response was for government to de-link itself from the water supply business. This could be done by relinquishing the management to stakeholders (mainly the consumers) or by privatizing water services. Given the limitations of relying on community self-help water projects, privatization was considered a viable option, albeit not without influence from the global North. It has been shown that privatization in Kenya was an initiative of the German donor institutions. Secondly the high concentration of 'Northern-based' institutions supporting one of the policy instruments for pro-poor water provision underscores the hegemonic nature of water governance in Kenya under the privatization paradigm. It appears from this case study that privatization does bring risks in terms of failing to address welfare issues for the poor.

This chapter has outlined and discussed the policy framework that may be useful in ensuring the welfare of the poor within the paradigm of water privatization, especially as provided for in the Water Act of 2002. Concerning participatory management approaches, the poor or their representatives have not been appointed to the boards of public water agencies. It has become apparent that representation of the poor in the various public water boards has been ignored by the constituting authorities, while this representation is mandatory for ensuring the needs of the poor are met. Secondly, whereas the interests of the poor have been considered in the National Water Services Strategy, the pro-poor strategies have not been implemented, especially by the Water Services Trust Fund – the only statutory body created by the Water Act 2002 to implement pro-poor water supply and development programs.

Further the Water Services Regulatory Board has come up with a tariff structure that it claims will balance 'commercial, social and ecological interests', thereby applying the concept of social tariffication. Nevertheless further research needs to be done to establish whether this is the true scenario. The current and potential role of alternative water suppliers must be recognized and supported by the Act, so that they can supplement the formal or official providers. However, alternative suppliers should only be considered as a stopgap measure. Policy measures should seek to ensure good-quality formal provision for all, otherwise the poor are left as captive consumers of 'informal' rather than standard services. Lastly contractual clauses and alternative water supplier strategies do not seem to have been applied at all. Therefore it is apt to conclude that the policy instruments for pro-poor provision have not been effectively employed.

The lessons we learn from the Kenyan case study are not entirely new. Overall, the case follows the global trend where privatization of water is often a hegemonic project recommended or influenced by global donor institutions – so much effort is employed in drafting frameworks for pro-poor provisions, but toward which little or no actual attention is paid.

Notes

1 Based on O. A. K'Akumu, Privatization of the urban water supply in Kenya: policy options for the poor. *Environment & Urbanization*, 16(2) (2004), 213–22. Reproduced by permission of SAGE Publications Ltd., London, Los Angeles, New Delhi, Singapore and Washington, DC. Copyright © K'Akumu, 2004.

2 Unaccounted-for water is a common feature of water supplies in the Global South. The World Bank estimated the unaccounted-for water at one-third (see World Bank, 2004) while Kirkpatrick *et al.* (2006) confirmed by empirical analysis for Africa at 29 and 35 percent for private and public suppliers respectively

References

Ahmed, N., and Sohail, M. 2003. Alternate water supply arrangement in peri-urban localities: *awami* (people's) tanks in Orangi township, Karachi. *Environment and Urbanization,* 15(2), 33–42.

Alder, G. 1995. Tackling poverty in Nairobi's informal settlements: developing an institutional strategy. *Environment and Urbanization,* 7(2), 85-108.

Anton, D. J. 1993. *Thirsty Cities: Urban Environments and Water Supply in Latin America,* Ottawa: International Development Research Centre.

Bakker, K. 2003. Achipelagos and networks: urbanization and water privatization in the South. *Geographical Journal,* 169(4), 328-41.

Bakker, K. 2010. *Privatizing Water: Governance Failure and the World's Urban Water Crisis,* Ithaca, NY: Cornell University Press.

Bhattacharyya, A., Parker, E., and Raffie, K. 1994. An examination of the effect of ownership on the relative efficiency of public and private water utilities. *Land Economics,* 70(2), 197–209.

Budds, J., and McGranahan, G. 2003. Are debates on water privatization missing the point? Experiences from Africa, Asia and Latin America. *Environment and Urbanization,* 15(2), 87–114.

Carpenter, G. 2003. Making markets work for clean water. In *Balancing Competing Water Uses: Present Status and New Prospects: Proceedings of the 12th Stockholm Water Symposium,* Stockholm: Stockholm International Water Institute.

Collignon, B., and Vezina, M., 2000. *Independent Water and Sanitation Providers in African Cities: Full Report of a Ten-Country Study,* Washington, DC: Water and Sanitation Program.

Donde, F. O. 1997. *Water Supply Situation in Kenya: Partnership in the Water Sector for Cities in Africa,* report of the Cape Town consultants, Nairobi: United Nations Centre for Human Settlements.

Eberhard, R. 2001. *Supply Pricing of Urban Water in South Africa: Theoretical Approaches to Urban Water Pricing – A Review,* Working Paper 1, Cape Town and Johannesburg: Palmer Development Group.

García-Sánchez, I. M. 2006. Efficiency measurement in Spanish local government: the case of municipal water services. *Review of Policy Research,* 23(2), 355-72.

Hardoy, J. E., Mitlin, D., and Satterthwaite, D. 2001. *Environmental Problems in an Urbanizing World: Finding Solutions for Cities in Africa, Asia and Latin America,* London: Earthscan.

Hukka, J. J. 2003. Refuting the paradigm of water services privatization. *Natural Resource Forum,* 27(2), 142–55.

Jaglin, S. 2002. The right to water versus cost recovery: participation, urban water supply and the poor in Sub-Saharan Africa. *Environment and Urbanization,* 14(1), 231–46.

K'Akumu, O. A. 2004. Privatization of urban water supply in Kenya: policy options for the poor. *Environment and Urbanization,* 16(2), 213–22.

K'Akumu, O. A. 2006. Privatization model for water enterprise in Kenya. *Water Policy,* 8(6), 539–57.

K'Akumu, O. A. 2008. Mainstreaming the participatory approach in water resource governance: the 2002 water law in Kenya. *Development,* 51(1), 56–62.

K'Akumu, O. A., and Appida, O. 2006. Privatization of urban water service provision: the Kenyan experiment. *Water Policy,* 8(4), 313–24.

Kinnersley, D. 1994. *Coming Clean: The Politics of Water and the Environment,* London: Penguin Books.

Kirkpatrick, C., Parker, D., and Zhang, Y. 2006. An empirical analysis of state and private-sector provision of water services in Africa. *World Bank Economic Review,* 20(1), 143–63.

Munga, D., Kitheka, J. U., Mwaguni, S. M., Barongo, J., Massa, H. S., Mwangi, S., Ong'anda, H., Mdoe, F., and Opello, G. 2005. *Vulnerability and Pollution of Groundwater in the Kisauni Area, Mombasa, Kenya,* Project on Assessment of Pollution Status and Vulnerability of Water Supply Aquifers in African Cities, Final Report, Mombasa: UNEP/UNESCO/UN-HABITAT/ECA. Available at: http://www.unep.org/groundwaterproject/Countries/Kenya/Report/April2005_full.pdf (accessed Nov. 2012).

Mwaguni, S. M. 2002. Public health problems in Mombasa District: a case study on sewage management. M.Sc. University of Nairobi.

Onjala, J. 2002. *Good Intentions, Structural Pitfalls: Early Lessons from Urban Water Commercialisation Attempts in Kenya,* CDR Working Paper 2.2, Copenhagen: Center for Development Research.

Postel, S. 1997. *Last Oasis: Facing Water Scarcity,* New York: Norton.

Republic of Kenya. 1996. *Welfare Monitoring Survey II: 1994 Basic Report,* Nairobi: Central Bureau of Statistics, Office of the Vice-President and Ministry of Planning and National Development.

Republic of Kenya. 2000. *Second Report on Poverty in Kenya: Incidence and Depth of Poverty,* Nairobi: Human Resources and Social Services Department and Central Bureau of Statistics, Ministry of Finance and Planning.

Republic of Kenya. 2001. *1999 Population and Housing Census,* vol. 1, *Population Distribution by Administrative Areas and Urban Centres,* Nairobi: Central Bureau of Statistics and Ministry of Finance and Planning.

Republic of Kenya. 2002. *The Kenya Gazette,* suppl. 107(Acts No. 9), 935–1053.

Republic of Kenya, 2007. *The National Water Services Strategy (NWSS),* Nairobi: Ministry of Water and Irrigation.

Republic of Kenya, 2010a. *The Constitution of Kenya, 2010,* Nairobi: National Council for Law Reporting with the Authority of the Attorney General.

Republic of Kenya, 2010b. *2009 Kenya Population and Housing Census,* vol. 1B, *Population Distribution by Political Units,* Nairobi: National Bureau of Statistics.

Republic of Kenya. 2011. *2009 Kenya Population and Housing Census,* vol. 15, *Analytical Report on Housing Conditions, Amenities and Household Assets,* Nairobi: National Bureau of Statistics, Ministry of State for Planning, National Development and Vision 2030.

Solo, T. M. 1999. Small-scale entrepreneurs in the urban water and sanitation market. *Environment and Urbanization,* 11(1), 117–32.

Stottman, W. 2000. The role of private sector in the provision of water and wastewater services in urban areas. In A. K. Biswas and J. I. Uitto (eds), *Water for Urban Areas: Challenges and Perspectives,* pp. 156–99, Tokyo: United Nations University Press.

UN-Habitat. 1989. *Conservation of Drinking Water Supplies: Techniques for Low-Income Settlements,* Nairobi: United Nations Centre for Human Settlements.

UN-Habitat. 1998. *Privatization of Municipal Services in East Africa: A Governance Approach to Human Settlements Management,* Nairobi: United Nations Centre for Human Settlements.

UN-Habitat. 2003. *Water and Sanitation in the World's Cities,* London: Earthscan.

UN-Habitat. 2007. *UN-HABITAT and the Kenya Slum Upgrading Programme*, Nairobi: United Nations Human Settlements Programme.

UN-Habitat. n.d. *Kisumu City Development Strategies (2004–2009),* Kisumu City: Kisumu City Council and Centre for Development and Planning Management. Available at: www.unhabitat.org/downloads/docs/3589_41974_kisumu_cds.pdf   (accessed   Sept. 2012).

World Bank. 2004. Reforming Infrastructure: Privatization, Regulation, and Competition, World Bank Policy Research Report, Oxford: Oxford University Press.

World Health Organization (WHO). 2010. Global Task Force on Cholera Control: Cholera Country Profile: Kenya. Available at: http://www.who.int/cholera/countries/ KenyaCountryProfile2010.pdf (accessed Sept. 2012).

14 Privatization, marketization, commoditization as dominant themes in water governance

A response

Shiney Varghese

Taking the water sector as the lens, the three chapters and framing note presented in this section focus on one of the key concepts developed over the last 20 years: the increasing focus on the private sector as central to global water governance. The idea that water is an economic good was first articulated in 1992 in the Dublin Principles (1992), which said: 'Water has an economic value in all its competing uses and should be recognized as an economic good.'[1] This fourth principle has often been cited as having provided the rationale for various policies that have since been introduced in water sector.

In her framing note, Leila Harris introduces a very helpful distinction between the concepts of privatization, marketization, commoditization, etc. as distinct issues, and how *unbundling* them may be key to understanding the dominant water governance paradigm. In her chapter on 'Variable histories and geographies of marketization and privatization' (Chapter 11), she concretizes the argument further by exploring the different trajectories of the water governance experienced in the United States (private to public), France (public to private) over the last century, and juxtaposes these with various Southern experiences of privatization. What emerges from her article is that, while in all these cases the existing system is identified as inefficient and in need of change, the similarities stop there.

In '(Dis)connecting the flow, steering the waters' (Chapter 12), Hillary Waters proceeds in a similar vein and explores Zambian water governance experiences from the 1930s to the present. She stresses that neoliberal privatization is only the most recent moment in the long history of private control of water resources. Dispossession of local communities had proceeded earlier in the 20th century by other means – including straightening the Zambezi river and filling up the swamps in the 1930s, and building the Kariba Dam in the 1950s. Across these phases, she points out, water governance is characterized by the recognition of some water uses (and actors) over others, in the name of 'apparent objectivity' that is 'often created through the use of scientific or "expert" language that "unbundles" or "abstracts" water from its socio-political context' (Waters, Chapter 12).

Yet with increasing urbanization and unprecedented growth in informal settlements, water supply and sanitation has become one of the biggest challenges in most developing countries. In the chapter on 'Privatization of the urban water supply in Kenya' (Chapter 13), O. A. K'Akumu looks at this water crisis experienced by urban communities such as those in Nairobi, and shows how the Water Act of 2002, with its emphasis on participatory water governance, has failed to deal with the crisis. He speculates that if affected communities were represented in the water governance structures, the outcome may have been different, while he and others have recognized participation as one of the hegemonic instruments of the contemporary water governance (see K'Akumu, Chapter 13; Goldin, Chapter 16).

All three case studies in this section implicitly remind us that, for most of last century, water management was dominated by the view referred to sometimes as the 'state-hydraulic paradigm' (see Sneddon, Chapter 2; Baker, Chapter 3), which often included the sense that water was to be made freely available for meeting the needs of legitimate water users.[2] As Hillary Waters's chapter reminds us, this usually excluded those who were already marginalized – we see similar trajectories regarding *aadivasis* (also referred to as tribals) in India, blacks in Zambia or South Africa, or indigenous groups in Bolivia. But following the recognition by the 1980s that there was a crisis in clean water availability in many parts of the world, this 'supply-management' oriented water governance began facing constraints.

The chapters also remind us that the simultaneous unbundling of water from its socio-economic context, and its association with concepts of efficiency (in the context of crisis) and expertise (in the context of participation), pave the way for ideas related to privatization and commodification of water (along with the use of market instruments) to become hegemonic in the realm of water governance. Further, the chapters implicitly recognize that the reforms which have been carried out since the sense of crisis emerged have been informed by what I would call an imperial ecological sensibility – a sensibility that evaluates ecological resources in terms of value, and presumes that the crisis was caused by a failure to value water. It was professedly to remedy this failure that the privatization, commodification and marketization of water has often been introduced.

To extend the spirit of these chapters, which by and large refuse to talk of a monolithic water sector, it may be helpful to stress that local specificities, including the history of water appropriation contributes to the 'variegated' (Sneddon, Chapter 2; Harris, Chapters 10, 11) ways in which privatization is experienced locally. A brief review of water-related struggles by local communities show that they recognize the specificities of their situation and accordingly adopt varied strategies both spatially and temporally. Many of them arose in opposition to initiatives in which water was abstracted from its socio-economic and cultural context and diverted for activities deemed to be more 'efficient', and/or to scale up economic benefit – both in the case of water services and water as a resource. This is the case for many of the anti-dam struggles across the world (including the Narmada Bachao Andolan, NBA, in India in the 1980s, perhaps the first localized anti-dam struggle to forge alliances with national and international solidarity networks). Even as these movements share an understanding of the processes of abstraction and diversion of water, their strategies and forms of resistance are often articulated in different ways, depending on the location and geopolitical realities: as an environmental campaign, a campaign to protect culturally important spaces, a campaign to protect homes and livelihoods, or a combination of these. Temporally too they vary: the campaigns are adept in shifting their focus in response to the new realities on the ground.[3]

Similarly, in the Bolivian water privatization experience, the forms of resistance that developed were influenced not only by the fact that Bolivia is largely an indigenous nation, but also by prehistories of water governance. While Bolivia was highly indebted to International Financial Institutions (IFIs), and while it did have its share of extractive industries (and was in these senses part of the global economy), it did not have a well-established water infrastructure. Water governance was mostly in the realm of self-organized local organizations. In the medium-sized city of Cochabamba, the community-led Association of Potable Water Community Systems of the South Side of Cochabamba, or ASICASUR, was responsible for over 40 percent of water supply. The farmers around Cochabamba city were also heavily invested and interested in the governance of the region's limited water resources. Both these groups saw the World Bank imposed privatization as a threat to their own interests, as the private entity Aguas del Tunari was awarded exclusive right to water resources in Cochabamba, including current infrastructure as well as to any future sources they might need to supply to their customers! When the privatization also resulted in water rates increases for consumers of the utility (reported to be between 40 and 200 percent), and ASICASUR members were billed for their water, Cochabambinos were out on the streets protesting. Oscar Olivera, a factory worker and union organizer who was familiar with mass mobilization, emerged as one of the key leaders of the movement that included unions, farmers, city residents, civil society groups and progressive civil society leaders. It was the coalition of these multiple groups, *la coordinadora*, with some support from international solidarity networks, that forced the country's leadership to withdraw from the contract (Shultz, 2003: 4).[4]

The privatization experience in South Africa was very different from that in Bolivia. Given its history of apartheid and international isolation, it was not indebted to IFIs such as the World Bank advocating for water privatization as part of structural adjustment programs (SAPs). Yet, as an arid, still developing country that had to deal with water scarcity early on, the newly independent nation was quick to take up the doctrine of water as an economic good. The Bank made sure that the new country was familiar with its prescription.

What made the uptake of such doctrine distinctive in this context was that the emphasis on the economic viability of the water supply sector, and on water as an economic good, occurred in parallel with a move towards the constitutional recognition of a right to water. Once the ANC-led government introduced payment for water services as a policy option, it was implemented in various municipalities. This resulted in water prices going up and becoming unaffordable, especially for those in the townships of cities such as Johannesburg. It appeared as if the new state was experimenting with different forms of water governance. For example, the state sought to apply market instruments in publicly owned (but independently managed) water utilities such as Johannesburg Waters, which then entered into a contract with Suez (a French water multinational), resulting in a form of governance closer to a public–private partnership. The use of prepaid meters and payment for water services were rationalized in the name of economic viability, as if there were no other options.

When a cholera outbreak in August 2000 killed over 200 people and infected thousands in KwaZulu-Natal (one of the poorest provinces in South Africa), communities in the area and campaigners calling for free access to water for basic domestic needs were quick to point out that prepaid water meters and forced water cut-offs were primarily responsible for the outbreak. They were joined by South African Municipal Workers' Union (SAMWU), which had been opposing water privatization, and civil society groups questioning neoliberal trends in governance more generally. As this happened barely three months after the Bolivian water protest, in which one of the protesters was shot dead, the world took note of the negative implications of privatization. A nascent international solidarity network (which later evolved into what is now known as the global water justice movement) gained strength from these struggles and worked to ensure that these struggles were not ignored in the global arena.

Partially in response to the cholera outbreak and the negative attention it attracted (besides other domestic concerns), South Africa introduced the policy of 'free lifeline', which allocated 25 liters per person per day and 6,000 liters per month for a family (assuming eight members in the family). However, even this proved inadequate. Poorer households of the community often had more members, and according to activists in the Coalition Against Water Privatization, they often would go through their quota in less than two weeks, and then would have no access to safe water unless they were able to pay for it. Moreover, the incremental price was disproportionately high for those consuming just above the lifeline, and the block tariff system was skewed in favor of those who consumed very large quantities of water (Bond, 2006).[5]

The struggles against bottled water of the last two decades are marked by a similar diversity, with the exception perhaps of their shared opposition to the commodification of water in broad senses. In North America and Europe, most of the opposition has been driven by a rejection of consumerism and the appalling generation of huge amounts of plastic waste. To a lesser extent, some of the opposition has also been leveraged in an attempt to express solidarity with those opposing bottling plants in local communities. These campaigns could take place either nationally or internationally (examples include the Stop Nestle Campaign, a coalition that has come together in several towns across USA to challenge Nestle's effort to appropriate their water, with some towns passing local laws establishing the fundamental 'right to water for people and nature' and the 'rights of nature').[6] In India, by contrast, the opposition has not been directed to bottled water as a consumer product so much, but to the impacts of the bottling plants threatening the right to water for domestic use and basic livelihoods. Such struggles have often been led by the already marginalized *aadivasis* (indigenous groups) as with the case of Plachimada, Kerala (Varghese, 2010).[7]

Just as there are differences in governance practices, then, there are varied registers along which the privatization battles are fought. While these struggles have helped to slow or arrest the advancement of particular forms of governance practices that played out in those moments, neoliberal approaches continue to pervade the water governance realm. For example, the Water Resources Group (based at the International Finance Corporation) has emerged as a leading group in extending the idea of water as an economic good to other areas of water use, such as agriculture and global water governance (Varghese, 2012).[8]

Another crucial issue is raised by Waters (Chapter 12), who points out that the neoliberal ideology selectively applies the notion of payment for services to some sectors such as domestic water supply and sanitation, but rarely for corporate sectors. Thus, in general, the Zambian mining sector does not pay towards the cleaning up of the pollutants. Zambia is not alone in this. Even as nations around the world are eager to treat water as an economic good, they are all too often not asking polluters to pay for their water use, and to clean it up.

Once again, ironically, the neoliberal framework has come up with an answer: the notion of water as an economic good is now extended to other areas including functions of nature: improved water quality, or rather water quality credits, is increasingly becoming a tradable commodity. Rather than requiring the polluters to lower their impact on water quality so as to meet water quality regulation standards, trading would allow polluters to pay another entity who would then reduce their own impact on water quality.[9] The polluters can buy cheap credits, and continue polluting, without reducing their pollution footprint!

When the right to water and water for ecosystems is recognized within a framework in which water is treated as primarily an economic good, then the former often becomes secondary. For these policies to function, they need to be 'unbundled' from the commodified framework of water governance. The notion of hegemony that is explored through these chapters can hopefully help us do this, and develop policies that when applied on the ground can help uphold the right to water.

Notes

1 The fourth principle of the Dublin Principles (1992) goes on to say that 'Within this principle, it is vital to recognize first the basic right of all human beings to have access to clean water and sanitation at an affordable price. Past failure to recognize the economic value of water has led to wasteful and environmentally damaging uses of the resource. Managing water as an economic good is an important way of achieving efficient and equitable use, and of encouraging conservation and protection of water resources.' Equity and water stewardship seem to be the main concerns behind this principle, yet only the economic elements of this principle have often been taken up in terms of implementation.

2 I borrow the term from Neda A. Zawahri, and Oliver Hensengerth (2012) who use it in their recent study on domestic environmental activists and the governance of the Ganges and Mekong Rivers in India and China.

3 E.g. in the 1990s the NBA shifted its focus away from World Bank (once they were successful both in getting the Bank to withdraw from funding the dam, and in influencing the outcome of the World Commission of Dams). Their focus has since been to hold the state and central governments accountable to the official promises regarding the height of the dam and rehabilitation packages.

4 In the interests of transparency, I should add that the Institute for Agriculture and Trade Policy that I am affiliated with was part of the international solidarity network that supported the anti-water privatization efforts in Bolivia and South Africa. Daily dispatches from Jim Schultz, Director of Democracy Center in Cochabamba, helped the world keep up with the developments in Cochabamba.

5 See above; Patrick Bond (2006; at the time with municipal services project, University of the Witwatersrand, Johannesburg) played a similar role in the context of South Africa.

6 Ruth Caplan, Alliance for Democracy, Washington, DC, email conversation, Oct. 2012. For more information see Stop Nestle Waters (2012).

7 Personal Conversations with Mylamma (the *aadivasi* leader of the struggle) and others in the Coca-Cola Virudha Samara Samiti (2002–5). For details, see the box in IATP's letter to the United Nations Independent Expert on Right to Water (Varghese, 2010)

8 I analyze this trend in the context of India in *Corporatizing Water: India's Draft National Water Policy* (Varghese, 2012).

9 The United States Environmental Protection Agency (EPA) sees water trading as a tool to reduce pollutants at a lower cost. The assumption behind this proposal is that industries would find it cost efficient to pay another entity to help reduce the total maximum daily load (TMDL) instead of investing in technologies that would help them further limit their pollution. For more information see EPA (2012).

References

Bond, P. 2006. *When Commodification Annuls the Human Right to Water*. Available at: http://www2.ohchr.org/english/issues/water/contributions/universities/UniversityofKwaZulu-Natal.pdf (accessed Oct. 2012).

Dublin Principles. 1992. *The Dublin Statement on Water and Sustainable Development*. Available at: www.wmo.int/pages/prog/hwrp/documents/english/icwedece.html (accessed July 2012).

Environmental Protection Agency (EPA). 2012. *Water Quality Trading*. Available at: http://water.epa.gov/type/watersheds/trading.cfm (accessed Oct. 2012).

Shultz, J. 2003. *Bolivia's War Over Water,* Cochabamba, Bolivia: Democracy center. Available at: http://www.uchastings.edu/faculty-administration/faculty/roht-arriaza/class-website/docs/law-and-development/law-and-development09-bolivias-war-over-water.pdf (accessed Oct. 2012)].

Stop Nestle Waters. 2012. Stop Nestle Waters.org Available at: http://stopnestlewaters.org/about (accessed Oct. 2012).

Varghese, S. 2010. *Submission to Ms. Catarina de Albuquerque, Independent Expert on the Issue of Human Rights Obligations Related to Access to Safe Drinking Water and Sanitation, Economic Social Cultural Rights Section,* Geneva: UNOG-OHCHR. Available at: http://www.ohchr.org/Documents/Issues/Water/ContributionsPSP/IATP.pdf (accessed Nov. 2012).

Varghese, S. 2012. *Corporatizing Water: India's Draft National Water Policy,* Minneapolis, MN: Institute for Agriculture and Trade Policy. Available at: http://www.iatp.org/files/2012_02_28_IndiaNWP_SV_0.pdf (accessed Oct. 2012).

Zawahri, N. A., and Hensengerth, O. 2012. Domestic environmental activists and the governance of the Ganges and Mekong Rivers in India and China. *International Environmental Agreements: Politics, Law and Economics*, 12(3), 269–98.

15 Hegemony does not imply homogeneity

Thoughts on the marketization and privatization of water

Karen Bakker

Let me begin this commentary by returning to the first question posed in the introduction to Part III, which frames the discussion of the privatization and marketization of water in terms of the concept of hegemony: 'Is it helpful to suggest that ideas related to market instruments, or privatization, have become hegemonic in the water governance realm?' (Harris, Chapter 10). By this, the author meant: 'Is the concept of hegemony useful?' My answer to this first question would be a qualified 'yes': it is helpful, but analytically insufficient, to deploy a concept of hegemony on its own. In order to fully understand the development and uptake of privatization and marketization, I suggest that we need to grapple with two additional concepts: ideology and discourse.

Why? Because the evolution of resource regulatory frameworks is simultaneously discursive and material (e.g. entailing inter-related processes of socio-economic restructuring, technological and infrastructural change, and environmental change). In other words, resource governance is inherently (but by no means solely) a discursive practice, as well as an institutional framework embodying rules that define knowledge and legitimize authority – implicated in (contested) ideologies of water, power and nature.

Here, I follow Hajer in defining discourse as 'a specific ensemble of ideas, concepts, and categorizations that is produced, reproduced, and transformed in a particular set of practices and through which meaning is given to physical and social realities' (Hajer, 1995: 44). Discourse is constituted by practices through which concepts and categorizations, as well as narratives, are (re)produced and transformed (Hajer, 1995). Discourse does not exist in isolation; it is embedded within particular institutional configurations of power, knowledge and accepted authority – in short, discourse is a practice through which competing ideologies are enacted. Where ideology serves a legitimating function by offering 'sets of reasons for material conditions' (Eagleton, 1991: 209), discourse is a practice by which ideologies are created, deployed and contested. Framing resource governance as (in part) the social negotiation of the exploitation of a dynamic resource landscape (via laws, regulations, norms, customs and other social institutions) thus requires an analysis of the relationship between the discursive, social and material dimensions of socio-environmental change. It is in this sense of 'deep discursivity', as well as in a social and material sense, that regulation entails the production as well as exploitation of resources. As such, governance is enacted by individuals, or groups of individuals, who cohere (perhaps temporarily) around shared 'storylines' – sets of (often contested) ideas which unite people in particular ways not only of communicating about, but also of producing knowledge of, a problem, issue or event. Governance thus inevitably (re)inscribes ideological as well as political alliances and configurations.

Here we can begin to appreciate the constantly evolving character of governance: as a practice, governance is 'inscribed from within with a multiplicity of ideological "accents"; and it is in this way that it sustains its dynamism and volatility' (Eagleton, 1991: 195). This dynamism is inherent, rather than incidental, as governance is one of the principal processes via which social negotiation of contradictions inherent in the accumulation–regulation nexus is played out.

Framing privatization/marketization as a process of ongoing 're-negotiation of resource governance' enables us to grapple with the specific mechanisms and pathways by which certain ideologies and discourses become hegemonic (for a time), and to identify counter-hegemonic discourses and practices, which compete with, and may eventually unseat, 'master narratives' by which resources are governed.

This brings us to the second question posed in the introduction to Part III: 'how does the hegemony of these ideas affect water governance, particularly as it plays out in varied locales?' (Harris, Chapter 10). Here, I would suggest, we might add an additional question in light of the above analysis: 'how do certain practices of water governance discursively create and reinforce particular ideological hegemonies, and how and why does this vary across locales?' It is the 'why' in this question that particularly interests me. Why, for example, are privatization and marketization initiatives often so similar around the world, despite significant local differences that might have reasonably led to different models being adapted and adopted? And why do we find such emblematic cases of resistance to water privatization in Bolivia but not in Brazil – which has had as many (if not more) privatization initiatives? These are issues worthy of empirical study, such as that presented by Waters (Chapter 12) and K'akumu (Chapter 13). These chapters raise important issues: the impact of privatization and marketization on the poor; the relationship between privatization, urban infrastructure and urban land use; the poor 'fit' of generic (one is tempted to say 'hegemonic') models of private-sector provision and commercialization of water supply in local contexts; the historical (often colonial) origins of private involvement, which in many locales predates the 'Washington Consensus' heyday of the 1980s and 1990s; the existence of multiple modes of water supply which complicate simplistic public/private binaries; and the power imbalances (within both conventional international development frameworks and developmental states) which enable certain models of resource management and water supply management to be transmitted, replicated and imposed in multiple locales; and the political challenges faced by local anti-privatization coalitions which are multi-scalar in nature.

This brings me to the third question posed in the introduction to Part III: 'Does the notion of hegemony enable us to appropriately account for differences regarding these practices in space and time?' (Harris, Chapter 10). Here, my answer would be a qualified 'no'. I say this despite my belief that the concept of hegemony is relevant, and indeed important to the debate over water privatization and marketization. As Sneddon (Chapter 2) notes, following Goldman (2007), hegemony is a useful analytical tool for explaining why certain concepts come to dominate governance practices – for example, to explain the sudden surge in private-sector activity within developing countries in the 1990s (Goldman, 2007). But the concept of hegemony does not, in my opinion, enable us to 'appropriately account for difference in space and time'. This exploration of difference is, of course, a pressing task. But in order to undertake this task, I believe we must look elsewhere.

We might begin with reframing the issue as one of variegation (Bakker, 2010a). A key question raised in the introduction is: 'How is geo-institutional *variegation* (Brenner *et al.*, 2010) systematically produced and accentuated, and in what ways is it articulated with the neoliberalization of water, and specific practices related to privatization, commodification or marketization?' In response, I would argue that we cannot fully account for privatization and marketization if we do not examine broader processes of neoliberalization, and if we have not accounted for the commonalities and differences in patterns of 'actually-existing neoliberalisms' across different types of resources in different places. Having identified these commonalities and differences, we need to theorize their emergence in the context of distinct neoliberal experiments. The difficulty is, of course, that these experiments are neither entirely homogeneous (and generically reproduced) nor entirely heterogeneous (and unique); this creates both epistemological and methodological challenges. Rather, as I have argued in detail previously (Bakker, 2010a), local experiences of the neoliberalization of nature reflect the interplay of inherited institutional lineages, policy landscapes, local economic and political dynamics, and the multi-scalar dynamics of regulatory restructuring. This variegated landscape means that hegemony does not (and cannot) imply uniformity: hegemony does not imply homogeneity – which the chapters (taken as a whole) demonstrate. This is the analytical nut we need to crack – and this is the central task of the chapter authored by Harris (Chapter 11).

In Harris's chapter, the concept of variegation is deployed to analyze the variable historical and geographical expressions of privatization and marketization of water supply. This is an admirably ambitious task for a single book chapter. Harris's quick tour of developments in Europe, North America and the global South sketches out some of the key trends, players, issues and politics – invaluable context for situating the case studies provided by K'akumu and Waters. As I have argued elsewhere (Bakker, 2010b), and as Harris reiterates, the rise of 'green neoliberalism' is the backdrop against which private-sector provision of water supply – its failures and successes, its discursive representations and contestations, and its multiple expressions in diverse locales – must be understood. We may then have a more comprehensive understanding of the dynamics by which hegemony – however troubled, however temporary – is enacted, imposed, resisted and perhaps ultimately transcended.

References

Bakker, K. 2010a. The limits of 'neoliberal natures': debating 'green neoliberalism'. *Progress in Human Geography,* 34(6), 715–35.

Bakker, K. 2010b. *Privatizing Water: Governance Failure and the World's Urban Water Crisis,* Ithaca, NY, and London: Cornell University Press.

Brenner, N., Peck, J., and Theodore, N. 2010. Variegated neoliberalization: geographies, modalities, pathways. *Global Networks,* 10(2), 1–41.

Eagleton, T. 1991. *Ideology: An Introduction,* London: Verso.

Goldman, M. 2007. How 'water for all' policy became hegemonic: the power of the World Bank and its transnational policy networks. *Geoforum*, 38(5), 786–800.

Hajer, M. 1995. *The Politics of Environmental Discourse,* Oxford: Oxford University Press.

Part IV
Participation

16 The participatory paradigm

Anathema, praise and confusion

Jacqueline A. Goldin

Introduction

With the growing concern about civil wars, revolutions and the rise of authoritarian regimes from the late 1960s onwards (Clark, 2003; Freire, 1972) political notions of and investments in civil society have amplified. Historically, liberals called for greater political freedom, civil rights and the democratization of all repressive regimes (Clark, 2003: 17). As Clark (2003) suggests, links were being made in the 1980s between economic growth and political freedom, with calls for nothing less than a fundamental reconfiguration of the relationship between state and citizen. Specific to water, over six decades ago Selznick (1949) proposed that localized systems would offer more viable solutions to environmental and developmental concerns in the context of the Tennessee Valley Authority, suggesting that they could more easily adjust to change and enable problem solving. Later, Chambers (1997), building on the work of Paulo Freire on *Adult Education Methods* (1972), proposed his participatory rural appraisal (PRA) and participatory development methodology, saying that 'they (the poor) can do it'. With these new techniques, Chambers and contemporaries cemented participation within the development pantheon (Williams, 2004) and participatory discourse moved from the 'margins to the mainstream' (ibid.). As such, participation has increasingly become a 'modern' idea that is difficult if not impossible to contest. In keeping with our volume's themes, one might say that 'participation' – in terms of water-oriented governance and development – has become a hegemonic concept (cf. Cooke and Kothari, 2001).

Following from these initial movements, it has become increasingly comfortable in development discourse to make a link between participation and decentralized administrative structures, whether at a municipal, village or other local levels. A frequently cited benefit of such decentralized regimes was the idea of increased proximity between decision-makers and those affected by governance decisions. This was later merged with ideals of democratic participation and greater access to local knowledge, ignoring leakages or incongruities that might thwart the comfortable logic that implies that more participation means more democracy and vice versa. The twinning of increased democracy and increased participation was taken up by Crocker who claims that 'authentic development occurs when groups at whatever level become subjects who deliberate, decide and act in the world rather than being victims of circumstance or objects of someone else's decisions, the tools of someone else's designs' (2008: 339). Unlike the somewhat controversial scarcity/crisis and marketization/privatization discourses, participation is an unabashedly normative ideal. Taken together, newly invigorated forms of participatory processes in the environmental sphere have created a novel relationship between state and citizen, representing a shift from government to governance. Even with these good intentions, sites across the developing world bear the marks of failed projects touted as 'participatory' that have not fully, or meaningfully, involved stakeholders at multiple scales (Agrawal and Gibson, 1999; Goldin, 2010; Ostrom, 1995).

Part of our concern in this section is to consider the meaning and implications of the shift towards participatory governance in the water realm and the problematics around participation as a hegemonic concept. In his exposé of the Tennessee Valley Authority, Selznick saw impulses towards multi-stakeholder participation as holding promise, but recognized that they could also serve as co-optation mechanisms whereby new actors were brought into bureaucratic structures of an organization as a means of averting any threats to its stability and 'business as usual' activities. Thus, participation can serve power interests rather than enabling a process of bringing people into decision-making processes that genuinely shape the development activities affecting their lives (see discussion of the Teshie water board in Accra in Morinville and Harris, Chapter 19; cf. Cooke and Kothari, 2006).

Four fatal flaws

There is imprecision about what participation means. It means different things to different people. I propose that there are several reasons for this imprecision and find it helpful to isolate 'four fatal flaws' (FFFs) related to the concept: (1) participation is enmeshed with notions of decentralization and devolution, and as such there is a lack of precision about the term that tends to be lost in some of these broader discourses and shifts; (2) it is too often supply driven, rather than demand driven; (3) vagueness about what participation means provides a space where participation can mean different things to different people, constituting a failure to articulate core principles in terms of what meaningful participation should look like; and (4) it results in a thrust towards isomorphism where the focus is on form rather than substance. I take up each of these points in turn.

First, decentralization and devolution, although not the same in meaning, both imply an impulse downwards where the state abrogates decision-making to lower levels, often without the concomitant human and financial capital. Amartya Sen (1999) in his *Development as Freedom* puts considerable emphasis on what he terms 'public reasoning', claiming that people value different things and they should be given opportunities (capabilities) to do and to be (functionings) what they choose to be and to do. In the water sector the implication is that people closest to the natural resources on which they depend should be given the opportunity to make decisions about that resource. However, too often decentralization and devolution by state actors constitutes nothing short of an unconfortable shifting of the state's responsibilities and a failure to commit the financial and human resources required for participatory practices (Goldin, 2003, 2010).

My second point is that participation too often remains supply, rather than demand, driven. As such, there tends to be a strong impulse for top–down logics, or for policies that fan out from a 'center'. We see this retrenchment of centralized institutions through the cooptation of participatory logics by centralized states, as well as by the Bretton Woods Institutions (BWIs). The BWIs, for instance, have increasingly called on participatory approaches as the right thing to do and in so doing have placed conditionalities on developing countries that would not qualify for donor aid unless they embraced participatory practice. This is ironic because participatory practice has historically been deeply embedded *within* developing country contexts, often infused with spiritual prayer, ritual, debate and dissent at the grassroots level. There are significant questions about the efficacy of participatory models of water use and management that are generated by external agents rather than from within community contexts (see Morinville and Harris, Chapter 19; Barnes, Chapter 17).

Thirdly, the idea of vagueness regarding participation is interrogated by others, including Goldin (2003, 2010), Marais (2001), Rahnema (in Williams, 2004), Selznick (1949) and Williams (2004). For Selznick, vague policy is vulnerable to misinterpretation and to manipulation by elites. Rahnema (in Williams, 2004) considers the concept of participation to have been politically 'tamed' (cf. Goldin, 2003). Marais (2001), in writing about the political and social transformations of recent decades in South Africa, posits that vagueness is not just incidental because it is a factor that deliberately allows for concessions and compromises between old regimes and newer forms.

Fourthly, hegemonic discourses of participation tend to be isomorphic, with a focus on form rather than substance. These forms are also often generic and have not always been framed specifically to suit the water sector. Essentially, many participatory projects are expected to include the same elements in their basket of activities and to comply with a checklist approach. Where differences might exist, and where elements do not fit into the mold, these hegemonic models are slow to adapt, and can even result in failure or what Iris Marion Young (1990) refers to as a misrecognition of difference and diversity. This causes symmetry, across and within country contexts, because we see participation cemented in form, rather than in substance. Actors driving hegemonic discourses of participation are struggling to control an impulse for order and sameness. This is heightened by the fact that the world of water remains predominantly 'technical', with agendas driven by engineers rather than social scientists. Social dimensions are more vigorously and carefully dissected in other disciplines such as economics, sociology, anthropology, political studies or health.

Grounding our views on participation

In the water sector, as elsewhere, ideals of deep democracy, encrypted into the four Dublin Principles of 1992, have proliferated (Goldin, 2005; Savenije and van der Zaag, 2000). Of relevance here are two principles: principle two states that 'water development and management should be based on a participatory approach, involving users, planners and policy-makers at all levels'. Principle three states that 'women play a central part in the provision, management and safeguarding of water'. Where did these ideas originate and why are there so few cases where the goals of participatory development, listening to new voices, and finding new ways of doing, are achieved in a meaningful fashion? Why, even with many 'failures' in this regard, are these hegemonic discourses so persistent? What is it about participation that gives it staying power, whilst at the same time makes it so difficult to practice?

Harris, in her framing chapter on privatization and marketization (Chapter 10) draws our attention to symmetry and likeness in the way that privatization manifests despite such different contexts. Sneddon, in Chapter 2, shows how hegemonic discourses manifest themselves in real rather than idealized spaces. There are examples along these lines in Part IV as well, where the periphery maintains its force and impulses to control from the core are contested. The three case studies here all scrutinize the way that discourses and practices of decentralization, localization and participation represent an ongoing struggle to redress imbalances in power and knowledge, including how these struggles augment or limit opportunities to deepen democratic ideals in particular locales.

We read, for instance, in the chapter by Barnes (Chapter 17), about 'incompleteness' of the participation discourse where it deliberately excludes female irrigators. In the case of Egypt, Barnes proposes that power and gendered politics determine the 'who and how' of inclusion. In Kadirbeyoglu and Kurtic's chapter on irrigation management by water user associations in Turkey (Chapter 18), participatory discourse is prominent but not meaningfully applied, and as such contributes to the perpetuation of hegemony. This case shows that rural communities are by no means passive in their refusal to accept the unequal playing field and their participation is manifest in their struggles to resist the hegemony of water governance in the face of devolution and privatization processes. Participation from the bottom–up has meaning in this context, as rural voices clamor for recognition, with villagers insisting on their right to refuse hydroelectric plants or changes in their water flow. Here, thus, we see intersections between participation and hegemonies related to water privatization (Part III). Morinville and Harris in their chapter on Accra, Ghana (Chapter 19), show that participation faces particular opportunities and limits in relation to given institutional forms, as well as in relation to broader political and economic changes, such as those associated with neoliberal water governance. In their look at Local Water Boards in urban Accra, they unpack some of the openings and closures with respect to participatory governance processes. These authors also challenge the ways that participation is often narrowly understood in relation to formal institutions, rather than embracing a broad understanding of the diverse ways that local people 'participate' in water-related issues in their communities.

Conclusion

Following the critical approach for which this volume strives, the chapters in this Part look specifically at the way in which participatory discourse and practice has woven itself into particular spaces in the global South. Highlighting examples from Africa (Ghana) and the Middle East (Turkey and Egypt) we are primarily concerned with the way in which hegemonic discourses, such as those related to participation, can lead to unexpected and at times perverse impulses. In light of our discussion of hegemony (Sneddon, Chapter 2), we pay particular attention to who benefits from the failure of participatory models of water governance. We are also interested in the ways that these practices might be improved, particularly to make participatory water governance more meaningful or sustainable, enabling citizens to be involved in decisions that affect their lives. In terms of similarities across contexts, power and politics are remarkably predictable, often leading to vicious cycles of inclusion and exclusion, disenfranchising some and enriching others – all too often along lines of gender, race or class. Lest I myself fall prey, in this framing chapter, to the temptation of brushing over difference and inequality with an impulse to order participatory discourses, I must remember that hegemonic discourses change as they disrupt or stifle everyday practices. I and my fellow authors in this Part suggest that uneven contexts are contested by individuals and groups who create new patterns of belonging (participation) through resistance, by finding new identities or similar processes. I do not propose that we reinvent a new form of participation – that would run the risk of becoming yet another hegemonic discourse – but rather that we revisit existing participatory discourse and challenge the issue of power and elite capture head-on. Deliberate attention to recognition of difference (within the current participation paradigm) is likely to give citizens new opportunities to create patterns of belonging, better suited to shift lines of power for advantage, rather than disadvantage, particularly for impoverished and marginalized populations.

We see in the Parts on crisis and scarcity and marketization/privatization in this volume, how 'big ideas', such as these and the one we are concerned about here, may dissipate and lose their hold, particularly as they penetrate localities in the South. In a similar sense we cannot presume that participation started at the center and traveled to the periphery, moving from the global North to the South. We are reminded that the global South is deeply differentiated and that there are variegated forms of 'traditional' or 'indigenous' participatory practices across the South that themselves have – or have not – worked towards the types of emancipatory and sustainability projects described above. Today, participatory discourse is the bedfellow of other hegemonic ideals in the jigsaw of 'modernity' and like the discourses of crisis and scarcity, privatization and marketization, goes hand in hand with the retreat of the state as central controls, with their checks and (im)balances, are replaced by more localized controls.

What discomfort do the normative claims of participation have in cycling back to the periphery? How has the droning refrain for participation been fitted into water reform processes and what promise does it hold for equity and inclusiveness? What disconnects are there between the global general (and vague) refrain for participation and the way this has been taken up by the water sector? What disconnects are there in taking up a discourse at a global level and in implementing it at the local level? This framing chapter, and the three chapters that follow in this section, scrutinize the confusing and contested terrain of participatory practice in water governance. While everything has changed in the public documents about decentralization, participation and so forth, power relations and economic structures remain. This suggests strongly that we need to remain vigilant to ensure that the ideal of participation does not go down in history as just another tool for keeping some in – and others out.

References

Agrawal, A., and Gibson, C. 1999. Enchantment and disenchantment: the role of community in natural resource conservation. *World Development*, 27(4), 629–49.

Chambers, R. 1997. *Whose Reality Counts? Putting the First Last Intermediate,* London: Technology Publications.

Clark, D. 2003. *Visions of Development: A Study of Human Values,* Northampton, MA, and Cheltenham: Edward Elgar.

Cooke, B., and Kothari, U., eds. 2001. *Participation: The New Tyranny,* London: Zed Books.

Crocker, D. 2008. *Ethics of global Development: Agency, Capability and Deliberative Democracy.* Cambridge: Cambridge University Press

Dublin Principles. 1992. *The Dublin Statement on Water and Sustainable Development.* Available at: www.wmo.int/pages/prog/hwrp/documents/english/icwedece.html (accessed July 2012).

Freire, P. 1972. *Cultural Action for Freedom,* Cambridge, MA: Harvard University Press.

Goldin, J. A. 2003. Washing away the sins of the past. *International Journal of Public Administration*, 26(6), 711–30.

Goldin, J. A. 2005. Trust and transformation in the water sector. Ph.D. University of Cape Town.

Goldin, J. A. 2010. Water policy in South Africa: trust and knowledge as obstacles to reform. *Review of Radical Political Economics,* 42(2), 195–212.

Marais, H. 2001. *South Africa, Limits to Change: The Political Economy of Transition,* New York: Zed Books.

Ostrom, E. 1995. Incentives, rules of the game, and development. In M. Bruno and B. Pleskovic (eds), *Annual World Bank Conference on Development Economics 1995,* Washington, DC: World Bank.

Savenije, H., and van der Zaag: 2000. Conceptual framework for the management of shared river basin; with special reference to the SADC and EU. *Water Policy,* 2, 9–45.

Selznick: 1949. *TVA and the Grassroots: A Study of Politics and Organization,* Berkeley, CA: University of California Press.

Sen, A. 1999. *Development as Freedom,* New York: Knopf.

Williams, G. 2004. Evaluating participatory development: tyranny, power and (re) politicization. *Third World Quarterly,* 25(3), 557–78.

Young, I. M. 1990. *Justice and the Politics of Difference,* Princeton, NJ: Princeton University Press.

17 Who is a water user?

The politics of gender in Egypt's water user associations

Jessica Barnes

It is a crisp winter's day, early in 2008, and a group of five men are sitting in the guest room of a farmer's house in a village in northern Egypt. The room is recently decorated, with a green mat on the floor, ornate armchairs and plaques on the wall with verses from the Koran. The men are gathered for one of the first meetings of a newly elected water user association (WUA).

I enter the room with Mohamed and Saida, two community organizers from Egypt's Ministry of Water Resources and Irrigation, and Noha, a member of the association whom we collected on our way. Mohamed goes to join the men at one end of the room, and I sit with the two women at the other end. The men start to discuss the problems occurring along their irrigation canal. They talk about a section of the canal that has become blocked with sediment and weeds. The blockage is impeding the flow, with the result that some farmers are not receiving enough water. They need the ministry to bring an excavator to scour out the blockage. One man, acting as secretary, takes notes.

A few times during the discussion Noha interjects with a comment, but the men pay little attention to her. She grows increasingly frustrated. After about half an hour, Noha starts talking quietly to Saida. She says that she is angry because she would like to be secretary of the water user association but the other members have said that she cannot be. She feels that whenever she makes a suggestion, the men ignore her. One of the men notices that Noha is talking to Saida and asks what she is saying. Noha starts speaking in a strong tone, anger simmering beneath her words: 'You don't agree that a woman should be with you. You don't give a woman an opportunity to talk. You don't want any women in the management committee!'[1]

In this ethnographic moment, we see the dynamics of participation in action. We see how participation – a theme that has become hegemonic within international water management circles (see Goldin, Chapter 16) – translates into practice on the ground. The group gathered together in the farmer's guest room comprises the management committee of a water user association that was formed through an internationally financed project. This project was one of a number of donor-funded initiatives that have sought to promote participatory water management in Egypt since the 1980s, through the establishment of WUAs, of which there are now over a thousand in Egypt.[2] The WUAs are designed to help improve management of the water distribution network, which channels water from the Nile (the source of 96 percent of Egypt's water) through over 48,000 km of canals, mostly to feed agricultural lands (where 90 percent of the water is consumed). While Egypt receives more than 55 billion cubic meters of water a year from the Nile, many farmers do not receive sufficient water to grow the number or type of crops that they would like to. As is often the case (see Mahayni, Chapter 4), this scarcity is a function, primarily, of the distribution system's failure to match supply and demand rather than fundamental water insufficiency. The rationale behind the water user associations – as articulated in the many documents produced by these donor projects – is that they will help the ministry pinpoint problems within the infrastructural system, such as places where canals are blocked, banks eroded or weirs broken. In addition, they will help resolve conflicts, like when farmers take other people's water allocations. The WUAs will, therefore, improve the efficiency with which water flows through the canal network, with the result that more farmers will receive the quantity and quality of water they need.[3] It is for this reason that members of the management committee have gathered to discuss the problems along their canal. The secretary writes up the list of problems, which the WUA will then pass on to the district engineer, in the hope that the ministry will address these issues during its next annual maintenance period.

The scene in the farmer's guest room captures the patchiness of participation. The fact that many do not participate in what are meant to be participatory institutions – a phenomenon that Bina Agarwal (2001) describes as 'participatory exclusions' – has been extensively documented in the literature on WUAs (see Kadirbeyoglu and Kurtic, Chapter 18; Morinville and Harris, Chapter 19; and also Hunt, 1989; Mosse, 2003; Pellissery and Bergh, 2007). In this case, as in many others, the limits to participation are drawn in part along gender lines (Harris, 2005; Meinzen-Dick and Zwarteveen, 1998). There is only one woman to five men in the management committee meeting, and as that woman states, she does not feel like her voice is being heard. The men in the WUA do not give her a space to express her feelings, nor is she allowed to stand for the post of secretary and record the WUA's priorities in an official report. She becomes angry at her exclusion, the strength of her emotion clearly indicating the lack of participatory parity in this setting. Hence not only is the number of women in the WUAs limited, but the dynamics that play out during WUA meetings preclude the participation of those women who do attend.

Many factors can limit female participation in a WUA. In the Egyptian case, meetings are often held at locations or times that are not conducive to women's attendance. Indeed the reason why we transported Noha to the meeting was because of the inconvenience of its location in relation to her house. Had we not collected her, she may well have not gone to the meeting. On other occasions, women are not told that meetings are taking place. In fact, later in this meeting the men sought to undermine Noha's commitment to the WUA by pointing out that she had failed to attend previous meetings, to which she replied that she was not aware that there had been any meetings.

However rather than focusing on the factors that shape participation after a WUA is formed, this chapter looks at factors that come into play during the preliminary stages of establishing a WUA. A number of authors have identified the fact that 'rules of membership' of participatory institutions are often biased against women (Meinzen-Dick and Zwarteveen, 1998; Agarwal, 2001). Since most analyses of WUAs have looked at associations that have already been established, though, they have tended to take these rules as a given. My interest here is in how these rules come into being. Who writes them? How are they communicated to the target population? What are some of the ways in which they may be contested? Tracing the origins of these rules helps explain how the people gathered in the farmer's guest room came to represent the water users in this area, why there was only one woman present at the meeting, and why the men were not interested in her opinion.

By focusing on how these rules were set, enforced and challenged during the process of establishing WUAs in Egypt, I draw attention to the role of a group that has been largely missing from studies of WUAs – those who coordinate the establishment process. In contrast to forms of communal interaction that evolve organically through the shared use of a water source, such as a pump (Hopkins, 1999) or canal (Trawick, 2001), WUAs are communities that are often coordinated 'from above'. Hence those who do this work of coordination play an important role. In cases where the WUAs are being established by a government, the coordinators may be mid-level government bureaucrats. In cases where the impetus for WUA establishment is coming from international donor agencies, the coordinators are likely to be the international consultants or local staff who run the donor projects.

The chapter draws on a year of ethnographic observation that I conducted in Egypt with a participatory water management project in 2007–8. This project worked in association with the Ministry of Water Resources and Irrigation (hereafter 'the ministry') to establish almost a hundred water user associations throughout one of Egypt's provinces between 2007 and 2010.[4] Project activities were implemented by a team of male and female 'community organizers' under the leadership of a project manager (an expatriate consultant) and project director (a ministry engineer). Some of the community organizers were agricultural engineers seconded from the ministry; others, most of whom held degrees in social work from the local university, were recruited by the project manager. The male community organizers came from the city where the project was based and from villages around the province; the female community organizers were all from the city. I argue that these people who coordinated the establishment of the WUAs, as well as the particular way in which they understood participation, were key to determining what participation came to mean for the associations and their members. They were the ones to translate the concept of participation – a buzzword of the international water management community – into an on-the-ground reality.

This chapter therefore speaks to the question raised by Sneddon (Chapter 2) about how concepts such as participation travel and how they are molded and modified in specific circumstances and locales. The chapter shows, first, how different parties debate and challenge the rules of participation according to their contrasting understandings of what it means to be a water user. Second, the chapter demonstrates how those who coordinate the establishment of the WUAs shape what the WUAs come to be through their communication to the community members of what it means to participate. I argue that these interactions and negotiations, which take place during the foundational stages of participatory water management, have profound consequences for how participatory processes subsequently unfold.

How do women use water?

Panning across a bucolic scene of fields and irrigation canals, the camera focuses on a woman dressed in a *galabiya* (the long tunic commonly worn in rural Egypt), who explains that she is a widow. 'I do all the work,' she says. 'A man just turns on the pump then leaves. When a plot takes its fill, I stop it. And so on till I'm done.' The camera cuts to a close-up of a man, also wearing a *galabiya*. He speaks adamantly. 'A woman here can only do certain tasks,' he declares. 'She can't irrigate. She might have to gird up her dress and our customs and traditions wouldn't permit that.' (Most Egyptian farms are flood irrigated, which means that the farmers have to direct the water across their fields by building up and breaking down small dams of earth until the surface is entirely covered.) The camera shifts back to the woman. With her back to the camera, she takes off her brightly patterned *galabiya,* leaving a plain brown one below. She picks up an axe and starts raking away a dam of earth. The water begins to flow from the irrigation ditch onto her field.

I press stop and the image freezes on the screen. It is March 2008 and I am giving a lecture to the project team on gender.[5] The lecture began with me asking the group of community organizers and ministry engineers gathered in the large meeting room to write down what they understood by the term gender. Responses ranged from a one-word definition – 'women' *(harim)* – reflecting the popular association of gender as meaning women's issues, to the Arabic term for gender – *al-noᶜ al-igtimaᶜi* – which translates literally and not particularly revealingly, as 'social type'. Most people, though, wrote something about men and women having different roles and responsibilities, so I am intrigued to see how they respond to this video clip.[6] To my surprise, they show no surprise. We know that women irrigate, they say. There is a pause, before the caveat comes. But, they add, not here in this province. In this province, they explain, it is very rare for women to irrigate.[7]

The question of whether or not women irrigate cuts to the heart of who should participate in a WUA and on what basis. The WUAs established by this project included two types of water users, which it termed agricultural water users and residential water users. The project defined the former as farmers, who draw water from the canals to irrigate their fields, and the latter as residents of the villages that the canals pass through, who use water from the canals for domestic purposes.

While these categories are not by definition gendered, they came to be understood by the project team in this way. In this simplified understanding, agricultural water users are men and residential water users are women. Farmers (*fellahin*), in other words, are a distinct category from women (*sitat*). Indeed I never heard anyone use the word farmer with a female case ending (*fellaha-fellahat*). The project guidelines fixed the number of residential representatives in each WUA as between 10 and 20 percent the number of agricultural representatives. This weighting reflected the fact that the WUAs' primary focus is irrigation. The rules of membership therefore not only set the terms on which women would participate in the WUAs – as residential representatives in an institution designed to improve irrigation management – but implicitly limited the ratio of women to men in the WUAs.

I turn now to trace the origin of these rules. The first WUAs established in Egypt during the 1980s did not include any women at all. This gradually came to be seen by the donors and consultants funding and managing development projects in Egypt as a limitation. Complete exclusion of one sex from a so-called participatory institution does, after all, undermine its participatory nature. Evaluation reports of these early projects also noted that people use canal water not only to irrigate but also to wash clothes and dishes and even, sometimes, to drink. People know that this water is poor quality, but in the absence of a reliable water supply within the homes, as is the case in many rural households, they have little alternative. In light of these domestic uses of canal water and their impact on water quality, evaluations of the early projects advised that the WUAs should take non-agricultural uses of water into consideration as well. In the second round of WUA projects, project managers therefore saw the inclusion of women as residential representatives as a way to address both these deficiencies. The WUAs would contain women and those women would represent domestic water concerns. Thus the WUAs' attention to domestic use was not to be an end in itself but a way of securing a sufficient quantity and quality of water for irrigation.

During the planning stages of this project, the manager was told by the funding agency that the project should adopt this same method of defining WUA membership by user type so as to be consistent. This need for coordination between donor projects is a topic of increasing emphasis within the international and bilateral agencies working on water issues in Egypt. Developing a unified model for WUA establishment throughout Egypt, they argue, will signify that participatory water governance is not just a project-based initiative, but rather a national program to which the water ministry is truly committed.

However both the consultant managing the project and the project director seconded from the ministry remained sceptical that adopting a gendered classification of water user was the best mechanism for ensuring full participation. The fact that both of these individuals were women may well have influenced this perspective. One day, shortly after the project began, I accompanied the manager to a meeting at the office of the agency funding the project. 'A key question', she commented to the program officer with whom we met, 'is how to get more women's representation in the WUAs.' She went on to explain what she saw as being the root of this limited participation. 'It is a problem that women are only involved as representatives of residential areas. This is how it is done in the other projects, but I would like to rethink it … It would cause an upheaval, but if you never challenge the method, you will never improve!'[8]

The consultant's desire to change the rules of membership for the WUA was hampered, though, by a lack of proof. Having worked on resource management projects around the world and attended many workshops on gender awareness, she had a sense that women probably irrigated as well as men, but she had no data. So she asked me, as a student affiliated with the project, to conduct a study of gender and water management in the province. I set out with the female community organizers from the project team on a quest to find women farmers. Where were the *fellahat* – this category that nobody referred to? Would we find any women who irrigated?

We selected a purposive sample of female farmers from five villages. Some of these women farmed land that was in their husband's name, as their husbands were working overseas or had passed away. Other women had never married and farmed land that they themselves rented or owned. In addition, we surveyed women who helped their husbands in the fields, as we considered these women, also, to be farmers. By means of comparison, we selected a similar sample of male farmers.

Many of the women we talked to described the role they played in agriculture and irrigation. One woman whose husband is working in the Gulf and whose son is working in Cairo talked in detail about how she irrigates their land. 'Our water is on Wednesdays. Our neighbors dam the irrigation ditch and I go and open it up. Then when the land has drunk I dam it again … We irrigate the top first, then the lower parts of the land, so that all the land will drink equally.' Indeed of the 25 women we surveyed, nearly half said that they irrigated the land themselves. While this was lower than the proportion of men, it is most likely an underestimate. Women often undervalue their own contributions to agricultural water management, seeing themselves as just 'helpers' rather than as the primary irrigators (Meinzen-Dick and Zwarteveen, 1998; Radwan, 2005). One woman who we talked to explained that she works with her husband to farm five acres, but that her husband is responsible for irrigation. It was only on further questioning that she acknowledged, 'I can irrigate during the day if my husband is not present.' Similarly, although she told us that her husband maintains the irrigation ditch, when we asked what she would do if she saw a blockage in the ditch she responded, 'If the man is not here, I can do it.' To her it was just common sense that she would step in and irrigate if her husband was not available. 'Isn't this our livelihood?' she said to us.

When, however, I conveyed the survey results to the project team in a formal presentation, they were met with scepticism. One engineer raised his hand. 'These cases where women irrigate are very rare,' he stated. Another joined him. 'It is only in marginal areas, in the areas of Arab populations' – people in this province use the word 'Arab' to refer to communities of Bedouin origin, which they often consider to be 'backwards' – 'or in fruit growing regions that you find women irrigating,' he asserted.[9] Just as they did during the lecture, the engineers dismissed the significance of women's role in irrigation and continued to question the notion that women might also participate in the WUAs as agricultural representatives. In doing so, they played into prevailing stereotypical ideas about the gendered division of labor and what kinds of male and female behavior are appropriate (Meinzen-Dick and Zwarteveen, 1998; Radwan, 2007). Interestingly, even among the female project staff who had helped carry out the survey and spoken to female farmers with me, the notion that women play a minor role in agricultural water use persisted. 'There really aren't very many women who farm,' I heard one of the female community organizers tell a visiting consultant. Even if what she meant by this was that there are few women who farm on their own, it was a puzzling comment given that she had spent a whole day with me interviewing women who participate in farming activities in a variety of ways.[10]

One could interpret the continuation of these skewed perspectives as ignorance – a detachment of government officials and project workers from rural realities. But to do so would be to disregard the fact that many of the male project staff actually came from rural backgrounds, as do many of the ministry engineers. Such a characterization would also be a misrepresentation. Even people living in rural areas, who are obviously aware of the fact that women go to the fields, would sometimes reply to my questions by saying that women do not farm. 'The land is for the men, it's not our business,' one woman told me.[11] During many conversations with rural residents, they would explain that women do farm, but only in other areas. There is, certainly, spatial variability in the degree of female participation in farming. Women tend to be more of a presence in the fields of northern Egypt than they are in the traditionally more conservative south (Hopkins and Saad, 2004: 11). But the insistence that women in this province do not farm, when clearly some do, deserves closer examination.

Rather than reflecting ignorance, I argue that the repeated assertions that women do not farm and irrigate reflect instead the fact that farming is not a particularly celebrated work for women in Egyptian society.[12] Most of the women who take primary responsibility for the work in the fields do so because they have no alternative. Their husbands have died or are working overseas and they do not have the money to employ laborers to do the work of tending the crops and irrigating the land. Gender therefore intersects with other lines of inequality. Female farmers are often poor, elderly and uneducated. They are the kind of women that it is easy for ministry officials, project staff and villagers to overlook. As one female community organizer said explicitly, 'If there are women who farm, they tend to only have very small pieces of land and are uneducated, so they aren't very important.'[13] Such women, in her view, have little role to play in participatory water management. They are low-status, not 'model' farmers who can represent the interests of other agricultural water users in the WUA.

Despite the project manager's repeated efforts, she was unable to challenge these stereotypes and open up the agricultural water user category for women. This failure was not only due to the difficulty of convincing the project staff that women do farm and so can represent agricultural areas. It was also because female farmers were not particularly interested in representing agricultural interests in the WUAs. At the start of my fieldwork, I assumed that everyone would want a chance to participate. As someone who has studied development and water management at graduate school in the United States, I have been trained in just the kinds of hegemonic concepts that this book analyzes. I had a notion that giving people an opportunity to participate in making decisions that affect them and their livelihoods is a good idea. I could relate to propositions like that of Agarwal (2001: 1624) that participation is 'important both in itself, as a measure of citizenship and a means of empowerment, and for its potential effects on equity, efficiency, and sustainability'. The more I talked to rural women, though, I realized that they did not necessarily share this perspective. As other authors have shown, participation, or rather a particular notion of participation – in this case, involvement in a WUA – can be a burden. Attending meetings takes time away from other activities of household maintenance and income generation (see e.g. Meinzen-Dick and Zwarteveen, 1998). Further, it potentially underscores an aspect of these women's identity and everyday realities that they may not want to celebrate – their marginal position within society and the fact that they have little choice but to undertake low-status irrigation and agricultural labor (cf. Harris, 2006).

In our survey of female farmers, we asked them if they would like to participate in the WUA. Most of them said no. One woman elaborated, 'No, am I a man? I'm not free. I'm a widow. You need a woman who is educated. Would men listen to me?'[14] In this comment, she drew attention not only to her gender but also to her social status as an uneducated woman, which she saw as placing her in a position where she did not think that she would be an effective participant. She had no problem with others representing her interests.

When I came to present this part of the survey results to the project team, one of the senior ministry engineers became animated. He wanted to know the exact percentage of female farmers who did not want to participate. He shouted across to the project director on the other side of the room, 'See! It's not our fault [that there aren't many women in the WUAs], they don't want to participate.'[15] This does not mean that these women are voiceless. They have their own mechanisms of making their voice heard (see also Zwarteveen *et al.*, 2010). If they see ministry engineers in the field, they approach them and make their claims. Or they approach other influential members of the community to make claims on their behalf. But they are not interested in the WUA as a forum for participation. They are well aware of how they are likely to be judged or dismissed in such a setting.

Thus, the rule that women should be incorporated in the WUAs as representatives of the residential areas persisted, despite the project managers' efforts to challenge it. In the next section, I examine how the community organizers communicated this rule to rural people, ultimately shaping the nature of women's participation in the WUAs.

Don't you care about sewage?

I leave the project office with Fatima, one of the female community organizers. We drive into the countryside and through fields of sorghum, maize, cotton and rice, soon arriving at the village of Latifa where Fatima has scheduled a meeting for women to elect a representative to the local WUA. We enter the guest room of one of the village houses, which lies just a short distance from the canal. We sit down on the two armchairs that are placed along one wall. Women from the village begin to file in. They are wearing dark colored *galabiyas,* with loose headscarves around their heads; a few have their faces covered with a full veil. Fatima, dressed in a long form-fitting turquoise skirt and jacket, with a matching headscarf and handbag, stands apart from them, marked by her dress as urban, educated, different. Unlike Fatima, the village women all slip off their sandals as they enter and sit down on the plastic mat covering the floor.

Fatima starts her speech. 'My name is Madame Fatima, and I come from the project in the "The Irrigation" (*al-rai*) [this is how people commonly refer to the ministry]. We're coming to do something called a water user association (*rabita mustakhdami al-mai*). An association (*rabita*) is like a cooperative (*gamaʿiya*), but not for agriculture or social affairs but for irrigation.' She describes the establishment process. She explains, first, 'We go to the people who irrigate from the canal. Those are the men.' The order of her words is not incidental; the irrigators are always first. She comes, then, to the women's piece of the WUA. 'Just as a canal irrigates agricultural land,' she says, 'so it also goes through villages.'

To demonstrate the importance of women in the residential domain of water use, she asks the group a series of questions. 'Have you ever seen a man throw rubbish in the canal? Are men responsible if a child falls in the canal? Have you ever seen a man wash dishes in the canal?' To each, there is a chorus of 'No!' The domestic domain is thereby bounded as a female one. Fatima continues. 'If you put sugar in a glass of water, what happens to the water?' The women reply that the water becomes sugary. 'And if you add dirt?' On cue, the women complete that the water becomes dirty. She makes her point, therefore, that the disposal of solid waste and sewage into the canal degrades the quality of water that then flows onto the fields.

Fatima moves straight from this discussion of water quality to introducing the meetings that embody what the WUA is and what it does. 'So,' she explains, 'we do meetings in villages and choose a woman who can talk about the problems of the canal in the village.' By framing her comments in this way, Fatima underscores the linkage between women's participation and water quality issues. Before doing the election, though, she says that she would like to hear the women's problems. The women respond that their main problem is the lack of irrigation water. This is not what Fatima expects to hear. It confounds her preconceptions of women as domestic water users who are mostly concerned about the water they can access for household use. She does not ask any follow-up questions, but instead, redirects the conversation. 'Do you have problems with rubbish?' she asks. 'Does anyone wash dishes in the canal? Does anyone put wastewater in the canal?' While these practices are not uncommon in the province, the women reply that no, everyone in Latifa has good drinking water in their homes and septic tanks to dispose of their wastewater. In essence, this group of women does not fall into the project's category of residential water user. They do, of course, use water for residential purposes, but their main interest in the canals is not as a source of domestic water but as a source of irrigation water.

Fatima persists regardless, following the procedures that the project has set in place. She explains that they need to select a female residential representative for the WUA management committee. The women choose someone and Fatima hands out a packet of laundry detergent to everyone who has attended the meeting – a gift designed to thank the women for their time and to encourage attendance, which also, subtly, reinforces their role as housewives who are interested in canal water for household tasks such as laundry. As we leave, however, an old woman grabs my hand. 'Oh on the prophet, bring us water, the land is so dry!' she implores, clearly hoping that I might have more influence than I do. I am struck by the contrast between the meeting and this parting impression. While on Fatima's insistence, the meeting has revolved around issues of water use in the home, the old woman's take-home message is about water scarcity in the fields.[16]

This ethnographic scene reveals how the actors driving the participation agenda communicate the notion to rural women as they introduce the idea of the WUA. For the women gathered in the room, this was their first encounter with participatory water management. It was through meetings like this one, which the female community organizers arranged with rural women around the province, that they led women to talk about residential concerns. They achieved this through the language that they used and the way in which they structured their meetings. Sometimes they would ask leading questions. Other times they would speak on the women's behalf. On one occasion, for example, I heard a community organizer ask a group of women, 'What are your problems?' only to answer straight away herself, 'sewage and rubbish?' The inflection in her voice indicated a question mark, but the answer was already clearly self-evident to her.[17]

The significance of this preliminary step in the establishment of WUAs is that it creates certain expectations. The issues that the community organizers emphasized to the women as being their chief concerns do not fall under the remit of the Ministry of Water Resources and Irrigation, which is the ministry formally responsible for establishing and interacting with the WUAs. The Ministry of Irrigation does not build drinking water treatment stations, install sewage pipes or arrange waste collection systems. These tasks are the responsibility of the drinking water and sanitation company and the local municipalities, which have no relationship with the WUAs. Thus the community organizers told the female representatives to expect things that the WUAs, designed to improve participation in irrigation management, will never be able to deliver. In addition, while these domestic concerns relating to the canals can be very problematic, they are often not the priority for farming communities, as the old woman's comment to me at the end of the meeting illustrated. Hence women who participate in the WUAs as representatives of residential water use are bound to be disappointed.

When their interests are not met, female participants lose faith in the WUAs. One community organizer reported, for example, how two women on a WUA management committee had suggested building a wall alongside their canal as a safety measure. But the male majority of the committee voted this out as a priority issue for work during the maintenance period, judging that their own irrigation concerns were more pressing. As a result, the women felt that their voices were not being heard and subsequently stopped attending meetings. By enacting the roles expected of them by the project, these women found themselves in a marginal position relative to the dominant function of the WUAs.[18]

Over the course of the project, the female community organizers, who were responsible for getting women to participate in the WUAs, also became frustrated. In one case, for instance, an organizer worked with a WUA representative from one village to try and increase the village's drinking water supply, after many women from the village complained that the supply was insufficient. This was the kind of 'domestic concern' that the female community organizers championed and the organizer was keen to demonstrate that the WUA could have a positive impact on the women's everyday lives. In this instance, the domestic usage was not one directly related to the use of canal water, as intended in the project's conceptualization of why it was important to include residential water users in the WUAs, but rather related to the water flowing (or rather, not flowing) into the villagers' homes through drinking water pipes. This was precisely the kind of slippage that occurred, though, through the project's framing of the female domain of water use as a residential one. The organizer took on the case as a personal mission, helping the WUA representative from the village write a petition, and accompanying her to present it in a meeting with the director of the drinking water company. After hearing the dire situation in this village, the director promised that a tanker would visit the village twice a week to supplement the supply. The women left, satisfied, but the tanker never arrived. Faced with a heavy demand on limited tankers, the director evidently prioritized other areas. Ultimately, the claims of the WUA, even when backed by the water ministry itself, held little weight with the semi-private company that provides drinking water. The disappointment in the village was acute and the organizer was embarrassed. She said that she doubted that she would be able to work further with these women after failing to deliver what she had promised.

This marginalization of the water-related issues deemed to be 'female' impacted the dynamics of the project team, as the female community organizers began to feel that their work was being sidelined. I attended one meeting, for example, in which the members of a WUA gathered together to elect representatives for the management committee. The meeting comprised eighteen men and one woman. The woman sat at the back of the room with the female community organizer and did not participate in any of the discussion. When the election took place for the management committee, on which this lady became the female representative by virtue of being the only woman present, she was not party to any of the decisions. Only at the end of the meeting, after the men had chosen the committee and selected a president, secretary and treasurer, did one of the male community organizers turn to the woman and ask, 'Do you agree?' His tone and manner was such that it would have been difficult for her to say that she did not. As we drove away from the meeting, the female community organizer was sullen. She said she was fed up with the 'gender work'. 'There were only words for the men, few words for the women,' she complained. There had not been any discussion of drinking water provision, sewage connections or rubbish collection – the issues that she saw as the priority concerns of the women in the WUA. 'I've lost all hope in my work,' she said.[19]

The way in which participation is structured and communicated at the outset is hence critical for determining the participants' expectations. These expectations play a key role in how the participants approach the participatory process, and ultimately shape the success of the participatory institutions. Participatory governance thus moves far beyond the theorizations of its advocates as it is enacted in practice.

Conclusion

This chapter has focused on one specific locale where international donors, working in partnership with a national water ministry, are seeking to implement the notion of participatory water governance. From the conference halls of international water forums and publications of international agencies and academic journals, where repeated iteration of the same phrases establishes water user participation in governance as one of *the* solutions to water problems, it is in scenes such as those I describe in this chapter that participation takes on, or fails to take on, meaning for participants. One of the most frequently cited critiques of participation is the fact that it is incomplete. In focusing on one dimension of this incompleteness – the marginalization of women from the WUAs – I show the significance of the establishment process for setting the terms of participation. In this case, as in many others, the rules of entry into the WUA are biased against women. But rather than the analysis stopping there and taking those rules as a given, the chapter has explored how those rules came into being, through an active process of negotiation between the different parties involved in the WUA establishment. This analysis thus brings to light the multiplicities reflected within a hegemonic concept like participation – the different understandings of who the participants are and what it means to participate. It draws attention to the people who carry the concept from place to place, communicating to those who are meant to participate what participation means, and in doing so, shaping the terrain for participation. It shows, also, how ideas about participation are always articulated through and circumscribed by other hegemonic understandings, such as societal interpretations of gender norms.

In their introduction to this volume, Goldin, Harris and Sneddon (Chapter 1) note the way in which hegemonic concepts manifest themselves in particular places in different ways. This chapter argues that efforts to promote participation could benefit from closer attention to how the concept travels and, in the process, evolves. It is in these spaces of implementation that participation gains its meaning. It is in these spaces that it impacts people's lives.

Notes

1 Fieldnotes, 17 Feb. 2008.
2 While international donors working in Egypt have also sought to promote other concepts that have become hegemonic in water management circles, like marketization, these efforts have been less successful. The Egyptian Ministry of Water Resources and Irrigation has, for example, resisted pressure from the donors to introduce charges for water, despite the argument that this form of marketization can help increase the efficiency of water use (see Harris, Chapter 10).
3 As of yet, none of the donor projects have encouraged the ministry to transfer responsibility for the operation and maintenance of the canals to the WUAs. The notion of participatory water management in this case thus remains limited to one of involvement in decision-making, rather than actually running the system. For more on the contrasting ways in which donors, consultants, engineers and farmers understand the concept of participation and the role of the WUAs as participatory institutions, see Barnes (forthcoming, Ch.3).
4 I keep the project anonymous in order to protect the identity of my informants.
5 The project manager asked me to give a series of lectures to the project team as part of my affiliation with the project.
6 The clip was from the short documentary film, *She Cultivates, She Irrigates*, produced by the Dutch-Egyptian Advisory Panel Project on Water Management in the late 1990s.
7 Fieldnotes, 2 March 2008.
8 Fieldnotes, 17 Jan. 2008.
9 This is a strikingly similar rhetoric to that presented by Harris (2006), in which she describes Arab farmers in southeastern Turkey as stating proudly that Arab women do not irrigate but Kurdish women might do, highlighting intersections between ethnicity and gender.
10 Fieldnotes, 23 April 2008.
11 Fieldnotes, 14 June 2007.
12 Harris (2006) also documents the lower prestige accorded to women who work in the fields in her analysis of irrigation in southeastern Turkey.
13 Fieldnotes 23 April 2008.
14 Fieldnotes, 11 March 2008.
15 Fieldnotes, 1 July 2008.
16 Fieldnotes, 16 June 2008.
17 Fieldnotes, 9 March 2008.
18 Fieldnotes, 26 March 2008.
19 Fieldnotes, 20 Feb. 2008.

References

Agarwal, B. 2001. Participatory exclusions, community forestry, and gender: an analysis for South Asia and a conceptual framework. *World Development,* 29(10), 1623–48.

Barnes, J. forthcoming. *Cultivating the Nile: The Everyday Politics of Water in Egypt,* Durham, NC: Duke University Press.

Harris, L. M. 2005. Negotiating inequalities: democracy, gender, and politics of difference in water user groups of southeastern Turkey. In F. Adaman and M. Arsel (eds), *Environmentalism in Turkey: Between Democracy and Development?*, pp. 185–201, Aldershot: Ashgate.

Harris, L. M. 2006. Irrigation, gender, and the social geographies of the changing waterscape in southeastern Anatolia. *Environment and Planning D: Society and Space,* 24(2), 187–213.

Hopkins, N. 1999. Irrigation in contemporary Egypt. In A. Bowman and E. Rogan (eds), *Agriculture in Egypt: From Pharaonic to Modern Times*, pp. 367–87, London: British Academy.

Hopkins, N., and Saad, R. 2004. *Upper Egypt: Identity and Change*, Cairo: American University in Cairo Press.

Hunt, R. 1989. Appropriate social organization? Water users associations in bureaucratic canal irrigation systems. *Human Organization*, 48(1), 79–90.

Meinzen-Dick, R., and Zwarteveen, M. 1998. Gendered participation in water management: issues and illustrations from WUAs in South Asia. *Agriculture and Human Values*, 15(4), 337–45.

Mosse, D. 2003. *The Rule of Water: Statecraft, Ecology, and Collective Action in South India*, New Delhi: Oxford University Press.

Pellissery, S., and Bergh, S. 2007. Adapting the capability approach to explain the effects of participatory development programs: case studies from India and Morocco. *Journal of Human Development*, 8(2), 283–302.

Radwan, H. 2005. *User Participation through Water Boards: An Evaluation of the Effectiveness of the Representative Assembly of Water Boards*, report produced for the Water Boards Project, Cairo: Ministry of Water Resources and Irrigation.

Radwan, H. 2007. *Female Farmers in Egypt: Their Water Management Interests and Coping Mechanisms*, Technical Report, 45, Water Boards: Integrated Irrigation Improvement and Management Project, Cairo: Ministry of Water Resources and Irrigation.

She Cultivates, She Irrigates. 1998. [video] Produced by the Dutch-Egyptian Advisory Panel Project on Water Management. Cairo: Advisory Panel Project (APP) Egypt.

Trawick, P. 2001. Successfully governing the commons: principles of social organization in an Andean irrigation system. *Human Ecology*, 29(1), 1–25.

Zwarteveen, M., Udas, P., and Delgado, J., 2010. Gendered dynamics of participation in water management in Nepal and Peru: revisiting the linkages between membership and power. In K. Berry and E. Mollard (eds), *Social Participation in Water Governance and Management: Critical and Global Perspectives*, pp. 69–94, London: Earthscan.

18 Problems and prospects for genuine participation in water governance in Turkey

Zeynep Kadirbeyoğlu and Ekin Kurtiç

Introduction

Focusing on the case of Turkey, this chapter assesses the extent to which participation of rural/local communities in water governance is possible. The specific examples of hydroelectric power plants and irrigation both shed light on the diverse ways that participation, or the lack of it, manifest themselves in the context of rural Turkey. Our interest in irrigation is linked to recent trends to decentralize the management of irrigation infrastructure, from centralized state bureaucracies to local communities. Our examination of hydroelectric power plants (HPPs) is also linked to the commercialization and privatization processes (see Part III), since the central state distributes licenses to companies to build the HPP infrastructure, with the guarantee that the national grid will purchase the energy produced at a certain price. This process also has clear links to privatization processes, in that licenses are being handed over to private companies, although the mechanisms in rural areas are distinct from those in urban areas, the latter of which is the focus of most studies of water privatization (Bakker, 2010). With these two cases – hydroelectric power plants and irrigation development – we explore the extent to which there is participation of local communities in the processes of decision-making and implementation in water governance. By doing so, we also ask whether or not participation is used within the hegemonic water governance discourse and what the consequences of its presence or absence might be.

Our analysis shows that hegemonic water governance in Turkey is not unified and single-layered. The two cases illuminate that water governance operates through different tools, strategies and discourses. For example, while the policies regarding the HPPs are defined and implemented in a top–down manner, leaving almost no space for genuine participatory processes, irrigation management is decentralized, engaging more directly with the discourses and practices of participatory governance. We argue that participation lies at the heart of the hegemony in water governance in HPPs and irrigation, albeit in different forms: while in the former case rural communities refuse to participate in the HPP construction processes and challenge the hegemonic discourses and practices, in the latter, participation is used as a key tool to legitimize and sustain hegemonic water governance. Thus, we claim that, although hegemonic water governance in Turkey exhibits a neoliberal character in terms of the ways in which it is decentralized and privatized, it also entails multiple pathways towards and layers of participation (see also Harris and Islar, forthcoming).

It is clear that the conditions in Turkey are connected to broader regional or global contexts. As discussed in the privatization and marketization section of this volume, water has become a commodity and its character as a public good has been increasingly transformed into private property in the neoliberal era (Bakker, 2007, 2012; Mitchell, 2012). The management of water as an economic good was encoded in the international arena at the International Conference on Water and the Environment (ICWE) in Dublin in 1992 through the Dublin Principles, which calls for efficient use and protection of the resource. The framing chapters by Mahayni and Harris in this volume (Chapter 4 and Chapter 10 respectively) reveal the construction of a scarcity discourse through an emphasis on water crisis, which then augments market and private property mechanisms that claim to bring about efficiency in water governance. For instance, the World Water Forum, which is organized by the World Water Council – whose major sponsors and participants are big water companies and government representatives from all over the world – highlights privatization of water services as *the* efficient and appropriate vehicle for the good governance of water in line with 'green neoliberal' policies of the World Bank and the IMF (Goldman, 2007; see also Sneddon, Chapter 2).[1]

Given the above-mentioned global trends, we need to briefly highlight the socio-political and historical peculiarities of Turkey in order to better understand the reflections of global trends in this local context. The top–down modernization strategy that the Republic of Turkey adopted in the 1920s aimed at creating a modern society within an authoritarian and centralized political framework (Köker, 1995: 58). The strong, centralized and highly bureaucratic state apparatus (Özbudun, 2000) was a continuation of the distrust of local autonomy inherited from the Ottoman Empire (Heper, 1985), and such a centralized structure was seen as necessary for rapid economic development (Esmer, 1989). The centralized developmentalist strategies of the state that followed often left out the possibility for participation of a majority of population. Whether rural or urban, actors whose lives were to be affected by major development projects found out about such projects only at the implementation stage, without being given the right to affect the course of the projects. The neoliberal turn, gaining pace in the 1980s, was coupled with the emphasis attributed to citizen participation in development projects throughout the world, particularly involving an emphasis on decentralization. But the question of whether decentralization entails a space for genuine participation by local communities in Turkey is yet to be answered. Looking at the water governance in Turkey, it is crucial to note that the central state and its developmentalist approach remain dominant and effective in determining the rules of the game concerning hydropower. Given this context, this chapter is interested in the articulation between concurrent processes of privatization, decentralization and participation.

As indicated by Sneddon in the introductory chapter on hegemony, the term 'governance' is linked to questions of power and authority that are key concerns for the construction of hegemony. Orlove and Caton (2010: 405) argue that 'the term governance is useful, but its association with the notion of management may presume the agreement of all parties on the goals that they share and on the values that they place on water' and thus may gloss over 'the debates and conflict over these goals'. In line with this argument, a reflection on the question of water governance must necessarily delve into the sphere of politics and interrogate the power relations between actors and collective social entities. Such interrogation must also involve issues of consent, as well as open conflict that challenges existing hegemonies.

In this sense, we believe that governance is closely related to politics and power relations that are always in the making. The focus on water especially requires such a framework since it connects humans and non-humans within a dynamic hydro-social cycle through social and natural flows (Swyngedouw, 2009). To capture this connectivity, it is necessary to deal with the relations between different actors or collective social entities. This point brings us to the importance of the idea of participation as well as related questions of who decides, who uses and who has access to water, and who is affected – and in which ways – by the changes and modifications in a hydro-social cycle. By looking at the role of local communities in water governance, we will show how different modes of participation, or the lack of it, may contribute to or challenge the construction of hegemonies that order the hydro-social cycle in particular ways.

What do we mean by 'participation'? In what ways does participation relate to the hegemonic understanding of water governance? Answering these questions requires a perspective wide enough to include various manifestations of participation, from tyranny (Cooke and Kothari, 2001) to transformation (Hickey and Mohan, 2004). According to Arnstein's ladder of participation (1969: 217), therapy and manipulation appear as the two bottom rungs, in which the aim is to 'enable powerholders to "educate" or "cure" the participants', corresponding to a lack of participation. The middle rungs are informing, consultation and placation, which are categorized as 'tokenism' where citizen voices are heard but this does not guarantee their active involvement in decision-making. Arnstein refers to the top rungs of the participation ladder as 'citizen power', which corresponds to 'partnership, delegated power, or citizen control' (ibid.).

As illustrated in Arnstein's categorization, there are many ways in which participation is constructed and put into practice. Therefore, it is not surprising that there is an ever-increasing importance attributed to participation, even by dominant institutions and actors. Not only can participation have a strong potential either to hide or to reinforce the manifold oppressions and injustices of a given context (Cooke and Kothari, 2001), but it can also be 'a Foucauldian exercise of power that rewrites the subjectivity of the Third World's poor, disciplining them through a series of participatory procedures, performances and encounters' (Ferguson, 1994, cited in Williams, 2004: 93). For instance, Birkenholtz (2009: 208) shows how decentralization and participation in groundwater management in India are in fact designed to construct 'self-conducting and willing subjects' who give consent to neoliberal transformations that cause them material harm.

Therefore, participation may easily become a mechanism through which hegemonic discourses and practices are constructed, legitimized and consented to.

Despite being tokenistic, participatory practices may also result in transformations in line with Gallagher's (2008) argument that governmental power which operates through persuading people to engage in self-conduct and subjection is a very subtle and effective mechanism of power but may result in the consolidation of independent agency, since it improves people's ability to govern themselves. 'Different spaces of participation, both within and against or outside the state' (Williams, 2004: 97), are bound to have varying qualities and thus the link between the political space and the people's capabilities can further call the power of the state into account. Similarly, Hickey and Mohan (2004) focus on the transformative effects of participation in development, considering participation's link to existing power structures and political systems. They emphasize that participation which questions existing power structures may have a transformative impact on those structures or relations.

In sum, this chapter focuses on the role of participation or lack of it in constructing, reproducing, challenging or resisting hegemonic neoliberal water governance in Turkey. For this purpose, in the following section we first explain how and why HPPs came onto the agenda. By dealing with the HPPs as cases that reveal neoliberal hegemonic water governance combining privatization with developmentalism, we ask whether or not local communities who live near the rivers can have an impact on decision-making and implementation processes. We then focus on irrigation management in Turkey by critically questioning the way decentralization is constructed and practiced in terms of the design of organizations and the power distribution within local communities. By approaching Water User Associations (WUAs) as examples of 'centralized decentralization' going hand in hand with marketization, we show that genuine participation of local communities in irrigation management remains lacking. All in all, we argue that, whereas participation is used to reinforce this hegemonic understanding in the case of irrigation, local people's refusal to participate in the procedural meetings necessary for the construction of HPPs and their continued resistance to the projects may challenge hegemonic approaches to water governance in novel ways.

Water in the making: how do powers of the river flows and of socio-political context intersect in the case of hydroelectric power plants in Turkey?

Nearly all of Turkey's rivers and streams – approximately 10,000 km – are slated to be dammed by 2023 (Şekercioğlu *et al.*, 2011). Since the 1950s, large and small dams have been constructed throughout Turkey for the purpose of energy production and/or irrigation as part of statist, top–down development projects.[2] Yet in the last decade, projects designed for energy production have shifted from large dams to run-of-the-river hydroelectric power plants (see also Erensu, Chapter 6) which led to a drastic increase in their numbers (see Figure 18.1). Unlike large dams, they function without reservoirs, or with very small reservoirs. River waters are taken from the riverbed into pipes or tunnels and energy is generated by falling water. From the point where one power plant finishes, another power plant can take the water again into another set of pipes. In this way, on a single river, from its source until its mouth, several or even dozens of power plants can be built. Although promoted as environmentally benign, this is expected to have serious negative impacts on livelihoods and ecosystems (Şekercioğlu *et al.*, 2011), largely due to the fact that water is confined in pipes and does not flow in its riverbed. Recent HPP projects have been planned, built and managed by private companies that are authorized for 49 years through the licenses distributed by central state institutions. 'In a few years, 25 river basins have become sites for private hydropower development' (Islar, 2012: 379). All in all, HPPs are pivotal as intersection points between the power of the river flows and of socio-political domains. In other words, HPPs provide critical cases that enable elaboration of the manifold ways in which power webs operate between different actors involved in water governance.

> Turkey can only make use of one third of its waters. We prepared all the plans to reach to the level of using all the potential of our water resources until 2023. We will change the saying 'Water flows, Turk watches'.
>
> (Radikal, 2010a)

> We don't have enough petroleum, nor natural gas. We have water, and it flows in vain. While water flows in vain, we cannot just watch it.
>
> (Zaman, 2010)

These quotes reflect the position of government officials on current water governance in relation to hydropower. Freely flowing river waters are framed as 'wasted' resources and if these resources were to be properly used, the argument goes, they could foster economic development. As others have argued, the HPP policies represent a recasting of the state management of rivers, not necessarily the state's total retreat from this realm (Harris and Islar, forthcoming). Developmentalist state discourse continues to be dominant in the efforts to legitimize these policies (see Erensu, Chapter 6; Islar, 2012). Where do the local communities who live in the vicinity of these rivers stand in this picture? What is their role in determining water policies and their implementation? Where are the local communities' priorities, preferences or opinions located in the flows of socio-political power? In other words, if governance 'looks at the balance of power and the balance of actions at different levels of authority' (Sneddon, Chapter 2), in what ways do local communities participate in socio-political flows that shape water governance?

We answer these questions by examining the ways in which hegemonic water governance is constructed discursively and in practice and in the reactions of the local communities. The only allegedly participatory step, in some HPPs, is the People's Participation Meetings (PPMs) required for the preparation of Environmental Impact Assessment Reports.[3] In many localities, refusing to

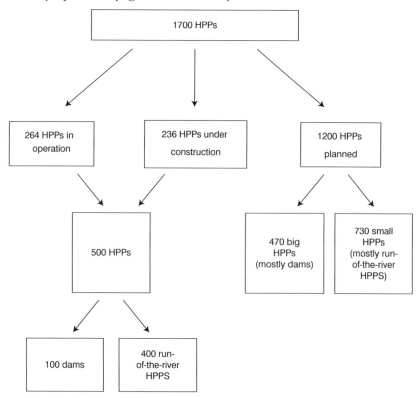

Figure 18.1 Turkey's hydroelectric power plants (HPPs) in numbers (source: Çevre ve Orman Bakanlığı Devlet Su İşleri Genel Müdürlüğü, 2011: 53)

participate in the PPMs became one of the tools for resisting the HPPs. By focusing on the conflicts between local communities, the state and private companies, we show that resistance against HPPs indicates that non-participation is in fact a way of participating. This is one of the mechanisms available to the communities by which to be involved in water governance. Although hegemony implies a kind of willing consent on the part of those being governed, it does not exclude the possibility of resistance to an all-encompassing hegemony. By not giving their consent to and struggling against the hegemonic water governance in the case of HPPs, rural communities engage through a slightly different means: non-participation, public protests, marches and litigation. Therefore, our argument is that local communities' resistance opens up a new space of participation by challenging and questioning the hegemonic and top–down water governance that has effectively sidelined meaningful participation in decision-making and implementation processes.

In order to better understand the contemporary situation, it is helpful to give a brief overview of the way in which hydropower took shape over previous decades in Turkey. From the 1950s until the early 1980s, investment in large dams came from public sources (Kibaroglu *et al.*, 2009). In 1984 Law No. 3096 was enacted to regulate the permission given to private companies to produce, distribute, transport and sell electrical energy. According to this law, the government may decide to transfer these functions in a given region to the private sector for a period of 99 years. In 2001 Electricity Market Law No. 4628 was enacted and aimed at creating a strong, transparent and independently regulated electrical energy market. This law formed the foundation of the Energy Market Regulatory Authority (EMRA) and defined the methods for privatization of electrical energy production and distribution. In line with this privatization and marketization process, in 2003 the government promulgated the Legislation for Agreement upon the Right of the Use of Water, which regulates the conditions and content of the agreement to be signed between the private companies producing hydroelectric energy and the State Hydraulic Works (Devlet Su İşleri, or DSI). According to this legislation, companies may apply for the projects developed and announced by DSI or they may apply to DSI with their own projects. Once their application and feasibility reports are approved by DSI, they apply for the approval of the EMRA. Upon approval of their application, the company obtains a license for hydroelectricity production for a period of 49 years. According the Law on the Utilization of Renewable Energy Resources for the Purpose of Generating Electrical Energy (No. 5346), put into force in 2005, the purchase of the hydroelectricity by the state is guaranteed (Kibaroglu *et al.*, 2009).

The above stated decision-making and implementation procedures also regulate the input from communities living close to the rivers where HPPs are constructed. Involvement is required in the form of People's Participation Meetings in Environmental Impact Assessment (EIA) preparations. Where it applies, private investors have to present the EIA's report on the project to the Ministry of Environment and Urban Planning. According to the Regulation on Environmental Impact Assessment No. 26939, when an EIA is required,

> the meeting for people's participation is organized by the owner of the project in the locality where the project is going to be realized on the date decided together with the Ministry in order to inform people about the investment and get their opinions and proposal about the project.
>
> (Budak and Güneş, 2011: 374)

Given that it is the companies themselves that are responsible for this engagement process, in practice the companies often use these meetings only to inform people without asking for feedback from them. As explained in the report of the Union of Chambers of Turkish Engineers and Architects, even in instances where people participate in People's Participation Meetings (PPMs) to express their negative opinions about projects, the EIA procedure continues uninterrupted. In fact, it is very rare to see the cancellation of a project by the Ministry based on an unfavorable EIA report (TMMOB, 2011).[4]

The façade of participation, which ignores voices from below, is exemplified by a recent participatory process undertaken in a village in the north-east of Turkey in Gümüşhane. In this case, the village headman declared that they, as the local people, did not accept the projects and would not participate in the meeting. The director of this meeting then responded that in the report of the meeting it would be stated that local people did not participate but that an informative meeting was carried out.[5] Another exemplary case that helps us question the meaning of 'participation' in these meetings happened in Erzurum, in eastern Turkey. While local people were demonstrating against the construction of an HPP, and as the tension in the public participatory meeting increased, the governor intervened with the following words: 'You should help those coming to your region with the purposes of HPP construction. Otherwise you are going to be in trouble.'[6] With instances of this type, we can understand the PPMs are examples of 'tokenism' (Arnstein, 1969) in the sense that they are described as instances for consultation, yet the way they are practiced corresponds to the lowest ladder of participation, where people are seen as passive actors to be educated or even threatened into giving their consent. In these circumstances there is an increasing need to consider what non-participation of the people as a way of protesting against this tokenism or manipulation means.

These 'sham meetings' do play an important role in the struggle against HPPs since people use them as a tool to show their reactions to HPPs (see also Erensu, Chapter 6). The head of the Platform of Sister/Brotherhood of Rivers[7] declared that: 'As local people and peasants, we will not participate in EIA information meetings and we will make sure that our position against these projects will be recorded in the minutes. On the other hand, in the meetings we get to participate, we will submit our documents and knowledge and demonstrate the irrevocable damage that these projects will bring to our natural living spaces.'[8] Other examples abound, as in the case of Rize in the north of Turkey, where peasants broke into the EIA meeting, claiming that people who were present in the meeting room were not local villagers, but that they had been brought there by the company from other places. Similarly, in İkizdere the EIA meeting was interrupted by local community members who claimed that those holding the meeting were not the people from İkizdere, but government and company representatives.[9] In cases where a genuine space for participation in decision-making processes is hindered through diverse mechanisms such as disregarding the oppositional opinions of local communities, threatening them if they protest against the HPPs or attempting to hold the PPMs in the absence of villagers, non-participation in PPMs or preventing the PPMs to take place become important tools of resistance available for local communities.[10]

Local communities' resistance strategies are not limited to non-participation. Villagers expressed their protest to the Prime Minister by turning their backs on him when he came for the inauguration of an HPP in Fırtına Valley located in the Black Sea Region (Hamsici, 2010: 146). They hindered EIA information and participation meetings in the district of İkizdere. Villagers in Fındıklı attacked the cars of the expert committee and company representatives with eggs and stones (Hamsici, 2010: 115). Other ways of showing frustration and disapproval of these schemes included, as was the case in Yuvarlakçay, camping in tents and keeping guard near the construction site in order to prevent the construction machines from entering the site and beginning their work (see also discussion in Özesmi, Chapter 8).[11]

State representatives' responses to local communities' resistance also take diverse forms, varying from public declarations and speeches to actions that include direct violence by the police,[12] trials[13] and new regulations.[14] The government declarations shed light on the different strategies the state adopts when dealing with rural unrest and protests, ranging from persuasion to absorption and denial. Prime Minister Erdoğan declared in Rize:

> In different parts of the world, there are environmentalists. You ask them 'what do you do?' and you see that they don't have any appropriate manageable occupation. To be environmentalist is what they do to use their free time. I am *daniska*[15] of the environmentalists. I am the real environmentalist.
>
> (Radikal, 2008)

Stigmatizing rural communities as ignorant and naïve people who are being manipulated by environmentalists or other political groups is also a very common tactic used by the government to delegitimize these resistances in the eyes of the broader public. Together, these governmental and corporate tactics constitute attempts to inhibit and enclose potential spaces for participation. Hegemonic water governance in the case of HPPs operates through top–down strategies of privatization and commercialization of rivers based on aggressive developmentalist endeavors. Although this hegemony is strongly questioned and challenged by the resistance of local communities and their supporters nation-wide, the ways in which the state responds highlight how power is used when consent cannot be assured, namely, direct violence, legal force, co-option and delegitimization. Whether or not these struggles will culminate in transforming hegemonic water governance, in the sense of building effective counter-hegemonies, is yet to be seen.

Decentralization in irrigation management: genuine participation?

It is important to examine irrigation and participation, given that agricultural production accounts for more than 70 percent of water use in Turkey[16] and given that participation of users in irrigation management is increasingly emphasized as part of decentralization reforms of recent decades. This section traces the history of decentralization in irrigation management in Turkey and shows that it was introduced as a manifestation of the hegemonic understanding of water governance which seeks to render irrigation schemes more efficient. Even though privatization of irrigation schemes is not yet on the agenda, decentralization reforms in irrigation operation and maintenance have been carried out in line with an increasing neoliberal approach to water governance.

Agrawal and Ostrom define decentralization as 'any act by which the central government cedes rights of decision-making over resources to actors and institutions at lower levels in a politico-administrative and territorial hierarchy' (2001: 488). The logic of decentralization often involves the assumption that local-level units are more easily accessed, monitored and pressured by individuals and groups (Goldin, 2010; Chapter 16). Decentralization can disperse political power and help create new civic spaces, enabling individuals to develop democratic skills and practices. Hence, decentralization can be associated with increased participation in local decision-making, greater efficiency and democratization (Goldin, 2010). However, whether or not these positive outcomes associated with decentralization materialize depends on factors such as institutional design and the distribution of power within local communities. In cases where the local context is disregarded, or where institutional dynamics are not well thought through, decentralization can aggravate power inequalities.

Key concerns that often remain underplayed in dominant discourses related to natural resources decentralization include unanticipated and unwelcome outcomes, such as 'elite capture' in decentralized institutions (Mohan and Stokke, 2000; Bryld, 2001; Dasgupta and Beard, 2007), the reinforcement of existing inequalities or corruption. Hadiz (2004) suggests that, to ensure the viability of decentralized structures, the World Bank often works only with the existing elite in a given collective, rather than disturbing the existing social order by establishing a more egalitarian institution for water governance. Practices such as this increase the likelihood of elite capture of decentralized structures. Research on decentralization also reveals that the discourse usually portrays the process as being clear-cut, whereas the reality is often very messy. This is exemplified by the case of Indonesia discussed by McCarthy, who shows that the Indonesian government passed in the same year the Regional Autonomy Act, which would presumably give more powers to the district and municipal governments, and the new basic forestry law. The forestry law allows the Forestry Ministry to retain central control over forests since 'the forestry law failed to detail the specific government agencies or levels of government that had responsibility for particular administrative functions' (McCarthy, 2004: 1204).

In the case of Turkey, the decision to decentralize irrigation management was taken by the state, following recommendations by the World Bank[17] and inspired by the Mexican example (Palerm-Viqueira, 2004) where the Bank has promoted the decentralization of irrigation since 1989 (Whiteford and Melville, 2002: 17). Officials from Turkey's central state agency, State Hydraulic Works (DSI), travelled to Mexico several times under the guidance of the World Bank in order to observe the functioning of that system (Svendsen and Nott, 1999). In Turkey, the operation and maintenance of irrigation infrastructure was transferred to water users starting in 1993 (Kudat, 1996). The formal rules of the decentralization of irrigation management – such as the statute determining the associations' structure and areas of action – were decided by DSI as a blueprint for all irrigation schemes across Turkey. This 'centralized decentralization', in the sense of creating identical organizations across the board and centrally devising their statutes, goes a long way towards determining how water user associations (WUAs) currently operate.

With the construction of new institutional forms such as WUAs, farmers are now confronted with an organization that is composed of individuals from their own and neighboring villages. Ideally, WUAs should be governed by local users who have been elected to an executive committee, and monitored by a council of representatives elected by the farmers themselves. In practice, the associations have often become non-representative organizations benefiting the powerful few and not allowing the participation of all water users within this representative structure. Initially, WUA councils were dominated by elected local authorities such as mayors and headmen of villages. This was deemed to be more efficient than electing all the representatives among water users. However, this type of organization clearly did not challenge existing power structures.

As in many other contexts, WUAs were expected to increase efficiency of water use. As such, they are clearly linked to hegemonic discourses of scarcity, the topic of Part I of this book (Mahayni, Chapter 4), particularly given that farmers pay for the maintenance of the system and have an incentive to conserve water. This also resonates with the second main theme of the book, i.e. marketization (Harris. Chapter 10). The decentralized structure of irrigation operation and maintenance transformed from being a financial burden on the DSI to being a self-sufficient operation organized within the WUA structure. Although, as this section shows, there is little meaningful participation and WUAs provide support for marketization in the irrigation realm, it is also the case that farmers largely consent to this water governance norm because it enables them to affect the pricing of water – the issue about which there is the most extensive debate in WUA councils (Kadirbeyoglu, 2008). In this way, decentralization shows the articulation between participation mandates and other elements of hegemonic water governance in Turkey (i.e. pricing and marketization). This case also shows how highly variable hegemonic practices of water governance can be as they interact with social and political relations in specific places.

Research on WUAs shows that inequalities such as unequal distribution of land and resources negatively affect how farmers are treated by the associations (Kadirbeyoglu, 2008). There is unequal enforcement of fees, which fluctuate depending on the socio-economic status of farmers. This is documented by an in-depth study of one of the associations in Urfa (Halcrow-Dolsar, 2000: 3–28). In a similar vein, a comprehensive study of irrigation associations in Turkey claims that the Chair of the WUA can annul the penalties and extend the payment deadlines for some farmers (Baran, 1996). Even in contexts where there is no mention of corruption within the associations or no complaint about unequal enforcement of fees, there were complaints that powerful farmers could influence the distribution of water. For instance, in a WUA in Söke, even though the order of water distribution is determined through a lottery, farmers claimed that they had to be present at the draw in order to ensure there was no trickery in their absence. Farmers stand up for themselves by being present and not allowing the system to marginalize or intimidate them (Kadirbeyoglu, 2008).

Discussions of WUAs in Turkey have also noted that bureaucrats and WUA personnel look down on farmers because they are seen as uneducated (Harris,

2005; Aygüney, 2002). Some scholars even use the analogy of children who are given a 'superb modern instrument' (farmers who are entrusted with the operation of the irrigation infrastructure) (Yalman, 1971: 196), which they then use to over-irrigate and cause environmental problems such as soil salinization and rising water tables (Karlı and Çelik, 2003: 27). This contempt for farmers, who are supposed to be the key actors and beneficiaries of decentralized irrigation associations, shows that many of the dimensions of their participation and engagement through these mechanisms are tokenistic rather than meaningful.

Even with evidence suggesting such difficulties, DSI has chosen to represent the decentralization of irrigation management as a successful project. For the most part, this celebratory tone is based on the evaluation of the WUAs using functional and technocratic criteria. The director of the DSI Operation and Maintenance Department is satisfied with the result of these transfers, as the following statement indicates:

> We have transferred the operation and maintenance of 94 percent of the irrigation schemes and not even one was returned to us [through the revocation of the WUA either because the users did not want to manage or through disciplinary action by the DSI as a result of bad management]. This is a great success. ... The WUA personnel are not appointed from the center. It creates employment. It is managed by a council. The farmers select the councilors. These were the multiple aspects of self-organization and self-management. We have, thus, provided a democratic opening.
>
> (Kadirbeyoglu, 2008: 109)

From this narrow framing (and from the state's perspective), WUAs are unproblematic. Yet they have significant problems in terms of participation of different agents: the exclusion of women, social oppression and exclusion of the farmers who are stigmatized as being uneducated and ignorant actors, economic inequalities within the rural communities and the impact of the central state's policies and decisions (Harris, 2005; Kadirbeyoglu, 2008). In setting up these decentralized institutions, little attention was given to inclusivity and to the minimization of inequalities. Kibaroglu *et al.* (2009) summarize the criticisms of the opposition coalition against the irrigation associations, who claim the impossibility of farmers' participation and the ignorance of local conditions in this top–down decentralization model. We agree that decentralization in the field of irrigation does not really allow for meaningful participation. This is also in line with Fung and Wright (2003) who claim that the democratizing potential of participatory practices is only realizable if they engender the ability to challenge the wealthy and educated groups who tend to dominate decentralized decision-making. In the absence of such countervailing powers, decentralization tends to serve the powerful and reinforces hegemonic understandings and operations of water governance. Despite such a negative evaluation, it should not be forgotten that decentralization can also open up new spaces for challenging hegemonies. However, in the case of Turkey, this does not seem to be the case at the moment.

Concluding remarks

What does the study of the intersection between the flows of rivers and the flows of socio-political power tell us in terms of participation? Water governance in Turkey, as illustrated in the case of hydroelectric power plants, shows us that privatization and commodification of river water – which previously was not commodified – has now taken root and goes hand in hand with top–down developmentalist discourses and practices. Yet as Williams (2004) explains, referring to the work of Moore and Putzel (1999: 96), 'despite increased globalization and privatization of development, developmental activities of states remain key sites for struggle as it is here that there's a chance that forms of recognized authority can be called into account'. Similarly, despite the obstacles inherent in the current hegemonic water governance framework in Turkey, local communities nonetheless find spaces to assert their needs, ideas and ideals. As such, resistance can effectively constitute a form of participation by other means. Indeed, rural communities make their voices heard via direct actions at the construction site or through court cases. This case brings us to the spaces of resistance that may question, challenge, weaken or destroy the hegemonies. Yet these forms of participation do not remain uncontested by the state. Protesters have been silenced by court decisions and their form of participation has been stigmatized and branded as 'nonsense' and as illegitimate by government representatives.

Irrigation management in Turkey is supposedly democratic, aligning water governance practices with participatory irrigation structures at the institutional level. WUAs have served to reduce the financial burden of irrigation on DSI's budget. In so doing, participatory governance serves broader marketization and privatization hegemonies (see Harris, Chapter 10). Genuine participation in irrigation schemes in this context is still largely absent. To move forward towards more meaningful participation would certainly begin with what Goldin (Chapter 16; 2012) refers to as the recognition of difference. Although DSI has seemingly adopted a new paradigm that is demand-driven, claiming that they will not build any infrastructure unless the local population demands it, the present-day practice still seems to follow largely from past top–down models.

By investigating participatory water governance across HPPs and irrigation schemes, we have highlighted linkages between hegemony and participation. As our opening epigraph attests, water does indeed link human beings, but it also creates novel webs of power that can be difficult to perceive. We put forward that both water hegemony and the responses to it are composed of multi-layered and complex practices and discourses operating through privatization, decentralization, developmentalism and participation. It is our hope that this chapter may also inspire further research to compare practices and experiences of using and accessing water with current transformations, in order to open up a space for more 'inclusive, sustainable and equitable' (Swyngedouw, 2009: 59) alternatives in the way humans interact with water.

Notes

1 It is noteworthy that the 5th World Water Forum (WWF) took place in Turkey in 2009.
2 The Southeastern Anatolia Development Project has been studied as an exemplary state-led top–down developmentalist project involving giant dams for the purposes of hydropower and irrigation (Çarkoğlu and Eder, 2005; Özok-Gündoğan, 2005).
3 These meetings do not take place in all the projects, since EIA is directly required only in HPPs that have installed capacity of 25 MW and above, corresponding to 46 percent of the HPP projects announced on DSI's website (DSI, 2012) This list covers only the projects that are developed by DSI and opened to applications of the private sector. The projects that are developed by the private sector itself are not included in the calculation of this percentage since their installed capacities are not yet announced on DSI's website. Moreover, for the HPP projects that have installed capacity between 0.5 MW and 25 MW, the Ministry of Environment and Urban Planning, based on the evaluation of these criteria, decides whether or not EIA is required.
4 To give precise numbers, in TMMOB's (2011) report it is stated that between 1993 and 2004 the Ministry approved 810 EIAs, whereas in the same period it gave negative decisions for only 16 EIAs.
5 See Haberler (2011).
6 See Radikal (2010b).
7 It is an independent civil entity composed of numerous local and national civil society organizations and movements struggling against HPPs in Turkey.
8 See Haberler (2011).
9 See İkizdere Derneği (2012).
10 For another case that explains non-participation as a way of resistance, see Birkenholtz's study (2009) on irrigation in India.
11 Resistance in Yuvarlakçay has been successful and it culminated in the withdrawal of the company. Thus Yuvarlakçay became an important symbol for the movements against HPPs.
12 Recently in Erzurum, the local community, in their protests against the project, faced violent reactions from the police and gendarmerie when the construction machines came along the river.
13 In Tortum, Erzurum, in Oct. 2011, the court decision resulted in the hindrance of rural people's right to take part in decision-making processes: the court banned 15 villagers from speaking with other villagers who had participated in the protests against HPPs.
14 Environmentally protected areas pose a crucial barrier for HPP construction projects and it is not surprising that the government made a very recent change (in 2010) in the Renewable Energy Law No. 6049, allowing for the construction of HPPs in environmentally protected areas and national parks as long as they are approved by the Ministry and or the regional conservation board. Islar (2012: 386) explains it as an example of 'accumulation by dispossession' where common resources are enclosed and transformed into exclusive places.
15 *Daniska* is a Turkish slang word meaning *the best, the most genuine.*
16 See Kadirbeyoglu and Ozertan (2010) for further details of agricultural use of water in Turkey.
17 WUAs have been the most frequently crafted institutions for irrigation management transfer. See e.g. Gorriz *et al.* (1995) for the case of Mexico, Sehring (2007) for the cases of Kyrgyzstan and Tajikistan; Veldwisch (2007) for the case of Uzbekistan.

References

Agrawal, A., and Ostrom, E. 2001. Collective action, property rights and decentralization in resource use in India and Nepal. *Politics and Society*, 29(4), 485–514.

Arnstein, S. R. 1969. A ladder of citizen participation. *Journal of the American Planning Association*, 35(4), 216–24.

Aygüney, N. 2002. Burdens of 'development' in southeastern Turkey: salinization and sociocultural disruption. MA Lund University.

Bakker, K. 2007. The 'commons' versus the 'commodity': Alter-globalization, privatization, and the human right to water in the global south. *Antipode*, 39(3), 430–55.

Bakker, K. 2010. *Privatizing Water: Governance Failure and the World's Urban Water Crisis,* Oxford: Oxford University Press.

Bakker, K. 2012. Commons vs. commodities: debating the human right to water. In: F. Sultana and A. Loftus (eds), *The Right to Water: Politics, Governance and Social Struggles*, pp. 19–45, Abingdon: Earthscan Routledge.

Baran, E. A. 1996. Sulama birlikleri kuruluş, görev ve sorunları (Responsibilities and problems of WUAs). Ph.D. TODAIE.

Birkenholtz, T. 2009. Groundwater governmentality: hegemony and technologies of resistance in Rajastan's (India) groundwater governance. *Geographical Journal*, 175(3), 208–20.

Bryld, E. 2001. Increasing participation in democratic institutions through decentralization: empowering women and scheduled castes and tribes through Panchayat Raj in rural India. *Democratization*, 8(3), 149–72.

Budak, S., and Güneş, A. 2011. *Temel* çevre *mevzuatı,* Istanbul: On Iki Levha Yayıncılık.

Çarkoğlu, A., and Eder, M. 2005. Development *alla turca*: the Southeastern Anatolia Development Project (GAP). In F. Adaman and M. Arsel (eds), *Environmentalism in Turkey: Between Democracy and Development?*, pp.167–84, Burlington, VT: Ashgate.

Çevre ve Orman Bakanlığı Devlet Su İşleri Genel Müdürlüğü. 2011. Çevre *ve Temiz Enerji: Hidroelektrik,* Ankara: Çevre ve Orman Bakanlığı Devlet Su İşleri Genel Müdürlüğü. Available at: http://www.ybtenerji.com/uploads/9/7/5/9/9759145/cevre_temiz_enerji.pdf (accessed Nov. 2012).

Cooke, B., and Kothari, U., eds. 2001. *Participation: The New Tyranny?,* London and New York: Zed Books.

Dasgupta, A., and Beard, V. A. 2007. Community driven development, collective action and elite capture in Indonesia. *Development and Change*, 38(2), 229–49.

DSI. 2012. *Hidroelektrik Santral Projeleri Listesi*. Available at: http://www2.dsi.gov.tr/skatablo/Tablo1.htm (accessed July 2012).

Esmer, Y. 1989. Allocation of resources. In M. Heper (ed.), *Local Government in Turkey: Governing Greater Istanbul,* London: Routledge.

Fung, A., and Wright, E. O. 2003. Thinking about empowered participatory governance. In A. Fung and E. O. Wright (eds), *Deepening Democracy: Institutional Innovations in Empowered Participatory Governance,* New York: Verso.

Gallagher, M. 2008. Foucault, power and participation. *International Journal of Children's Rights*, 16(3), 395–406.

Goldin, J. A. 2010. Water policy in South Africa: trust and knowledge as obstacles to reform. *Review of Radical Political Economics,* 42(2), 195–212.

Goldin, J. A. forthcoming. From vagueness to precision: raising the volume on social issues for the water sector. *Water Policy*.

Goldman, M. 2007. How 'water for all!' became hegemonic: the power of the World Bank and its transnational policy networks. *Geoforum*, 38(5), 786–800.

Gorriz, C. M., Subramanian, A., and Simas, J. 1995. *Irrigation Management Transfer in Mexico: Process and Progress,* Washington, DC: World Bank.

Haberler. 2011. *Rize ve Artvin'de,* Çed *Toplantılarına Protesto Hazırlığı.* Available at: http://www.haberler.com/rize-ve-artvin-de-ced-toplantilarina-protesto-2876255-haberi (accessed June 2012).

Hadiz, V. R. 2004. Decentralization and democracy in Indonesia: a critique of neo-institutionalist perspectives. *Development and Change*, 35(4), 697–718.

Halcrow-Dolsar. 2000. *GAP sulama sistemlerinin işletme bakımı ve yönetimi – taslak sonuç raporu* (GAP irrigation systems management, operation and maintenance: final report), Ankara: GAP.

Hamsici, M. 2010. *Dereler ve İsyanlar* (Rivers and riots), Ankara: NotaBene

Harris, L. 2005. Negotiating inequalities: democracy, gender, and politics of difference in water user groups of Southeastern Turkey. In F. Adaman and M. Arsel (eds), *Environmentalism in Turkey: Between Democracy and Development?*, pp. 185–201, Burlington, VT: Ashgate.

Harris, L., and Islar, M. forthcoming. Neoliberalism, nature, and changing modalities of environmental governance in contemporary Turkey. In Y. Atasoy (ed.), *Global Economic Crisis and the Politics of Diversity: Trans/Regional Variations, Mixed Responses, New Tensions,* Basingstoke: Palgrave Macmillan.

Heper, M. 1985. *The State Tradition in Turkey,* Beverley, North Humberside: Eothen Press.

Hickey, S., and Mohan, G., eds. 2004. Towards participation as transformation: critical themes and challenges. In S. Hickey and G. Mohan (eds), *Participation: From Tyranny to Transformation?*, pp. 3–25, London and New York: Zed Books.

Islar, M. 2012. Privatised hydropower development in Turkey: a case of water grabbing? *Water Alternatives*, 5(2), 376–91.

İkizdere Derneği. 2012. İkizdereliler *ÇED toplantısını bastı!* . . . Available at: http://www.ikizderedernegi.org/ced_tepki.php (accessed June 2012).

Kadirbeyoglu, Z. 2008. Decentralization and democratization: the case of water user associations in Turkey. Ph.D. McGill University.

Kadirbeyoglu, Z., and Ozertan, G. 2010. Neoliberal policies, challenges and the road ahead. In F. Adaman and G. Ozertan (eds), *Rethinking Structural Reform in Turkish Agriculture: Beyond the World Bank Strategies*, pp. 169–87, New York: Nova Science Publisher.

Karlı, B., and Çelik, Y. 2003. *GAP alanında tarım kooperatifleri ve diğer* çiftçi örgütlerinin *bölge kalkınmasındaki etkinliği* (Agricultural co-operatives and other farmer organizations' role in development in the GAP region), Şanlıurfa: TEAE (Agricultural Economics Research Institute).

Kibaroglu, A., Baskan, A., and Alp, S. 2009. Neo-liberal transitions in hydropower and irrigation water management in Turkey: main actors and opposition groups. In D. Huitema and S. Meijerink (eds), *Water Policy Entrepreneurs: A Research Companion to Water Transitions around the Globe*, pp. 287–304, Cheltenham: Edward Elgar.

Köker, L. 1995. Local politics and democracy in Turkey: an appraisal. *Annals of the American Academy of Political and Social Science*, 540(1), 51–62.

Kudat, A. 1996. *Social Assessment: Participatory Irrigation Management in Turkey,* Washington, DC: World Bank.

McCarthy, J. F. 2004. Changing to gray: decentralization and the emergence of volatile socio-legal configurations in Central Kalimantan, Indonesia. *World Development*, 32(7), 1199–1223.

Mitchell, K. R. 2012. The political economy of the right to water: reinvigorating the question of property. In F. Sultana and A. Loftus (eds), *The Right to Water: Politics, Governance and Social Struggles*, pp. 78–94, Abingdon: Earthscan Routledge.

Mohan, G., and Stokke, K. 2000. Participatory development and empowerment: the dangers of localism. *Third World Quarterly*, 21(2), 247–68.

Moore, M., and Putzel, J. 1999. *Thinking Strategically about Politics and Poverty*, IDS Working Paper, 101, Brighton: Institute of Development Studies, University of Sussex.

Orlove, B., and Caton, S. 2010. Water sustainability: anthropological approaches and prospects. *Annual Review of Anthropology*, 39(1), 401–15.

Özbudun, E. 2000. *Contemporary Turkish Politics: Challenges to Democratic Consolidation*, Boulder, CO: Lynne Rienner.

Özok-Gündoğan, N. 2005. 'Social development' as a governmental strategy in the Southeastern Anatolia Project. *New Perspectives on Turkey*, 32, 93–111.

Palerm-Viqueira, J. 2004. *Irrigation Institutions Typology and Water Governance through Horizontal Agreements*. Available at: http://dlc.dlib.indiana.edu/dlc/bitstream/ handle/ 10535/1771/Palerm-Viqueira_Irrigation_040525_Paper608a.pdf?sequence=1 (accessed Jan. 2012).

Radikal. 2008. *Erdoğan, Rize'de santralleri savundu*. Available at: http://213.243.16.15/ Radikal.aspx?aType=RadikalDetayV3&ArticleID=895007&CategoryID=78 (accessed March 2012).

Radikal, 2010a. *Çevre ve orman ve maliye bakanından açıklama*. Available at: http://www. radikal.com.tr/Radikal.aspx?aType=RadikalDetayV3&ArticleID=991598&Category ID= (accessed Feb. 2012).

Radikal, 2010b. *Vali'den köylülere tehdit gibi uyarı: Yardımcı olun yoksa canınız yanar . . . * Available at: http://www.radikal.com.tr/Radikal.aspx?aType=RadikalDetayV3&Cate goryID=85&ArticleID=981932 (accessed Feb. 2012).

Sehring, J. 2007. Irrigation reform in Kyrgyzstan and Tajikistan. *Irrigation and Drainage Systems*, 21(3–4), 277–90.

Şekercioğlu, C. H., Anderson, S., Akçay, E., Bilgin, R., Can, Ö. E., Semiz, G., Tavşanoğlu, C., Yokeş, M. B., Soyumert, A., İpekdal, K., Sağlam, İ. K., Yücel, M., and Dalfes, H. N. 2011. Turkey's globally important biodiversity in crisis. *Biological Conservation*, 144(12), 2752–69.

Swyngedouw, E. 2009. The political economy and political ecology of the hydro-social cycle. *Journal of Contemporary Water Research and Education*, 142(1), 56–60.

Svendsen, M., and Nott, G. 1999. Irrigation management transfer in Turkey: process and outcomes. *EDI Participatory Irrigation Management Case Studies Series*. Available at: http://www.inpim.org/files/documents/sve_turk.pdf (accessed Jan. 2012).

TMMOB. 2011. *Hidroelektrik santraller raporu* (Hydroelectric power plants report), Ankara: Mattek.

Veldwisch, G. J. 2007. Changing pattern of water distribution under the influence of land reforms and simultaneous WUA establishment. *Irrigation and Drainage Systems*, 21(3), 265–76.

Whiteford, S., and Melville, R. 2002. Water and social change in Mexico: an introduction. In S. Whiteford and R. Melville (eds), *Protecting a Sacred Gift: Water and Social Change in Mexico*, San Diego, CA: Centre for US–Mexican Studies.

Williams, G. 2004. Towards a repoliticization of participatory development: political capabilities and spaces of development. In S. Hickey and G. Mohan (eds), *Participation: From Tyranny to Transformation?*, pp. 92–109, London and New York: Zed Books.

Yalman, N. 1971. On land disputes in Eastern Turkey. In G. L. Tikku (ed.), *Islam and its Cultural Divergence*, Urbana, IL: University of Illinois Press.

Zaman, 2010. Eroğlu: Baraj, gölet ve hidroelektrik santrali yapılmasına karşi çıkmak çılgınlık. Available at: http://www.zaman.com.tr/newsDetail_getNewsById.action?ha berno=964530&title=eroglu-baraj-golet-ve-hidroelektrik-santrali-yapilmasina-karsi-cikmak-cilginlik&haberSayfa=0 (accessed March 2012).

19 Participation's limits

Tracing the contours of participatory water governance in Accra, Ghana

Cynthia Morinville and Leila M. Harris

It's four o'clock on a sunny Monday afternoon in Ghana's capital city of Accra. A man is setting up rows of chairs in a small office. Behind a desk at the back of the room, Florence is busy reading papers and reviewing notes. Women and men walk in the small office one by one, quietly greet one another. Florence, the chairperson, carefully assesses the crowd to make sure everyone is present before she welcomes them. She asks one representative to lead them into prayer and then outlines the agenda of this week's Local Water Board meeting. The next hour and a half is spent discussing the progress of the Board's work, their objectives and next report deadline for their funding agencies. In the words of the chairperson, they 'talk about activities, what [has been] done, [and] the way forward.'[1]

In line with the other chapters presented in Part IV, we focus on participatory water governance as it unfolds in a particular locality. Specifically, we look at the case of Local Water Boards (LWBs) established throughout the last decade in underserved communities of urban Accra, Ghana[2] with interest in their potential to foster transformation in terms of water access and governance. Participation has been increasingly recognized and promoted in the realm of water governance as a way to empower communities and ensure better outcomes. We look not only at the specific articulations and forms that 'participation' takes across several neighborhoods of Accra, but in line with the themes of the book, we are interested in the importance and role of participation as a 'hegemonic' construct. As such, we are attentive to the ways that the concept has been promoted in Accra, how local organizations and development agencies engage with it, as well as the intersection with other operational hegemonies, such as privatization and marketization. We first engage in a brief discussion of participatory resource management, highlighting how certain concepts or forms of participation gain privilege in development and water governance agendas. We then turn to our case study and examine how Accra's LWBs function and what spaces these have, or have not, created for participation. Our focus on LWBs provides an entry point to think through the limits of participation in several ways – the limits of LWBs in fostering participation and the limits of participation in bringing about transformation. Last, and in line with this volume's focus on hegemony, we look at the delimitation of participation – or how the boundaries and contours of what is rendered visible and intelligible (as well as what is not) might be circumscribed by current participatory frameworks. Even though our discussion emphasizes participation's limits, we nonetheless argue that it remains an important concept for water governance.

We draw mostly on primary research implemented in Accra during the summer of 2011,[3] including a series of semi-structured interviews conducted with community members, NGO staff, utility representatives and government officials; as well as field observations recorded during LWB and NGO staff meetings. We focus on formal participation as well as informal engagement in water governance in four communities of Accra: Ayidiki, Nima, Sukura, and Teshie (see Figure 19.1). We also bring in data from a comparative survey of informal settlements[4] in the contexts of Accra (Ashaiman and Teshie) and Cape Town (Phillipi and Khayelitsha) conducted with local partners in early 2012.[5]

Participatory resource governance

Participation has, since the 1980s, evolved to a mainstream discourse in development theory and practice (Hickey and Mohan, 2004). Objectives of fostering participation and invocations of the 'local' are now routinely found in development agendas and projects supported by international financial institutions (IFIs). As communities are directly involved in rule establishment and enforcement, it is often argued that participation will overcome the disjuncture between top–down policies and localities, improve outcomes by bringing in local knowledges, as well as lead to more effective monitoring (e.g. Ostrom, 1990). Some have further suggested that participatory approaches are critical for poverty alleviation (Ahmad, 2003). Participatory principles spelled out in the Dublin Principles (1992) and the Bonn Recommendations for Action (2001) similarly suggest that policies affecting water access should be developed on the basis of consultations with those affected (see also Goldin, 2010; Chapter 16). Despite such claims, the evidence with respect to the manifold benefits of participatory governance remains thin (e.g. Cooke and Kothari, 2001). Cleaver, in a rather fierce critique of the concept, argues 'participation has ..., become an act of faith in development, something [believed] in and rarely questioned' (2001: 36).

Critical perspectives on participation

In line with these critiques, an increasing body of work has called participation into question (see also Goldin, Chapter 16; 2010). It has been argued that theories of participation and development practitioners too often romanticize communities (Cleaver, 2001). The ability of communities to realize change is taken for granted or assumed to be contingent on the establishment of organizations or institutions, rather than on the performance of these organizations or other measures. This is often in line with an excessive focus on the 'local', ignoring the multi-scalar fabric through which power relations are established and reproduced. Hickey and Mohan further maintain that we have 'an insufficiently sophisticated understanding of how power operates and is constituted and thus how empowerment may occur' (2004: 11). As such, there are important issues regarding the appropriate scale for participatory governance, particularly as taking on the issue of multi-scalar power relations significantly affects possibilities for 'empowerment' in any sense of the term.

Other critical voices have raised yet further concerns, including the ways that these efforts articulate with neoliberalism and devolution efforts. For instance, some have suggested that devolution and participatory approaches may effectively involve a downloading of responsibility to communities, constituting a significant burden for marginalized groups (e.g. Walker, 1999; Ribot, 2002; Kesby, 2005). From an equity perspective, it might be inappropriate to ask the city's poor and marginalized to deal with water governance challenges in the absence of higher level institutions, especially given the capacity, time and resources required (Harris, 2009). In this sense, the collection edited by Cooke and Kothari (2001) suggests that participation might represent a new 'tyranny' that ushers in new modes of governmentality wherein people govern themselves to advance power-laden agendas (cf. Ekers and Loftus, 2008). Many remain concerned about the risks of participatory governance, whether in entrenching power dynamics or perpetuating inequalities through mechanisms such as 'elite capture' or 'participatory exclusions' (Kesby, 2005; Agarwal, 2001; Goldin, 2010; Harris, 2005, 2009; Ribot, 2002; see also discussion of four fatal flaws by Goldin, Chapter 16).

Added to these concerns, a focus on 'formal' participation can also lead to 'bean counting', such as focusing on attendance or numbers of groups represented at meetings. Theorists draw attention to the importance of meaningful or genuine participation (particularly with respect to gender, caste, class, race, and so forth; see Morales and Harris, in process). Goldin (Chapter 16) argues that we must attend to difficult-to-measure 'intangibles' such as emotions and the ways that these sentiments play into possibilities for participatory governance. We must therefore be aware of the factors influencing participation, but also acknowledge that participation often occurs outside of formally recognized spaces. This echoes feminist scholars who have long been calling for an appreciation of the 'informal' or 'alternative' spheres of engagement (e.g. Staeheli *et al.*, 2004; McEwan, 2000).

Lastly, Cleaver (2001) reminds us that, as participatory mechanisms and empowerment become themselves central objectives of development, these concepts might lose their radical, challenging, and transformative edge. In sum, while there has been a great push to further participatory approaches, the expected results have often not materialized. Ideas around participation have served to reinforce a romanticized view of 'community', or they have led to the adoption of narrow approaches focused on formal institutions, or fixated on the 'local' rather than engaging in multi-scalar approaches. More attention to power dynamics, as necessary corollaries of empowerment, need to be highlighted, particularly to better understand the role of institutions in fostering or constraining meaningful participation. All told, the promises and also the potential pitfalls of participatory governance are multifarious. We engage, in the remainder of this section, with concerns related to hegemony and their intersection with theories of participation, before we move on to explore their materialization on the ground through an analysis of Accra's LWBs.

Hegemonies and alternatives

As discussed by Sneddon, hegemonic ideas 'limit the terms of debate, create little space for conflicting ideas ... and tend to become the dominant frame of reference' (Chapter 2). Hegemonic practices or discourses often circumscribe (and thus limit) our understanding of both causes and solutions to various technical, institutional, and natural concerns (ibid.). Given Hickey and Mohan's (2004) concern that participation is often couched as a technical tool, we must query the degree to which hegemonic understandings of participation render the issues involved as largely 'technical', and outside the domain of social or historical influence. In other words, are hegemonic ideas of water governance over-focusing on the establishment of formal institutions, in a technical or instrumental sense, and less on the ways in which inequalities, social differences, or other social and political processes continue to affect governance?

Certainly, some forms of participation do go beyond head counts at meetings and, as such, are likely to hold more potential for transformation or democratic inclusion than other forms. While we aim to contribute to critical perspectives on these issues, we also argue that the concept of participation continues to hold great potential – particularly if we are able and willing to map out and recognize its limits more fully.

Accra's Local Water Boards

We now turn to an exploration of Accra's LWBs. Our intention is to engage with broader questions around participation as introduced above, as well as to discuss the role of hegemony in conditioning (1) the spaces opened or foreclosed for participation (limits *to* participation), (2) the possibilities for transformation created through these mechanisms (limits *of* participation), as well as (3) the ways in which participation in this context is currently conceptualized and operationalized (participation's *delimitations*[6]). We first provide a short discussion of Accra's drinking water landscape.

Context description

Ghana's capital city, Accra, is a fast-growing urban center facing considerable planning challenges that, as the population is expected to increase more than twofold in the coming decade, will likely be heightened (Government of Ghana, 2011).

The study sites selected through the 2011 field season can be considered as low-income or informal settlements, with Teshie being a long-term settlement

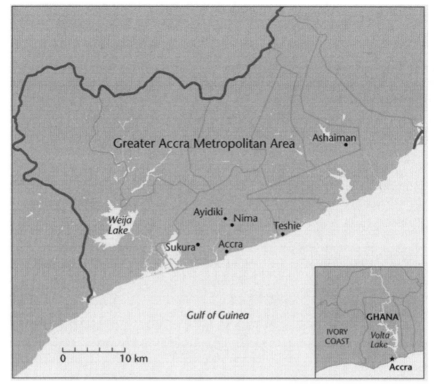

Figure 19.1 Map of the Greater Accra Metropolitan Area (cartography by Eric Leinberger, 2012)

occupied by low-income indigenous residents. Ayidiki, Nima, and Sukura are newer areas predominantly occupied by low-income migrant communities (Agyei-Mensah and Owusu, 2010; Weeks *et al.*, 2007; Songsore and McGranahan, 1998). Ashaiman, the last community involved in this study as a survey site, represents a mixed-income low-to-middle density area on the outskirts of the Greater Accra Metropolitan Area (GAMA).

The Ghana Water Company Limited (GWCL) is the main provider of drinking water in Accra. Approximately half of the population of Accra is not served by a municipal connection (Adank *et al.*, 2011). Unconnected households and those affected by shortages often rely on secondary and tertiary providers (many of whom obtain their water directly from the GWCL and then sell it for a profit). The full list of alternative water provision options includes tanker services; water vendors or kiosks; sachet[7] or bottled water; hand-dug wells; boreholes; and direct access to rivers and streams. As we discuss below, several of these modes of access (e.g. public or private water tanks) may be mediated by NGOs or community entities (LWBs) operating in those communities. Estimates regarding water access across Accra vary considerably. In Table 19.1, we provide a comparison between figures

Table 19.1 Water access in Accra, Ghana: comparison of our data focused on underserved areas with previously reported data for the Accra-Tema Metropolitan Area

	Lundehn and Morrison 2007 *Based on Accra-Tema Metropolitan Area**	*EDGES 2012 Survey* *Based on underserved communities of Teshie and Ashaiman***
Private access	35.9 %	9 % (4% in house connection and 5% private tank)
Shared / communal access	44.9 %	44 % (16% in-yard connection; 13% communal standpipe and 15% public water tank)
Vendors	– (None reported)	47 %
Tanker service	7.3 %	–
Boreholes	11.8 %	–

* Lundehn and Morrison, 2007, based on Ghana Statistical Service, 2002.
** Our survey purposefully targeted underserved communities.
Note: There is some overlap between categories, as public water tanks could also be reported as vendors (since they sell water), and often those or private tanks rely on tanker services to fill them.
Source: Harris et al. (2012); Lundehn and Morrison (2007, based on Ghana Statistical Service, 2002

for the Accra-Tema region offered by Lundehn and Morrison (2007) in the first column and data from our survey conducted in the underserved communities of Teshie and Ashaiman in the second.

With respect to the general water governance trends of interest for this volume, Accra is a clear example of a Southern context required to privatize urban water provision through World Bank loan conditionalities (see Harris, Chapters 10 and 11). The privatization has drawn heavy criticism, for instance, from commentators who suggest this undercuts Ghanaian democracy (Yeboah, 2006; Whitfield, 2006), and from protesters who rallied against it, particularly in response to the rapid increase in tariffs (an initial rise of 95 percent) in preparation for the concession (reported by Amenga-Etego and Grusky, 2005: 282). Ultimately the protest movement, the National Coalition Against the Privatization of Water (NCAP), was able to delay the concession, but not prevent it (ibid.; see Whitfield, 2006, for further details). The recent privatization phase of Accra's water is also significant given longer-term structural adjustment policies and the IFIs' influence in the Ghanaian context (e.g. Konadu-Agyemang, 2000). Privatization, in this sense, follows many similar policies intended to reduce Ghana's debt burden, which in turn have important implications from social policy and inequality perspectives (cf. Arthur, 2002). In a context of aggravated inequality, and under the pressures of protest movements, the private Aqua-Vitens Rand Limited consortium (AVRL), who won the concession bid, pledged that it would not operate for profit, but in pursuit of the Millennium Development Goals. However, after the initial five years of operation (2006–11), the Government of Ghana decided not to renew AVRL's contract, citing failure to meet goals (see Ghana News Agency, 2011a, 2011b).

Accra's Local Water Boards

Participatory water governance has long been on the agenda, both for the GWCL and AVRL. As discussed in this section, the LWBs, initiated in 2007 and currently operational across urban Accra, are one of the key efforts under way. LWBs generally involve elected representatives from a number of interest groups (e.g. women, youth, elders) within a community to a total of 10–15 members. LWBs were initially established in partnership with the utility company (Ghana Water Company Limited) and, more recently, have been established with NGOs such as CHF-Ghana.[8] Three of the communities where research was conducted in 2011 had an operational LWB: Teshie, Nima, and Ayidiki. Teshie's water board was the first to be established by the GWCL in 2007 as part of a pro-poor initiative.[9] The utility later established LWBs in six other communities of Accra, including Nima in 2008. CHF-Ghana (hereafter CHF) became involved with Nima's LWB in 2009. The NGO selected Nima as an area of focus – together with several other communities – given the community's poor water and sanitation access. CHF based their activities on Nima's LWB model and established similar boards[10] in several other communities of Accra, including Ayidiki in 2010.[11]

While a stated primary goal of the LWBs is to promote local participation, the boards are also responsible for the administration of a certain portion of the water available in the community. For instance, the LWB in Teshie is responsible for the administration of a tanker as well as several water kiosks, with the board hiring a driver for the tanker and vendors for each kiosk. The tanker is filled at a provision point administered by the GWCL, where water is paid for up-front by the LWB. The LWB in turn facilitates the distribution of the water to several kiosks where vendors sell it to community members at a fixed price established jointly by the board, the GWCL, and Public Utility Regulatory Commission (PURC).

Water kiosks in Nima and Ayidiki are slightly different than the ones found in Teshie. No tankers are involved and the kiosks rely on a direct connection to the mains. Water is nonetheless stored in polytanks[12] to avoid problems associated with inconsistent delivery. The GWCL charges the board for the water as it is stored, and the board employs vendors who sell it by unit-volume to community members. Nima's LWB, with the financial help of CHF (in turn funded by USAID and the Bill and Melinda Gates Foundation), has plans to add two boreholes to supply the community in times of shortage. Furthermore, LWBs can also facilitate the process of getting private latrines, or private connections to the network. It is important to note that not all such activities go through the organization and not all water flowing through a community is administered by the LWB. Individuals connected directly to the mains are not reliant on the extensions provided by the board, and many other private vendor services might also operate within these communities.

From participation to transformation

In the following discussion, we highlight, through participants' own words and vignettes, some of the limits *to* and *of* participation, but also some of participation's *delimitation* in terms of the ways that participation is understood and articulated. While we treat these issues as somewhat distinct, we also recognize that they are fundamentally linked.

Each board is based on the voluntary work of its members and, as such, echoes challenges and concerns raised in the literature suggesting participatory governance may represent a significant burden for communities, or for certain segments of the population. For instance, while the organizational schemes may include a dividend redistribution system to be paid to the board members with any profits generated, the reality is that this rarely occurs. In the case of Teshie, the tanker at the center of the board's activities is ageing and increasingly plagued with mechanical problems. The board simply does not have the funds to pay for repair services and water distribution can be interrupted for several days. Board members rarely realize any financial benefits from their involvement. An experience of the work burden was apparent in a conversation with an LWB youth representative:

> This board is not paid. It is a volunteer job that we are doing. It's not being paid and look at me I'm a young guy, right. Abandon my jobs and sit in meetings and stuff like that … It is very challenging … I'm a designer and construction man. You abandon your work that you have to do on your [computer] and come sit here three or four hours … discussing issues that would bring this community ahead … But, I've [also] learn[ed] a whole lot from it … not [every]thing that you do [has] to collect money or something like that. You have to sometime also volunteer some of your time to do this communal work and you're pleased to do that.[13]

Further limits to participation also arise from the heavily procedural nature of water-related development in Accra. Despite the existence of the boards to facilitate this process, the steps one must go through in order to obtain a connection or acquire a permit for a connection or a latrine are considerable. The process typically involves the landlord, the LWB, the NGO, a micro-finance organization, the utility, as well as the sub-metro, which must sanction the development plans. This complex and long process, often taking several months to a year, may both discourage participation itself and, in turn, limit the LWB's potential to broker improvements regarding water access or infrastructure. This was evidenced by this quote from an LWB member describing the working relationship with the sub-metro:

> Well for the municipality helping us, there is a bit of collaboration but not much at all … it's not helpful … We mainly work with CHF, the water company and the sub-metro. But what I'm saying is that the sub-metro it's a

challenge, it's very difficult because as a government initiative to get Accra as a millennium city, we were thinking that this intervention from CHF and USAID, there [would] be some speed ... But you don't see that, you don't see that coming from the sub-metro. There is something, I cannot describe.[14]

On the other hand, the LWBs clearly serve as a channel for communication between the community and the utility. Even as there might be significant issues with respect to who serves on the board (i.e. regarding representation or elections procedures), part of the board's function is to communicate the needs of the community to the utility. This sentiment was expressed by one LWB chairperson:

> There is a lot of collaboration because they know us, we also know them. They call us, we call them. We have meetings concerning water related programs in the community. So for instance, when they were doing the pipe laying they had to disconnect a particular group line and these community members came here to complain to us. We also called GWCL to lodge the complaint and they came and rectified it.[15]

This function appears critical, given that the GWCL is generally not present in underserved communities and may also have limited knowledge of these areas. In this sense, the LWB may facilitate community engagement, offering possibilities to hold the utility accountable. It was clear through interviews that the LWBs have become a point of reference in the community, a go-to organization when issues regarding water arise. Interaction between the utility and community through the LWBs may contribute to building trust to the extent the communications are frequent, or productive. It is interesting to note, however, that data from a survey we conducted in 2012 suggest that there is not a great deal of familiarity with the activities around NGOs' efforts on water issues (this was evident from the respondents surveyed in Teshie – only two respondents out of 120 reported knowing of any NGOs working on water issues there; Harris *et al.*, 2012). Also, a representative from the utility reported that communications between the boards and the GWCL are typically reactive, arising when there is an issue rather than as part of regular exchange – in short, interactions are best described as ad-hoc and problem-rooted.[16] LWBs do however bring, to a certain extent, the utility's presence into the community, both in providing water beyond Accra's centralized network, but also, in some instances, serving as a point of payment for water.[17] As such, the LWBs can act as an extension of the utility's presence and influence in informal settlements where its integration has historically been unsuccessful.

It is significant that *all* LWBs investigated as part of this research were established by an agency external to the communities. This clearly limits their ability to represent community members in a grassroots sense. In all cases, the communities were selected *a priori* by the GWCL or CHF, most often due to experiences of acute water stress. This pre-selection not only limits the possibilities for bottom–up and participatory governance, but it also raises questions regarding the role of external actors. Consider a discussion between a representative of the primary NGO involved with one of the LWBs and a member of the board during one of our visits to the board's office.

> During a progress assessment meeting, the NGO representative was inquiring about the progress made on awareness-raising regarding sanitation and waste disposal. The board member candidly answered the question and started listing the streets that had been patrolled – pointing in the direction of the location where the work had taken place. The NGO representative did not seem pleased with the answer and asked, while pointing in another direction, when they were going to patrol a particular street and why they had not done so already. The board member explained that they had started where they considered the situation regarding hygiene and sanitation to be most acute. The NGO representative acknowledged that work there was indeed needed, but made clear that it was essential that they patrolled the other streets mentioned since delegates from the funding agencies would soon visit the neighborhood. It was anticipated that the NGO and partners would walk the main streets rather than areas further within the settlement.

The work conducted by the board does not only have to correspond to the objectives of the NGO, but is also clearly accountable to other stakeholders. Situations such as this clearly illustrate yet other limits of the LWBs, including the ways that participation can be instrumentalized as it becomes mainstreamed (or hegemonic). This is particularly true when large funding agencies become involved (in this case USAID and the Bill and Melinda Gates Foundation). In a Community Debrief Session we held in 2012, where we gathered representatives from three of Accra's LWBs to discuss the results of our work with the boards, allusions to the strictness of donors was brought up, including the ways in which board members and NGO staff feel limited in their potential to respond to community concerns rather than being accountable to donor interests and conditions of funding providers (see Hailey, 2001, for a discussion on tokenism through external agencies' influence).

Furthermore, the presence of a LWB does not immunize the communities from being affected by water shortages and availability issues – representing yet another limit of participation. Frequent disruptions may result in the community losing confidence in the board or the utility, as well as in the potential for participatory mechanisms altogether. In this sense, the infrastructural, water quality, and availability challenges can also circumscribe the potential of the LWBs. Take for example the case of a water vendor:

> During an episode whereby there was a technical problem with the board's tanker, the water vendor hired to administer one of the kiosks decided that the board and the utility company were not holding their end of the bargain and turned to a private tanker service to supply his kiosk. The vendor maintains that the kiosk is now his to manage independently, even though the infrastructure (kiosk and polytank) was paid for by the board. When asked directly whether

the polytank belongs to the LWB, he replied by acknowledging that they had provided it, but that it doesn't belong to them anymore. He also suggested that disagreements and quarreling made the LWB difficult to work with, pointing to inevitable challenges associated with participatory governance.[18]

During our visit to the community, as well as through interviews with board members, the behavior and actions of this particular vendor were quickly dismissed; he had left the organization and was no longer a participant in the established participatory mechanisms that were in place for the neighborhood, but this did not exclude him from providing water to his customers and maintaining the status of vendor. As an autonomous vendor, he interacted directly with private tanker services and was able to circumvent some of the limitations imposed by the board, or difficulties with service interruptions. Similarly, the establishment of a second board in the community, in partnership with a different organization, has created an important division whereby both entities question and dismiss the legitimacy of the other board.[19] Both the vendor's disengagement from the board as well as the quarreling between the two boards pose interesting questions for theories of participation. Does the vendor's continuing engagement with water delivery constitute a form of participation, or since he no longer works within the remit of the board, are his activities in fact working against the principles of participatory water governance? The sense that he is working in conflict with participatory mechanisms was emphasized by members of the board, but is it possible that his actions also constitute an alternative mode of participation? This situation provides an illustration of the ways that hegemonic forms of participation can become rigid and delimited – excluding other modes of engagement with water provision and governance. Indeed, in considering participation's limits in relation to hegemonic notions of participatory governance, we argue that it may become difficult, if not impossible to recognize, or validate, that which falls outside those dominant frameworks. Some of these engagements could, nonetheless, hold transformative potential for alternative community participation and access to water. The flourishing sachet water industry can similarly be understood as a series of engagements that extends water access to underserved areas, albeit at a premium (see also Stoler *et al.*, 2012; Morinville, in process, for discussion). Clearly, sachet water provision is not a community-based project. It can nonetheless be understood as a way through which the residents of Ghana directly engage in extending water access, with clear implications for water governance – defined as decision-making and processes that determine water use, quality and access.

These issues again beg the question of what comes to be defined as genuine participation and what other forms of engagement in water use and access might be meaningful yet underexplored? At its core, this is about opening up investigations to query what is meant by participatory water governance, and what practices and engagements fall beyond such recognition. Is participatory water governance only about making formal institutions that are transparent and accountable to local communities, or might it involve multiple engagements of communities in determining water use, access, or quality, and also articulating concerns or meeting their water-related needs? If it is at least in part the latter, than we can imagine that both the story of the rogue water vendor and the sachet industry could be key to understanding what participation 'means' in lived everyday senses in urban Accra.

There are yet other considerations related to the limits of hegemonic notions of participatory governance that deserve mention. Consider the case of Sukura, the fourth community we worked with during the 2011 field season. In the absence of a pre-selected and formally sanctioned LWB, community members in this district have to organize themselves differently in order to engage the utility in dialog. The Sukura community worked on a Community Scorecard project to grade the utility for the services they receive, and the GWCL engaged in a self-assessment of their services. They later met together to discuss discrepancies in the grading and issues affecting the community.[20] First, even as these types of direct engagement appear promising, again they were facilitated by an external agency, in this case the Coalition of NGOs on Water and Sanitation (CONIWAS). Second and more importantly, while the community is engaged in water governance processes through the Community Scorecard program, it is interesting to consider the history of their engagement:

> Sukura is an in-migrant Muslim-majority community. In 2001, the community was subjected to police raids twice in the same week after which community members organized themselves. In the words of one of our key informants: 'Some of us began to say no, no, no, we will not allow this. So we began organizing ourselves also to have our own kind of resistance.' The Integrated Social Development Center (ISODEC) was at the same time organizing its anti-privatization campaign and networked with community leaders from Sukura to facilitate the establishment of a Local Action Committee (LAC). Water became one of the focal issues of the community group advocating for social change within the neighborhood. The committee later worked with CONIWAS on the Community Scorecard program.[21]

This example points to the broader political context in which community participation in water governance is embedded. As such, it is clear that we must consider the politics of privatization, development, or colonialization as issues that are all potentially important to how and why participation might unfold in particular ways (see also discussion in Goldin, Chapter 16, and Harris, Chapter 10).

In this sense, we can also question the many factors that drove the establishment of LWBs, rather than focus narrowly on their current expression (for a similar point, see Barnes's analysis of the factors that conditioned the establishment of WUAs in Egypt, Chapter 17). As mentioned above, the first board was implemented in Teshie in 2007. Interviews with utility representatives, LWB members, and community leaders seem to suggest that the community of Teshie has historically been vocal regarding water access. The LWB was established in part as a response to the demands of the community who had previously organized under other forms to engage the utility and government.[22] The Teshie case is thus of interest when considering the issue of hegemony in relation to participatory governance. In this example, the formalization of the LWB was used to contain and circumvent a situation where there had historically been vocal protest and dissent.

Conclusions

This chapter has sought to understand hegemonies of participation as they work on multiple registers in the context of water governance in urban Accra. Through the examples presented above, we have considered some conceptual issues related to hegemony in both the discourse and practice of participation. As Goldman reminds us, 'genealogies and biographies do matter' (2007: 798), and it is clear from our discussion that characteristics and specifics of localities do not only influence the possibilities for participation, but also the possibilities for transformation and the potential to create counter-hegemonies. While our focus here is on the LWBs and 'formal' examples of participation, we also aim to illustrate how formal and informal manifestations are likely to be closely interwoven. It is clear that the LWBs are offering some important functionality with respect to fostering participatory water governance. However, we must not only question the limits of such participation, but we need to scrutinize what lies beyond that which is formally recognized as participatory.

Notes

1   Interview with LWB chairperson, 14 July 2011.
2   The area of interest for this chapter includes the entire Greater Accra Metropolitan Area as depicted in Figure 19.1; we refer to the city simply as 'Accra' throughout the chapter.
3   A nine-week field season was conducted by Cynthia Morinville from June to Aug. 2011. Follow-up work was conducted by three members of our research team in 2012, including both authors of this chapter.
4   The term 'informal settlement' is used in this chapter even as they are formally recognized settlements by the municipality. All communities investigated through this research correspond to the UN-Habitat's definition of 'slums'.
5   This survey was conducted with the support of the Center for International Governance Innovation and in partnership with A. Darkwah and J. A. Goldin in Ghana and South Africa respectively. 243 surveys were conducted in Ashaiman and Teshie (Accra), and 256 in Khayelitsha and Phillipi (Cape Town). Only data related to the Ghanaian sites are mobilized in this chapter.
6   The term delimit is defined as the action of determining limits or boundaries, especially with regards to 'zones' or 'areas'. The French definition for 'delimiter' indicates the word can also mean to circumscribe, as with a thesis topic. In this chapter, we accordingly use the term 'delimitation' to signify the boundaries or the contours of participation as a concept.
7   Sachets are small bags of 500ml of water, heat-sealed at both ends and manufactured locally.
8   CHF-Ghana is one of approximately 65 NGOs working on water and sanitation related issues in Ghana (interview with CONIWAS official, 20 July 2011).
9   Interview with GWCL official, 19 July 2011; interview with LBW member, 11 July 2011.

10 Boards under CHF administration are called 'Water and Sanitation Boards' (WSB). In order to limit confusion we maintain the use of Local Water Board (LWB) throughout. It is interesting to note that discussions are under way regarding whether or not to change the denomination from 'board' to some other term (such as team) in light of previous confusion and questioning around the LWBs' legitimacy, given the frequent dissolution of 'all boards' at times of political turnover.

11 Interview with CHF staff, 13 July 2011.

12 Polytanks are large water storage tanks made of plastic (polyethylene). It is common for wealthier households to own a tank and thus avoid experiencing intermittent supply.

13 Interview with LWB member, 25 July 2011.

14 Interview with LWB member, 14 July 2011.

15 Interview with LWB chairperson, 14 July 2011.

16 Interview with GWCL official, 19 July 2011.

17 The LWB typically collects only the money for the water it sells directly. Bills to consumers enjoying a direct connection to the pipe network must be paid to the utility. While prepayment for water provided by the LWBs can help overcoming challenges such as those associated with non-revenue water, this does not necessarily alleviate concerns related to affordability.

18 Interview with LWB vendor, 22 July 2011.

19 Interview with PURC official, 12 July 2012.

20 Interview with NCAP activists, 1 July 2011; and interview with CONIWAS official, 20 July 2011.

21 Interview with LAC member, 1 July 2011.

22 Interview LBW member, 11 July 2011.

References

Adank, M., Darteh, B., Moriarty, P., Osei-Tutu, H., Assan, D., and van Rooijen, D. 2011. *Towards Integrated Urban Water Management in the Greater Accra Metropolitan Area: Current Status and Strategic Directions for the Future,* Accra: Switch/RCN Ghana.

Agarwal, B. 2001. Participatory exclusions, community forestry, and gender: an analysis for South Asia and a conceptual framework. *World Development,* 29(10), 1623–48.

Agyei-Mensah, S., and Owusu, G. 2010. Segregated by neighborhoods? A portrait of ethnic diversity in the neighborhoods of the Accra metropolitan area, Ghana. *Population, Space, and Place,* 16(6), 499–516.

Ahmad, Q. K. 2003. Towards poverty alleviation: the water sector perspectives. *International Journal of Water Resources Development,* 19(5), 263–77.

Amenga-Etego, R. N., and Grusky, S. 2005. The new face of conditionalities: the World Bank and water privatization in Ghana. In D. A. McDonald and G. Ruiters (eds), *The Age of Commodity: Water Privatization in Southern Africa,* pp. 275–91, New York: Earthscan.

Arthur, P. A. 2002. Ghana: industrial development in the post-structural adjustment program (SAP) period. *Canadian Journal of Development Studies/Revue canadienne d'études du développement,* 23(4), 717–42.

Bonn Recommendations for Action. 2001. Available at: www.weltvertrag.org/e375/e719/e1042/InternationalConferenceonFreshwater_2001_RecommendationsforAction_ger.pdf (accessed July 2012).

Cleaver, F. 2001. Institutions, agency and the limitations of participatory approaches to development. In B. Cooke and U. Kothari (eds), *Participation: The New Tyranny,* pp. 36–55, London: Zed Books.

Cooke, B., and Kothari, U. 2001. *Participation: The New Tyranny,* London: Zed Books.

Dublin Principles. 1992. *The Dublin Statement on Water and Sustainable Development.* Available at: www.wmo.int/pages/prog/hwrp/documents/english/icwedece.html (accessed July 2012).

Ekers, M., and Loftus, A. 2008. The power of water: developing dialogues between Foucault and Gramsci. *Environment and Planning D: Society and Space,* 26(4), 698–718.

Ghana News Agency. 2011a. Ghana Urban Water Limited takes over the management of urban water. *Modern Ghana,* 10 June.

Ghana News Agency. 2011b. Aqua Vitens failed. *Modern Ghana,* 10 June.

Goldin, J. A. 2010. Water policy in South Africa: trust and knowledge as obstacles to reform. *Review of Radical Political Economics,* 42(2), 195–212.

Goldman, M. 2007. How 'water for all!' policy became hegemonic: the power of the World Bank and its transnational policy networks. *Geoforum,* 38(5), 786–800.

Government of Ghana. 2011. *2010 Population and Housing Census: Provisional Results. Summary of Findings,* 3 Feb., Accra: Ghana Statistical Services.

Hailey, J. 2001. Beyond the formulaic: process and practice in South Asian NGOs. In B. Cooke and U. Kothari (eds), *Participation: The New Tyranny*, pp. 88–101, London: Zed Books.

Harris, L. M. 2005. Negotiating inequalities: democracy, gender, and politics of difference in water user groups in southeastern Turkey. In F. Adaman and M. Arsel (eds), *Environmentalism in Turkey: Between Democracy and Development?*, pp. 185–200, Aldershot: Ashgate.

Harris, L. M. 2009. Gender and emergent water governance: comparative overview of neoliberalized natures and gender dimensions of privatization, devolution, and marketization. *Gender, Place, and Culture,* 16(4), 387–408.

Harris, L. M., Darkwah, A., Goldin, J. A., and UBC EDGES Research Collaborative. 2012. Water Access and participatory governance survey of households in informal settlements of Accra, Ghana and Cape Town, South Africa.

Hickey, S., and Mohan, G. 2004. *Participation: from Tyranny to Transformation, Exploring New Approaches to Participation in Development,* London: Zed Books.

Kesby, M. 2005. Retheorizing empowerment-through-participation as a performance in space: beyond tyranny to transformation. *Journal of Women in Culture and Society,* 30(4), 2037–65.

Konadu-Agyemang, K. 2000. The best of times and the worst of times: structural adjustment programs and uneven development in Africa: the case of Ghana. *Professional Geographer,* 52(3), 469–83.

Lundehn, C., and Morrison, G. M. 2007. An assessment framework for urban water systems: a new approach combining environmental systems with service supply and consumer perspectives. In G. M. Morrison and S. Rauch (eds), *Highway and Urban Environment: Proceeding of the 8th Highway and Urban Environment Symposium*, pp. 559–77, Dordrecht: Springer.

McEwan, C. 2000. Engendering citizenship: gendered spaces of democracy in South Africa. *Political Geography,* 19(5), 627–51.

Morales, M., and Harris, L. in process. Participatory natural resource management, identity, and subjectivity. Manuscript in preparation.

Morinville, C. in process. Accra's intricate waterscape: sachet water, small-scale private service providers, and everyday social fabric. Manuscript in preparation.

Ostrom, E. 1990. *Governing the Commons: The Evolution of Institutions for Collective Action,* Cambridge, MA: Cambridge University Press.

Ribot, J. 2002. *Democratic Decentralization of Natural Resources: Instituting Popular Participation,* Washington, DC: World Resources Institute.

Songsore, J., and McGranahan, G. 1998. The political economy of household environmental management: gender, environment and epidemiology in the Greater Accra Metropolitan Area. *World Development*, 26(3), 395–412.

Staeheli, L. A., Kofman, E., and Peake, L. 2004. *Mapping Women, Mapping Politics: Feminist Perspectives on Political Geography,* New York: Routledge.

Stoler, J., Fink, G., Weeks, J. R., Appiah Otto, R., Ampofo, J. A., and Hill, A. G. 2012. When urban taps run dry: sachet water consumption and health effects in low income neighborhoods of Accra, Ghana. *Health and Place*, 18(2), 250–62.

Walker, A., 1999. Democracy and environment: congruencies and contradictions in southern Africa. *Political Geography,* 18(3), 257–84.

Weeks, J. R., Hill, A. G., Stow, G., Getis, A., and Fugate, D. 2007. Can we spot a neighborhood from the air? Defining neighborhood structure in Accra, Ghana. *GeoJournal*, 69(1–2), 9–22.

Whitfield, L. 2006. The politics of urban water reform in Ghana. *Review of African Political Economy*, 33(109), 425–48.

Yeboah, I. 2006. Subaltern strategies and development practice: urban water privatization in Ghana. *Geographical Journal*, 172(1), 50–65.

20 Reclaiming global citizenship

A perspective from Catalan water justice activists

Annelies Broekman

In Spain, as in many other Mediterranean countries, water management during the last century was largely perceived as a task for the government. The goal has been to ensure supply for all possible users and to use water as a strategic tool for economical and social development of the country (Estevan, 2008; Aguilera Klink, 1994). This approach lead to the massive construction of hydraulic infrastructure, such as dams and irrigation and water transfer channels, with the aim of distributing water far and wide within the territory in the name of economic progress (Ministerio de Medio Ambiente, 1998; see Baker (Chapter 3) and Erensu (Chapter 6) for discussion of what is commonly referred to as the 'hydraulic mission').

Indeed, the foundations of Spanish traditional water management, much of it based on Joaquim Costas's vision from the 1920s, is characterized by expressions such as 'Water as a motor for development', the 'Need for water solidarity' and the idea that waterworks are of 'General interest to adjust water cycle to the needs of the people', where the underlying idea is protection against the 'Capricious unfairness of nature' (del Moral and Saurí, 1999; Arrojo and Naredo, 1997). As a result of policies of this type (some of which can certainly be considered hegemonic), the hydrological functionality of the Iberian Peninsula's water bodies has deteriorated and serious conflicts are resulting from an overexploitation of water resources (Sánchez, 2003; Llamas Madurga, 2005).

As with other cases elsewhere across the globe, many grassroots movements came into existence in Spain, driven by the desire to defend the livelihood of people against the destruction caused by these large-scale infrastructural projects across the country. This happened in Catalonia, where around 2000 the Xarxa per una Nova Cultura de l'Aigua (XNCA – Network for a New Water Culture) was created to give support to the fight of a local movement called Plataforma en Defensa de l'Ebre (PDE – Platform in Defense of the Ebro River). Its aim is to defend the Ebro Delta region – one of the most important cradles of biodiversity in Europe – and make sure that its vital water would not be transferred to supply the industrial agriculture in the Southern Murcia Region (Ibáñez *et al.*, 1999; Martínez and Esteve, 2002).

This New Water Culture Network, which gathered many grassroots organizations throughout Catalonia, was inspired by the committed foundation of university professors founded in 1998 (Fundación Nueva Cultura del Agua – FNCA), who laid the basis for a 'New Water Culture' – and new policy principles (Martínez Gil, 1997; Estevan and Naredo, 2004; Subirats, 2004; Arrojo, 2006). This foundation created an interdisciplinary committee, which published in 2004 a European declaration of basic policy principles for responsible water governance.[1] The framework this declaration generated triggered a paradigm shift, now referred to as the New Water Culture, as an attempt to respond to technocratic hegemony. This critique shares some elements of the vision cited in Sneddon (Chapter 2): 'the main causes for this unacceptable state of affairs are neither technical nor "natural" but rather are, broadly speaking, of a social and political nature'. In order to link the technical aspects with their political nature, the declaration indicated how management strategies should be oriented according to the 'functions' of water: (1) water for life (free for people and ecosystems –guaranteed above all uses as a human right), (2) water for citizenship (social right –managed by public economy for general interest), (3) water for economic growth (legitimate private interest –managed under economic rationality), calling for a strong response against illegitimate and illegal water uses. The implementation of these guiding principles challenged Spanish traditional water hegemony, and induced a strong call for active participation of society as a tool to create a counter-hegemonic discourse. These new concepts gave a framework to many social movements to promote an holistic approach based on: (1) the recovery and conservation of the Catalan water bodies and related ecosystems, (2) the revision of the economic rationality of investments to address water demands, (3) the study of water demand allocation as well as consumption-reduction strategies and (4) the preservation of cultural and spiritual values linked to water.

This New Water Culture movement has been one of the most important and successful resistance movements in Spain. Resistance resulted in the abrogation of the National Hydrological Plan, and the cancellation of the aforementioned River Ebro water transfer project. This movement laid the basis for territorial awareness and a social organization of resistance that is to this day very much alive (Arrojo, 2001; Tello Aragay, 2000). An activist perspective grounded in these grassroots struggles forms the basis for the discussion that follows in this chapter.

We want to indicate that it is possible to collectively construct this New Water Culture, overcoming administrative barriers. Much of this can be done by enriching citizen participation as well as through an appropriate modification of management practices in order to integrate diverse views and priorities into decision-making processes. Nevertheless, this case demonstrates that the real obstacle for this to happen is the administration not being able to represent the interests of society as a whole. Instead, what occurs is that the administration is co-opted by private economic interests. Even when there is appropriate legislation, an economic elite has been able to impose a hegemony that maintains a vision focused on infrastructure, as well as commodified visions of water management.

Water framework directive (WFD) and citizen participation in Catalonia

The history as described here examines the role of grassroots water justice movements in Catalan water policy, setting the scene for an investigation of why the Catalan government considered citizen participation between 2006 and 2010 to be such an important tool for enhancing Catalan sovereignty and for overcoming the so-called 'Spanish hydraulic structuralism' approach in water management.

The Agència Catalana de l'Aigua (ACA – Catalan Water Agency, a public company created by the Environmental Department of the Catalan autonomous government in 1999), in collaboration with the General Directorate for Citizens' Participation of the autonomous government of Catalonia (Generalitat), embraced the new EU Water Framework Directive (WFD – CE/2000/60 of the European Parliament and of the Council of 23 October 2000, establishing a framework for the Community action in the field of water policy). This directive provided an opportunity to introduce a counter-hegemonic discourse (ACA, 2009), particularly given the strong emphasis in the language on participation and community involvement, as well as the focus on ecological concerns. In sum, the WFD invited the Spanish state to change its national policy, and forced it to adapt its political narrative, taking account of the need to restore and maintain the ecological functionality of its water bodies.

Since 2000, the ACA has worked intensively to adopt the narrative of the WFD, and (I believe genuinely) tried to reform its water management model in order to integrate economical, social and environmental aspects into the sustainable management of the hydrological system. In addition, the Catalan government took the opportunity to develop 'Public Participation Processes' as required by the European directive, with a special effort to create a space for interaction with citizens to develop a new water policy for Catalonia – a region that claims independence from the Spanish national state. A successful implementation of the WFD would have demonstrated the ability to manage political issues at EU level, perhaps even in ways that would outpace the Spanish national government, effectively proving that Catalonia is a trustworthy candidate to become the 28th EU member state. Moreover, active democratic practices aimed to increase feelings of 'belonging to' Catalonia, while distancing its citizens from the Spanish central government. Water is of high political relevance in Catalonia, and invokes territorial defense and other linked struggles. For example, if the Spanish government does not allow a reduction in the volume of water abstracted from the Ebro River, a great part of the delta region will disappear, as will the livelihood of the people living there (Ibáñez *et al.*, 1999).

For many, the WFD was an opportunity to contest and replace the old economic and infrastructure-dominated hegemony that had long dominated Spanish hydraulic management (see Swyngedouw, 1999) and, legitimized under this European directive, to integrate their visions into a mainstream policy reform process. It drove forward the principle that it is necessary for all people to participate actively in the transition process to new water policies through an intersectoral and multi-stakeholder dialog, coordinated yet decentralized throughout the territory. The theoretical/political concept behind this approach is 'deliberative democracy', a decision-making process based on a closer relation between the administration and the people, allowing for a direct dialog and transparent sharing of information (DIBA, 2007).

As a result of the above elements, Catalan public participation processes between 2006 and 2010 have been considered the most ambitious and avant-garde in Spain (Espluga *et al.*, 2011). The processes, characterized by high complexity, were designed to overcome many of the classical problems related to citizen participation in governance as documented in the literature on that subject (see Goldin, Chapter 16). We outline only a few of these problems here, which set the stage for a discussion of current hegemonic struggles over water governance in Catalonia.

Overcoming barriers of legal and territorial authority

ACA has full legal authority *only* where river basins flow entirely within its regional territory (*Cuencas Internas*), but its authority has also been exercised in river basins like the Ebro River Basin, which flows through nine autonomous communities (*Cuencas Intercomunitarias*). In this case, ACA holds shared competences with the Confederación Hidrografica del Ebro (CHE – Hydrological Confederation of Ebro River).

A wide debate is currently ongoing on how to reformulate the legal authority on water resources management in the Spanish state in order to comply with EU laws and overcome the conflict between autonomous communities and the central state. The participatory processes outlined by the ACA – developed also in the Ebro River Basin in an adapted format – made the contradictions between the Spanish hydro-hegemony and the Catalan legitimized counter-hegemony very clear. The Ebro territory represents a direct battlefield between visions on water policy: shared competences evidenced that the participation processes developed by the Ebro River Basin Authority were less coherent with WFD principles than the one adopted by the ACA. The approach of the Ebro River authorities in dealing with citizen participation confirmed their approach to water management, as they did a mere public consultancy, where every sector could list its demands, without problem-solving debate on how to deal with the environmental problems of the river. The ACA instead tried to bring forward these issues, empowered by the fact that this is what is actually required by the WFD legislation.

Participation in the design

It is remarkable that the processes that emerged in much of Catalonia were designed in close collaboration with social movements. In fact, the development of the structure of the participation processes was worked out by means of an agreement between the ACA and the NGOs Fundación Nueva Cultura del Agua (FNCA) and the Xarxa per una Nova Cultura de l'Aigua (XNCA), since all three organizations focused on the implementation process of the WFD. The agreement generated a stable workgroup on participation, characterized by continuous collaboration right up to the implementation strategy and follow-up of the various participatory projects over the four-year period (2006–10).

The XNCA has participated in all participation sessions with several mandates: as a monitor to report the quality of the development of the participation techniques, it was able to provide feedback to the workgroup with the ACA, and as a stakeholder representing the member organizations of its network. This formula provided an opportunity to make technical changes during the implementation phase of the process, and to enhance the information flow between the different local water justice movements. This information flow allowed the introduction of an integrated perspective pertaining to territorial water-related conflicts, otherwise separated within the sphere of each Catalan River Basin. For example, the movements of River Ter could not participate in the River Llobregat participation process, but as both rivers supply Barcelona, their problems are related. The XNCA could bring the voice of the Ter people to the Llobregat, and vice versa.

Adaptation of the structure of the administration

In order to allow high-quality participation to unfold, the administration had to adapt its structure to meet the demands associated with the new participatory mechanisms. The WFD prescribes mandatory participation processes for the revision of the River Basin Management Plan, which takes place every six years of the European implementation calendar. To have these processes be constructive and effectively reach the goals set, a continuous interaction with citizens is needed. Therefore the statutes of ACA were modified to create permanent structures for interaction with citizens, as is the case with the creation of a 'Department for Participation in the Water Administration Agency' and 'River Basin Councils'. These structures promote the making of interaction protocols and legal frameworks, as well as the allocation of human resources needed to follow up on the implementation process between periods of revision of the River Basin Management Plan.

Where we are today: a battle of hegemonies

The recent history of water reform in Catalonia reflects the lingering struggles over two different visions of water governance, and is directly tied to the rapidly shifting political and economic conditions in Spain and Europe more broadly. The official calendar of the WFD's implementation deadline was in 2009. By November 2011 the Catalan River Basin Management Plan had finally been completed and was approved by Parliament – just the day before Catalan governmental elections. Aware of the political situation in the Spanish state with respect to the WFD implementation, and as a political gesture to protect Catalonia from critique that was being levelled against Spain, the plan was also immediately and directly forwarded to the European Commission. Indeed, the Spanish state had been convicted by European Supreme Court of Justice – just a month prior on 4 October 2012 – because of lengthy delays related to the management plan approval. Another legal process also had started that similarly focused on the incorrect implementation of the WFD participation guidelines. Today Catalonia is still the only Spanish autonomous community that handed over its River Basin Plans, which are now being evaluated by the Commission. Yet, as detailed below, progress along these lines has not been able to continue, for a range of reasons.

After the elections, the whole process came to a standstill in just a few months. In fact, immediately after the elections of the new Catalan government, all reference to citizen participation was eliminated from Catalan governmental activities, and even the official website that was used for interaction with citizens was shut down, with the argument that it was too expensive to maintain (even though the participation department reported this cost at 30 euros per month).

The recent economic 'crisis',[2] compounded by the shift of parties with the new government, together led to the freezing of measures included in the Catalan Water Basins Management Plan, which is currently undergoing an unforeseen 'revision process' without any participatory involvement, based primarily on economic criteria. The current economic crisis, rather than broad participation as had been worked out in the past decade, is affecting the basic elements for policy design and the implementation of water policies. Public debt is opening the doors for private actors to get involved in water management functions. For example, multinational corporations such as Suez are managing some of the most sensitive parts of the water supply system.[3] Indeed, the recent privatization of Aguas Ter Llobregat (ATLL) – a public company for bulk supply to the Barcelona Metropolitan Region (114 municipalities) – includes strategic management features, such as the quantity of water that the company may withdraw from all different sources for the next 50 years. If any change were needed (except when drought emergency is officially declared) the Catalan government would be obliged to refund the company for its lost profits. This clearly will impede the ability of the government to enforce the recently approved management plan, as well as its legal duties according to the European WFD. The role of technocratic hegemony and the hydraulic mission that historically was the purview of the Spanish state have now, it seems, been taken up more centrally by private actors.

At present, Spanish and Catalan water management is in a transitional phase, moving from that a state hegemony to a 'private hegemony' of sorts. This hegemony is exercised through the idea that companies are better managers than public authorities, even if this claim is largely without evidence (see Part III above). A widespread political discourse has discredited public service, blaming the institutions for economic hardships now being experienced. Ironically, Suez is now paying high dividends to its shareholders through Barcelona water revenues (estimated at 389 million euros in 2009).[4]

In the current context, Catalan water governance is increasingly (or again) focused on private interests and technocratic premises. Even if the word 'participation' is still used, it does not actively define current water governance processes in Catalonia. Participation as a concept is, in this context, effectively emptied of substance. This backs up other chapters of this section that suggest that citizen participation narratives may be present in form, but not always imply an effective change in democratic quality. High-quality citizen participation processes, which had been promoted by the Catalan government between 2006 and 2010, are currently losing this battle of hegemonies.

The loneliness of the state or speaking new terms, using old ideas

The Catalan case is interesting because of the counter-hegemonic potential of policies orientated towards collective capacity-building process in ways that promised to formulate a new concept of citizenship and that aimed to overcome uncomfortable administrative frontiers. It was a real attempt to challenge the balance of power at different levels of authority and to develop a new governance model for Catalonia, beginning with the water management realm.

The participation processes meaningfully influenced the final management plan and helped to move towards conflict resolution. For example, an agreement was signed in which the government promised to minimize the pressure on the River Ter, 80 percent of which is diverted to the Barcelona Metropolitan Region. The ACA also brought many issues to the table in the Ebro Basin, establishing a special Commission to develop an environmental flow proposal to present to the River Ebro Authorities.[5]

As a social movement, we participated intensively and actively in these processes, even though perfectly aware that these practices could have led to a diffusion of social resistance and the imposition of consensus policies. We considered this as an opportunity to withdraw from the old Spanish hydraulic hegemony based on unbalanced power relations and, with the legitimacy of the new European directive, to integrate our visions of a New Water Culture into the mainstream policy reform process.

Even though this is in some parts a success story, the case also confirms Goldin's idea that top–down participation as a normative ideal has not proven to be effective and does not necessarily change business-as-usual politics. Indeed, in this case, the initiative taken by the ACA and the General Directorate for Citizens' Participation seriously irritated other departments of the same government, including the agriculture, industry and zonal planning authorities: as water management is binding for all other sectors, new visions in water policies affect the economic interests of those they represent.

The case of the EU WFD implementation process shows how citizen participation is disappearing as a result of state governance morphing into non-state governance, which we may call 'private'. No genuine citizen participation, as referred to in deliberative democracy, can take place in a context where the state is not genuinely working in society's interest: the fact that the Catalan government is undergoing the privatization of its functions transforms its political power, which gets concentrated in the hands of an economic elite which actually *embodies* the government. As a consequence, to talk about genuine citizen participation in water governance may be an oxymoron. Even if the European Commission takes legal action to defend our rights to be active citizens and participate in decision-making, the decision against the government means that the fines levied will be paid by public tax revenues, not by those responsible for the reasons behind the conviction.

In this context, when we read the idea that participation is seen as a tool for the state not to be alone in a decision-making process, we argue that it is not the state, but rather the citizens that are alone. Unless governmental functions are restored under citizen control, 'non-participation is in fact a way of participating' (Kadirbeyoglu and Kurtic, Chapter 18; cf. Morinville and Harris, Chapter 19), calling for 'different spaces of participation, both within and against or outside the state' (Williams, 2004: 97, cited in Kadirbeyoglu and Kurtic, Chapter 18).

If a kind of global citizenship, as suggested in the title of this chapter, is in the making at the beginning of the 21st century, the decisive question seems to be whether that citizenship is the product of a state-governed legal determination, or of a non-state citizenship which is based on self-organization of communities in order to overcome the capture of the state by other interests than society's well-being. An interesting example is the experience of the collectivized Barcelona Water Company during the Spanish Civil War (Gorostiza *et al.*, 2012). After the company was returned to the original owners after the war, it became evident that many of the management objectives that could not be reached before the war had in fact been accomplished by the Workers Committee, who had set service quality as a priority over economic interest. This example gives hope that, even in times of considerable hardship, water governance challenges can be effectively overcome through collective action. This experience and the positive experience of participation that we enjoyed for several years in Catalonia both speak to the power of participation and the ability to promote new forms of water governance, and new ways of effectively achieving social or ecological goals. To be a citizen means to participate, and in this situation of serious discredit of current sovereign states, we call on global active citizenship as a way to enhance water justice.

Notes

1 See European Declaration for a 'New Water Culture' (2012).
2 We put the word 'crisis' in quotation marks because it is our belief that our current economic situation has to be considered as a fraud of an economic elite against citizens. More concretely, the economic situation of the water management agency, featuring over 1,250 million euro debt, which justifies the current privatization process, was a deliberate plan and approved by Catalan Parliament in 2008.
3 For more information on our struggle against privatization of the whole water cycle in Barcelona, please visit http://plataformaaiguaesvida.wordpress.com, or contact internacional@xnca.org. Audiovisual material is available in english at http://www.latele.cat/water.
4 https://plataformaaiguaesvida.wordpress.com/2012/10/16/np-el-pastis-de-laigua-de-catalunya-en-venda.
5 Only traces of the work of this commission are still accessible through the official website: http://www20.gencat.cat/portal/site/territori/menuitem.c6e8d3be598ec9745f13ae92b0c0e1a0/?vgnextoid=1acda2144b775310VgnVCM1000008d0c1e0aRCRD&vgnextchannel=1acda2144b775310VgnVCM1000008d0c1e0aRCRD&vgnextfmt=default#Blocbebb11831a959210VgnVCM2000009b0c1e0a.

References

Agència Catalana de l'Aigua (ACA). 2009. *Memória 2009*. Available at: http://aca-web.gencat.cat/aca/documents/ca/publicacions/memoria2009/memoria_aca_2009_ebook/index.html#/4 (accessed Nov. 2012).

Aguilera Klink, F. 1994. Agua, economía y medio ambiente: interdependencias físicas y necesidad de nuevos conceptos. *Revista de Estudios Agrosociales*, 42(167), 113–30.

Arrojo, P. 2001. *El Plan Hidrológico Nacional a debate*, Bilbao: Bakeas.

Arrojo, P. 2006. *El reto ético de la Nueva Cultura del Agua*, Zaragoza: Fundación Nueva Cultura del Agua.

Arrojo, P., and Naredo, J. M. 1997. *La gestión del agua en España y California*, Bilbao: Bakeas.

Diputacío Barcelonas (DIBA). 2007. *Seminario Internacional de la Democracia Participativa: Actores Políticos y Movimientos Sociales*, Diputació Barcelona. Available at: http://www.diba.cat/documents/523487/523545/participacio-fitxers-publicacions_papers-papers18_es-pdf.pdf (accessed Nov. 2012).

European Declaration for a 'New Water Culture' (2012). *Declaration*. Available at: http://www.unizar.es/fnca/euwater/index2.php?x=3&idioma=en (accessed Nov. 2012).

Espluga, J., Ballester, A., Hernández-Mora, N., and Subirats, J. 2011. Public participation and institutional inertia in water management in Spain. *Reis*, 134(3), 3–26.

Estevan, A. 2008. *Herencias y problemas de la política hidráulica española*, Bilbao: Bakeas.

Estevan, A., and Naredo, J. M. 2004. *Ideas y propuestas para una nueva política del agua en España*, Bilbao: Bakeas.

Gorostiza, S., March, H., and Saurí, D., 2012. Servicing customers in revolutionary times: the experience of the collectivized Barcelona Water Company during the Spanish Civil War. *Antipode*, 00(0), 1–18, (early view). Available at: http://onlinelibrary.wiley.com/doi/10.1111/j.1467-8330.2012.01013.x/abstract (accessed Nov. 2012).

Ibáñez, C., Prat, N., Canicio, A., and Curcó, A. 1999. *El delta del Ebro, un sistema amenazado*, Bilbao: Bakeas.

Llamas Madurga, M. R. 2005. Una causa radical de los conflictos hídricos en España. *Tecnología del Agua*, 259, 72–6.

Martínez, J., and Esteve, M. A. 2002. *Agua, regadío y sostenibilidad en el Sudeste ibérico*, Bilbao: Bakeas.

Martínez Gil, F. J. 1997. *La nueva cultura del agua en España*, Bilbao: Bakeas.

Ministerio de Medio Ambiente. 1998. *Libro Blanco del Agua en España*, Madrid: Centro de Publicaciones Secretaría general Técnica Ministero de Medio Ambiente.

Moral, L. del, and Saurí, D. 1999. Changing course: water policy in Spain. *Environment*, 41(6), 12–36.

Sánchez, A. 2003. Major challenges and future groundwater policy in Spain. *Water International*, 28(3), 321–5.

Subirats, J. 2004. Ciencia y ciudadania en la nueva cultura del agua. Proceso de cambio y participacion social. Presentation at IV congreso Iberico de Gestión y Planificación del Agua, Tortosa, Spain, Dec.

Swyngedouw, E. 1999. Modernity and hybridity: nature, *regeneracionismo*, and the production of the Spanish waterscape, 1890–1930. *Annals of the American Association of Geographers*, 89(3), 443–65.

Tello Aragay, E. 2000. Los próximos veinticinco años del movimiento ecologista (y los anteriores). In E. Grau and P. Ibarra (eds), *Una mirada sobre la red: Anuario de movimientos sociales*, pp. 221–46, Barcelona: Icaria Editorial and Tercera Prensa.

Williams, G. 2004. Towards a repoliticization of participatory development: political capabilities and spaces of development. In S. Hickney and G. Mahon (eds), *Participation: From Tyranny to Transformation?*, pp. 92–109, London and New York: Zed Books.

21 Participation, water and the edges of capitalism

Eric Sheppard

Water has consistently posed among the biggest challenges for nature–society relations. It is essential to sustaining most life-forms occupying earth's ecosystems, requiring that it be harnessed, at least temporarily, by these entities. Yet its availability is highly geographically uneven, and its fluidity makes it difficult to pin down. The hydrological cycle, however reshaped by human affairs, is just that: Water is always on the move, preferably downhill, with individual H_2O molecules spending limited time under human control and constantly evading our attempts to capture them for our livelihood practices (and the other species bodies that we depend on). In short, water's agency profoundly shapes (more than) human possibilities.

Human societies long have developed sophisticated cultural beliefs and practices for entraining and directing water to where it is needed. Consider, for example, the *subak* governance system developed in Bali for ensuring that upstream and downstream rice farmers gain access to the water they require. Widely studied since Dutch colonial rulers encountered it and still in use, the *subak* is a complex, territorial, participatory governance system combining social, technological, cultural and religious features (Geertz, 1980; Suradisastra *et al.*, 2002; Jha and Schoenfelder, 2011). Consider also Dutch *waterschappen* (water boards), which emerged in the 13th century to share responsibility for controlling the flow of water in a landscape constantly threatened by inundation. *Waterschappen* not only raised levies to pay for flood control, but also shaped the nature of the highly decentralized Dutch nation-state as it emerged in the 18th century. Thus participatory governance can be highly variegated and independent of state formations, by contrast to the much narrower contemporary state- and institution-led visions of participation documented in this Part – a modern idea, as Goldin (Chapter 16) puts it.

These three empirical studies trace the emergence of similar discourses, norms and practices of participatory governance across three countries, touching on each key phase of entraining water: trapping it 'in the wild' (hydroelectric power in Turkey), redistribution for food production (Turkey and Egypt) and allocation to urban residents (Accra). In these studies, the mantra of participation has accompanied neoliberalization – a trend that has been widely noted well beyond the domains of development and water taken up in this book. Thus Nikolas Rose argues that discourses of community became influential in the UK under what he calls 'late liberalism'. When, under neoliberalism, individuals are presumed to take responsibility for their own welfare, citizenship – the marker of both individual rights and responsibility to the collective – is not simply conferred by the state. Rather, citizenship inheres in and derives from individuals' active engagements with specific 'zones of identity' (Rose, 1999: 178), or communities. These communities are presented as stakeholders, whose perspectives should be incorporated via deliberative democracy (participation). With respect to development, participatory governance has become a hegemonic discourse in many domains (e.g. Cooke and Kothari, 2001).

Describing how governance coevolved with European liberalism and neoliberalism, Foucault made the influential point that (neo)liberal states practice what he dubbed governmentality (Lemke, 2001), through 'government at a distance' (Rose, 1999). In liberal societies, where individual autonomy is valued, nation-states arrange affairs in such a way as to ensure that citizens and other residents behave appropriately by framing the 'conduct of conduct' – i.e. how citizens govern themselves. In the progressive liberalism of European social democracies, the state took a proactive role through its social welfare institutions. Under neoliberalism, market principles have emerged as inner regulators of the state, of individuals and of community participation. This is entirely consistent with the observation across all three chapters that, while directed towards the local, participation effectively emerges as a governmental norm from beyond the local.[1]

The authors underline Barnes's important argument that to understand how participation works/fails (cf. Goldin's four fatal flaws, Chapter 16), it is necessary to unravel the originary hegemonic/governmental moment shaping participation, examining what it comes to mean in particular geographical contexts. As these chapters also show, the geography of the emergence of participation as a component of water governance does not simply play out across scales, from the national to the local as in Foucault's analysis, but also from global North to South. Key institutions in the global North develop principles (e.g. the Dublin Principles) for, and put in place conditions requiring, participatory water governance in the South. Morinville and Harris trace the role of Bretton Woods conditionalities, the Ghanaian state and international NGOs in bringing into existence, tasking and constraining Local Water Boards in Accra, Ghana. This is a well-worn story of Gillian Hart's (2002) big-D Developmentalism, whereby actors grounded in Europe and North America frame what the South should do (ignoring the rich traditions of variegated indigenous participatory practices across the global South).

At the national scale, Kadirbeyoglu and Kurtic demonstrate how the long-standing modernist Turkish state dictates and legitimizes participation, enforcing it when desired participants dissent from its presuppositions. Locally, Barnes details how local discourses articulating around gendered norms about men's and women's work and who uses water for which purposes, make it all but impossible for women's voices to be included. While some might assert that neither of these are about North–South linkages, much depends on what these terms are taken to mean (Sheppard and Nagar, 2004). Any regional division of the globe into North versus South (cf. World Commission on Environment and Development, 1987) must be suspect, given those living very prosperously in otherwise impoverished regions, and those living precariously in wealthy ones (the precariat; Standing, 2011). In this de-regionalized, fractal reading of North–South spatiality, the Turkish state stands in for Northern developmentalism. In the early years of the Republic, the young Turks saw their role as secular modernizers of a multi-ethnic religious empire. The state's contemporary pressure on Turkish farmers who do not conform to its dictates, on the grounds that they do not know what is good for them, is similarly hierarchical: classic coercive developmentalism (Guha, 1997).

In Egypt, Barnes portrays a struggle between outsiders (including herself) who wish to empower local women, against those (mostly local men but also women) who articulate an alternative, in some sense Muslim, view of women's roles. Barnes's account draws out well the paradoxes of participatory governance running through the three chapters. On the one hand, participation is about empowering those living precariously – and who can be against that? It brings concrete benefits, as in Morinville and Harris's discussion of how Local Water Boards in Accra improve water delivery. On the other hand, with the prosperous determining the frames within which participation (and empowerment) come to be defined, new limits are enacted – limits that seem all too familiar. The chapters thus reconfirm the many studies revealing the failures of participation *tout court*, from therapy to placation (Kadirbeyoglu and Kurtic, Chapter 18), to external constraints on participation (Morinville and Harris, Chapter 19), to the marginalization of subgroups (women and the precariat more generally) within always already heterogeneous communities (Joseph, 2002; Young, 1990). Barnes's study of Egyptian Water User Associations poses further North/South paradoxes. She describes how Western/Northern views of gender are marginalized, along with the (particularly precarious) village women. Can Western feminism empower those living precariously, or is this developmentalism redux (Mohanty, 2003)? Can the extreme patriarchy she documents be dismissed simply as Muslim traditionalism and fundamentalism (the current *bête noire* for proponents of northern hegemony), only curable through development? Or do these perspectives reflect particular local genderings – variants on struggles that cut across religion, culture and place – that are hard to discern through Western feminist perspectives (Johnson-Odim, 1991)?

A related theme, brought out particularly in the Turkey and Accra case studies, is what to make of grassroots actions that do not fit well-worn, imported definitions of participation. When the private vendor in Accra hires a private tanker service, or when Turkish villagers and activists protest run-of-the-river hydroelectric power plants, are they engaged in participatory activities? These chapters raise this question, notwithstanding the dismissal of such actions as beyond the participatory pale by those implementing participation. In so doing, the authors laudably challenge state-led definitions of participation, revealing hegemony at work. When consent fails, as grassroots actions dissent from the participatory norm, both the state and consenting participatory groups invoke coercion to reassert hegemony.

As argued throughout the book (cf. Sneddon, Chapter 2; Goldin, Chapter 16), hegemonic processes cut across the domains of scarcity, privatization and participation, continually struggling to suture them into a coherent and acceptable developmental imaginary. In other domains of participation such as community forestry, the complementarities are particularly clear: state- and World Bank-induced participation reinforces the commodification of nature in part through granting program participants access to nature's use values (Paudel, 2012). As these chapters show, participatory water governance need not entail the production of water as a commodity. Nevertheless, participation is tendentiously framed by external actors as reducing scarcity, improving efficiency, and as being consistent with other logics of neoliberal market rule. Neoliberalization has ridden on the back of successfully propagating its own particular hegemony: a mainstream economic theory asserting that well-functioning markets, supplemented by 'good', market-friendly governance, are capable of eliminating poverty and clearing markets such that supply matches demand (Peck, 2010). This has gained broad consent, notwithstanding the deepening socio-spatial inequality and economic crises that have accompanied privatization and deregulation, particularly in recent years. The details of neoliberalization vary across space and time, reflecting local context, resistance and contestation, and its intersections with other political-economic regimes (Leitner *et al.*, 2007a). Nevertheless, when participatory governance is framed in these ways, it reinforces 'good' governance by incorporating the perspectives of particular stakeholders. This suturing further underwrites trajectories of, and reinforces consent to, neoliberalization.

Actually existing markets do not function like this, however, particularly for the Southern precariat. When their participation is enrolled into neoliberalizing capitalism, too often this reproduces the processes of socio-spatial uneven development and inequalities that long have accompanied globalizing capitalism. This is compounded for nature–society relations because biophysical processes can never be fully commodified or marketized, creating sustainability challenges that market-oriented governance proposals (e.g. carbon trading or full-cost pricing) cannot resolve (Bumpus and Liverman, 2007; O'Connor, 1991). When participatory water governance is restricted to and presented as a means of tweaking capitalism to address inequity and unsustainability, non-capitalist forms of participatory governance are ruled out of order. This delegitimizes a whole host of 'Southern' alternative imaginaries and practices to (neoliberal) capitalism (Leitner *et al.*, 2007a). Such alternatives range the spectrum from participatory practices predating capitalism (e.g. the *subak*), to 'rogue' capitalism (e.g. Accra's water handler), diverse non-capitalist management practices (e.g. *Waterschappen*) and active resistance to capitalist water extraction, distribution and consumption (e.g. Turkey's hydroelectric activists). It is commonly believed that such alternatives exist only in capitalism's periphery, with resistance driven by precariousness and exploitation. Yet such alternatives in fact are quite commonplace (Gibson-Graham, 2006), and, as Paudel (2012) shows for Nepal, successful participatory governance may actually catalyze anti-capitalist resistance (in this case, exemplary community forestry projects bred Maoist revolution).

Finally, there are the questions of spatiality. As described in these chapters, and prescribed by its proponents, participatory water governance is a downscaled form of governance, to be practiced locally. The authors' methodological focus on territorial context reinforces such localized thinking. Yet scholars have come to appreciate that local events are profoundly shaped by how local participants are interconnected with the rest of the world, often in distinct ways that can be generative of heterogeneity and conflict within local communities (Massey, 1991; Sheppard, 2011). When participation is localized, each community seeks to solve its particular problems with the implication that broader processes and possibilities are neglected. These chapters show how the hegemonic processes framing and eliciting consent for participation come from the outside, but have little to say about how participation can extend beyond the local scale. Critical analysis of the kind of participatory water governance discussed here must go beyond the local, tracing the trans-local mobilities of participatory governance policy (Peck and Theodore, 2010; Roy, 2010) and examining participatory practices and imaginaries capable of traveling beyond localities (Featherstone, 2003). Trans-local activism will be vital if participatory water governance is to escape the localist trap set by its advocates, disrupting its top–down capitalist framing.[2]

Notes

1 The close parallels between Foucauldian governmentality and Gramsci's discussion of hegemony and consent should be clear.
2 I am grateful to Jacqui Goldin, Leila Harris and Chris Sneddon for comments on an earlier draft, without imputing to them any responsibility for lingering deficiencies in my arguments.

References

Bumpus, A. G., and Liverman, D. M. 2007. Accumulation by decarbonization and the governance of carbon offsets. *Economic Geography*, 84(2), 127–55.

Cooke, B., and Kothari, U. 2001 *Participation: The New Tyranny?* London and New York: Zed Books.

Featherstone, D. 2003. Spatialities of transnational resistance to globalization: the maps of grievance of the Inter-Continental Caravan. *Transactions of the Institute of British Geographers*, 28(4): 404–21.

Geertz, C. 1980. Organization of the Balinese Subak. In E.W. Coward Jr. (ed.), *Irrigation and Agricultural Development in Asia*, pp.70–90, Ithaca, NY: Cornell University Press.

Gibson-Graham, J. K. 2006. *A Postcapitalist Politics*, Minneapolis, MN: University of Minnesota Press.

Guha, R. 1997. *A Subaltern Studies Reader, 1986–1995,* Minneapolis, MN: University of Minnesota Press.

Hart, G. 2002. *Disabling Globalization: Places of Power in Post-Apartheid South Africa,* Berkeley, CA: University of California Press.

Jha, N., and Schoenfelder, J. W. 2011. Studies of the Subak: new directions, new challenges. *Human Ecology*, 39(1), 3–10.

Johnson-Odim, C. 1991. Common themes, different contexts: third world women and feminism. In C. T. Mohanty, A. Russo and L. Torres (eds), *Third World Women and the Politics of Feminism*, pp. 314–27. Blooomington, IN: University of Indiana Press.

Joseph, M. 2002. *Against the Romance of Community,* Minneapolis, MN: University of Minnesota Press.

Leitner, H., Peck, J., and Sheppard, E. 2007a. Squaring up to neoliberalism. In H. Leitner, J. Peck and E. Sheppard (eds), *Contesting Neoliberalism: Urban Frontiers*, pp. 311–28, New York: Guilford.

Leitner, H., Sziarto, K. M., Sheppard, E., and Maringanti, A. 2007b. Contesting urban futures: decentering neoliberalism. In H. Leitner, J. Peck and E. Sheppard (eds), *Contesting Neoliberalism: Urban Frontiers*, pp. 1–25, New York: Guilford.

Lemke, T. 2001. The birth of bio-politics: Michel Foucault's lecture at the Collège de France on neo-liberal governmentality. *Economy and Society*, 30(2), 190–207.

Massey, D. 1991. A global sense of place. *Marxism Today*, June, pp. 24–9.

Mohanty, C. T. 2003. *Feminism without Borders: Decolonizing Theory, Practicing Solidarity,* Durham, NC: Duke University Press.

O'Connor, J. 1991. On the two contradictions of capitalism. *Capitalism, Nature, Socialism*, 2(3), 107–9.

Paudel, D. 2012. The double life of development: peasants, agrarian livelihoods and the prehistory of Nepal's revolution. Ph.D. University of Minnesota.

Peck, J. 2010. *Constructions of Neoliberal Reason,* Oxford: Oxford University Press.

Peck, J., and Theodore, N. 2010. Mobilizing policy: models, methods, and mutations. *Geoforum*, 41(2), 169–74.

Rose, N. 1999. *Powers of Freedom: Reframing Political Thought,* Cambridge: Cambridge University Press.

Roy, A. 2010. *Poverty Capital: Microfinance and the Making of Development,* New York: Routledge.

Sheppard, E. 2011. Geography, nature and the question of development. *Dialogues in Human Geography*, 1(1), 46–75.

Sheppard, E., and Nagar, R. 2004. From East–West to North–South. *Antipode*, 36(4), 557–63.

Standing, G. 2011. *The Precariat: The New Dangerous Class,* New York: Bloomsbury Academic.

Suradisastra, K., Sejati, W. K., Supriatna, Y., and Hidayat, D. 2002. Institutional description of the Balinese Subak. *Jurnal Litbang Pertanian,* 21(1), 11–18.

World Commission on Environment and Development. 1987. *Our Common Future,* Oxford: Oxford University Press.

Young, I. M. 1990. *Justice and the Politics of Difference,* Princeton, NJ: Princeton University Press.

Part V
Conclusion

22 Placing hegemony

Water governance concepts and their discontents

Christopher Sneddon, Leila M. Harris and Jacqueline A. Goldin

This volume has explored the spread, uptake and effects of three sets of concepts – linked ideas of scarcity, marketization and participation – that have in recent years achieved hegemonic status within theories and practices of water governance. Our intent has not been to provide definitive explanations of these concepts and their application to the numerous water-related challenges confronting humankind. We express a more modest aim: to shed light on the multiple ways that water governance initiatives employ certain hegemonic ideas, enacted, or 'placed', in specific sites of the global South, with distinct effectiveness and responses. We use this conclusion to reflect on the themes highlighted in the case studies, commentaries and framing chapters. Rather than summaries of each contribution, we instead focus on what we perceive to be critical sites of integration, as well as those areas of the book where more needs to be explored, or which could be elaborated in different ways. Our conclusion is thus organized around: variegation regarding the uses of hegemonic concepts; how hegemonic concepts in water governance are linked; techniques of resistance; and the tensions that emerge when thinking across activist and academic fields of knowledge. Tactically, we hope this will generate numerous points of discussion and stimulate future research that will account for the profound and subtle ways in which hegemonic concepts in water governance are crafted, transmitted and contested.

Integrating themes

An initial integrating theme is provided by Harris's treatment, following Brenner *et al.* (2010), of the geo-institutional variegation characteristic of how neoliberal policies, related to marketization and privatization, have been enacted and resisted differently in distinct locales (Chapter 11). We contend that a focus on variegation is quite critical to a deeper understanding of how hegemonic concepts function. While recognizing that certain hegemonic ideas related to scarcity/crisis, marketization and participation are prominent features of water governance in the global South, our case studies insist that the encounter between global discourses and the policy environments, political-economic dynamics and material landscapes of specific locales inevitably distorts and reorients those discourses and produces disconnects and 'friction' (see Tsing, 2005). In other words, hegemonic concepts do serve certain focal points of institutional power, but the pathways between the concepts' application by particular actors and the policy and material changes that follow are always case-specific, following particular historical, geographical, institutional or biophysical characteristics and differences. Some examples from our chapters illustrate this point.

K'Akumu (Chapter 13), for instance, provides an incisive view of the institutional body charged with implementing water privatization in Kenya. This reinforces the need to stay cognizant of the details of different pathways and institutions of water governance, and how they reveal different forms of hegemonic relations. The influence of the PLC (Public Limited Corporation) model, imported as a privatization and commercialization package into Kenya under the guidance of German development partners, cannot be understated. Conceived initially as a pilot project for urban water supply, the Kenyan government eventually absorbed this approach within national law. Subsequently, many of the provisions of the 2002 law were adapted to provincial and local-level urban contexts, where the stipulations regarding privatization were undoubtedly transformed by local political, economic and technological contexts. It becomes quite clear that, although the overarching framework of water supply law is informed by a hegemonic understanding of privatization, there can be no definitive fashion with respect to how this circulates outward towards provision and reception of water in Kenya's urban neighborhoods.

On occasion, changing political-economic conditions can alter the pathways by which hegemonic ideas travel, thus speaking to the importance of temporal and spatial variability in determining how water governance is adapted to different places. For example, Turkey had already embraced hegemonic ideas regarding river basin development as a path towards modernization, but it took the energy crisis of the early 2000s to alter these pathways and mobilize a different kind of hegemony (Erensu, Chapter 6). The Turkish state has played a critical role in determining how hegemonic ideas related to scarcity and privatization have played out on the ground; in this case, in the implementation of small-scale hydroelectric projects, especially along the Black Sea coast in northern Turkey. In examining the variegation of hegemonic concepts as they travel, it is thus crucial to keep in mind both the spatial and temporal dimensions of difference.

A second major integrating theme in our volume concerns how hegemonic water governance concepts (represented by our three themes) are intimately connected to both other water governance approaches as well as to broader discourses and practices within development circles – e.g. neoliberalism, or sustainable development. These practices and discourses reinforce each other in particular ways, and also exist alongside one another in tension. Among the other effects of this broader constellation of ideas, these concepts and approaches may be selectively deployed and operationalized, particularly to advance the power or hegemony of certain institutional or social actors. As Harris explains (Chapter 10), one of the key means of interpreting the rise of privatization and marketization of water is to consider the ways that these diverse practices are often 'bundled', understood as one and the same even though these concepts refer to distinct processes and outcomes. Waters (Chapter 12) takes up this notion of 'bundling', pointing to the integration between private water and ideals of public health in colonial-era Zambia. More recently as well, there is another linkage between privatization of urban water supply systems and the political influence of the mining industry in the country's Copperbelt. One of the consequences of the bundling of water privatization with these different actors and pathways is that 'private water' is linked to other power relations (e.g. control over crucial resource sectors), a move that causes water itself to become radically separated from the multiple social and ecological networks important to those contexts. We see this sort of bundling, and radical unbundling that proceeds as a consequence, as a salient part of the story with respect to how modern engineering expertise surrounding water in effect redefines water as a highly utilitarian 'resource' (see Baker, Chapter 3). This 'abstraction' of water from its complex and contingent surroundings (following Linton, 2010) is a common theme, and is taken up by both Waters (Chapter 12) and Erensu (Chapter 6). Erensu, in particular, notes the alienation of water from socio-ecological relations and its conversion to 'modern water', a conceptualization prevalent throughout the 20th century.

With respect to the interrelations between the hegemonic concepts that interest this volume, there are several examples where those concepts become strongly linked and intermeshed. As we see in K'Akumu's case of water supplies in Nairobi (Chapter 13), the inequities promulgated by privatization can in many instances be overcome, at least in theory, by more participatory management. This participatory dimension was in fact written into Kenya's water supply legislation. The incorporation of participation into Kenya's water policies was thus reactive, yet must also be understood as itself a reflection of global trends centered on efforts to democratize and decentralize water governance. Conversely, it is also remarkable that in the Kenya case the broad emphasis on marketization has spawned other market-based tools, such as social tariffication, to address the shortcomings of water provision for the urban poor. Moreover, as K'Akumu highlights, such strategies may only be effective contingent on the poor's greater *participation* in water user groups and representation within water forums. Participation in fact becomes the single most crucial factor whereby the urban poor might challenge the hegemony of market-oriented strategies of water provision.

The intersections between participation and marketization are also apparent in the case of Turkey (as explored by Kadirbeyoglu and Kurtic, Chapter 18). For example, the power of flowing water is effectively privatized through the implementation of hydroelectric power plant (HPP) development. The abstraction of water from its ecological and social networks, and the shortchanging of participatory processes, facilitates this process. These convergences and associated power dynamics do not pass unnoticed. Instead, these coalitions and convergences provide animus for the protest movements, as they react with resistance and a strong push for greater levels of participation in water management decisions (see response commentaries by Ozesmi, Chapter 8, Varghese, Chapter 14, and Broekman, Chapter 20, all of whom deal with tensions between marketized water and participatory governance). What is interesting for the Turkish case in particular is how what is going on in Turkey is clearly linked to institutional and political changes happening elsewhere. As Erensu explains (Chapter 6), the European Union and global focus on green energy provides the impetus for HPPs and the range of changes under way in the Black Sea case. Similarly, while the Turkish government is playing a strong role in all of these changes, we see learning and cross-fertilization encouraged by the IFIs and other institutions, for instance, sending Turkish planners and farmers to Mexico to better understand devolved and participatory irrigation management (Chapter 18). Bauer (2004) demonstrates the power of this type of horizontal hegemony (geographic dispersion) in the case of the Chilean state's embrace of marketization and privatization of water resources and the subsequent diffusion of this model throughout Latin America and to other contexts of the global South (see Harris, Chapter 11). In all of these senses, we see the fundamental ways that these diverse hegemonies are clearly linked, as well as the ways that these practices are intricately related to a range of other discourses and practices across time and space.

Apart from linkages to broader development discourses and practices, we also find ample evidence suggesting that hegemonic concepts related to water governance are frequently enmeshed within broader ideas about nature–society relations. A case in point is Mahayni's examination of water scarcity in Damascus (Chapter 5). Here, we see that the framing of scarcity as 'driven' by certain processes becomes a crucial tool in the construction of hegemonic concepts. As outsiders, when we read a report on Syria's or Damascus's water situation we tend to accept, without question, that the crisis is driven by population growth, climate change and agricultural misuse. Our acceptance of these common framings in turn furthers the hegemony of scarcity as a simplified narrative. Scarcity is rendered as the obvious result of seemingly straightforward demographic, biophysical and political-economic processes and is defined exclusively as a physical reality rather than a condition constructed through a complex set of vulnerabilities, inequities and political contests. By tracing the situation of Damascus in relation to a broader history and geography that includes the history of political power and Ba'ath party rule in Syria, as well as demographic shifts linked to rural agricultural transformation throughout the countryside, Mahanyi allows us to read the 'crisis' of water in Damascus as much more than a biophysical change. As a result, the complex geographical and historical relations that enabled the 'crisis' to emerge are made visible.

Another integrating theme is that of resistance. Lest we forget, hegemony is ultimately about the maintenance of power relations:

> Hegemony consists in the formation of a coalition of top–down forces activated by a common consciousness in which those at the bottom are able to participate. Counterhegemony arises when bottom–up forces achieve a common consciousness that is clearly distinct from that of hegemonic power.
> (Cox, 2001: 56)

Several of the cases show how seemingly 'emancipatory' projects, such as those associated with participatory governance, are oftentimes linked to broader hegemonic projects such as privatization. This begs a difficult question: if participatory projects are embedded within a pre-given water strategy, one that includes e.g. marketization as a prominent feature, are they in fact abetting hegemonic power relations? The case of Local Water Boards (LWBs) in Accra, Ghana (Morinville and Harris, Chapter 19), speaks directly to this conundrum. LWBs provide an intriguing lens to examine the possible limitations of participatory water governance, in part because these local bodies are (simultaneously) contested internally, delimited by state and transnational regulations and actors, *and* a source and vehicle of counter-hegemonic impulses. Moreover, as the cases regarding Accra, Kenya's urban centers, rural Turkey, rural Egypt and Catalonia (Broekman, Chapter 20) all highlight, 'participation' is frequently an extraordinarily power-laden pathway, being directed from outside, yet importantly affecting people's everyday lives. In addition, certain forms of participation may be invisible (or not remarked upon) within a more hegemonic conception of participation (which is hegemonic by virtue of its connection to specific global and national actors). Again, this point is accented in the analysis of Chapter 19 (Morinville and Harris). If only certain types of engagement are recognized as participatory, what does this mean for the consolidation of particular forms of power, or the ability to resist those power complexes through counter-hegemonic movements or concepts?

In a related vein, there is a real need to zero in on the distinct ways that hegemonic concepts are, if not formally resisted, received and transformed by communities and individuals. A case in point: Barnes's analysis of water user associations (WUAs) in Egypt (Chapter 17) shows how participation is not always hegemonic in the same way on the ground; how participation as enacted and performed within each site (whether rural Egypt or elsewhere) is unique, and offers multiple examples of how hegemonies are both solidified and, at the same time, weakened. The members of WUAs in Egypt accepted participatory reforms as long as these reflected how they defined themselves – as women, or as poor – in relation to water. Moreover, those community members in charge of coordinating WUAs behave as key interlocutors of how participatory decision-making is interpreted at the neighborhood level. Barnes's case also offers an interesting contrast to the Kenyan experience, where the rhetoric of participation captured within national legislation has yet to filter down to the urban poor, or for that matter, with the case of Accra, Ghana, where participation is enacted through particular institutions (LWBs) that serve to extend water access in some areas, but also bring with them new forms of exclusion, and new forms of hegemonic understandings in terms of what 'counts' as participatory.

Water governance and hegemony: future directions

There is a real danger in allowing our focus to fall so heavily on the *ideas* associated with hegemonic concepts in water governance. Specifically, might we be neglecting the material interests of those actors in a position to most benefit from implementation of policies or projects that we call hegemonic, or the material effects of those projects on landscapes and people? One of Gramsci's central concerns revolved around the need to clarify how hegemony – set in motion within elite political circles – is 'made real' through the material and everyday practices that influence human lives and livelihoods (Ekers and Loftus, 2008). Undoubtedly, even as we are interested in exposing some of the actors and interests who benefit from particular water governance practices and understandings, we could similarly go further to shed light on the water governance ideas and practices that coalesce within discourses of scarcity, marketization and participation. Waters' contribution (Chapter 12) is one example of work that makes progress regarding the nebulous beneficiaries of water privatization in Zambia. While tracing such linkages is difficult, we know it is something that could, and should, be done more effectively. Hegemony is a way of thinking through power, so in this sense, we remain only somewhat satisfied with the degree to which our contributions have actually been able to trace and analyze these circuits of power and influence.

Another noticeable omission in our collection is a fuller discussion of the divide between academic and activist knowledge and practice. Rather than brush it under the rug, we wish to acknowledge this tension in the hope of developing a fruitful dialog for overcoming what for many of us is an unhelpful incapacity to communicate. It is clear from reading our case-study chapters against the activist and civil society responses that in some ways we are speaking the same language, and in other ways we are dealing with dramatically different assumptions and realities. Anna Tsing captures this tension when she discusses how some of the 'most critically aware scholarship fails us' because theory 'has followed its own specifications' (2005: 266). It does so by overgeneralizing, demonstrating how 'each local situation' is nothing more than an 'exemplification of a self-fulfilling global scheme' (ibid.). In a sense, theory addresses itself to the task of conceptual refinement rather than to 'urgent local dilemmas or to far-reaching collaborative visions'. As a result, theory often 'has had less and less to say to activists, visionaries, and the public at large' (ibid.). This gap between theory and practice is apparent in the frustrations expressed by Ozesmi (Chapter 8) concerning the need to strip away some of the conceptual posturing around water governance and begin the difficult task of resisting a hegemonic capitalist development model that threatens the resilience of water–society relations in Turkey and elsewhere. Aquatic ecosystems and the humans that depend on them cannot wait for theoretical advances when confronted by destructive pressures. We see similar tensions implicit in discussions of water justice activism offered by Varghese (Chapter 14), or the challenges facing activists involved in participatory governance around Barcelona (see Broekman, Chapter 20). In this last case especially, we are forced to confront the reality that, although many academic analysts see participatory water governance as another mechanism that often ushers in power relations and hegemonies (see discussion by Goldin, Chapter 16), this is clearly something that activists require and will continue to fight for. In the case of participatory involvement in Catalonia, the effort to engage activists was difficult, yet ultimately meaningful. Now that those opportunities have been taken away with a new political regime, and in the face of fiscal challenges following the economic crisis, it is all the more apparent that activists value and will continue to fight for participatory governance mechanisms. In the absence of such opportunities, transparency and accountability are all the more elusive.

Even though we recognize some of the shortcomings of our approach, and of our volume, we are convinced that the volume has offered a great deal in terms of working through some of the broader patterns and dynamics of contemporary water governance. Most certainly, there is something to be said for a project that can identify broad patterns of hegemonic ideas at work in water governance while remaining faithful to the idea that contextual specificities and place-bound realities also matter. This attention to broad shifts and patterns, as well as to local realities, is especially crucial to identify and communicate counter-hegemonies, or different types of resistances. For both Sheppard (Chapter 21) and Bakker (Chapter 15), concepts and academic discourse should always be in dialog with the aims of social movements and the activist community, whether surrounding questions of water governance or broader concerns over neoliberal development approaches. Likewise, the global water justice movement – which remains somewhat fragmented yet increasingly unified in its resistance to the hegemonic project of privatization and top–down water governance in general (see Davidson-Harden *et al.*, 2007) – can hopefully uncover useful arguments and strategies of opposition to and in articulation with academic communities.

As a final example of the value of theoretical engagement, Bakker's commentary (see Chapter 15) opens up an important line of inquiry that deserves further attention. In essence she argues that the connections between hegemonic concepts of water governance – such as scarcity, or marketization – and water governance in actual practice – policies, management initiatives, distribution and consumption – are more mutually constitutive than perhaps is recognized and acknowledged in work on water–society relations. How do such practices feed back into and fortify (or weaken) hegemonic ideas in distinct places and at distinct times? Intriguingly, we see an example of this in Musemwa's arguments regarding the historical evolution of scarcity as a framing concept in the early evolution of water governance institutions in colonial Zimbabwe (Chapter 7). The drought conditions and narratives of water scarcity (promulgated by the region's farmers and elites) that characterized water politics in south-western Matabeleland in the early and middle 20th century actually helped *produce* the hydraulic bureaucracy of Southern Rhodesia. This in turn established a strong institutional mechanism for promoting water scarcity as a prominent hegemonic narrative. The case thus provides a specific example of the co-constitution of different hegemonic concepts, discourses and institutions or pathways.

In conclusion, we are not suggesting that hegemony is the only framework for examining water governance in the early 21st century. Nor is it always the most appropriate lens through which to identify and understand salient elements of water–society relations. Still, we contend that our focus on certain hegemonic concepts does bring to the fore an important and neglected dimension of water governance: that of the relations of ideology, power and co-constitutive practices amongst a variety of critical agents in struggles over water. These agents – whether international water professionals, community associations, government officials, water activists or academics – are connected by virtue of their entanglements within the dominant ideas regarding water governance. We also find that hegemony provides a sense of the interactions and connections of practices and discourses across diverse times and places, rather than solely recognizing their influence and import in particular locales. As such, we find it fruitful to interrogate broad conceptual issues, as well as detailed empirical dimensions, to trace and understand the tensions and consistencies that bind them. Overall, we hope that the structure of this book, and the involvement of contributors from diverse academic and activist communities, has furthered this project, and in so doing, brought together different ways of analyzing and understanding water governance realities and futures. The concepts that form the focus of our analyses – scarcity/crisis, marketization/privatization and participation – do not spring out of the ether as the most objective, rational means of addressing water challenges, even if at times they are portrayed that way. As the writings in this book have shown, hegemonic concepts have distinct histories and geographies and serve specific interests in society in ways that demand attention and, in many instances, contestation and reform. To the extent that analyses of hegemonic concepts can reveal those networks of power and ideology that by definition work most effectively when hidden, then the present volume will have made a genuine contribution to working towards more socially and ecologically just modes of water governance.

References

Bauer, C. 2004. *Siren Song: Chilean Water Law as a Model for International Reform,* Washington, DC: Resources for the Future.

Brenner, N., Peck, J., and Theodore, N. 2010. Variegated neoliberalization: geographies, modalities, pathways. *Global Networks*, 10(2), 1–41.

Cox, R. 2001. The way ahead: toward a new ontology of world order. In R.W. Jones (ed.), *Critical Theory and World Politics*, pp. 45–60, Boulder, CO: Lynne Rienner Publishers.

Davidson-Harden, A., Naidoo, A., and Harden, A. 2007. The geopolitics of the water justice movement. *Peace, Conflict and Development*, 11. Available at: http://www.peacestudiesjournal.org.uk/dl/PCD%20Issue%2011_Article_Water%20Justice%20Movement_Davidson%20Naidoo%20Harden.pdf (accessed June 2012).

Ekers, M., and Loftus, A. 2008. The power of water: developing dialogues between Foucault and Gramsci. *Environment and Planning D: Society and Space*, 26(4), 698–718.

Linton, J. 2010. *What is Water? The History of a Modern Abstraction*, Vancouver: UBC Press.

Tsing, A. L. 2005. *Friction: An Ethnography of Global Connection,* Princeton, NJ, and Oxford: Princeton University Press.

Index